International money and banking

As the interdependence of world economies deepens and widens apace, the dynamics of banking and finance are constantly changing. New regulations are introduced, new markets opened up and financial innovations ensued, all of which have important implications for global banking business.

This is the first major text with a comprehensive up-to-date treatment of both international money and banking. It systematically analyses workings of international money, leading up to the question of a monetary union. It deals comprehensively with the structure of exchange, money and Euro-currency markets, covering the basics of such areas as exchange rate determination, market arbitrage, product innovations and global market integration process. It also examines the international bank regulatory environments, including emerging principles of regulatory jurisdiction in light of US and European Community experiences. It covers major banking activities like international portfolio management, trade finance, country risk analysis, loan syndication and debt-service resolutions. While its scope is international, the book also contains brief summaries of topics for closed economies.

The book is designed to provide the student with an essential survey of international money and banking, in both theory and practice, and it includes questions and exercises to facilitate class discussion and to aid review of topics. It will be essential reading for all those studying international business and finance at undergraduate and MBA levels, and it will be a useful handbook for practitioners involved in international banking and finance.

Taeho Kim is Professor of Economics and International Banking at the American Graduate School of International Management, popularly known as Thunderbird, in Arizona, USA.

International money and banking

Taeho Kim

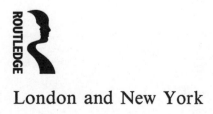

London and New York

First published 1993
by Routledge
11 New Fetter Lane, London EC4P 4EE

Simultaneously published in the USA and Canada
by Routledge
29 West 35th Street, New York, NY 10001

Reprinted 1995

Typeset in Times by
Mathematical Composition Setters Ltd, Salisbury, Wiltshire

Printed in Great Britain by T.J. Press (Padstow) Ltd,
Padstow, Cornwall

British Library Cataloguing in Publication Data
A catalogue record for this book is available from the
British Library

Library of Congress Cataloguing in Publication Data
A catalogue record for this book is available from the
Library of Congress

ISBN 0-415-05943-7 (hbk)
ISBN 0-415-05944-5 (pbk)

Contents

Figures

Tables

Preface

This book is intended as a textbook in international money, banking, and finance and is based on lecture notes originally developed for a one-semester course in international banking at the American Graduate School of International Management. It has evolved as a cumulative result of over a decade of teaching and research in this field.

Despite the fact that the money and banking markets in individual countries are becoming increasingly interdependent, we find that most textbooks in the field treat the subject matter as if each economy were a closed one. Even when international topics are incorporated, at least in some books, it is often done seemingly in an afterthought fashion.

This book is suitable for use as a textbook in an MBA-level course in international money and banking. It is also suitable for a course in international finance offered by Economics Departments if Chapters 3, 10, 11, 12, 13, and 14 are omitted. In addition, it may serve as a reference book for bankers and financiers who wish to become familiar with some analytic treatment of topics and techniques in this field. As for prerequisites, some basic understanding of money and banking is helpful. Calculus is marginally used in Chapters 2, 4, 7, and 12, although it is by no means necessary to understand the topics conceptually.

In developing the original set of notes into a book, I had two general objectives in mind. The first was to produce a reasonably self-contained money and banking textbook with an international dimension. For this purpose, I have introduced a summary of closed-economy topics at the beginning of some chapters, where necessary. Such chapters then proceed to concentrate more on international topics.

My second objective, sometimes difficult to reconcile with the first because of the need to allocate limited pages among competing topics, was to produce a book which incorporates recent significant developments in international banking as much as possible. Yet, special attention has been paid in order not to exclude important traditional topics.

This book reflects many suggestions and insights provided by numerous bankers and economists in the field. The initial insights on the actual workings of the international banking market were provided by guest speakers who participated in the three-week International Banking Conferences which were organized as special winter courses under the auspices of the Bankers' Association for Foreign Trade. In each conference which I coordinated for three years (1982–4), over twenty speakers participated, including people from major multinational banks, the IMF, the World Bank, and the US bank regulatory agencies. I also had opportunities to visit London financial institutions, as well as foreign branches and offices of various countries of origin in Hong Kong, Singapore, Seoul, and Beijing. Over several years, I also benefited from seminars and programs in international banking at Baylor University, the University of Hawaii PAMI, and the University of Virginia Center for International Banking Studies, in which I participated as either a lecturer or a faculty fellow.

In writing this textbook, I realize that I owe a debt to the valuable graduate training in economics that I received at the University of Colorado under the Fulbright graduate fellowship program. I am also grateful for the conducive environment fostered at the American Graduate School of International Management, where I was able to initiate and experiment with an untested course in international banking over a decade ago and where I have received generous encouragement and research support, without which literally I could not have produced this book.

My greatest debt is to the students who took my course in international banking without a suitable textbook and suffered most. In addition, I am grateful to reviewers of my earlier drafts, who provided me with valuable comments, preventing me from falling into too much of an America-centric approach or into technical pitfalls. Of course, any remaining errors or imbalance in coverage are mine. I am also grateful to the Routledge editorial staff for their outstanding editorial help and advice. My special thanks go to Francesca Weaver and Jennifer Binnie.

Finally, I am deeply grateful to my wife Myong, daughter Grace, and son Edward for their enthusiasm, tolerance, and subtle pressure, without which the completion of this book might have been further away.

Taeho Kim
April 1993

Part I

Basics of money and banking in an open economy

Chapter 1

Introduction to international money and banking

INTERDEPENDENCE OF THE WORLD ECONOMIES

The movement toward greater economic interdependence among nations has been one of the mega-trends in the world economy since the end of the Second World War and particularly since the mid-1970s. However, such a trend was initially less apparent to a nation like the United States with an economy that is relatively large and self-sufficient. On the other hand, to smaller countries like Belgium and Luxembourg, having an average propensity to import exceeding 50 percent and being members of the European Community, or to newly industrializing countries that have vividly experienced the benefit of a rapid rise in foreign trade, the interdependence of world economies has been very apparent.

Regardless of the size and characteristics of national economies, the evidence of interdependence among nations is aplenty and filled with everyday news: for example, an immediate drop in share prices of multinational banks in response to a debt-service moratorium announced by a Latin American government; almost spontaneous chain reactions in the world-wide stock markets to the US stock market crash in 1987; the plunging of the US dollar value in response to a German central bank's discount rate hike; the up-and-down reactions of the European currency unit (ECU) bond market to the Maastricht Treaty and the subsequent Danish rejection, and so on.

To a larger extent, the acceleration of interdependence of world economies has been reinforced by the internationalization and globalization of the financial markets, particularly the banking markets. Thus, no longer can the subject matters of money and banking be dealt with properly without taking into account the interdependence of world economies. At the macroeconomic level, understanding the interactions among different economies is a key to prescribing correct policy measures. At the microeconomic level, an understanding of the evolution of the domestic banking market into an integral part of a single global financial market is important to explain the behavior of banks. Also, from a bank management point of view, an understanding of increasingly open and competitive banking environments is essential for the strategic planning of any bank, whether it is a domestic or an international bank.

Measurement of the openness of an economy

How can we then measure the openness of an economy? The openness of an economy is the degree of its exposure to the rest of the world. Openness and interdependence are often used interchangeably. However, the concept of interdependence of an economy requires not only an openness of the economy to the rest of the world as a requisite, but also a two-way causality relationship between the economy in question and the rest of the world.

The degree of openness of an economy can be measured by comparing the size of external transactions to that of domestic transactions, for example by the ratio of international trade (exports, imports, or both) of the economy to its gross domestic product (GDP) or gross national product (GNP).

GDP is the value of the final goods and services produced within a nation, regardless of whose residents produced them, during a given period, whereas GNP is the value of those goods and services produced by the residents of a given nation, regardless of where they produced them, at home or abroad. Thus, the divergence of GDP and GNP can also be used as an index of the degree of openness of the economy, particularly to measure the degree of factor movements indirectly.

In interpreting the ratio of GDP to GNP, some caution is in order. Even if the ratio is unity, that does not mean that the economy is closed. For example, if factor income paid out abroad and factor income received from abroad are the same, the ratio will be unity even though the amount of such income may be large. In general, however, if GDP is larger than GNP, the economy is utilizing more foreign factors of production for domestic production. Developing countries with a significant presence of foreign direct investment are likely to have greater GDP than GNP. Countries sending their workers for overseas employment may experience a GDP that is less than their GNP.

The degree of openness can also be measured by using financial market data, for instance the ratio of foreign financial assets held to total financial assets owned by residents of a nation. Table 1.1 shows the openness of sample countries, including the United States and its major trading partner countries.

Analytic definition of economic interdependence

As noted earlier, the concept of economic interdependence focuses on both openness and two-way causality between the activities of one economy and those of another economy (or the rest of the world).

Table 1.1 Openness of economies of sample countries (1990)

Country	Ranking in trade with USA	EX/GDP	IM/GDP	EXIM/GDP	GDP/GNP	FA/TA	FL/TL
Bel-Lux	14	0.638	0.648	1.286	1.009	0.558	0.697
Canada	1	0.227	0.215	0.441	1.037	0.134	0.193
France	8	0.184	0.199	0.383	–	0.370	0.398
Germany	3	0.275	0.231	0.506	0.983	0.163	0.093
Italy	9	0.156	0.167	0.322	1.012	0.106	0.163
Japan	2	0.097	0.080	0.177	0.992	0.139	0.194
Korea	7	0.271	0.290	0.561	1.007	0.059	0.064
Netherlands	11	0.474	0.454	0.929	0.991	0.362	0.299
Singapore	12	1.519	1.755	3.273	0.981	0.393	0.390
UK	5	0.191	0.230	0.421	0.991	0.450	0.489
USA		0.073	0.095	0.168	0.992	0.086	0.118

Sources: IMF (1992) *International Financial Statistics*, January; IMF (1991) *Direction of Trade Yearbook*
Notes: EX, exports of goods; IM, imports of goods; EXIM = EX + IM; FA, foreign financial assets held by banks; FL, banks' liabilities to foreign residents; TA, total financial assets of banks; TL, total liabilities of banks.

Now let us examine the concept of economic interdependence in a formal analytic context. First, let us assume that in a closed economy (denoted by 1) there is one ultimate policy goal (Y_1), which is influenced by one policy instrument (X_1), the previous level of economic activity (Y_{-1}), one non-policy factor (Z_1), and an error term (e_1). Then the outcome of the ultimate policy goal, say the level of GNP, can be expressed as follows:

$$Y_1 = b_1 X_1 + c_1 Y_{-1} + d_1 Z_1 + e_1. \tag{1.1}$$

In this case the causality is relatively clear, as long as the coefficients b_1, c_1 and d_1 are statistically significant.

Now, in the case of two economies, economy 1 (denoted by subscript 1) and economy 2 (denoted by subscript 2), the relations among variables such as ultimate target variables (Y_1, Y_2), policy instruments (X_1, X_2), non-policy variables (Z_1, Z_2), previous levels of economic activities (Y_{-1}, Y_{-2}), and error terms (e_1, e_2) can be expressed as follows:

$$\begin{bmatrix} a_{11} & a_{12} \\ a_{21} & a_{22} \end{bmatrix} \begin{bmatrix} Y_1 \\ Y_2 \end{bmatrix} + \begin{bmatrix} b_{11} & b_{12} \\ b_{21} & b_{22} \end{bmatrix} \begin{bmatrix} X_1 \\ X_2 \end{bmatrix} + \begin{bmatrix} c_{11} & c_{12} \\ c_{21} & c_{22} \end{bmatrix} \begin{bmatrix} Y_{-1} \\ Y_{-2} \end{bmatrix}$$

$$+ \begin{bmatrix} d_{11} & d_{12} \\ d_{21} & d_{22} \end{bmatrix} \begin{bmatrix} Z_1 \\ Z_2 \end{bmatrix} + \begin{bmatrix} e_1 \\ e_2 \end{bmatrix} = \begin{bmatrix} 0 \\ 0 \end{bmatrix}. \tag{1.2}$$

If all the circled coefficients are zero, these two economies are completely independent or equivalent to closed economies. If the circled coefficients on the first row are zeros but those on the second row are nonzeros, the relationship is a one-way street similar to the American perception of the US economy during the period immediately following the Second World War. Now, if some of the coefficients on both rows are no longer zeros, then the relationship becomes more of a two-way street, each economy dependent on the other. Obviously, each coefficient associated with an explanatory variable represents the degree of influence exerted on the dependent variable.

At the microeconomic level, increasing economic interdependence signifies increasing integration of domestic and foreign output as well as input markets. For example, banks produce their output using different national currencies at facilities located in any part of the world. Managers of certain multinational banks are recruited worldwide and assigned to banking facilities in different countries. Their customers may be third-country residents.

MONEY AND BANKING IN AN OPEN ECONOMY

In the field of money and banking for a closed economy, we commonly study functions of domestic money, how the size of the aggregate domestic money stock is determined (money supply process), how the money stock affects the economy (transmission process), and how and to what extent the central bank influences the whole process. These are topics for the study of monetary environments. In addition, we study microscopic aspects of banking such as banking industry structure, bank regulations, activities of banks, and optimization behavior of banks.

In the field of international money and banking where an international dimension is added to domestic money and banking, we must first consider multicurrency environments. The precise conditions of multicurrency environments are determined by both domestic and foreign government actions as well as by market forces, which are occasionally reinforced by external shocks. Thus, it becomes increasingly difficult for economic policy makers to achieve their policy goals, partly because policy effects may be washed out and partly because the choice of policy tools becomes more constrained by external factors.

For banks, such unsettled monetary environments cause greater uncertainty. In addition, banks face national differences in bank regulations. Although there has been a concerted effort toward harmonization of bank regulations in recent years among industrial countries, including the Basle Accord and European Community (EC) regulatory harmonization, regulatory environments are still distinctively different from country to country. Such differences create distorted comparative advantage among banks of different countries.

The upper or lower panel of Figure 1.1, viewed separately, represents the case of a closed economy. The upper panel shows a simplified version of

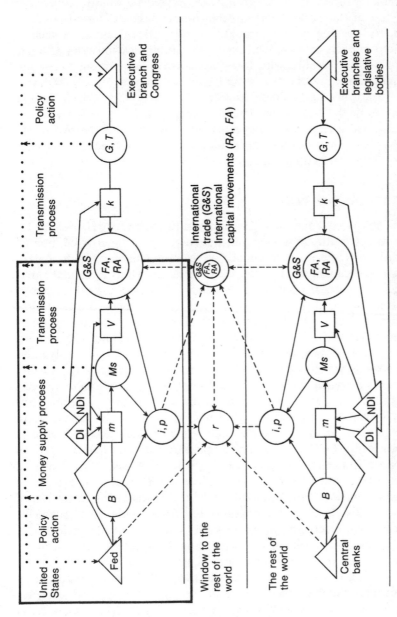

Figure 1.1 Monetary and fiscal policy processes: · · ▶, market signal; ──▶, closed economy; ──▶, new relations in open economy; *B*, base money; DI, depository institutions; *FA*, financial assets; *G*, government expenditures; *G&S*, goods and services; NDI, non-depository institutions private sector; *i*, interest rates; *k*, expenditure multiplier; *m*, money multiplier; *Ms*, money stock; *p*, price level; *r*, exchange rates; *RA*, real assets; *T*, taxes; *V*, velocity of money

the monetary process in the United States. When the window of contact with the rest of the world opens up, the country becomes interdependent. The window opening occurs through several different channels such as exports and imports of goods and services or purchases and sales of financial and real assets dealing with foreign residents. In addition, to support such transactions, buyers and sellers may go to the foreign exchange markets to acquire or liquidate foreign currencies. The broken lines in Figure 1.1 show the transactions caused by the added international dimensions. As noted earlier, when the economy is exposed to the rest of the world, the direction of causality becomes less clear. In subsequent chapters, we will examine these topics in more detail.

THE PLAN OF THE BOOK

This book consists of four parts. The first part of the book presents a bird's-eye view of international money and banking. Since the crux of international banking is international finance, we start in Chapter 2 with analysis of international capital movements. We examine the effect of capital movement on income redistribution and the characteristics of different types of international capital flows, including capital flight. Chapter 3 provides the theory of international banking as a synthesis of theories of foreign direct investment. We proceed to examine the segmented banking and product market matrices, using a taxonomic approach. In Chapter 4 we study international money, which is particularly important as it shapes the monetary environments in which international banks operate. In addition to key currencies and gold, we pay special attention to artificial currency units including special drawing rights (SDRs) and ECUs for private transactions. The discussion of artificial currency units leads us to an examination of a possible use of the ECU to construct an optimum currency area. We present the European Monetary Union, as envisaged in the Maastricht Accord, as such a possibility. In Chapter 5, we analyze the international balance of payments statements, their structure and the economic interpretation of balances. We also examine the relationship between balance of payments and international indebtedness and between exchange gap and savings gap. Finally, we discuss the role of commercial banks in international transactions, as recorded in the balance of payments.

The second part of the book consists of the structure and workings of a number of interrelated markets – foreign exchange markets, Eurocurrency markets, and US and UK money and banking markets, where commercial banks play a major role. We will first examine the structure of foreign exchange markets in Chapter 6. We are interested in not only the physical structure of the market but also contractual arrangements of products in the market. Chapter 7 covers arbitrage activities of banks in the exchange market and other exchange-related services provided by banks. Chapter 8 deals with the Eurocurrency market. We first discuss two alternative approaches to explaining the development of Eurocurrency markets, namely the balance of payments approach and the regulatory difference approach. We also note the importance of differentiating between regulatory cost differences and regulatory constraint differences. After reviewing the workings of the market, we examine the question of whether the Eurocurrency market is inflationary or not.

Since a market is a place where certain products are traded, in Chapter 9 we direct our attention to new product developments under the heading of international financial innovations. We examine causes of supply and demand for international financial innovations and recent major developments. We then extend our analysis to the role of innovations in financial market integration, to national monetary policy implications, and to International Monetary Fund (IMF) operational implications. Chapter 10 provides an overview of the US money and banking markets. Similarly, Chapter 11 presents an analysis of the UK system. Both chapters may serve as reference points for comparative analysis of the banking market structure, the bank regulatory framework, and the role of banks in the monetary policy process, not only in the UK and the United States, but also in other countries.

The third part of the book covers international bank regulations. Chapter 12 provides an analytic framework for evaluation of international bank regulations. The topics include classification of banking regulations by their impacts rather than by *de jure*, emerging principles of regulatory jurisdictions, and the optimum bank regulation. Then, we turn our attention to US regulations in Chapter 13. We study US regulations governing both US banks having international operations and foreign banks operating in the United States. Chapter 14 covers the EC regulatory framework for credit institutions, as predicated by the Second Banking Directive. We also examine issues arising from the reciprocity requirements.

The final part of the book examines selective activities of international banks, namely international portfolio investment, international trade finance, and international lending. In Chapter 15, we first analyze several basic models of portfolio investment. We then examine the effects of including foreign financial assets in a portfolio. Finally, we discuss the role of banks in international portfolio management. Chapter 16 covers international trade finance. In this chapter, we first examine how different methods of payment shift risks and trade financing costs between the seller and the buyer. We next study the required documentation for international trade transactions. We then take a look at how various methods of payment result in alternative methods of trade financing, including nonconventional methods of financing. In the final chapter we study three sequentially related topics: country risk analysis, international bank lending, and debt restructuring issues. We will pay particular attention to two alternative approaches to the resolution of debt problems, namely the concerted renegotiation approach and the market-oriented approach.

METHODOLOGICAL NOTES

This book presents basic principles, theories, and practices for a sound understanding of international money and banking. Although the US institutional settings are used as a frame of reference, the EC and other individual country settings are also incorporated to the extent possible. As cited in the preceding section, the book deals with both macro-finance and micro-finance topics.

Where practical, the book introduces concepts applicable to a closed economy first and expands them suitably to an open economy. The book also attempts to give a balanced coverage of theory and practice. International banking practices are evolutionary optimization behaviors of banks, given institutional constraints. The institutional constraints themselves are in turn shaped by repeated practices. Some of the topics covered are fairly recent developments, which require new theoretical underpinnings. Thus, in some instances, we may employ untested hypotheses in order to facilitate our discussion.

Review problems and exercises are provided at the end of each chapter. When a class is organized in two-tier sessions, one for primary lectures and the other for review and discussions, these questions may serve as convenient tools for such review sessions.

The Basic readings give the most relevant references, clearly identifying the particular concepts or theories which are presented in the chapter. The Further readings are for students who are interested in pursuing the subject matter further.

REVIEW PROBLEMS AND EXERCISES

1. What is the difference between openness and interdependence of an economy?

2. If the GDP/GNP ratio is used as a measure of openness of an economy, what sort of inference can you make for each of the following cases?
   (a) GDP/GNP > 1
   (b) GDP/GNP = 1
   (c) GDP/GNP < 1

3. Differentiate the meaning of widening of interdependence and deepening of interdependence.

4. Using equation (1.2) on page 5, show a case of one-way dependence and a case of two-way interdependence.

5. Using Figure 1.1, elaborate the monetary process in a closed economy. Specifically, answer the following:
   (a) What sort of policy tools can the Federal Reserve use to influence the size of base money?
   (b) How does the money stock influence the economy (such as GNP growth rate and rate of inflation)?

BASIC READING

Bryant, R. C. (1980) *Money and Monetary Policy in Interdependent Nations*, Washington, D.C.: Brookings Institution.

Bryant, R. C., Henderson, D. W., Holtham, G., Hooper, P. and Symansky, S. A. (eds) (1988) *Empirical Macroeconomics for Interdependent Economies*, Washington, D.C.: Brookings Institution, Chapter 1.

Grassman, S. (1980) "Long-term Trends in Openness of National Economies," *Oxford Economic Papers*, 32: 123–33.

Hervey, J. L. (1986) "Internationalization of Uncle Sam," *Federal Reserve Bank of Chicago Economic Perspectives*, May–June: 3–14.

Javanovic, M. N. (1991) *International Economic Integration*, London: Routledge.

Rivera-Batiz, F. L. and Rivera-Batiz, L. (1985) *International Finance and Open Economy Macroeconomics*, New York: Macmillan, Chapter 1.

FURTHER READING

Das, D. K. (ed.) (1993) *International Finance*, London: Routledge.

Hollerman, L. (1960) "What Does 'Dependence' Mean in International Trade?" *Kyklos*, 13: 102–8.

Kenen, P. B. (1985) "Macroeconomic Theory and Policy: How the Closed Economy was Opened," in Jones, R. W. and Kenen, P. B. (eds) *Handbook of International Economics*, Vol. 2, Amsterdam: North-Holland, 625–77.

McKibbin, W. J. and Sachs, J. D. (1991) *Global Linkages: Macroeconomic Interdependence and Cooperation in the World Economy*, Washington, D.C.: Brookings Institution.

Pardee, S. E. (1987) "Internationalization of Financial Markets," *Federal Reserve Bank of Kansas City Economic Review*, February: 3–7.

Chapter 2

International capital movements

INTRODUCTION

International capital movement is one of the central topics in international money and banking. Each capital movement affects international monetary environments. Moreover, behind each capital movement banks are almost always involved either as financial dealers, or as brokers, or simply as bookkeepers. When we say international capital movement, it does not necessarily mean a physical cross-border movement of financial assets. Rather it means a change in ownership of financial assets between residents of different countries. That is, a resident of one country is selling financial assets (borrowing), while a resident of another country is buying financial assets (lending). Therefore, "investment in country A" means purchase of financial instruments issued by residents of country A. Such a transaction enables the buyer of financial assets to trade off her current use of real resources for her future use. At the same time it permits the seller of financial assets to exchange his future use of real resources for his present use by importing goods and services financed by the resident of the other country.

We first look at the effect of international capital movements on functional income distribution in both capital exporting and capital importing countries. The distributional effects of capital movement have often been a source of heated political debate, because capital outflows are viewed as exporting domestic jobs and shrinking the labor share of the income pie. After examining these effects and allocative efficiency issues, we will turn our attention to the characteristics of different types of capital movements, namely short-term capital movements, portfolio investment, and direct foreign investment.

INTERNATIONAL CAPITAL MOVEMENT AND ECONOMIC WELFARE

Let us now examine a basic model of foreign capital flow. It is assumed that

(a) the diminishing marginal product of capital holds, that is, as the size of capital increases while other factors of production are held constant, the marginal productivity of capital will eventually diminish; and (b) the functional distribution of income is determined by the marginal productivity. Given the above, we can determine the direction of capital flow, the amount of flow, and the impact of such flow on income distribution at home and abroad.

In Figure 2.1, curve AA' represents the marginal product of capital in country 1, whereas curve BB' represents the marginal product of capital in country 2. These curves are determined by each country's level of technology and other factors complementary to capital. In isolation, the amount of capital in country 1 is OF and in country 2 it is O'F.

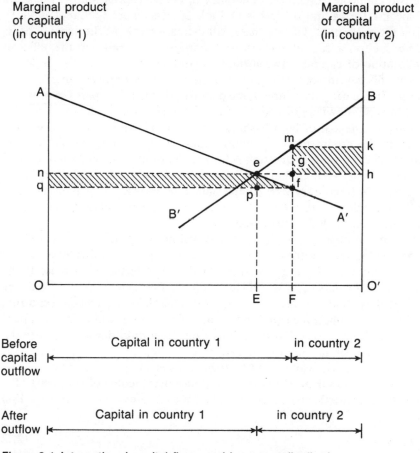

Figure 2.1 International capital flows and income redistribution

The total amount of income in country 1 is represented by the area OFfA, whereas the total amount in country 2 is the area O'FmB. According to the marginal productivity theory of income distribution, the share of income distributed to capital owners in country 1 is the area covered by OFfq which is determined by the marginal productivity of capital Ff multiplied by the amount of capital OF.[1] The share for the owners of labor factor of production is the residual part under the capital productivity curve, qfA.

Since the marginal product of capital in country 1 is lower than in country 2, capital will flow out from country 1 to country 2 seeking a higher rate of return. The amount of flow will be FE, so that the marginal products in these two countries will become equal. After the movement of capital, the capital owners of country 1 will gain their share partly at the expense of labor and partly because of more efficient reallocation of capital between the two countries. Likewise, in country 2, before capital inflow, the share of income for capital owners is O'Fmk and the share for labor is kmB. After the movement, labor's share will increase partly at the expense of its home country's capital owners and partly as a result of the efficient reallocation of capital between the two countries.

Not only causing redistribution of income, the free movement of capital will result in a net gain of area fgme on a worldwide basis, part fge of which goes to capital owners of country 1 and part gme goes to labor owners of country 2. The loss of labor's share in the capital exporting country is the basis of the argument that capital export is partly responsible for job export. Then, a welfare question is how to distribute the net gain of capital outflow fge between capital and labor in country 1.[2] A similar argument would apply to country 2 to compensate capital owners for their loss due to capital inflow. Table 2.1 summarizes the effect of international capital movement on income distribution.

Indeed, another way to look at this welfare question is which welfare target the capital exporting country should maximize, worldwide welfare or its own country's welfare – welfare measured in terms of income. If the objective is to maximize worldwide income, free capital flows should be permitted so that the rate of return on capital in the capital exporting country (i_1) will become equal to the rate of return on capital in the capital importing country (i_2). However, this same condition does not ensure the maximization of income of the capital exporting country. In effect, it is necessary to restrict capital outflows before reaching the condition $i_1 = i_2$.

Let us take a look at why it is so. Suppose that income of country 1 (Y_1) consists of domestic-source income (Y_{11}) and foreign-source income (Y_{21}) so that

$$Y_1 = Y_{11} + Y_{21} \tag{2.1}$$

Table 2.1 Redistribution of income due to international capital flows

	Before capital flow	After capital flow	Gain or loss
Country 1			
Labor	qfA	neA	Loss of **qpen** to domestic capital owners investing at home
			Loss of **pfe** to domestic capital owners investing abroad
Capital	OFfq	OEen + EFge	Gain of **qpen** + **pfe** from domestic labor
			Gain of **fge** from worldwide efficient allocation of capital
Country 2			
Labor	kmB	heB	Gain of **hgmk** from domestic capital owners
			Gain of **gme** due to worldwide efficient allocation of capital
Capital	O'Fmk	O'Fgh	Loss of **hgmk** to domestic labor

Now, Y_{11} is a function of the total endowed capital of country 1 (K_1) less foreign investment (I),

$$Y_{11} = f(K_1 - I) \tag{2.2}$$

whereas Y_{21} is a function of two variables, namely the amount of foreign investment (I) and its rate of return (i_2):

$$Y_{21} = i_2 I. \tag{2.3}$$

Then

$$Y_1 = f(K_1 - I) + i_2 I. \tag{2.4}$$

In order to find the maximum value of income Y_1, we differentiate Y_1 with respect to I and set the result equal to zero, as follows:

$$\frac{dY_1}{dI} = -\frac{df}{dI} + i_2 + I\frac{di_2}{dI} = 0. \tag{2.5}$$

Since df/dI is the marginal product of capital in country 1, that is, $df/dI = i_1$, equation (2.5) yields

$$i_1 = i_2 + I\frac{di_2}{dI} \tag{2.6}$$

which is the condition needed for the maximization of income in country 1. We note that di_2/dI is negative, because a diminishing marginal rate of return is assumed. Therefore condition (2.6) implies that

$$i_1 < i_2. \tag{2.7}$$

That is, the amount of capital outflow needed to maximize the income of the capital exporting country will be less than the level which will maximize the worldwide income. Thus, the capital exporting country may have to reduce capital outflows instead of permitting free outflows. At what point should the country stop outflows then? It depends on the magnitude of $I\,di_2/dI$ in equation (2.6). Table 2.2 gives a numerical example. Column (1) shows the amount of foreign investment. The rate of return on investment in the capital exporting country is shown in column (2). Note that the rate of return (measured in marginal product) is increasing because less capital becomes available at home as a result of foreign investment. Likewise, the rate of return on investment in the capital importing country, listed in column (3), is decreasing because more capital becomes available as a result of foreign capital influx. The optimal capital outflow to maximize income of the capital exporting country is at 40 where $i_1 = i_2 + I\,di/dI = 11.6$ percent, which satisfies the condition in equation (2.6). On the other hand, the optimal amount of foreign investment to maximize the worldwide income is about 65 where $i_1 = i_2$, which is about 14 percent. Thus, the capital exporting country should intervene by imposing a penalty, for example a foreign investment tax, amounting to 5.2 percent.

In Chapter 12, we will reexamine this optimization question to determine the optimum burden of international bank regulation from a banking capital exporting country's point of view.

Table 2.2 Determination of optimal amount of foreign investment

Foreign Investment I (1)	Rate of return in country 1 i_1 (%) (2)	Rate of return in country 2 i_2(%) (3)	$(I/\Delta I)\Delta i_2$ (%) (4)	(%) (3) + (4)
20	9.1	19.5	–	–
30	10.4	18.1	– 4.2	13.9
40	11.6	16.8	– 5.2	11.6
50	12.7	15.6	– 6.0	9.6
60	13.7	14.5	– 6.6	7.9
70	14.6	13.5	– 7.0	6.5
80	15.6	12.6	– 7.2	5.4
90	16.1	11.8	– 7.2	4.6

Note: Figures under Column (4) are based on the value of I which represents a new level of investment rather than the previous level.

SHORT-TERM CAPITAL INVESTMENT

Interest arbitrage

When the economy is open, the investor faces two investment alternatives, to invest at home or to invest abroad. Let us assume that the investor is risk neutral and guided by the maximization of the terminal value. Then he will compare the interest rate at home and that abroad, taking into account foreign exchange gains or losses from exchange rate movements. Suppose he has $1 million investment funds and faces the following market conditions:

r_{00} is the spot exchange rate, $1.2000 per pound;
r_{01} is the one-year forward exchange rate, $1.1880 per pound;
i_d is the domestic (US) interest rate, 8 percent;
i_f is the foreign (UK) interest rate, 10 percent.

For the notation of exchange rates, the first subscript indicates the time of contract and the second the time of delivery (Figure 2.2). Thus, $1 million invested at home for one year becomes $1.08 million:

$$\$1 \text{ million}(1 + 0.8) = \$1.08 \text{ million}. \tag{2.8}$$

On the other hand, investment in the UK market requires three steps: (a) conversion of $1 million into pounds at the spot rate, (b) investing sterling pounds in the UK money market instrument, yielding, say, a 10 percent return, and (c) converting investment proceeds back into dollars at the forward rate which is set at the beginning of the investment through a forward contract. Then, $1 million invested in the UK money market becomes $1.089 million:

$$\$1 \text{ million} \times (£1/\$1.2)(1 + 0.10) \times \$1.188/£1 = \$1,089,000. \tag{2.9}$$

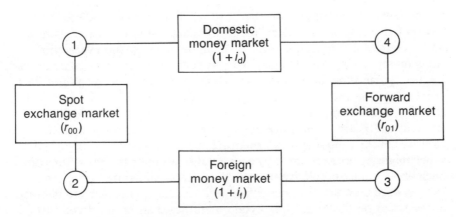

Figure 2.2 An interest rate arbitrage mechanism

In general, the direction of short-term international capital movement will be determined by the terminal value of each investment alternative. The short-term funds will flow out of the US money market into the UK market if

$$\frac{1}{r_{00}} (1 + i_f)r_{01} > 1 + i_d. \tag{2.10}$$

Alternatively, funds will flow into the US market if

$$\frac{1}{r_{00}} (1 + i_f)r_{01} < 1 + i_d. \tag{2.11}$$

The equilibrium condition where the investor becomes indifferent between investing at home or abroad is obtained when

$$\frac{1}{r_{00}} (1 + i_f)r_{01} = 1 + i_d. \tag{2.12}$$

As shown in equations (2.10) and (2.11), to take advantage of interest rate differentials in the different national markets by investing in the market where the interest rate is higher and borrowing in the market where the interest rate (including foreign exchange gain $(+)$ or loss $(-)$) is lower is termed an interest arbitrage. More precisely, this is a case of covered interest arbitrage, covered by a forward contract. It is this arbitrage that restores the market equilibrium promptly, leaving no room for further profit for a while. Figure 2.3 shows the recent experience in the covered interest rate arbitrage between the US dollar and three other major currencies. The narrow band around zero with covered arbitrage indicates how efficient the market is.

Speculative short-term capital movements

For a number of countries, however, certain short-term capital movements have posed substantial problems for their balance of payments adjustment. Some short-term capital movements are motivated by the expectation of gains or the avoidance of losses from sudden exchange rate changes, as frequently happened in the 1930s as well as in the post-Second World War years under the IMF fixed exchange rate system. When an investor anticipates a devaluation of the home currency, he will purchase foreign currency at the present low price and invest abroad without committing a forward contract, hoping to sell the foreign currency later at a higher price which might be brought about by actual devaluation of the home currency. Such an action is speculative because the outflow of capital is not covered by a forward contract. In other words, it is speculative because profitability is calculated on the basis of expectations rather than on fixed contractual terms. Thus, at the time of expected devaluation, there will be an exodus

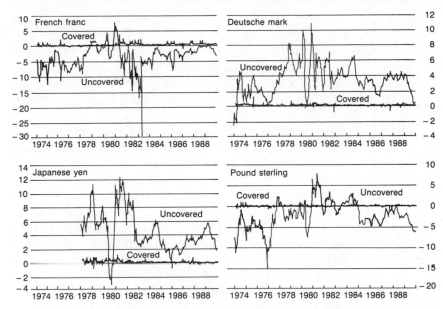

Figure 2.3 Covered and uncovered interest rate differentials: an indicator of market efficiency (US dollar versus other currencies). The uncovered differential is the three-month US Eurodollar deposit rate minus the corresponding three-month Eurocurrency rate, as specified. The covered differential is the uncovered differential minus the three-month forward rate
Source: IMF (1991) *Determinants and Systemic Consequences of International Capital Flows*, Washington, D.C., p. 9

of short-term capital from the home country. But that is precisely the time when the home country needs capital inflows. In the short run, such sudden outflows create a shortage of international liquidity in the country, giving pressure for devaluation of the home currency even though originally such a devaluation was unwarranted. Sudden outflows of capital also cause depletion of official reserves, leading to further instability in the exchange markets.[3]

Capital flight

Another type of short-term capital movement, so-called capital flight, is somewhat more difficult to define. Capital flight is private short-term capital outflows from developing countries, outflows which avoid official measurement or detection.

Comparing with speculative capital movement, we find that capital flight is different in several aspects, namely the direction of flows, purposes, and morality. First, the direction of speculative capital flows is in two ways depending on the direction of expected changes in foreign exchange rates. If a devaluation of the home currency is expected, short-term capital will flow out from the home country. On the other hand, an expected revaluation will cause inflows. Capital flight is one-way movement flowing out from developing countries. The fled capital usually remains abroad. Second, the motive of speculative flows is mainly to take advantage of expected rate changes, whereas the motives of capital flight are varied but are mainly defensive in nature, "fleeing" from unfavorable investment environments in developing countries. Recall Figure 2.1. Capital flight from country 2 occurs when the rate of return, real or perceived, becomes low, pressing curve BB' downward to shift the equilibrium point e below point f. Unfavorable investment conditions are real or potential, including (a) limited investment opportunities caused by regulatory constraints such as interest rate ceilings on deposits, (b) depreciation of the value of invested assets due to a high rate of inflation or frequent devaluation of the home currency and (c) restriction in the use of assets such as the imposition of foreign exchange control or expropriation. In short, the resident in the developing countries faces the possibility of losing the value of his assets in part or in total without appropriate compensation, whereas the risk on similar assets held abroad is perceived to be significantly less. Third, speculative capital movement does not necessarily avoid official detection or measurement, whereas capital flight intentionally does.

Besides the above definition, there are several variations in the definition of capital flight. For example, Cuddington (1986) defines short-term speculative capital outflows as capital flight, emphasizing the disruptive effects of such outflows on the country's balance of payments, outflows being caused most commonly by an over-valued exchange rate. On the other hand, taking a broader approach, the World Bank (1985) defines total private capital outflows from developing countries as capital flight, stressing the need of such capital at home. Lessard and Williamson (1987) define capital flight as resident capital that flees from the perception of abnormal risks at home, focusing on the importance of differences in perceived risks between resident capital owners and foreign capital investors. On the other hand, our definition can be classified as an approach based on a "derived measure," which derives its measured amount of capital flight by identifying part of a country's total stock of external claims which does not yield recorded investment income. Why is there such a part? It is due to the cumulative outflows of capital which have avoided official detection or measurement, fleeing from risks at home perceived to be greater than those abroad. This definition is based on works of Khan and Ul Haque (1985, 1987) and Rojas-Suárez (1991).

This avoidance of official detection creates difficulties in estimating the magnitude of capital flight. Khan and Ul Haque (1987) suggest two indirect methods for such estimation, as shown in Table 2.3. The first approach is to use simply gross private short-term capital flows plus net errors and omissions in the country's balance of payments account. Of course, this approach (suitable for the World Bank definition) covers all short-term capital outflows including those for speculative and nonspeculative purposes as well as those fleeing from economic or political uncertainties in the home country. The second approach (suitable for our definition) is to use the difference in magnitude between total private capital outflows and the part for which interest income is identified and reported. Table 2.3 shows the estimated capital flight of eight countries, using these two approaches. These countries are heavily indebted externally and presumably cannot afford short-term capital outflows; yet the table indicates a substantial accumulation of external claims.

Why are we concerned about capital flight? In the short run, the effect of capital flight is similar to that of speculative capital movements, causing instability in the exchange markets. In the long run, lessened availability of foreign financial resources means slower domestic capital formation and less technology transfer, all leading to slower economic growth. Also it is undesirable from a tax equity point of view, since the home government would not be able to tax undetected income generated from capital flight.

Table 2.3 Estimates of foreign debt and capital flight, 1974–82 (in billions of US dollars)

		Method 1		Method 2	
	Gross external debt (1)	Cumulative capital flight (2)	(2)/(1)(%) (3)	Cumulative capital flight (4)	(4)/(1)(%) (5)
Argentina	43.6	15.3	35.1	31.3	71.8
Brazil	90.5	− 0.2	− 0.2	3.9	4.3
Chile	17.3	− 1.9	− 11.0	− 0.7	− 4.0
Korea	37.1	0.6	1.6	8.1	21.8
Mexico	85.6	32.7	38.2	29.4	34.3
Peru	11.6	1.2	10.3	3.8	32.8
Philippines	23.3	?	?	8.4	36.1
Venezuela	31.8	10.8	34.0	15.6	49.1

Source: Khan, M. S. and Ul Haque, N. (1987) "Capital Flight from Developing Countries." Finance and Development, 24 (1): 4
Notes: Method 1, private short-term capital plus net errors and omissions; method 2, total private capital flows minus private capital flows calculated on the basis of reported interest income.
A negative sign indicates capital inflow.
?, not estimated.

Thus, capital flight implies a loss of resources which could have been used to increase domestic investment and to mitigate balance of payments problems including external debt-service problems. The potential detrimental effect of capital flight can easily be seen when we take a look at the actual magnitudes involved. The total amount of capital flight for a group of highly indebted developing countries (Argentina, Bolivia, Chile, Colombia, Ecuador, Gabon, Jamaica, Mexico, Nigeria, Peru, the Philippines, Venezuela, and Yugoslavia) in 1978 was estimated to be $47.30 billion, equivalent to 66 percent of their total external claims and 42 percent of their total external debts. The magnitude of capital flight steadily increased over a decade. In 1988 the total amount reached $184.01 billion, which was equivalent to 77 percent of their total external claims and 51 percent of their total external debt.[4] Such a high percentage of capital flight indicates the need for concerted efforts to win back the confidence of resident capital left abroad. Concerted efforts may include macroeconomic policy measures (such as reduction in government deficits, lower inflation, and removal of foreign exchange controls) as well as microeconomic policy measures (such as removal of tax-like restrictions on investment).

Then, what are the conduits used for deploying assets abroad avoiding official detection? Capital flight is accomplished commonly by under-invoicing exports and overinvoicing imports, or by simply not reporting fees and commissions paid by foreign residents which are kept abroad, or by paying dummy fees and commissions by home residents to foreign residents, or even by outright smuggling of foreign currencies or foreign exchange-earning commodities.

INTERNATIONAL PORTFOLIO INVESTMENT

International portfolio investment involves purchase of stocks or bonds issued by foreign companies or governments. It offers the investor long-term returns and diversified risk without the responsibility of management and control. In 1988, for example, total portfolio investment reported in the balance of payments accounts by IMF member countries amounted to SDR 202.1 billion ($272.0 billion), whereas the short-term lending was SDR 258.8 billion ($348.3 billion).[5]

A bulk of portfolio investment has been made in industrial countries. Many of these countries have witnessed simultaneous inflows and outflows of portfolio capital. On the other hand, portfolio investment has not provided much finance for developing countries, mainly because of impeding restrictions imposed by host countries, such as a minimum holding period requirement, higher capital gains taxes, foreign exchange controls, discriminatory treatment of foreign investors, and under-developed secondary markets. Nonetheless, the portfolio investment climate in developing countries is improving for a number of reasons. For example, in many developing countries, companies have outgrown their capital markets and need new sources of capital injection. The traditional sources of bank loans have become scarce. Equity capital does not require a periodic fixed amount repayment, thereby giving less pressure on the country's balance of payments. In addition, the World Bank group and other regional development banks have actively been promoting domestic stock and bond markets.

Now let us consider an individual investor's position. For short-term financial investment abroad, the type of risk associated with such investment is by and large foreign exchange rate risk. Therefore, if an investor wishes to cover his position, he is likely to engage in interest-arbitrage-type investment. On the other hand, if he wishes to assume risk, he may engage in speculative investment. However, in the case of portfolio investment, an investor must consider additional risks such as credit risk of the debtor (more explicitly) and country risk, in addition to foreign exchange rate risk.

How can an investor reduce his international portfolio risk? It has been shown that if the investor divides his available funds and invests in several different international financial assets simultaneously, he may be able to reduce risk. It is entirely possible to achieve such diversification through investing in a domestic company which in turn diversifies internationally.

The investor behavior of risk diversification can explain observed two-way international capital flows. For example, if security A is available in one country while security B (with about the same average yield as security A but less directly related to the yield on security A) is available in another country, investors in the first country may be better off by investing some of their available resources in security A and some in security B instead of investing all in security A. Likewise, investors in the second country may be better off by investing some in security A and some in their country's security B.

In summary, as we examined in the previous section, the interest arbitrage model can explain the international financial movement which is caused by yield differentials. However, it cannot explain observed two-way portfolio investment flows which take place even when the rates of return in both countries are about the same. Accounting for risk diversification can explain such flows.

In Chapter 15, we will study the portfolio theory of international investment in more detail and examine the effects of international portfolio diversification.

DIRECT FOREIGN INVESTMENT

Direct foreign investment is investment made to acquire a lasting interest in an enterprise operating in a country other than that of the investor. In this instance the investor has an effective voice or control in the management of the enterprise. What percentage of share ownership can constitute an effective voice is still an open question.[6]

According to the IMF report, in recent years direct foreign investment by member countries has dramatically increased. In 1988 it reached SDR 109.4 billion ($147.2 billion), which is over five times the SDR 21.6 billion ($23.8 billion) in 1982.[7] Although individuals do make direct foreign investment, for example by purchasing commercial banks in another country, a study by the World Bank shows that the bulk of direct investment is done by a relatively small number of large firms. The 380 largest multinational corporations had foreign sales of about $1,000 billion in 1980, almost $3 billion per firm.[8] These are the firms making large foreign sales associated with direct foreign investment. As Table 2.4 shows, the US-based multinational corporations (MNCs) had foreign sales and purchases (exports and imports) of $609.8 billion in 1986, which was 52.3 percent of total US trade. The table also shows that the total assets of foreign subsidiaries of US multinational corporations amounted to $932 billion in 1986, employing 6.3 million workers abroad then.[9]

Why does direct foreign investment take place? In the case of portfolio investment, an investor does not have an effective voice or control over management of the invested enterprise to influence the rate of return on her investment. However, in the case of direct investment an investor does have

Table 2.4 Size of nonbank US multinational corporations (in billions of US dollars)

	1977	*1982*	*1985*	*1986*
Total assets				
MNCs worldwide	2,033.4	3,493.1	4,297.0	4,746.1
Foreign affiliates	490.2	751.5	834.6	932.3
Total sales				
MNCs worldwide	2,060.3	3,284.2	3,482.2	3,474.7
Foreign affiliates	648.0	935.8	895.5	930.7
Total employees (millions)				
MNCs worldwide	26.081	25.345	24.532	24.124
Foreign affiliates	7.197	6.640	6.419	6.263
US exports associated with US MNCs				
Total exports by US MNCs			171.9	171.0
of which to their foreign affiliates			69.6	71.3
US imports associated with US MNCs				
Total imports by US MNCs			153.6	147.1
of which from their foreign affiliates			68.2	65.6
US trade associated with US MNCs as				
percentage of total US trade			57.0	52.3

Sources: US Department of Commerce (1988) *Survey of Current Business*, June: 85, 87; *Federal Reserve Bulletin* (March 1988), A54

an effective voice to influence the outcome. A number of theories have been advanced, particularly since the 1950s, to identify and explain the basic causes of growth and the changing pattern of direct foreign investment, including the differential rates of return theory, the market size hypothesis, the product cycle theory, the industrial organization theory, the internalization theory, the currency area hypothesis, the customs area hypothesis, and an eclectic approach. [10]

The differential rates of return theory which was popular in the late 1950s argues that if expected marginal revenues are higher abroad than at home, given the same marginal cost of capital for investment at home and abroad, there is an incentive to invest abroad. This theory basically assumes that direct foreign investment is simply an international capital movement and it does not recognize that direct investment is more than that. In addition, this theory cannot explain why some countries are experiencing simultaneous inflows and outflows of direct investment, and empirical studies have not produced conclusive evidence to support this theory.

The market size hypothesis postulates that the market size measured by either sales volume of investor companies or income in the host country is the source of incentives to make direct investment. The available data are consistent with this hypothesis in terms of significance of correlation between direct investment and market size. However, without definitive theoretical underpinning, the significant correlation can also be interpreted to be superfluous.

The product cycle theory employs the notion that most products follow a life cycle. First, new products are introduced in the domestic market as innovations and eventually they are completely standardized, thereby becoming an easier target for competition. Direct foreign investment takes place when firms, facing saturation of the domestic market as the product matures, expand overseas and capture the remaining rents from development of the product. In addition, overseas expansion follows a certain geographical sequence according to the firm's familiarity with the markets. This hypothesis, first introduced by Vernon (1966), is empirically consistent with US direct foreign investment as well as UK and German experience. However, more recent evidence shows that firms introduce new products at home and abroad almost simultaneously. And the innovations do not necessarily start at home.

Hymer (1976) argued that the very existence of multinational firms rests on the monopolistic market imperfections arising from structural imperfections and transactions cost imperfections. The recognition of these two sources of imperfections has led to the development of two theories: the industrial organization theory and the internalization theory of direct foreign investment. The industrial organization theory (or monopolistic market theory) argues that, despite unfavorable conditions abroad for foreign entrants, multinational firms do have net advantage in competing against local firms because they have brand-name products, superior technology, marketing know-how, cheaper financial costs, and economies of scale. On the other hand, the internalization theory argues that direct foreign investment is a result of replacing market transactions with internal transactions. The need for such replacement arises when the entrant firms face greater imperfections in the foreign markets for intermediate inputs. From the acquisition of input to the delivery of output to customers, there are a number of transactions to be performed with outsiders (unaffiliated units) as well as with insiders (affiliates) of a firm. By replacing outsider transactions with insider transactions, a firm may reduce transactions costs, particularly when the market is imperfect. The benefits include avoidance of many-stage negotiations, delays and market uncertainty, minimization of government intervention through transfer pricing and changes of sourcing, and the ability to exercise discriminatory pricing. Also, through such internalization of transactions, a firm can reduce the external exposure of intangible assets, whose value is difficult to protect.

The currency area theory, advanced by Aliber (1970) and Heller (1981), argues that the pattern of direct foreign investment depends on the relative strength of various currencies. The stronger the currency of a certain country, the more likely it is that firms from that country will engage in foreign investment, and the less likely it is that foreign firms will invest in the domestic market. The strength of a currency is determined by the size of the capital market denominated in this currency, its exchange rate risks, the extent of overvaluation of the currency and the market's preference for holding assets in the currency. Empirical studies in line with this hypothesis have focused on testing whether an overvaluation of a currency has caused outflows of direct investment from the currency country and an undervaluation of a currency has caused inflows of direct investment from abroad. The findings indicate that the hypothesis is consistent with the experiences of the United States, the UK, Germany, France, and Canada, and more recently of Japan. We will examine the hypothesis in more detail in relation to international banking in Chapter 3.

Another important hypothesis of direct foreign investment is the customs area hypothesis which argues that, because of preferential treatment of the member countries within the customs area, firms outside the customs area tend to make direct investment in the area in order to substitute international trade.

Finally, an eclectic approach, advanced by Dunning (1988), synthesizes three hypotheses: the organization theory, the internalization theory, and the location theory. Our following discussion is an extension of the eclectic approach. We can identify three basic sources of comparative advantage which give incentives for direct foreign investment: (a) firm-specific advantage, (b) host-country-specific advantage, and (c) home-country-specific advantage.

The firm-specific advantages (captured in the industrial organization and internalization theories) refer to some unique advantages that a firm possesses to compete with host-country firms. Sources of such advantages may include product differentiation, technical know-how, marketing skills, economies of scale, and better access to essential input. These are the advantages typically enjoyed by firms in oligopolistic industries.

The host-country-specific advantages (captured in the market size and customs area hypotheses) cause firms to invest abroad and produce there rather than exporting. Such advantages lead to low-cost production because of low-cost labor, preferential tax and tariff treatments, reduced transportation costs, outright subsidies, and the like. In addition, foreign production *per se* brings about a risk diversification effect, as discussed on pp. 22–3. Risks stemming from uncertain profitability which might be reduced by multinational production include national business cycles, changes in government policies, and changes in the tastes of consumers.

The home-country-specific advantages (captured in the product cycle and currency area theories) include favorable research and development environments where innovations are fostered and a favorable relationship is maintained by the home government with the host government.

These advantages are dynamic in nature, changing over time. In Chapter 3 we will apply the above concepts of direct investment in explaining the expansion of international banks abroad.

SUMMARY

International mobility of capital increases the efficiency of the world economy as a whole and alters distribution of income in each country between capital owners and labor. The worldwide efficiency, however, does not guarantee maximum income for the capital exporting country.

It is useful to differentiate three types of short-term capital movements having different motives, namely interest rate arbitrage, speculative investment, and capital flight. When international investment risk is explicitly considered, like in the case of international portfolio investment, it is easier to explain why two-way capital flows between two countries may take place simultaneously. Finally, theories of direct foreign investment, such as the product-cycle theory, industrial organization theory, internalization theory, and currency area theory do capture certain aspects of investment behavior. However, they are not inclusive enough individually. We find an eclectic theory which combines several elements of the above useful. This approach will be used to explain the internationalization of banking in the next chapter.

REVIEW PROBLEMS AND EXERCISES

1. Using Figure 2.1, explain (a) why the organized labor in the United States opposes US investment abroad and (b) how the labor force in capital importing countries would benefit from such investment. What will the amount of deadweight loss be if capital flows are not permitted?

2. Given the following data, find the optimum amount of foreign investment for a capital exporting country. Also find the optimum amount from the worldwide efficiency point of view.

Foreign investment	Domestic rate of return (%)	Foreign rate of return (%)
10	7.0	14
20	8.0	13
40	9.0	12
30	10.0	11
40	10.5	10.5
50	10.8	10.0

3. The following information is given:

    Spot SFr 2.24/$1.00   US interest rate 10%
    One-year forward SFr1.90/$1.00   Swiss interest rate 3.7%

    (a) Which direction will international money flow?
    (b) How much profit (%) will the investor make from the interest arbitrage?

4. What are major differences between speculative capital movement and capital flight?

5. How can we measure the magnitude of capital flight?

6. How can we explain the international capital movement from a high-yield country to a low-yield country?

7. Explain the following theories or hypotheses of direct foreign investment:
    (a) the differential rates of return theory
    (b) the product cycle theory
    (c) the industrial organization theory
    (d) the internalization theory
    (e) the currency area hypothesis

NOTES

1 The marginal productivity theory of income distribution is also known as the product exhaustion theorem of income distribution. See, for example, Ferguson (1968: 321).
2 In the United States there is no formal policy mechanism through which adversely affected workers are compensated to share the gains of direct foreign investment. A program closest to this idea is the Trade Adjustment Assistance program which was created in 1962.
3 However, Friedman (1968: 436) argues that "the major aim of policy is not to prevent such changes from occurring but to develop an efficient system of adapting to them − of using their potentialities for good while minimizing their destructive effects."
4 See Rojas-Suárez (1991: 84).
5 See Goldstein et al. (1991: 4).
6 From an accounting point of view, over 50 percent ownership of shares of a company may be regarded as sufficient for exercising effective control. However, the IMF (1977: 137, 187−94) reports that in many countries a relatively low percentage of ownership frequently ranging from 25 percent down to even 10 percent is classified as direct investment.
7 See Goldstein et al. (1991: 4).
8 The World Bank (1985: 125).
9 See, for instance, Caves (1982) and Aharoni (1972: 3−20) for alternative definitions of a multinational corporation.
10 See Lizondo (1991) for a comprehensive survey of theories of direct foreign investment.

BASIC READING

Aliber, R. Z. (1970) "A Theory of Direct Foreign Investment," in Kindleberger, C. P. (ed.) *The International Corporation*, Cambridge, Mass.: MIT Press, 17−34.
Cuddington, J. T. (1986) *Capital Flight: Estimates, Issues and Explanations*, Princeton Studies in International Finance No. 58, Princeton, N.J.: Princeton University Press.
Dunning, J. H. (1988) "The Eclectic Paradigm of International Production: a Restatement and Some Possible Extensions," *Journal of International Business Studies*, 19 (Spring): 1−31.
Goldstein, M., Mathieson, D. J. and Lane, T. (1991) "Determinants and Systemic Consequences of International Capital Flows," in *Determinants and Systemic Consequences of International Capital Flows*, IMF Occasional Paper No. 77, Washington, D.C.: IMF, 1−45.
Heller, H. R. (1981) "International Banking in a Multicurrency World," in Hufbauer, G. C. (ed.) *The International Framework for Money and Banking in the 1980s*, Washington, D.C.: Georgetown University, 483−509.
IMF (International Monetary Fund) (1977) *Balance of Payments Manual*, 4th edn, Washington, DC: IMF, Chapters 18 and 19.
Khan, M. S. and Ul Haque, N. (1985) "Foreign Borrowing and Capital Flight: A Formal Analysis," *IMF Staff Papers*, 32 (4): 605−28.
—— (1987) "Capital Flight from Developing Countries," *Finance and Development*, 24 (1): 2−5.

Lessard, D. R. and Williamson, J. (1987) *Capital Flight and Third World Debt*, Washington, D.C.: Institute for International Economics.

Lizondo, J. S. (1991) "Foreign Direct Investment," in *Determinants and Systemic Consequences of International Capital Flows*, IMF Occasional Paper No. 77, Washington, D.C.: IMF, 68–82.

Rojas-Suárez, L. (1991) "Risk and Capital Flight in Developing Countries," in *Determinants and Systemic Consequences of International Capital Flows*, IMF Occasional Paper No. 77, Washington, D.C.: IMF, 83–92.

Simonds, R. R. (1978) "Modern Financial Theory," *MSU Business Topics*, Winter, 54–63.

Solnik, B. H. (1974) "Why Not Diversify Internationally Rather Than Domestically," *Financial Analysts Journal*, July–August: 48–54.

Takayama, A. (1972) *International Trade: An Approach to the Theory*, New York: Holt, Rinehart & Winston, 448–52.

Vernon, R. (1966) "International Investment and International Trade in the Product Cycle," *Quarterly Journal of Economics*, 80 (2): 190–207.

World Bank (1985) *World Development Report 1985*, New York: Oxford University Press.

FURTHER READING

Agarwal, J. P. (1980) "Determinants of Foreign Direct Investment: A Survey," *Weltwirtschaftliche Archiv*, 116: 5.

Aharoni, Y. (1972) "On the Definition of a Multinational Corporation," in Kapoor, A. and Grub, P. D. (eds) *The Multinational Enterprise in Transition*, Princeton, N.J.: Dawing Press, 3–20.

Boddewyn, J. J. (1985) "Theories of Foreign Direct Investment and Divestment: A Classificatory Note," *Management International Review*, 25: 1.

Caves, R. E. (1982) *Multinational Enterprise and Economic Analysis*, London: Cambridge University Press, Chapters 1 and 2.

Ferguson, C. E. (1968) *Microeconomic Theory*, Homewood, Ill.: Richard D. Irwin, Chapter 13.

Friedman, M. (1968) "The Case for Flexible Exchange Rates," in Cave, R. E. and Johnson, H. G. (eds) *Readings in International Economics*, Homewood, Ill.: Richard D. Irwin, 413–37.

Hymer, S. H. (1976) *The International Operations of National Firms: A Study of Direct Foreign Investment*, Cambridge, Mass.: MIT Press (based on a Ph.D. dissertation, 1960).

Kemp, M. C. (1962) "Foreign Investment and the National Advantage," *Economic Record*, 38 (1): 56–62.

Kindleberger, C. P. (1969) *American Business Abroad*, New Haven, Conn.: Yale University Press.

MacDougall, G. D. A. (1960) "Benefits and Costs of Private Investments from Abroad: A Theoretical Approach," *Economic Record*, 361: 13–35.

Sokoya, S. K. and Tillery, K. (1992) "Motives of Foreign MNCs Investing in the United States and Effect of Company Characteristics," *The International Executive*, 1 (1): 65–80.

Vernon, R. (1979) "The Product Cycle Hypothesis in a New International Environment," *Oxford Bulletin of Economics and Statistics*, 43 (November): 255–67.

Chapter 3

International banking

INTRODUCTION

In this chapter, we begin with the definition of a bank from regulatory as well as theoretical perspectives. From this, we may learn the underlying characteristics of commercial banks, which are the major players in international financial intermediation. We will then see how the functions of banks can be properly characterized when the international dimension is added. The international dimension includes location of parent banks and their banking facilities, residency of customers, and currency denomination.

After examining the significance of the role played by commercial banks in international direct and indirect finance, we turn our attention to the theories of international banking. Applying the theories of direct foreign investment, we provide hypotheses to explain (1) why certain banks of selective countries can compete better against banks of given host countries; (2) why banks maintain a vertical organizational structure and at the same time a horizontal structure with facilities in a number of different countries; and (3) what causes or accelerates internationalization of banking.

Finally, using a combination of different elements of international dimension, we classify the banking market into a number of distinctive submarkets ranging from the domestic market to the Eurocurrency market, the traditional foreign banking market, the indigenous foreign market, the entrepôt, and the all-inclusive international banking market. Such a classification will be useful for both regulatory policy makers and strategists of individual banks.

THE DEFINITION OF A BANK

The business of banks, or banking, is a fuzzy subset of financial services. Like other financial institutions, a major function of banks is to acquire funds from surplus economic units and channel such funds to deficit units, known as financial intermediation. Then, how unique is their intermediation function so that they can be called banks? As we shall see below, the uniqueness is largely due to the regulatory constraints imposed on so-called banks and it is not because of fundamental differences in the nature of their intermediation.

Regulatory definition of a bank

In the United States, for example, certain financial institutions such as non-bank banks can perform almost all the functions of commercial banks, yet they are not banks for regulatory purposes. Once out of the bank regulatory jurisdiction, such financial institutions can conduct business anywhere across the United States; they can have a new range of business activities; and they can be owned by any commercial entities. On the other hand, commercial banks do not have such a wide range of freedom.

There are three criteria which we may use to define a commercial bank: charter, activity, and deposit insurance.[1] First, the charter criterion asks whether or not an institution is chartered by regulatory authorities as a commercial bank. A strict application of this criterion implies that, once an institution is chartered as a bank, it is a bank irrespective of its activities.

On the other hand, the activity criterion defines a bank by what it does. For example, in the past the US regulatory authorities under the Bank Holding Company Act of 1956 (as amended) emphasized this approach, creating the control problem of elusive nonbank banks. According to this law, a financial institution was a commercial bank if it performed the three stipulated functions as a whole, namely accepting demand deposits, providing a payment clearing mechanism, and providing commercial loans. However, if at least one of these three functions was omitted, it was technically no longer a bank, becoming a so-called "nonbank bank." Since it was no longer a bank, it could avoid restrictive bank regulations.

The third criterion looks at whether an institution is insured for its deposits or not. Once it is insured by the government deposit insurance agency, it is a bank irrespective of its specific activities. This criterion has an element of the carrot-and-stick. That is, if a financial institution wishes to have its deposits insured, it must be prepared to submit itself to bank regulations. Today, in the United States, a bank is defined on the basis of the charter and deposit insurance criteria. This approach constitutes a departure from the earlier approach of the charter criterion combined with the activity criterion.[2]

The approaches taken in some other industrial countries are somewhat different from the US approach. For instance, in the UK, even the charter was less important. Before the Banking Act 1979, any company could take money on deposit. Whether a particular deposit taking company was a bank depended on the privilege accorded to it by the Bank of England and its reputation in the banking community. However, after the enactment of the

Banking Act 1979 and as amended in 1987, it became necessary to receive a formal authorization from the Bank of England to become a bank.[3] Nonetheless, the activity requirements are far less specific in the UK. On the other hand, the French approach emphasizes the activity criterion, similar to the earlier US approach, but it defines the banking activity broadly enough so that there is no reason to become a "nonbank bank-type" institution. In effect, banks are no longer differentiated from other credit institutions according to the Banking Act 1984 of France. A credit institution (établissement de crédit) is an institution that engages in at least one of the three banking activities: (a) taking deposits from the public, (b) providing credit, and (c) providing alternative means of payments (travelers' checks, bankers' drafts, credit cards, etc.). This approach is in line with the EC First Banking Directive 1977, which provided a basis for the subsequent EC financial market integration plan.

Theoretical definition of a bank

Then, from a theoretical point of view, how can we differentiate banks from other financial institutions? We are interested in grouping a particular subset of financial institutions as banks so that we can better explain and predict the behavior of such institutions. Thus, the definition of a bank that we are seeking here is essentially to identify unique attributes of banking activities.[4]

For this purpose, we may examine certain unique items found in a bank's balance sheet. First, on the banks' liabilities side, banks offer demand deposits which play a key role as a medium of exchange. In addition, such deposits enable banks to create their own money, known as "inside money," through the money multiplier process, as well as alternative means of payments through financial innovations. Nevertheless, this unique power is fading in the United States and other countries where nonbank financial institutions are also permitted to offer checkable deposits. However, to some extent deposits at banks are still different from those of other depository institutions, because deposits at banks are more likely to cause high-powered monetary expansion.

Alternatively, it is also argued that banks are unique only because they have monopoly power in the financial markets, the power which is created by restrictive entry. For example, upon its establishment, the market value of a new bank tends to surge immediately above the shareholders' contribution. This phenomenon is viewed as evidence of the value of such monopoly power to create bank money.[5] Thus, free entry would eliminate the monopoly power of banks, an essence of their uniqueness.

On the asset side, banks perform asset transformation functions. They change the size of deposits into different sizes of loans; they diversify their assets by "not putting all their eggs in one basket"; and they evaluate credit risk for uninitiated depositors and shareholders who may only have limited information in hand. The limited availability of information makes the credit evaluation function all the more important. In addition, having diversified investment and loan portfolios, banks can reduce risk on the rate of return on their assets. However, in these capacities banks are not much different from any other financial intermediaries. Perhaps a major difference may stem from the way that commercial loans are provided. Let us compare commercial lending and security issuance.

Before granting a commercial loan, a lending bank negotiates with a borrower on terms and conditions which are tailored to the latter's need. Thus the lending process tends to be personal. On the other hand, if the borrower is issuing securities to raise funds, she may not know her ultimate lenders until the securities are sold. Therefore there must be someone indirectly negotiating on behalf of potential lenders. This is usually done by an investment bank. Thus the relationship between the borrower and the lenders is impersonal. The promissory note presented by the borrower to the lending bank is expected to be kept by the latter until maturity and its confidentiality is to be honored, whereas securities are bought to be sold and the disclosure of information is encouraged. Finally, perhaps, the most important aspect is that a loan contract contains implicit contract elements, by which the bank is informally promising to provide loans on a continuing basis and ready to renegotiate terms and conditions, if necessary. The bank keeps customers captive in this way. Many international lending experiences in the 1980s attest to this situation. Securities buyers are one-time buyers – they do not supply funds on a continuing basis and they do not renegotiate terms and conditions. This then implies that commercial banks can lose their uniqueness should they securitize their loans and sell them off.

In summary, a commercial bank is a financial intermediary which offers demand deposits and commercial loans both of which in turn contain some unique features. Demand deposits enable the banking system as a whole to provide the payment settlement system and to create inside money as well as alternative means of payment. Implicit contractual elements in commercial loans enable banks to maintain a long-term relationship with their customers. In doing so, banks are indirectly providing credit evaluation services to their depositors and shareholders. However, the uniqueness of banks is becoming less important, as noted above in the French and EC regulatory framework for financial institutions.

International dimensions of banking

Now let us turn to the international business activities of banks, that is, international banking. Here, the national boundary becomes a critical criterion which defines the country of origin by which a bank is chartered; the host countries in which a bank's facilities are located; the countries in which bank customers reside; and the national currencies in which banking products are denominated. On the other hand, the formation of a regional monetary union (such as the European Monetary Union) in essence removes the importance of national boundaries, replacing them with the union boundary. Our discussion proceeds without the presumption of a union boundary.

The parent organization O_i, chartered in country i, may take one of several forms. In the United States, it can be a bank holding company or a commercial bank itself. A bank holding company is a company which controls at least one bank by its share ownership (25 percent or more) or its power to elect a majority of bank board members. In addition, there are also banking organizations specifically geared for international operations such as Edge Act corporations and Agreement corporations. An Edge Act corporation is an international banking corporation chartered by the Federal Reserve Board and exclusively engaged in international banking business. A state chartered international banking corporation becomes an Agreement corporation when it is acquired by a member bank. As a condition for approval by the Federal Reserve for such acquisition, the state-chartered corporation must enter an agreement with the Federal Reserve. The agreement provides a guideline to determine the permissible scope and nature of the corporation's international banking operations.

The banking facility B_j, located in country j, produces banking services. If the banking organization has facilities that produce banking services in two or more countries, it is a multinational bank. The type of production facilities that a banking organization should have abroad obviously depends on cost–benefit considerations – the costs of its operations and the benefits for the entire banking network.

There are several different setups with varying degrees of banking power: calling officers, representative offices, agencies, branches, and foreign subsidiaries in addition to the head office. Notice that if a calling officer is staying long enough in a particular country with some support facilities, the facility becomes the representative office which is essentially an office for liaison between the head office and customers and for information gathering and dissemination. When the representative office acquires lending powers, it becomes an agency; when an agency acquires deposit taking powers, it is then a branch.

The customers C_k of banking services, residing in country k, may again be classified in a number of ways depending on the nature of the products which they typically demand or the geographical location of each group of customers. Typically, commercial banks classify customers into government units, financial institutions, nonbank business firms (multinational corporations and local corporations), and individual households.

The banking products P_m, denominated in a national currency m (or mix of several currencies), can be classified into three categories: asset-based products, liability-based products, and fee-based products.

Thus, international banking involves four dimensions:

$\{O_i, B_j, C_k, P_m\}$.

If at least one subscript is different from the rest, it is an international banking service. Therefore, we may note that domestic banking is a special case of international banking where all the subscripts are the same.

From the regulatory viewpoint, which element is the most important among the four elements $\{O_i, B_j, C_k, P_m\}$ to serve as the basis of determining the country of primary supervisory responsibility? We will examine this question of regulatory jurisdiction in Chapter 12.

BASICS OF INTERNATIONAL FINANCIAL INTERMEDIATION AND THE ROLE OF BANKS

Since international banking is a subset of financial intermediation involving cross-border transactions, let us examine the meaning of financial intermediation more closely. A surplus unit SU is an economic unit (household, firm, or government unit) with total revenue exceeding total current expenditures during a given period of time, whereas a deficit unit DU is one with total expenditures exceeding total revenue. That is, for an SU, the following income statement condition must hold:

$$\text{revenue} - \text{expenditures} = \text{saving} > 0. \tag{3.1}$$

Similarly, for the SU, the following balance sheet conditions must hold:

$$\text{lending} + \text{investment} = \text{borrowing} + \text{saving}, \tag{3.2}$$
$$\text{lending} - \text{borrowing} = \text{saving} - \text{investment} > 0. \tag{3.3}$$

How then can an SU transfer its surplus funds to a DU? The SU can directly lend its surplus funds to a DU without involvement of a third party. We call this kind of arrangement direct finance. Another way to channel funds is that an SU first lends its funds to another economic unit, known as a financial intermediary FI, which in turn transfers the funds to a DU. This arrangement is known as indirect finance.

International direct finance

Even in the case of direct finance, there are usually additional market participants other than just DUs and SUs. They are brokers and underwriters who facilitate the matching of DUs and SUs. Brokers who match DUs and SUs do not hold debt instruments on their own account at any time. On the other hand, underwriters who purchase new security issues from DUs and sell them to SUs do hold such debt instruments on their own account temporarily between the time of purchase and the time of sale. If the period of holding becomes longer, the underwriter is indistinguishable from a lending intermediary. On the other hand, if the holding period approaches zero, the underwriter becomes almost indistinguishable from a broker.

In international direct finance, instruments used are typically bonds, commercial paper, and stocks, of which bonds are still the dominant form. In 1989, the total amount of gross issues of international bonds was $261.1 billion, whereas that of Euro-commercial paper and other notes was $6.9 billion. In bond financing, a variety of colorful names are used to signify the currency denomination, place of issue or residence of DUs. Eurodollar bonds are those dollar-denominated bonds issued outside the United States. Eurocurrency bonds including Eurodollar bonds issued in Japan are called shogun bonds if they are issued by foreign DUs. On the other hand, if bonds issued in Japan by foreign DUs are denominated in yen, they are called samurai bonds. Yankee bonds are similar to samurai bonds, the former being denominated in dollars and being issued by foreign DUs in the US market. In addition, an increasing number of multicurrency bonds, such as ECU-denominated bonds, have been issued in recent years. In the United States, the first ECU bonds were issued in 1984 by the EC.

As for the role of banks, international bond issues are usually arranged through an underwriting group consisting of a large number of banks, often a hundred or more, even if the amount of an issue is relatively small. These banks can place the new issues with speed, simplicity, and privacy, mostly through private placements. In the Euro-commercial paper market, banks provide similar underwriting services as in the Eurobond markets. In addition, banks are important buyers of lesser-name commercial paper.

International indirect finance

As pointed out earlier, three parties are involved in indirect finance, namely SUs, FIs, and DUs. What is then the role of FIs in financial intermediation? By borrowing funds on one hand and lending on the other, FIs perform several functions, such as the transformation of default risk, size, maturity, and interest rate risk.

First, since an SU lends its surplus funds to an FI such as a bank, this changes the source of default risk to the FI from an ultimate borrower DU. This change in the source of risk and the corresponding change in the degree of risk is called credit risk intermediation. As noted earlier, the ability of a financial intermediary, particularly a bank, to reduce credit risk stems from its efficiency in portfolio diversification and credit analysis. In addition, a bank deposit insurance, if available, effectively transfers the credit risk faced by depositors to other economic units.

Next, the FI rearranges the loan package to a DU, which may be different from the credit package received from the SU in terms of size, maturity, and interest rate risk. For example, banks receive relatively short-term funds and lend for longer term in response to the different maturity preferences of customers. Such a transformation is called maturity intermediation. Similarly, size intermediation in bank operations typically involves banks receiving small-sized deposit money from many customers and granting loans in larger size. However, in certain markets such as the Eurodollar interbank market, more or less no size intermediation takes place.

Another intermediation function is transforming fixed interest rate instruments to floating rate instruments, or vice versa, which results in the assumption by the FI of interest rate risk. A "cost (LIBOR) plus spread" type of pricing in the Eurocurrency loan market transfers interest rate risk directly to the DU, instead of the banks assuming such risk.

In addition to the above type of financial intermediation, banks perform additional intermediation functions with an international dimension. First, there is currency intermediation. The currency in which an SU wants to lend and the currency in which a DU wants to borrow may not be the same. Then, receiving funds in one currency, the bank may convert the funds into another currency on the foreign exchange market through either an outright purchase of a desired currency or a currency swap, and lend them out. When the loan repayment is received, it is converted back into the original currency through a reverse process.

Since more than one country is involved in international financial intermediation, the financial intermediary may select a particular country as a place of transactions where such transactions are least regulated or least costly. To execute such transactions, the original financial intermediary FI(1) may interject another intermediary (often its branch) FI(2) between itself and the SU or between itself and the DU in order to avoid certain regulatory restrictions. For example, taking deposits through a branch in the Cayman Islands and remitting such deposit funds back to the parent bank was once a common practice to avoid the Federal Reserve reserve requirements.[6]

$$\boxed{\text{DU}} \leftarrow \boxed{\text{FI(1)}} \leftarrow \overline{\underline{\text{FI(2)}}} \leftarrow \boxed{\text{SU}}$$

Among financial intermediaries commercial banks have been the major players in international finance. However, before 1970 banks lent developing countries relatively small amounts to finance their trade and to meet the needs of subsidiaries of multinational corporations located there. After 1970, banks became the fastest-growing and most flexible sources of international finance to developing as well as developed countries to meet the needs of their balance of payments deficits. Too rapid growth was accompanied by a major debt-service crisis that began in 1982. However, only during the setback years of 1984, 1985, and 1986 did international finance through bond issues exceed international lending volume. More recently, international bank lending resurged with gross lending of $373.7

Table 3.1 International bank assets by nationality of banks (in billions of US dollars)

Country	December 1979		December 1985		December 1989	
		%		%		%
France	123.6	11.1	244.0	9.0	432.1	8.4
Germany	69.3	6.2	191.2	7.0	435.8	8.5
Italy	29.6	2.7	113.3	4.2	?	?
Japan	45.4	4.1	707.2	26.1	1,967.2	38.3
Switzerland	59.1	5.3	109.2	4.0	?	?
UK	285.5	25.7	192.9	7.1	247.3	4.8
USA	263.9	23.8	590.2	21.7	727.4	14.2
Others	234.5	21.1	566.8	20.9	1,329.4	25.8
Total	1,110.9	100.0	2,714.8	100.0	5,139.2	100.0

Source: Bank for International Settlements (1982) *52nd Annual Report*, 138–9; (1988) *58th Annual Report*, 121; (1990) *60th Annual Report*, 135
Note: The international assets shown here are those of banking offices located in the following seventeen countries: Austria, Belgium, Luxembourg, Canada, Denmark, Finland, France, Germany, Ireland, Italy, Japan, the Netherlands, Spain, Sweden, Switzerland, the UK, and the United States. The international assets are the cross-border assets in all currencies plus the foreign currency assets loaned to local residents. The international assets of US banks also include the cross-border assets reported by US banks' branches in the Bahamas, the Cayman Islands, Panama, Hong Kong, and Singapore.

billion (or $330.0 billion of the net amount) in 1989, reaching a total stock of $5,139.2 billion as of the end of 1989. This total amount is almost equivalent to the size of the US GDP ($5,244.0 billion) in that year, as shown in Table 3.1. Although banks of five major industrial countries (France, Germany, Japan, the UK and the United States) have provided about three-quarters of the total international bank loans over the past decade, the market shares of these five countries have changed substantially. In 1989, the share of Japanese banks reached 38.3 percent from a mere 4.1 percent in 1979, whereas UK and US banks' shares decreased steadily from 25.7 percent and 23.8 percent in 1979 to 4.8 percent and 14.2 percent respectively in 1989.

THEORIES OF INTERNATIONAL BANKING

A theory of international banking needs to explain three broad questions related to the international banking pattern. The first question is why banks choose particular locations for their banking facilities. The second is why banks maintain a vertical organizational structure and at the same time a horizontal structure with facilities in a number of different countries. The third is to explain the underlying causes of internationalization and globalization of banking.

Sources of comparative advantage in international banking

What are the particular advantages enjoyed by certain banks from selective countries operating in given host countries? Recall the eclectic approach that we discussed in Chapter 2 to explain motives for direct foreign investment. Applying this eclectic approach, we can identify three sources of relative advantages which determine the location of international banking activity.

The host-country-specific advantages stem from a variety of advantageous banking environments encircled by a national boundary. Typically, such an advantageous environment is characterized by an absence or lack of bank regulations that results in lower operational costs, or by the existence of a banking community cluster that facilitates interpersonal contacts and reduces communication expenses.[7] Or, the banking system of the country is either underdeveloped or highly concentrated, creating monopolistic market characteristics, which may be manifested by a wider spread between the borrowing and lending rates. Robert Aliber (1976), for example, argues that with a high spread situation it would be easier for a bank of another country to enter such a market as long as the entrant can manage a narrower spread.

On the other hand, there are cases in which distinctive advantages are associated with the home country. The currency area theory of Robert Heller (1981) is a case in point. He points out that the amount of usage of a particular country's currency in principle is proportional to its economy's size, although some deviation may result from variations in the velocity of money or foreign demand for the currency. For over two decades after the Second World War, the use of the US currency was high. The large size of the US economy, the comparatively stable value of the dollar linked to the fixed exchange rate system and the practice of invoicing a large proportion of world exports in the dollar all contributed to a greater use of the dollar which in turn gave an intrinsic advantage for US banks until the early 1970s. Also a country where banking industry is highly developed has a pool of skilled workers ready to be placed overseas. These conditions give relative advantage in the factor endowment to the country of origin. Since the mid-1970s the US dollar has become a less dominant currency, whereas currencies of other major industrial countries, notably the Japanese yen and the deutsche mark, have emerged as competing international currencies. A rise of Japanese banks as a group was largely helped by strong Japanese yen. During the nine-year period 1981–9, Japan accumulated a current account surplus of $421.1 billion, while the United States experienced a total deficit of $788.6 billion. At the same time the yen value appreciated more than 67 percent *vis-à-vis* the US dollar during the period from 1979 to 1989. All of these strengthened the positions of Japanese banks.[8] This fact is also reflected well in the ranking of the largest banks worldwide, as

Table 3.2 The world's twenty-five largest banks (by assets in billions of US dollars)

	1979		1989	
Rank	Bank	Assets	Bank	Assets
1	Crédit Agricole (F)	105.00	Dai Ich Kangyo Bank (J)	388.87
2	BankAmerica Corp. (USA)	103.92	Sumitomo Bank (J)	377.21
3	Citicorp (USA)	102.74	Fuji Bank (J)	365.55
4	Banque Nationale de Paris (F)	98.86	Mitsubishi Bank (J)	362.94
5	Deutsche Bank (G)	91.19	Sanwa Bank (J)	350.20
6	Crédit Lyonnais (F)	91.09	Industrial Bank of Japan (J)	268.53
7	Société Générale (F)	84.91	Norinchukin Bank (J)	243.56
8	Dresdner Bank (G)	70.33	Caisse Nationale de Crédit Agricole (F)	241.98
9	Barclays Group (UK)	67.47	Banque Nationale de Paris (F)	231.46
10	Dai Ich Kangyo Bank (J)	66.58	Citicorp (USA)	230.64
11	National Westminster Bank (UK)	64.39	Tokai Bank (J)	225.78
12	Chase Manhattan Corp. (USA)	61.98	Mitsubishi Trust & Banking (J)	211.95
13	Westdeutsche Landesbank Girozentrale (G)	60.08	Crédit Lyonnais (F)	210.73
14	Fuji Bank (J)	59.83	Mitsui Bank (J)	206.87
15	Commerzbank (G)	58.27	Barclays Group (UK)	204.89
16	Sumitomo Bank (J)	58.02	Deutsche Bank (G)	202.26
17	Mitsubishi Bank (J)	57.34	Bank of Tokyo (J)	198.27
18	Sanwa Bank (J)	55.30	Sumitomo Trust & Banking (J)	197.94
19	Norinchukin Bank (J)	53.66	National Westminster Bank (UK)	188.54
20	Banco do Brasil (Brazil)	49.13	Long-Term Credit Bank of Japan (J)	183.33
21	Bayerische Vereinsbank (G)	48.28	Mitsui Trust & Banking (J)	179.96
22	Industrial Bank of Japan (J)	47.35	Taiyo Kobe Bank (J)	174.53
23	Banca Nazionale del Lavora (I)	46.38	Yasuda Trust & Banking (J)	171.73
24	Manufacturers Hanover Corp. (USA)	45.88	Société Générale (F)	164.81
25	Cooperatieve Centrale Raiffeissen- Boerenleenbank (N)	45.33	Daiwa Bank (J)	156.45

Source: *The Banker* (June 1980), 149; *Euromoney* (June 1990), 119
Note: F, France; G, Germany; J, Japan; I, Italy; N, the Netherlands.

shown in Table 3.2. Out of the world's ten largest banks, seven were Japanese in 1989.

The individual-bank-specific advantages stem mainly from the special bank–customer relationship. The existence of such advantages is a manifestation of market imperfections. The follow-the-customer hypothesis (Grubel 1977) or gravitational pull hypothesis (Métais 1979) asserts that a bank will follow its major customers going abroad. Such a bank then has considerable advantages, since it knows whom it is going to serve. It can reduce marketing expenses and marketing uncertainty; and it can reduce the time lag for granting loans as it already has credit information on the parent firm whose subsidiary the bank is going to serve.

The significance of individual bank advantages changes as the competitiveness of the market structure changes. Through the diffusion of banking technology and market information, the monopoly position will be reduced to an oligopoly level of competition and to monopolistic competition over the time. Then, the individual-bank-specific advantage disappears, converging to either a host-country-specific advantage or a home-country-specific advantage. If banks of many different countries tend to concentrate in that market, we may infer that it is due to the host-country-specific advantage. On the other hand, if banks of a particular country concentrate in the market, it may be due to the home-country-specific advantage.

Figure 3.1 shows the dynamic comparative advantage for banks of a banking services exporting country, which we designate as the home country. In Figure 3.1(b) the curve AC_1 represents the average cost of production of banking services by a representative bank in the home country. The curve is determined by specific advantages associated with this country. The second curve AC_2 represents the average cost of production in the foreign country by same bank. The steeper slope of the second curve reflects that, although it is disadvantageous to produce in the foreign country initially, it would become advantageous to produce there as the banking service exporting country bank learns how to do business there and expands its production over time. Figure 3.1(a) exhibits the change in the cost curve as a result of the combined cost reduction effects of learning and increased production. The curve AR_2 with a downward slope shows the average revenue in the foreign market, which becomes more competitive over time. If there is a downward deviation from the curve AC_2, it represents the individual-bank-specific advantage. We assume that the time horizon is sufficiently long so that the investment decisions are made on the basis of average cost and average revenue.

On the basis of the relationship between these three variables, namely AC_1, AC_2, and AR_2, we can classify four distinctive periods, as shown in Figure 3.1. Period I (characterized by $AC_2 > AR_2 > AC_1$) represents the time in which banks in the home country produce banking services exclusively at home and export such services to the foreign country. In

Cost

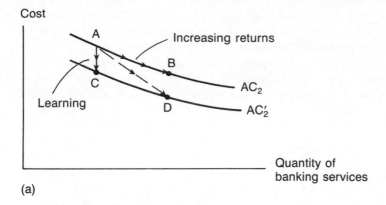

(a)

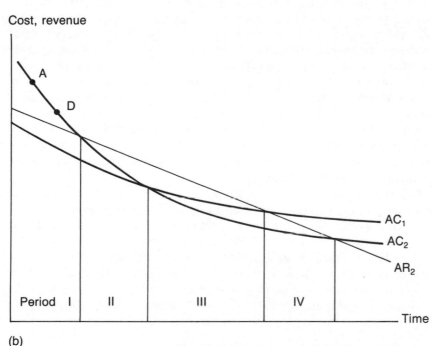

(b)

Figure 3.1 Dynamic comparative advantage in sourcing of banking services:
(a) learning versus increasing returns to scale in foreign banking;
(b) changes in relative advantage over time

period II ($AR_2 > AC_2 > AC_1$), banks in the home country can start establishing foreign facilities, thereby producing banking services both at home and abroad, although emphasis will still be on domestic production. In period III ($AR_2 > AC_1 > AC_2$), production of banking services at foreign facilities becomes greater than at home, implying that the proportion of international banking business is now greater than domestic banking. Finally, in period IV ($AC_1 > AR_2 > AC_2$), home country banks produce banking services exclusively abroad and import them for domestic services. This four-period cycle may repeat as new innovation starts at home, providing new competitive advantage for the home country again. We may call a theory which postulates the above cycle the location-cycle theory of international banking.[9]

Internalization of international banking transactions

Why does a bank produce its products through an integrated organization using foreign branches or foreign subsidiaries instead of sharing the production process at different stages with other firms? We can postulate that banks may find it advantageous to replace market transactions for certain intermediate input with internal transactions so that they can reduce transactions costs, protect the value of intangible assets, and exercise greater flexibility in banking operations. In order to internalize transactions, banks may have to establish overseas branches or subsidiaries.

Besides reducing transaction costs, the internalization of banking transactions also provides flexibility in transactions. For example, with internalization of transactions, the direction of flows of funds can be easily reversed depending on the place of need. Also, through a transfer pricing mechanism, the bank can execute regulatory arbitrage, taking advantage of regulatory variations in different countries.

The above examples are vertically integrated banking operations. The bank may also internalize the full value of its intangible assets. This rationale may be used to explain horizontally integrated banking organizations. For example, when it is difficult to control the transfer of a particular piece of banking technology, it would be easier for a bank to embody such technology in its own final products, price them accordingly, and sell them at different locations. Instead of selling a bank-developed cash management software, the bank may provide cash management services, for example.

Internationalization and globalization of banking

Since the early 1960s banking has become more and more "international." Many banks in the United States and abroad, particularly larger ones, have expanded their banking market into the international sphere and the character of banking business itself has become increasingly international.

The process of expanding banking activity abroad and replacing domestic banking business content by international content may be defined as internationalization of banking. After this stage is globalization of banking which may be defined as the process in which banking services become worldwide in terms of geographical coverage and universal in terms of the provision of banking services. The global coverage implies that there is no longer a one-way directional sense of 'from home to abroad'. The universal provision of banking services presumes the harmonization of banking rules and the removal of barriers so that all banking firms can compete in all markets. Thus, we may view internationalization as an early stage of globalization. In this section, we first examine a brief history of the internationalization of banking and then look at the main causes of internationalization in the past two to three decades and of globalization in more recent years.

A brief history of internationalization of banking

The origins of international banking are old and diverse. British foreign lending, for example, can be traced back even to 1571 when usury laws were imposed that limited the interest charged on domestic loans to a stipulated rate, thereby diverting financial resources from domestic lending to foreign lending.[10] International banking served the needs of foreign sovereigns and nobles; it grew with international commerce, providing private international trade financing; and again it has become a major source of government finance in recent years.

We may note that the process of internationalization of banking has been closely related to the interdependence trend of the world economy. The historical shifts of international money centers were symptoms of shifts in direction of relative dependence. As Baster (1935) points out, in the early nineteenth century the London money market became the international money center, owing to shifts of international banking activities from Germany and Holland after the Napoleonic War.[11] Then, the international connection of the London market to Europe began to expand rapidly. In this expansionary process, British banks were engaged in the massive undertaking to finance the industrialization of Europe.

European money centers such as Amsterdam, Hamburg, and Paris regained some international prominence in the late nineteenth century due to their central locations for transportation, commerce, and government seats. From 1914 on, New York emerged as a center for foreign reserves and a source of short- and long-term credit, directly competing against London for its supremacy. From 1936 on, and especially after the Second World War, the world financial leadership was increasingly accepted in the United States, first by the government and gradually by commercial banks with revived interest in lending abroad.

When we take a look at the recent internationalization of banking which began at a significant pace in the 1960s, there appears to be three waves of internationalization. At first, relatively large-sized US banks began rapid expansion of their overseas operations around the early 1960s as a natural course of extension of their domestic banking in response to the rising demand for international financial intermediation combined with their relative advantages. Then, a similar pattern of expansion was started by banks of other industrial countries, notably Canada, Japan, and Germany. Although banks from the UK and France experienced a substantial reduction in overseas presence in their former colonies in the 1950s and 1960s, they began expanding their presence in other industrial countries, notably the United States, in the 1970s. The third wave of internationalization came from banks of developing countries in the late 1970s. The fourth wave which may be regarded as the globalization of banking started after the Single European Act of 1986 within the European Community upon removal of barriers to international capital flows.

Causes of internationalization of banking

A number of important developments in the world economy in the past two to three decades have caused greater demand for and supply of international banking services; they include (1) conducive international banking (more generally international financial services) environments, (2) real economic growth in terms of GNP and trade volume, and (3) payments imbalances. Now let us examine each cause more closely.

To a great extent, the quickened pace of internationalization of banking can be attributed to the fact that the monetary, regulatory, and technological infrastructures have increasingly become conducive to internationalization.

An infrastructure may be defined as a societal or institutional arrangement which reduces the private cost of doing business or is conducive to doing business. The infrastructure needed for international banking may be tangible or intangible. The intangible structure consists of free capital flows and deregulation of financial services. The US postwar policy for free capital flows, the restoration of convertibility of European currencies in 1957, and a steady promotion of convertibility by the IMF have provided the basic monetary environment conducive to the growth of international banking. In addition, recent worldwide movements toward deregulation of the domestic financial services industry have further provided the regulatory infrastructure needed for internationalization and globalization of banking.

For example, the formation of a single market in the European Community attests to new opportunities for international banking. A study (1988) by the Commission of European Communities on the pricing of banking services by product line (consumer credit, credit cards, mortgages, letters of credit, foreign exchange, travelers' checks, and commercial loans) shows a checkerboard picture of efficiency across the Community countries. Great variations in pricing imply potential opportunities. Because of favorable conditions created from the formation of a single market, such as a reduced regulatory burden, increased competition, and advantageous economies of scale, the potential reduction in prices of these banking services was estimated to be from 4 percent to as high as 22 percent. After 1992 when banks are free to conduct banking business in any EC country, the Community will serve as a place of experimentation for the globalization of banking.

As for the tangible infrastructure, faster communications, data processing, and transportation facilities have reduced the psychological as well as the real-time distance of foreign markets. This has enhanced the perception of bank management that it can exercise effective management control over any overseas operations regardless of distance from the head office.

However, more fundamental causes of internationalization lie in changes in the real economies. Not only growing, the world economies have become more interdependent in terms of absolute scope and intensity. All of these require increased financial services.

The increasing size of the world economy demands a greater volume of financing and diversified financial services.[12] In 1960, for instance, the GNP size of the world economy (excluding nonmarket economies) was about $1.1 trillion, reaching $9.2 trillion in 1980 and $20.7 trillion in 1989. Also, the merchandise trade volume (exports and imports), an indicator of inter-dependence, grew at an annual rate of 7.2 percent during the period 1962–80, reaching $3.9 trillion in 1980 and $5.9 trillion ($2.9 trillion of imports and $3.0 trillion of exports) in 1989.

Not only the trade size but also the degree of imbalance in the balance of payments leads to a greater demand for international financing. Such imbalance was heightened by several factors such as the OPEC's major oil price hikes in 1973 and 1979, the difficulties in making necessary economic adjustments by many developing countries, and the untenable foreign exchange rate management by deficit countries. As a result, in 1980 for instance, the OPEC countries had $115 billion surplus in their current accounts whereas the industrial and non-oil developing countries had deficits of $44.8 billion and $58.9 billion respectively. For about a decade starting in 1973, international banks suddenly found themselves engaged in large-scale balance of payments financing, known as petro-dollar recycling. Such balance of payments deficits of some countries were not only caused by higher oil prices but also because of ambitious economic development plans with domestic investment plans that exceeded domestic saving plans by several percentage points as a percentage of GNP. Deficits were met by external borrowing, part of which was provided by international commercial banks.

The supply and demand conditions for banking services vary from country to country. In many developing countries there often exists a discrepancy between the real sector development stage which demands a certain level and type of banking services and the lagging financial sector development which is unable to fulfill that demand. This seems also the case of the current Eastern European economies. Such a gap creates an opportunity for foreign banks to step in. In addition, as the demand for financial assets is generally elastic with respect to changes in income, further opportunities may be created for foreign banks in the host country with higher economic growth.

There is also shareholder-driven globalization. Should a bank go abroad to diversify its asset portfolio? If bank shareholders have diversified themselves to eliminate unsystematic risk, then they will find little value in the lowered variability achieved by the bank. On the other hand, if they find it costly or otherwise difficult to diversify their portfolio, then the bank may be forced to diversify its portfolio internationally. As bank shareholders become aware of the availability of international diversification, the desire of bank shareholders to diversify their portfolio may become a cause of globalization of banking. We will examine the role of banks in international portfolio investment in Chapter 15.

TAXONOMY OF INTERNATIONAL BANKING

Classification of international banking markets

Now, let us return to the definition of international banking, which has four elements $\{O_i, B_j, C_k, P_m\}$. Although it is possible to pair these four elements in several different ways, pairing of $\{C_k, P_m\}$ and $\{B_j, C_k\}$ would be most useful for our study.

With the first set $\{C_k, P_m\}$, we can classify banking activities according to the currency composition of products (such as deposits and loans) and the residency of customers, as shown in the activity matrix in Table 3.3. Suppose that banks facing the matrix are those of country 1. Then, A_{11} represents domestic currency deposit-taking and lending. Since such transactions are with domestic customers, they are domestic banking business. On the other hand, A_{12} and A_{13} represent transactions with foreign residents in the domestic currency. This type of transaction is known as "traditional foreign banking," because domestic banks have long provided

Table 3.3 Banking activity matrix

Country of currency	Country of residence of customers		
	Country 1	Country 2	Country 3
Country 1	A_{11}	A_{12}	A_{13}
Country 2	A_{21}	A_{22}	A_{23}
Country 3	A_{31}	A_{32}	A_{33}

domestic currency facilities for foreigners to finance their international trade transactions. Next, all foreign currency transactions represented by A_{21}, A_{22}, A_{23}, A_{31}, A_{32}, and A_{33} are in effect Eurocurrency transactions. These are banking services provided by banks in foreign currencies, which are currencies other than those of the country in which the banks are located. Customers may be foreign as well as domestic residents. In Chapter 8, we will examine this Eurocurrency market more extensively. Related to the term Eurocurrency lending or deposit-taking is narrowly defined international lending or deposit-taking, which is a transaction with a foreign resident irrespective of currencies. Such a transaction is represented by A_{i2} and A_{j3}. This narrow definition is based only on the residency of customers. However, in the subsequent analysis we will use a broader definition of international banking meaning all types of transactions represented by the above matrix, except A_{11}.

Another useful approach is to classify the banking market according to geographical areas which are defined by residency of customers and location of banking facility, $\{B_j, C_k\}$ (Table 3.4). Each area is distinctive in terms of the bank regulatory structure, industry structure, and customers' demand for products.

The banking market represented by M_{11} is the domestic banking market in a geographic sense, where domestic banks provide banking services to customers in the home country. However, unlike the case of banking activity A_{11} that we discussed above, banks are assumed to provide deposit and credit facilities in both domestic and foreign currencies. This market therefore contains a so-called foreign sector.

M_{12} and M_{13} correspond to the traditional foreign banking markets. However, here again trade financing facilities provided by domestic banks are not necessarily confined to the domestic currency. On the other hand, M_{22} and M_{33} represent the foreign indigenous markets, providing services to local customers with facilities established there. We also call such a market an onshore market.

The markets represented by M_{21} and M_{31} fit more to the description of the Eurocurrency markets, serving customers in the home country including parent organizations by providing deposits and loan facilities in both home

Table 3.4 Banking market matrix

Location of banking facilities	Residence of customers		
	Country 1	Country 2	Country 3
Country 1	M_{11}	M_{12}	M_{13}
Country 2	M_{21}	M_{22}	M_{23}
Country 3	M_{31}	M_{32}	M_{33}

and third-country currencies. During the monetary crunch in the United States in 1969, for example, these outposts served as a major mechanism through which Eurodollars were rechanneled back to the United States. Finally, the markets M_{23} and M_{32} function as "entrepôt" or "turntable" business centers by taking foreign currency deposits from nonresidents and lending them back to other nonresidents.

In terms of the time sequence of market expansion, a bank may start out from the foreign sector services in M_{11} and expand its trade financing services in M_{12} and M_{13}. It may then establish offshore banking facilities in M_{21} or M_{31} to serve mainly domestic customers or domestic company subsidiaries. If the bank is a regional bank, it may go as far as this point. On the other hand, if this bank is a large money-center bank, it may expand its offshore banking business in M_{23} and M_{32} serving nonresident customers. Furthermore it may establish onshore facilities and localize its services to local customers in M_{22} and M_{33}.

Classification of banking products

Let us now take a closer look at a given particular market, say M_{12}. For our analysis it is convenient to decompose this market further by type of customers and by type of products $\{C_{kx}, P_{ms}\}$, yielding a segmented market matrix. The subscript x represents a type of customer of given country k, whereas s represents a product line of given currency denomination of m, as in Table 3.5.

The liability-based items represent sources of funds. Banks take deposits in a variety of forms from a variety of sources, such as deposits of official exchange reserves from foreign governments, S_{11}; correspondent banking balances from foreign banks, S_{12}; transaction balances, time deposits, and repurchase agreements from corporations, S_{13}; and transaction balances, time deposits, and savings deposits from household units, S_{14}. However, for international banking, banks have relied heavily on interbank time deposits and floating rate notes issuance for their major sources of funding. These are all interest-bearing liabilities, sensitive to interest rate fluctuations.

Table 3.5 Banking product line matrix

Products based on	Type of customers			
	Governments (1)	Banks (2)	Nonbank firms (3)	Individuals (4)
Liabilities (1)	S_{11}	S_{12}	S_{13}	S_{14}
Assets (2)	S_{21}	S_{22}	S_{23}	S_{24}
Non-balance-sheet (3)	S_{31}	S_{32}	S_{33}	S_{34}

On the other hand, the asset-based items represent uses of funds. Here again, banks allocate their financial resources in a variety of forms to a variety of customers. For international banking, banks have been particularly active in syndicated loans to foreign governments, S_{21}; interbank deposit placing, and overdraft facilities for foreign correspondent banks, S_{22}; short-term working capital loans, trade finance, and project-related loans to corporations, S_{23}; and consumer loans, S_{24}. Because of floating rate funding, banks tend to set their international loan rate on the basis of the cost of funds plus a spread (a certain add-on profit margin).

In recent years, banks have become increasingly interested in non-balance-sheet based (also known as fee-based) international banking services, partly because of the Third World country debt crisis and their need to improve their capital position. Banks are active in providing trust services (payment agent) and debt–equity swap management services to foreign governments, S_{31}; international collection and funds transfer for foreign banks, S_{32}; standby letters of credit, interest rate swap arrangements, cash management, foreign exchange exposure management, and portfolio management for corporations, S_{33}; and international investment management for individual investors, S_{34}.

Note, however, that the above activities are only representative samples. Banks do constantly produce new products, as we will examine in Chapter 9. In Part IV, we will study international banking activities in more detail.

SUMMARY

Commercial banks are financial intermediaries which offer demand deposits and commercial loans both of which contain some unique features, which may justify to differentiate them from other financial institutions. When a commercial bank operates internationally, it faces four distinctive international dimensions, namely the bank's home country, its facility location, residence of customers, and currency denomination of banking products. With a number of suitable combinations of these dimensions, we developed a taxonomy of international banking markets, which can, for example, clearly differentiate the traditional foreign banking market from the entrepôt or offshore market, and the international bank lending market from the Eurocredit market.

Based on theories of direct foreign investment, we developed an eclectic theory of international banking, describing dynamics of three sources of comparative advantage for banks to go abroad, namely, home-country-, host-country-, and firm-specific advantages. One main source of home-country-specific advantages comes from the home currency being used as international money, whereas host-country-specific advantages stem from regulatory differences. The individual-bank-specific advantages stem mainly from the special bank–customer relationship, which is characterized by the follow-the-customer hypothesis, the product-cycle theory, and the internalization theory, as we examined in the previous chapter.

REVIEW PROBLEMS AND EXERCISES

1. Discuss the three regulatory criteria used for the definition of a commercial bank. Why is it difficult to use the activity criterion?

2. Compare and contrast the regulatory definitions of a commercial bank used in the United States, the UK, and France.

3. What are major differences between borrowing through issuance of securities and borrowing from commercial banks?

4. Differentiate the following international banking markets:
   (a) traditional foreign banking market
   (b) international lending market (in a narrow definition)
   (c) Eurocurrency market
   (d) foreign indigenous market
   (e) entrepôt

5. Explain the kind of functions performed by commercial banks in
   (a) international direct finance
   (b) international indirect finance

6. Why are banks in a better position to reduce credit risk than economic surplus units?

7. Give examples of the regulatory (or location) intermediation performed by banks. Is such intermediation immoral?

8. What are the major underlying causes of the internationalization of banking?

9. Give examples of the following to explain the location choice of multinational banks:
   (a) host-country-specific advantages
   (b) home-country-specific advantages
   (c) individual-bank-specific advantages

10. Explain how banks may be able to protect the value of intangible assets or to reduce transactions costs by maintaining a vertically integrated organizational structure.

11. Identify each banking market by location of banking facilities and by residence of customers $\{B_j, C_m\}$.

12. Give specific examples of asset-based, liability-based, and fee-based international banking services in accordance with type of customer (financial institutions, corporations, government units, and individuals).

NOTES

1 See Clemente (1983).
2 See Chapter 10 for a more detailed presentation of US bank regulation.
3 See Chapter 11 for more details on the UK regulatory framework.
4 See Santomero (1984: 576–602) for a literature survey on fundamental characteristics of banks.
5 In recent years, however, the ratio of the market value to the book value of equity, known also as the Q ratio, of major banks in the United States has been below unity, indicating that the value of monopoly may no longer exist. On the other hand, the Q ratios in Japan, Germany, and Switzerland have consistently been higher than unity. See Aliber (1984: 673).
6 This practice was effectively terminated in October 1969 when a deposit received by a US domestic bank from a foreign source was classified as Eurocurrency liabilities subject to the reserve requirement.
7 See Kindleberger (1974).
8 Other factors contributing to the recent rapid growth of international lending by Japanese banks include the country's high saving ratio and low bank capitalization requirement, overseas expansion by Japan-based MNCs, and the removal of foreign exchange controls. See Pavel and McElravey (1990: 4).
9 See Vernon (1966) for the product cycle theory on which our discussion is based.
10 See Kindleberger (1974: 58).
11 See Baster (1935: 1–9).
12 For a comprehensive analysis of the relationship between economic growth and financial services, see McKinnon (1973).

BASIC READING

Aliber, R. Z. (1976) *The International Money Game*, 2nd edn, New York: Basic Books.
—— (1984) "International Banking: Survey," *Journal of Money, Credit and Banking*, 16 (4), Part 2: 661–78, 696–712.
Bank for International Settlements (1982, 1988, 1990) *52nd Annual Report*; *58th Annual Report*; *60th Annual Report*.
Baster, A. S. J. (1935) *The International Banks*, London: King. Reprinted in the Arno Press Collection (1977), New York: Arno Press.
de Boissieu, C. (1990) "The French Banking Sector in the Light of European Financial Integration," in Dermine, J. (ed.) *European Banking in the 1990s*, Oxford: Blackwell.
Bryant, R. C. (1987) *International Financial Intermediation*, Washington, D.C.: Brookings Institution.
Caves, R. E. (1982) *Multinational Enterprise and Economic Analysis*, Cambridge: Cambridge University Press.
Clemente, J. J. (1983) "What Is a Bank," *Federal Reserve Bank of Chicago Economic Perspectives*, January–February: 20–31.
Grubel, H. G. (1977) "A Theory of Multinational Banking," *Banca Nazionale Lavoro Quarterly Review*, 123 (December): 340–63.
Heller, H. R. (1981) "International Banking in a Multicurrency World," in Hufbauer, G. C. (ed.) *The International Framework for Money and Banking in the 1980s*, Washington, D.C.: Georgetown University, 483–509.
Hultman, C. W. (1990) *The Environment of International Banking*, Englewood Cliffs, N.J.: Prentice Hall.

Johnston, R. B. (1982) *The Economics of the Euro-Market: History, Theory and Policy*, New York: St Martin's Press.

Kim, T. (1984) "A Taxonomy of International Banking," in Kim, T. (ed.) *Proceedings of the 1984 International Banking Conference*, Glendale, Ariz.: American Graduate School of International Management, 87–99.

—— (1990) "Internationalization of Banking: With Special Reference to the Case of Korea," *Journal of Economic Development*, 15 (1): 63–82.

Kindleberger, C. P. (1974) *The Formulation of Financial Centers: A Survey in Comparative Economic History*, Princeton Studies in International Finance No. 36, Princeton, N.J.: Princeton University Press.

McKinnon, R. I. (1973) *Money and Capital in Economic Development*, Washington, D.C.: Brookings Institution.

Métais, J. (1979) "The Multinationalization Process of Commercial Banks: a View in Industrial Economic Theory," *Revue Economique*, 30 (2): 487–517.

Pavel, C. and McElravey, J. N. (1990) "Globalization in the Financial Services Industry," *Federal Reserve Bank of Chicago Economic Perspectives*, May–June: 3–18.

Pecchioli, R. M. (1983) *The Internationalization of Banking: The Policy Issues*, Paris: OECD.

Santomero, A. M. (1984) "Modeling the Banking Firm," *Journal of Money, Credit and Banking*, 16 (4), Part 2: 576–602, 696–712.

Stern, S. (1951) *The United States in International Banking*, New York: Columbia University Press. Reprinted in the Arno Press Collection (1976), New York: Arno Press.

Vernon, R. (1966) "International Investment and International Trade in the Product Cycle," *Quarterly Journal of Economics*, 80 (May): 190–207.

World Bank (1985, 1991) *World Development Report 1985*, New York: Oxford University Press, 110–24; *World Development Report 1991*, for recent statistics.

FURTHER READING

Baughn, W. H. and Mandich, D. (1983) *The International Banking Handbook*, Homewood, Ill.: Dow Jones-Irwin.

Cline, W. R. (1987) *Mobilizing Bank Lending to Debtor Countries*, Washington, D.C.: Institute for International Economics.

Khoury, S. (1980) *Dynamics of International Banking*, New York: Praeger.

Kim, S. H. and Miller, S. W. (1983) *Competitive Structure of the International Banking Industry*, Lexington, Mass.: D. C. Heath.

Lessard, D. R. and Williamson, J. (1985) *Financial Intermediation beyond the Debt Crisis*, Washington, D.C.: Institute for International Economics.

Park, Y. S. and Zwick, J. (1985) *International Banking in Theory and Practice*, Reading, Mass.: Addison-Wesley.

Tucker, A. L., Madura, J. and Chiang, T. C. (1991) *International Financial Markets*, St Paul, Minn.: West.

Chapter 4

International money

INTRODUCTION

A study of international money is in large part a study of international monetary environments in which international banks operate. In this chapter, we first review major functions of money in an open economy. We then examine the demand model of a key currency which reduces international transactions costs. Since it is desirable to compare a multilateral value of a key currency *vis-à-vis* a number of other national currencies, we discuss how to construct a foreign exchange index. The exercise is similar to the construction of a consumer price index.

We then analyze relative advantages and disadvantages of using national currencies, gold, and artificial currency units (such as SDRs and ECUs) as international money. Related to international money is the question of an optimum currency area. That is, what is the optimum economy's boundary within which a single currency should be used? We examine conditions needed to establish a single-currency area. We then discuss the Maastricht Treaty on the establishment of the European Monetary Union, which may be considered as an approximation of a theoretical optimum currency area.

FUNCTIONS OF MONEY

Functions of money in an open economy

Nations use their own national money for domestic transactions, even when their economies are open to the rest of the world. But which national money should they use to effect international transactions? One extreme case is where every nation's own money is used in international transactions. Then, there is no international money. The flexible exchange rate system corresponds to this situation. The other extreme is the case where one national currency or something else is used to perform three major functions of money in international transactions, including the unit of account function. This is the case of the fixed exchange rate system where the value of every country's national money is tied to the value of one particular country's money. Between these two extremes, there is a case where values of currencies of several countries may be fixed to the currency of one nation. We may call such a currency a *key currency*. Today, there is no national currency serving as an international money in the sense of the theoretical maximum. Rather there are several key currencies with some limited usages. Therefore, our discussion will be mostly based on key currencies. Like money in the domestic economy, a key currency performs three major functions as: a medium of exchange, a store of value, and a unit of account.

A medium of exchange

A key currency acts as a medium of exchange in international transactions. When exporting goods and services, exporters may invoice their claims in units of a certain key currency and receive payment accordingly. The use of such a currency reduces transaction costs. Let us look at Figure 4.1 which suggests three possible cases depending on the extent to which a key currency is used for transactions purposes. Case 1 shows that the key currency does not have a direct access to the goods and services market of country 1. Therefore, anyone who wants to buy products from such a country must convert a national currency into that country's money first. Case 2 represents the situation where both key currency and own national

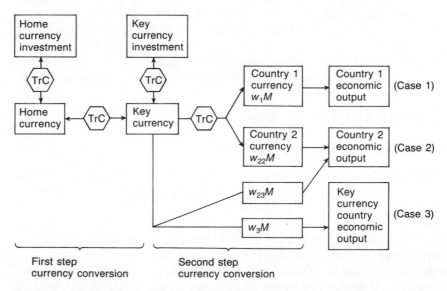

Figure 4.1 The role of a key currency in international transactions (TrC, transaction cost)

currency can be used to have access to that market. For example, during the period of the British–Irish monetary union, the pound sterling circulated freely in the Republic of Ireland alongside the local currency. Case 3 represents the situation where the key currency has direct access to its own country market.

By holding a key currency instead of the home currency for future international transactions purposes, the first step currency conversion needs can be eliminated. Likewise, the second step conversion needs can also be reduced, if not eliminated, thereby reducing transactions costs. Here, by transactions costs we mean the spread between a currency dealer's buying and selling rates plus the time and trouble one must go through in order to convert one national currency into another. In case 1, only the first step transaction cost is eliminated by using a key currency. In case 2, the second step transaction cost can also be eliminated, depending on the acceptability of the key currency. In case 3, no conversion transaction cost is at all involved. Later we will use the above cases in constructing models of demand for a key currency.

A store of value

A store of value function of international money has been utilized by private economic units as well as monetary authorities of countries. In either case, this function enables economic units to pursue an intertemporal optimal consumption pattern which may be different from a revenue pattern. Besides, a particular international money may appreciate in value relative to the home currency. Greater attention to policy prescription has traditionally been paid for the case of monetary authorities which hold key currencies as official reserves. A temporary excess of export proceeds, for example, may be kept in the form of foreign exchange reserves until domestic consumption and investment need is increased.

A unit of account

When a national currency is used as international money, the value of each of all other currencies may be expressed as a rate of exchange (number of units of international money per unit of one currency). Thus, we need $N - 1$ exchange rates when there are N national currencies. On the other hand, if there is no specific national currency serving as international money, we need $N(N - 1)/2$ foreign exchange rates just as in the case of a barter economy. The value of a key currency can be determined as an inverse value of the foreign exchange rate. Then, when a national currency is serving as an international numeraire, what would be the value of such a numeraire? This is expressed as an exchange rate index, similar to a price index, which we will examine on pp. 60–5.

Models of demand for international money by firms

International money (or key currency) is demanded because payments and receipts in international transactions cannot be perfectly matched in total sum or by currency. It is also held because there are nonzero transaction costs involved in converting the domestic currency into a foreign currency or vice versa.

Using the Baumol (1952) deterministic cash balance model, we may construct a model of demand for international money. Suppose that a multinational corporation receives an export revenue in a lump sum amount T in a key currency, which is to be invested in a key-currency-denominated financial asset. This corporation will use this receipt for the continuous payment of raw material imports from three countries, as represented in Figure 4.1. The key currency when invested would earn income at the interest rate i. Out of investment, a given amount M will be withdrawn and held in the key currency balance to make payment for the imports to the three countries with each receiving $w_i M$ where w_i is the respective weight. That is,

$$(w_1 + w_{21} + w_{22} + w_3)M = M \tag{4.1}$$

where w_1 is the weight for country 1 which require the conversion of the key currency into the local currency for the imports, w_{22} is the partial weight for country 2 representing the imports which require the conversion of the key currency into the local currency, w_{23} is the partial weight for country 2 representing the portion of imports made by payment in the key currency, and w_3 is the weight for country 3 in which the key currency is directly used. The average amount of the key currency balance held is $M/2$. The opportunity cost of holding this balance will be $i(M/2)$. The cost of converting the key-currency-denominated investment into the key currency balance ϕ is assumed to be fixed, regardless of the amount converted. Then, $T/(w_1 + w_{22} + w_{23} + w_3)M$ or T/M is the number of times the investment asset is liquidated. v_1 and v_2 are variable costs of converting the key currency into country 1 currency and country 2 currency respectively. Then the total cost TC is the sum of the opportunity cost, the fixed cost of investment conversion, and the variable costs of foreign currency conversion, as follows:

$$\text{TC} = i\,\frac{M}{2} + \phi\,\frac{T}{(w_1 + w_{22} + w_{23} + w_3)M} + v_1 w_1 M\,\frac{T}{M}$$

$$+ v_2 w_{22} M\,\frac{T}{M}. \tag{4.2}$$

The rule is to find M to minimize TC or to set $dTC/dM = 0$, where dTC/dM is the derivative of TC with respect to M.

$$\frac{dTC}{dM} = \frac{i}{2} - \frac{\phi T}{M^2} = 0.$$

Thus,

$$M = (2\phi T/i)^{1/2}. \tag{4.3}$$

Thus, the optimal key currency balance to be held does not depend on the variable conversion costs. Furthermore, the optimal balance does not have to increase in the same proportion as the size of total receipts (or transactions) increases.

If the firm is to invest its receipts in a financial asset denominated in its home currency instead of the key currency, it must first convert its key currency receipts into the home currency which is in turn invested. Later, the firm must withdraw an amount equivalent to M and convert it into the key currency balance. Thereafter the procedure will be the same as the previous case.

This kind of inventory model can also be used to characterize the demand for the cash balance by an international bank to meet deposit withdrawals. In such an application, T represents, for example, the total Eurocurrency deposit receipts which are to be invested in Eurocurrency securities, ϕ is the transaction cost for buying/selling such securities, and τ is the interest rate on the securities.

What if the bank is more concerned about the uncertain deposit withdrawals or payment outflows? If the bank knows the average size of Eurocurrency deposit withdrawal X and its variance σ^2, it can determine the optimal size of the precautionary cash balance E using the Chebyshev inequality. The precautionary balance is in excess of the average balance. The probability of a deposit withdrawal in excess of the average amount μ which is equal to or is to exceed any given amount of the precautionary balance is[1]

$$P[\,|\,X - \mu\,| \geqslant E] \leqslant \sigma^2/E^2. \tag{4.4}$$

The total cost of holding the precautionary balance is the sum of the opportunity cost and the expected cost of running out the precautionary balance:

$$TC = \tau E + \Phi P + 0(1 - P) \tag{4.5}$$

where τ is the interest rate on Eurocurrency securities and Φ is the cost of running out of the balance (which may be measured by a disadvantage in funding either by a higher than usual cost of borrowing or a lower than usual price of selling securities). Then,

$$TC < \tau E + \Phi(\sigma^2/E^2). \tag{4.6}$$

Differentiating with respect to E and setting $dTC/dE = 0$, we obtain

$$E = (2\Phi\sigma^2/\tau)^{1/3} \tag{4.7}$$

which is the optimal balance which in turn will minimize the total cost. Obviously, when the variance becomes greater the size of the precautionary balance must be increased but at a slower rate.

CONSTRUCTION OF AN EXCHANGE RATE INDEX

In a closed economy, as noted earlier, the value of money may be expressed by price indexes. Similarly, in an open economy the value of a key currency may be expressed by an exchange rate index, which is a weighted average of exchange rates of that currency against the currencies of selected countries. Since individual exchange rates vary in different directions by varying degrees, there is a need to have an aggregate index which tells us an overall change in the value of the key currency. That is, the rationale for the construction of an exchange rate index is to have a reliable measure of the change in the value of that key currency. Such an index can then be used as a measure of changes in competitiveness in international trade and investment, as well as as a measure to assess the need for policy adjustment.

In constructing an exchange rate index, we face several basic questions, which are similar to those posed for domestic price index construction, namely (a) which currencies to include, (b) how to determine an appropriate weight to be assigned to each currency, (c) which mathematical method to use for computation of the index, and (d) whether to use a real index or a nominal index. Domestic price index construction would not face the last question, however.

Now let us examine the case of the dollar functioning as a key currency. The Board of Governors of the Federal Reserve System and the Morgan Guaranty Trust Company of New York first developed their exchange rate indexes following the dollar float in March 1973. Subsequently, the IMF, OECD, and the regional Federal Reserve Banks (such as Atlanta, Dallas, and Chicago) also developed their own versions. The proliferation of construction of different versions is a result of different considerations given to the above four questions.

Choice of currencies

Which national currencies should be included in the index? While no group of currencies can be ideal for all purposes, the inclusion of a particular currency depends on our interest in the analysis of specific aspects of the economic interaction between the key currency country (the United States) and the country of the currency. Therefore, the selected currency should represent significant interaction of economic activity between the countries involved. Such interaction can be measured by the trade volume or capital flows.[2] In addition, the value of the selected currency should reflect market forces. This means that the country of the currency should have a relatively well-developed exchange market, where exchange rates can be freely determined by market forces.

For simplicity the number of currencies should be as few as possible. Thus, any currency linked to another currency which is already included in the group should be excluded in order to avoid redundancy. On the other hand, accuracy of the index to measure the comprehensive impact of a change in the value of the dollar requires the inclusion of as many currencies as possible. The number of currencies included in the existing indexes for the US dollar ranges from 10 to 131, the latter representing the total number of countries with which the United States is currently trading.

Choice of appropriate weights

Once the currencies are selected, weights must be assigned prior to averaging. Ideally, the weight assigned to each currency should reflect the importance of that currency in determining the general purchasing power of the dollar. More narrowly, different weights may be assigned depending on the particular economic problem being analyzed – such as trade impact, domestic price impact, or capital inflow impact. For simplicity, broadly based weights such as a country's share in international trade are appealing. Two trade weights have been widely used: bilateral and multilateral. Bilateral weights are determined by each country's share of total US exports plus imports. Thus, the bilateral weight BW_k for country k is

$$BW_k = \frac{USEX_k + USIM_k}{\Sigma \ USEX_j + \Sigma \ USIM_j} \tag{4.8}$$

where $USEX_j$ is US exports to country j, $USIM_j$ is US imports from country j, and $j = 1, ..., k, ..., n$ (all the countries included in the index). On the other hand, multilateral weights are the share of each country in the combined total trade of all the foreign countries whose currencies are included in the index. Thus, the multilateral weight MW_k for country k is

$$MW_k = \frac{WEX_k + WIM_k}{\Sigma \ WEX_j + \Sigma \ WIM_j} \tag{4.9}$$

where WEX_j is the worldwide exports of country j and WIM_j is the worldwide imports of country j.

Since bilateral weights emphasize trade between two countries, they do not capture the effect of trade competition in third-country markets. On the other hand, multilateral trade weights allow for such third-country market competition, but in some instances they may overstate its importance, from the point of view of the United States. However, if the US dollar plays the

Table 4.1 Weights of foreign currencies in indexes of the dollar's effective exchange rate

Country/currency	Multilateral weights	Bilateral weights
Germany/deutsche mark	0.208	0.101
Japan/yen	0.136	0.207
France/franc	0.131	0.047
UK/pound	0.119	0.080
Canada/dollar	0.091	0.401
Italy/lira	0.090	0.048
Netherlands/guilder	0.083	0.046
Belgium/guilder	0.064	0.034
Sweden/krona	0.042	0.016
Switzerland/franc	0.036	0.020
Sum	1.000	1.000

Source: *Federal Reserve Bulletin* (October 1978), 785
Note: As of May 1992 the Federal Reserve has not changed the above weights in spite of changing world trade patterns. See the footnote in *Federal Reserve Bulletin* (May 1992), Table A68.

role of the major key currency, it would be more useful to choose the weights which capture the third-country effect. The Federal Reserve reports the US dollar index based on the multilateral weights which are shown in Table 4.1.

Computational methods

Which technique should we use to average (or to aggregate) these various weighted exchange rates? There are two options – the arithmetic averaging technique and the geometric averaging technique. Of the two options available, analytic arguments strongly favor the geometric over the arithmetic averaging technique.

An arithmetic average merely multiplies each currency's weight in the index by the ratio of the base year exchange rate to the t year exchange rate and sums up these products

$$\text{index at time } t = 100\left(W_1 \frac{R_{10}}{(R_{1t})} + \cdots + W_n \left(\frac{R_{n0}}{R_{nt}}\right)\right) \tag{4.10}$$

where R_{j0} is the exchange rate at base year expressed as the number of key currency units (US dollars) per unit of foreign currency j and R_{jt} is the exchange rate in year t expressed as the number of key currency units per unit of foreign currency j. The major drawback of the arithmetic method is that it does not treat appreciation and depreciation of the key currency symmetrically. Changes in currencies whose value rose against the key currency would have a reduced impact on the index, whereas changes in currencies that fell against the key currency would have an increased impact. As a result, the arithmetic average imparts a systematic upward bias to the measurement of changes in the key currency's average exchange value.[3]

On the other hand, the geometric average yields more symmetric results between appreciation and depreciation of the key currency. Also it gives the same percentage change in an index even if the base period for the index is changed and even if the exchange rates in the index are defined in reciprocal terms. Thus, most of the recently developed indexes use the geometric approach:

$$\text{index at time } t = 100 \left(\frac{R_{10}}{R_{1t}}\right)^{MW1} \cdots \left(\frac{R_{n0}}{R_{nt}}\right)^{MWn}. \tag{4.11}$$

Nominal index versus real index

The real index further attempts to adjust the index by incorporating relative price changes in the United States against other countries in the index. Such additional adjustment need is based on the assumption that price changes are not immediately reflected in exchange rates. That is, although in the long run exchange rates adjust over time exactly to offset movements in relative prices, the short-term variability of exchange rates is usually not consistent with changes in relative exchange rates. Otherwise, there is no need to make this adjustment.

$$\text{real index at } t = 100 \left\{ \left[\frac{(R_{10}/R_{1t})(FPI_{10}/USPI_0)}{FPI_{1t}/USPI_t}\right]^{MW1} \right.$$
$$\left. \cdots \left[\frac{(R_{n0}/R_{nt})(FPI_{n0}/USPI_0)}{FPI_{nt}/USPI_t}\right]^{MWn} \right\} \tag{4.12}$$

where FPI_{nt} is the price index of country n at time t and $USPI_t$ is the price index of the United States (key currency country) at t.

How different are they?

A recent study by Jack L. Harvey and William A. Strauss (1987) compared twelve dollar indexes available in the literature. As shown in Table 4.2, those included are the Federal Reserve Board's trade-weighted dollar nominal index (FRB-TWD), its real index (FRB-TWDr); Morgan Guaranty's fifteen-country nominal index (M-G15n), its real index (M-G15r), its forty-country real index (M-G40); OECD's effective exchange rate index (OECD); IMF's effective exchange rate index based on the multilateral exchange rate model (IMF); Atlanta Federal Reserve Bank's index (ATLANTA); Dallas Federal Reserve Bank's nominal index (X-131), its real index (RX-101); Chicago

Table 4.2 Summary characteristics of various exchange rate indexes for the US dollar

Index name	Number of currencies	Trade weight period	Multilateral/ bilateral	Relative price adjustment (nominal or real)
			Index characteristics	
		Weighting scheme		
Federal Reserve Board (FRB-TWD)	10	1972–6	Multilateral	Nominal
Morgan Guaranty (M-G15n)	15	1980	Bilateral (trade in manufactures)	Nominal
Chicago Fed (7-Gn)	16	Moving average, 12 quarters	Bilateral	Nominal
IMF effective (IMF)	17	1972 (years through 1974); 1977 (years 1975 on)	Multilateral (Multilateral exchange rate model)	Nominal
Atlanta Fed (ATLANTA)	18	1984	Bilateral	Nominal
OECD effective (OECD)	22	Moving average, annual	Bilateral (double-weighted, based on manufactured goods production and trade)	Nominal
Dallas Fed (X-131)	131	Moving average, annual	Bilateral	Nominal
Federal Reserve Board (FRB-TWDr)	10	1972–6	Multilateral	Real, CPI based
Morgan Guaranty (M-G15r)	15	1980	Bilateral (trade in manufactures)	Real wholesale prices of manufactured goods, excluding food and fuels
Chicago Fed (7-Gr)	16	Moving average, 12 quarters	Bilateral	Real, CPI based
Morgan Guaranty (M-G40)	40	1980	Bilateral (modified to take into account US competitiveness in foreign markets for trade in manufactures)	Real wholesale prices of manufactured goods, excluding food and fuels
Dallas Fed (RX-101)	101	Moving average, annual	Bilateral	Real, CPI based

Source: *Federal Reserve Bank of Chicago Economic Perspectives* (July–August 1987), 8

Federal Reserve Bank's nominal index (7-Gn), and its real index (7-Gr). In comparing these indexes, they used two measures, namely correlation coefficients and recovery ratios. Except for the Dallas indexes which cover the largest number of currencies (131 in nominal index and 101 in real index), simple correlations between the various indexes indicated a high degree of similarity with each other. The correlation coefficients between the levels of the various nominal indexes were 0.960 or above and the correlations in terms of rate of changes of the indexes were also high – 0.952 or higher. Another measure they used was the recovery ratio which is defined as the ratio of the recorded decline in the index since the peak to the previous recorded increase from the trough. Based on the data covering the 1985–6 depreciation of the US dollar in relation to the 1980–5 appreciation of the US dollar, the recovery ratios in most cases were at about 0.70. In conclusion, these indexes except for the Dallas indexes appear to be strikingly similar, vindicating the original doubt raised against the ability of the Federal Reserve Board's index (FRB-TWD) to represent the relative strength of the US dollar. However, it remains to be seen whether the indexes can serve as a true measure of international competitiveness of the US economy.

TYPES OF INTERNATIONAL MONEY

Basically three types of money are being used for international transactions today: (1) national currencies as key currencies, (2) artificial currency units (such as SDRs and ECUs), and (3) gold. They are used for both official and private transactions as a means of international payment settlement, a store of value, and a unit of account. Sometimes, international money is termed vehicle currency emphasizing the function of payment settlement, or reserve currency emphasizing the official use of the store of value function. Not all the above three types of money perform the three major functions of money equally well. Their functions are evolutionary over time. Gold is now going through demonetization process by losing its two main functions and performing mainly a store of value function only, whereas some artificial currencies which were created to serve as numeraire in private transactions are acquiring additional functions of money and moving toward a fully fledged money. We may generally categorize their active functions as in Table 4.3.

Key currencies

Prior to 1914, the British pound served by and large as international money. After the Second World War and until the early 1970s the US dollar was undisputed in its role as international money, representing over four-fifths of total official holdings of foreign exchange reserves. However, coupled with the declining relative position of the US economy, two major changes in the

Table 4.3 Types of international money

Function of money	Key currency		Artificial currency units (SDR)		Gold	
	Official transactions	Private transactions	Official transactions	Private transactions	Official transactions	Private transactions
Means of payment	Yes	Yes	Yes	No	Yes	No
Store of value	Yes	Yes	Yes	Yes	Yes	Yes
Unit of account	Yes	Yes	Yes	Yes	No	No

international payment system which took place in the early 1970s have progressively reduced the predominant role of the US dollar. The United States terminated its dollar-for-gold convertibility in August 1971 and abandoned the fixed exchange rate system in March 1973. By contrast, currencies of other major industrial countries such as the deutsche mark and the Japanese yen began to surge forward to function as key currencies. Although it is difficult to ascertain the exact extent of uses of each key currency, we may use official holdings of reserve currencies as one proxy measure for official transactions, as shown in Table 4.4. For private sector transactions, available data show that the currency of invoice in international trade transactions is not always dominated by key currencies, but rather by the currencies of exporting countries whose uses appear to be more extensive than expected.[4] On the other hand, in international financial markets the extent of use of major key currencies appears to be dominant, but not to the same extent as shown by shares of official reserve holdings. For example, $275.2 billion or 45.7 percent of total 1989 cross-border lending and borrowing by banks in Western industrial countries was denominated in the US dollar, 16.5 percent in the deutsche mark, 11.3 percent in the Japanese yen, and the remainder in ECU, pound sterling, Swiss franc, and so forth.[5]

Table 4.4 Official holdings of reserve assets (excluding IMF reserve position-related assets) (in billions of SDRs)

	1975	1980	1985	1988
Key currencies	137.4	292.8	346.7	493.2
of which (%)				
US dollar	85.2	69.0	65.1	63.3
Pound sterling	4.1	3.1	3.2	3.1
Deutsche mark	6.6	15.6	15.5	16.2
French franc	1.3	1.8	1.2	1.7
Swiss franc	1.7	3.3	2.4	1.5
Netherlands guilder	0.6	1.4	1.0	1.1
Japanese yen	0.6	4.5	7.6	7.2
Unspecified currencies	–	1.4	3.9	6.0
SDRs	8.8	11.8	18.2	20.2
ECUs	–	47.7	38.0	50.0
Gold				
Quantity (million oz.)	1,018.0	953.0	948.9	945.2
Value at London market price	121.9	440.5	282.5	288.2
US dollars per SDR	1.17066	1.27541	1.09842	1.34570

Source: International Monetary Fund, *Annual Report*, 1981, 1986, 1988; various issues of IMF, *International Financial Statistics*

Requisites to become a key currency

What, then, makes a national currency become a key currency? It must have general acceptability internationally. The general acceptability can be increased by a number of requirements: (1) currency convertibility, (2) accessibility to a large economy which produces goods and services to satisfy global demand in a substantial way, and (3) accessibility to large well developed financial markets. What is currency convertibility? According to Joseph Gold (1971), it is possible to define the convertibility of any currency by determining three aspects: the extent of use of the currency, the extent of its exchangeability, and the extent of assurance of its exchange value. Table 4.5 shows the different definitions for convertibility used at different times. Before the establishment of the IMF in 1947, convertibility was determined by an official arrangement for a currency to be converted back into gold at a predetermined official price. Between 1947 and August 1971 the convertibility was defined by the IMF with reference to an official arrangement which permits (a) unrestricted use of the home currency for international current account settlement purposes, (b) exchangeability of the home currency for both prescribed foreign currencies (mostly key currencies) and gold at fixed rates which are either the rates (par value) permanently agreed upon between

Table 4.5 Definition of currency convertibility

	Conventional concept	3/47 – 8/71	8/71 – 3/73	Post 3/73	Theoretical maximum
It can be used without restriction for					
current account settlement		x	x	x	x
capital account settlement					x
It can be exchanged for					
some prescribed currencies		x	x	x	x
any other currency					x
gold	x	x			x
It can be used or exchanged at					
par value (expressed in gold)		x	x		
unilaterally fixed rate	x	x	x		
market value				x	x

Note: March 1, 1947, establishment of International Monetary Fund; August 15, 1971, suspension of convertibility of US dollar into gold; March 19, 1973, implementation of the floating rate system.

the currency country and the IMF or the rates temporarily fixed by the government of the currency without an IMF agreement. During these early post Second World War years, convertibility into gold was still regarded as an important criterion to satisfy the definition of convertibility. In March 1973, the system of fixing exchange rates against the dollar was terminated and this was followed by formal ratification through amendment of the IMF's Articles of Agreement in 1976. Therefore, during the transition period between August 1971 and March 1973, the gold convertibility requirement was dropped; since March 1973, fixed exchange rates have been replaced by the market exchange rates.

Although convertibility is a necessary condition for a national currency to be elevated to the status of international money, it is not a sufficient condition. According to the theoretical maximum of convertibility, a national currency is convertible if (a) it can be used for whatever transactional purposes and (b) it can be exchanged for any currency including gold at free market rates. Obviously, if a national currency approaches this theoretical maximum, it becomes more attractive as international money.

Another important requisite for becoming a key currency is that the currency must represent a relatively large economy (trade potential and investment potential). If several key currencies are available, two important questions arise. The first is what the optimum territory of each of such currencies is. The second is to what extent each currency can be substituted. These questions will be examined in the context of the optimum currency area on pp. 86–90.

The Nth currency issues

Related to a national currency becoming international money are basically two issues: a seigniorage problem and an asymmetric policy advantage problem.

Seigniorage was originally defined as the feudal lord's power to charge a fee to mint precious metal into coins. Now, it is defined as the difference in value between the value of the coin and its content (or cost of production). When the dollar money is created by the United States at practically zero cost and accepted by other countries as a means of international payment, the United States gains power to command the resources of other countries, accruing almost all the seigniorage to the United States. The United States, as the principal issuer of international money under the gold–dollar standard, was widely accused of abusing the seigniorage privilege by excessive monetary expansion, especially after the mid-1960s. This complaint in part prompted the search for a new means of international payment, resulting in the creation of the SDR under the auspices of the IMF.

Another problem related to international money is the asymmetric advantage it gives to its country of origin in conducting monetary policy. Suppose again that there are N countries with N currencies in the world where one currency serves as the Nth currency or numeraire. If the $N-1$ countries fix the value of their currencies against the Nth currency, there is no exchange rate left over for the Nth country to fix, thus freeing the Nth country from the responsibility of fixing any rate. What happens when each country tries, for example, to expand its economy by expansionary monetary policy? Let us look at a likely scenario for the Nth country and other countries.

In the case of the Nth country, a rise in money stock Ms will cause a decrease in the interest rate i, at least in the short run, which in turn has two effects. First, it increases the demand for foreign exchange (FX), as investment opportunities abroad become more attractive, resulting in depreciation of the value of the Nth currency (FXR). Second, it causes domestic real investment I to increase, leading to higher income Y at home. Since the monetary authority of the Nth country is not required to intervene in the foreign exchange market, it can let the effect of monetary policy take its full course (Figure 4.2). Unless the $N-1$ countries prevent the depreciation of the Nth currency, the Nth country will experience an increase in exports (EX) and a decrease in imports (IM), in addition to increased domestic investment. Under the fixed exchange rate system (equivalent to the existence of international money),[6] $N-1$ countries are obliged to fix their respective rates by purchasing the Nth currency when the the Nth currency depreciates. This means that these $N-1$ countries must expand their money supply until their home interest rates are driven down to the same level as that of the Nth country. Nonetheless, by doing so their economies will also expand.

On the other hand, if one of the $N-1$ countries tries to expand its money stock, its home interest rate will go down just as in the case of the Nth country, causing the value of its home currency to depreciate. In order to prevent this from happening, the central bank of this country must sell the Nth currency in exchange for its home currency – causing contraction of its

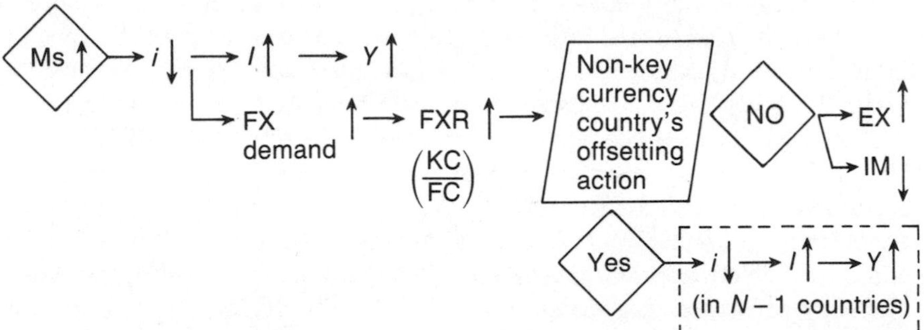

Figure 4.2 Monetary policy action taken by the key currency country (KC, key currency; FC, foreign currency)

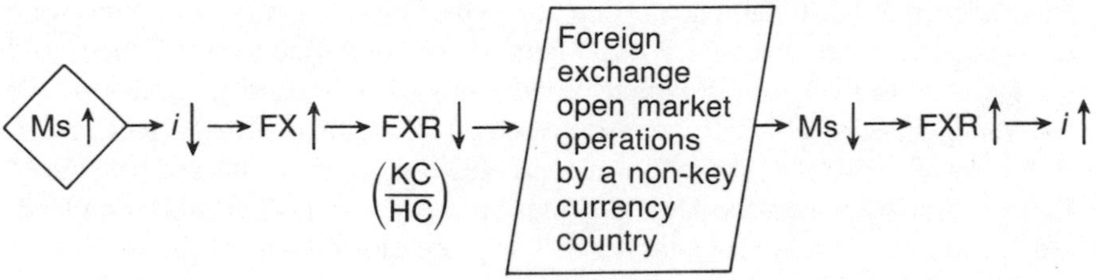

Ms ↑ → i ↓ → FX ↑ → FXR ↓ → $\left(\dfrac{KC}{HC}\right)$ → Foreign exchange open market operations by a non-key currency country → Ms ↓ → FXR ↑ → i ↑

Figure 4.3 Monetary policy action taken by a non-key currency country (KC, key currency; HC, home currency)

home money stock. The process will continue until the interest rate is driven up to the previous level (Figure 4.3).

Thus, while the *N*th country can freely use monetary policy to influence its economy with a resultant influence on other economies, the $N-1$ countries are left with their powerless monetary policy. This inherent asymmetry of policy advantage and seigniorage privilege places immense economic power in the hands of the country of origin of international money. This was indeed a major argument advanced in the 1960s and early 1970s for breaking up the gold–dollar system and adopting a floating rate system.

Gold

The gold standard in which currency is convertible into gold on request was formally initiated when the monometallic standard was adopted in England in 1816 for its domestic monetary system and was implemented by minting gold coins (with 123.27 grams being equal to 20 shillings) in 1821. This standard, more precisely the gold coin standard, was soon adopted by other countries and finally by the United States in 1879. When each country independently fixed its currency value in terms of amount of gold, the exchange rate between its currency and the currency of another country was automatically determined. For example, when one ounce of gold was $20.67 in the United States and £4.24 in England, the exchange rate between dollar and sterling would be $4.87 = £1. Thus any US resident who needed pounds sterling could buy at that rate. If the exchange rate was high enough, she would consider use of gold for payment by shipping gold to England, although she would incur a transportation cost of about $0.03 per ounce then. Similarly, if she wanted to sell pounds sterling for US dollars but the selling price was lower than $4.84, she would rather buy gold by spending £1 in England and import it and sell it for $4.87 to the US government which followed the gold standard.

This system worked rather well for about thirty-five years until the outbreak of the First World War in 1914. Then, in order to finance the war, no country was willing to tie its money supply to the stock of gold. After the war, countries led by England tried to revive the old system but they were unsuccessful largely because it became increasingly difficult to link their gold stock to the money supply which became out of hand and to return to the old value of gold which became quite distorted against other prices.

Meanwhile, in the United States in 1934 Congress enacted the Gold Reserve Act by which the United States returned to another gold standard, but this time a gold bullion standard. The price of gold was raised to $35 per ounce and the US government stood ready to purchase or sell gold bullion instead of gold coins at that price upon request from foreign governments. Gold coins and certificates were prohibited from circulation until this provision of the Act was rescinded in 1975. The gold bullion standard was incorporated into the gold–dollar standard which was the main stay of the IMF-sponsored international monetary system during the period from 1947 to 1971. Under this system, values of the $N-1$ currencies were fixed to the US dollar which in turn was tied to gold.

Over the last hundred years, the role of gold as international money has gradually diminished. But it was only in March 1975 that a drastic demonetization of gold began, as the world's monetary authorities decided to abolish the official price which had supported gold nominally as the standard of the international monetary system.[7]

Today, the US government treats its stock of gold as a commodity to be auctioned off from time to time at the prevailing market prices, as its need arises. This has been a substantial source of gold supply, as shown in Table 4.6. In international transactions gold is rarely used as an international vehicle currency but is still used as a reserve currency by monetary authorities. This is because today no government can compel other countries to accept gold as a means of payment. However, gold has been used extensively for industrial purposes in the private sector. It has also been conjectured that gold has been demanded for store of value purposes primarily to hedge

Table 4.6 Estimated market sources and uses of gold (in metric tons)

	1981	1983	1985	1987	1989
Production	975	1,115	1,235	1,385	1,655
Estimated net sales by Communist countries	300	100	250	300	300
Estimated changes in official gold stock (–, increase)	– 100	70	– 165	95	185
Net new gold loans				70	50
Estimated private demand	1,175	1,285	1,320	1,850	2,190

Source: Bank for International Settlements, (1986) *56th Annual Report*, 160; (1988), *58th Annual Report*, 184; (1990), *60th Annual Report*, 198.

December 1977 = 100

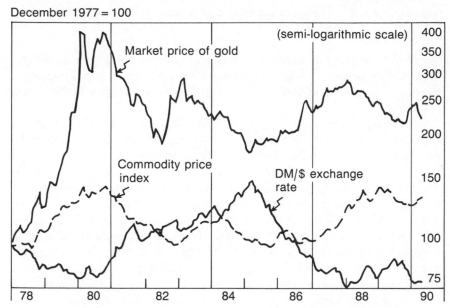

Figure 4.4 Gold price movements in comparison with commodity price and
deutsche mark–dollar exchange rate movements
Source: Bank for International Settlements (1990) *60th Annual Report*, 201

against inflation. The contemporaneous correlation between inflation and
gold prices is rather weak.

However, some non-dollar based investors appear to treat gold as an
alternative to dollar-denominated financial assets, as they increase their
purchase when the dollar weakens, thereby creating a fairly close inverse
relationship between the dollar price of gold and the value of the dollar
vis-à-vis major European currencies (Figure 4.4).

Artificial currency units

When the floating rate system was introduced in 1973, many international
investors, lenders, borrowers, and merchandise traders tried to avoid or
mitigate problems of foreign exchange rate fluctuations. One way to do so
was to use alternatives to fluctuation-prone key currencies. Since then, there
have been growing efforts to create substitutes which would provide a more
stable measure and store of value, resulting in a variety of artificial currency
units. Some of the efforts have been initiated by official agencies, while others
have been initiated by private institutions, particularly from the banking
industry.

An artificial currency unit (ACU) is a unit of account expressed as a weighted average of selected national currencies:

$$ACU = \Sigma \ w_i C_i$$

where C_i is one unit of national currency of country i and w_i is its weight. When the initial weight is fixed under given exchange rates, its value changes as soon as the exchange rate of any currency *vis-à-vis* another in the basket changes.

Obviously, if $w_i = 0$, the corresponding currency is excluded from the ACU. How each weight is determined is a matter of convention among the parties involved. Typically, in official ACUs, the weight (including zero) for the currency of a country is determined by one or more factors such as (a) the GNP of the country, (b) the international trade volume of the country, and (c) the role of the country's currency as international reserves. On the other hand, in private ACUs, factors considered may include (a) minimization of marketing cost by choosing constituent currencies familiar to prospective customers as in the case of the Arcru (see p. 85), (b) maximization of exchange gains by choosing only (traditionally) strong currencies, and (c) minimization of exchange rate risk by choosing several currencies whose exchange rates are negatively correlated. The optimal trade-off between objectives (b) and (c) is a topic in portfolio analysis which we will formally study in Chapter 15.

The official special drawing right

The official SDR is a fiduciary reserve asset created by the IMF, beginning in 1970, as a supplement to existing reserve assets (gold, foreign exchange, and reserve positions in the IMF). The official SDR is simply an accounting device. Let us consider how the Federal Reserve pays when it buys government securities from a commercial bank. The Federal Reserve simply credits the purchased amount to the account of the bank kept at the Federal Reserve, which the bank subsequently can freely use for any purposes. Likewise, when the IMF creates and allocates new SDRs, it simply credits the allocated amount to the account of the participant country but without any compensation. The recipient country can then use the account to settle financial obligations, to make loans, to make donations, or simply to keep as a store of value. The main restriction in using this account is that all the transactions to be settled by this account must be intergovernmental transactions between participant countries or between participant countries and the IMF and a dozen or so designated official organizations.[8] Thus, there is no common base at present where the official SDR and the private SDR can co-mingle.

During the period 1970–86 the IMF created and allocated a cumulative total of SDR 21.4 billion to its participant countries. The amount allocated to each country was determined on the basis of the size of the participant country's quota in the IMF. This allocative criterion was questioned by many low quota countries which by and large are poor countries. They claim that they are the ones who need new international money most and yet they receive least. Although the seigniorage gains of SDR creation are distributed more equitably than in the case of dollar creation, the allocative criterion remains debatable.

What is the obligation of the participant countries which are receiving free international money – SDRs? Just like any borrower paying interest on her borrowed money, they are levied with charges on their cumulative allocations. In addition, if requested by the IMF, they are required to accept SDRs in exchange for their currency. In such a case, the participant is obliged to hold SDRs up to a maximum of three times the net cumulative allocation it has received.

The SDRs also serve as a store of value. In order to promote this function further, the IMF pays interest to participants and other holders on their holdings of SDRs. The interest rate and the charges were initially set to be the same.[9]

As pointed out earlier, there is no common ground where the official SDR and the private SDR can interact. The only direct link they have is that they use the same valuation. The value of the SDR was initially expressed in terms of gold, SDR 35 being equivalent to one fine ounce of gold (or 1 SDR = 0.888 671 gram of fine gold). But it was also linked to the US dollar indirectly through gold so that SDR 1 was equal to $1.00. As shown in Table 4.7, in the middle of 1974 a new valuation method was adopted as the weighted average value of a basket of sixteen currencies representing countries that had shares in world exports of goods and services exceeding 1 percent during the five-year period through 1972. It was revised in the middle of 1978 using the same method, but this time based on the 1972–6 world export data. At the beginning of 1981, the size of the valuation basket was reduced to the currencies of the five countries having the largest shares of world exports of goods and services. This simplification was designed to promote uses of the private SDR. The valuation was again revised at the beginning of 1986 on the basis of each country's export performance during the period 1980–4. Thereafter, it was decided to readjust the SDR basket every five years. Accordingly, the latest revision was made effective on January 1, 1991.

At this time, it appears that the monetary authorities in the world are not in a hurry to create additional SDRs despite the fact that an announced objective of the IMF is to make the SDR become the principal reserve asset of the international monetary system. Issues such as inflationary concern and allocative criteria must be resolved before the resumption of SDR creation. To make the SDR the main reserve asset would require making the IMF a world central bank which would have control over world liquidity. No country would be willing to give up its central banking power to the IMF at this time.

Table 4.7 Units of currencies in the special drawing rights basket (percentage weight in basket at base period in parentheses)

Currency	Effective 1/1/1991		Effective 1/1/1986		Effective 1/1/1981		Effective 7/1/1978		Effective 7/1/1974	
US dollar	0.572	(40)	0.452	(42)	0.540	(42)	0.40	(33.0)	0.40	(33.0)
German mark	0.453	(21)	0.527	(19)	0.460	(19)	0.32	(12.5)	0.38	(12.5)
Japanese yen	31.800	(17)	33.400	(15)	34.000	(13)	21.00	(7.5)	26.00	(7.5)
French franc	0.800	(11)	1.020	(12)	0.740	(13)	0.42	(7.5)	0.44	(7.5)
British pound	0.0812	(11)	0.0893	(12)	0.071	(13)	0.05	(7.5)	0.045	(9.0)
Italian lira	—		—		—		52.00	(5.0)	47.00	(6.0)
Dutch guilder	—		—		—		0.14	(5.0)	0.14	(4.5)
Canadian dollar	—		—		—		0.07	(5.0)	0.071	(6.0)
Belgian franc	—		—		—		1.60	(4.0)	1.60	(3.5)
Saudi riyal	—		—		—		0.13	(3.0)	—	
Swedish krona	—		—		—		0.11	(2.0)	0.13	(2.5)
Iranian rial	—		—		—		1.70	(2.0)	—	
Australian dollar	—		—		—		0.017	(1.5)	0.012	(1.5)
Danish krone	—		—		—		—		0.11	(1.5)
Spanish peseta	—		—		—		1.50	(1.5)	1.10	(1.5)
Norwegian krone	—		—		—		0.10	(1.5)	0.099	(1.5)
Austrian schilling	—		—		—		0.28	(1.5)	0.22	(1.0)
South African rand	—		—		—		—		0.0082	(1.0)

Sources: IMF, Annual Report, 1974, 1978, 1981, 1986; IMF SDR Department

The private special drawing right

The private SDR consists of the same basket of currencies as the official SDR. However, the private SDR is different from the official SDR in a number of ways. The official SDR was created under an agreement by IMF member governments to supplement international reserves, whereas the private SDR was created by a contract entered into by the private parties involved for use as a numeraire. Therefore, the private SDR is not constrained by the rules governing the uses of the official SDR. At the same time, private SDR accounts cannot be transferred to the official accounts, or vice versa.

The private SDR as a numeraire started out when the Bank Keyser Ullman and the Chase Manhattan Bank office in London began accepting deposits in SDRs as an alternative denomination of deposits in mid-1975. The mechanics of taking SDR deposits is that a bank receives a certain national currency for deposit which is to be denominated in SDRs and redeems the deposit with interest at maturity either in the SDR constituent currencies as prescribed in the SDR basket or in any predetermined currency, all according to a deposit contract.

However, the development of the private SDR market was slow until the start of 1981. The market was estimated to be in the order of SDR 3 billion then. The attractiveness of the market was enhanced largely by the decision of the IMF to simplify the basket of the official SDR from sixteen to five currencies beginning January 1, 1981, as shown in Table 4.7. This decision not only facilitated public understanding of the SDR but also made it easier for banks to hedge their positions. Since, for banks, taking SDR deposits is equivalent to assuming multicurrency payment obligations, one way to hedge their multicurrency exchange rate risk is to find willing borrowers of the SDR in the same amount and maturity of each deposit. Because it is difficult to match their assets and liabilities in such a manner, banks may choose an alternative method of hedging, namely forward exchange contracts by which banks can purchase needed foreign currencies at predetermined contractual prices. The use of foreign exchange forward contracts depends on well developed forward exchange markets for each of the currencies involved. Prior to 1981, not all currencies in the sixteen-currency SDR basket had well developed forward markets, although each had its active spot markets. The 1981 IMF decision to simplify the SDR basket resolved this problem. Nonetheless, after the initial enthusiasm of the basket simplification, the use of the SDR tended to be less. This led to speculation about whether a larger number of currencies should be used. However, more fundamental causes of the less intensive use may be the steady appreciation of the US dollar in the early 1980s and the relative stability which prevailed in exchange markets, making the need for hedging in multicurrencies less.

An example of deposit taking in the special drawing right

Suppose a prospective depositor has $1 million, which she wishes to deposit in the denomination of the SDRs for one year. Basically, there are three steps involved: (a) determination of the initial deposit amount in SDRs; (b) calculation of the SDR interest rate; and (c) settlement of the redemption value in a prescribed currency.

In order to determine the initial deposit amount, we first need the conversion rate of the dollar to the SDR, which is the sum of the dollar values of the component currencies in the SDR. Given the spot exchange rates at the time of the deposit, as shown column (2) in Table 4.8, the conversion rate in column (3) can be calculated by summing the products of columns (1) and (2). With a conversion rate of $1.3428/SDR 1, the initial SDR deposit amount is:

$$\$1 \text{ million} \times (\text{SDR } 1/\$1.3428) = \text{SDR } 744,713. \tag{4.13}$$

Next, we need to calculate the SDR interest rate which is the weighted sum of the interest rates on the component currencies, with each weight equal to the percentage share of a currency's value in the SDR. Depending on which interest rates are used, banks use two alternative methods in the SDR rate calculation. One method is to use the interbank deposit rates in London, that is, the London Interbank Offered Rates (LIBORs), as shown in Table 4.9(a). In this approach the SDR interest rate is calculated as if the bank had received deposit money in the five component currencies in the proportion prescribed in the SDR. It does not make direct reference to the total cost of funds (interest payment plus exchange gain or losses) for the bank, although differences in the interest rates are the reflection of exchange gains or losses.

Table 4.8 Computation of US dollar – special drawing right exchange rates

| SDR component (1) | At the time of deposit | | | At the time of withdrawal | |
	Spot rate ($/FC) (2)	SDR in dollar (3)	Component weight (%) (4)	Spot rate ($/FC) (5)	SDR in dollar (6)
$0.5720	$1/$1	$0.5720	42.60	$1/$1	$0.5720
DM0.4530	$1/DM1.7199	$0.2634	19.62	$1/DM1.7600	$0.2574
¥31.800	$1/¥138.22	$0.2301	17.13	$1/¥137.50	$0.2313
FFr0.8000	$1/FFr5.8282	$0.1373	10.22	$1/FFr5.9200	$0.1351
£0.0812	$1.7238/£1	$0.1400	10.43	$1.6392/£1	$0.1331
SDR 1		$1.3428	100.00		$1.3289

Note: FC, foreign currency.

Table 4.9 Computation of special drawing right interest rates

(a) Using Eurodeposit rates

	LIBOR (%) (1)	Weight-based spot rates (%) (2)	SDR interest rate (%) (3)
$ deposit	7.0	42.60	2.9820
DM deposit	8.8	19.62	1.7266
¥ deposit	5.6	17.13	0.9593
FFr deposit	8.8	10.22	0.8994
£ deposit	11.1	10.43	1.1577
		100.00	7.7250

(b) Using forward exchange rates (Morgan formula)

	Spot ($/FC) (1)	Forward ($/FC) (2)	Discount/ premium[a] (3)	Covered rate (%)[b] (4)	Weight based on forward rate[c] (5)	SDR interest rate (%) (6)
$ deposit	1.0000	1.0000	0	7.00	0.4292	3.0044
DM deposit	0.58143	0.5714	−0.0173	8.73	0.1942	1.6954
¥ deposit	0.00723	0.00733	0.0138	5.62	0.1749	0.9829
FFr deposit	0.17158	0.16835	−0.0188	8.88	0.1010	0.8969
£ deposit	1.72380	1.65290	−0.0411	11.11	0.1007	1.1188
					1.0000	7.6984

Notes: [a] Discount = $[(2) - (1)]/(1) < 0$; premium = $[(2) - (1)]/(1) > 0$.
[b] $ deposit rate = 7.00%.
[c] SDR 1 (based on forward rate) = $1.3328.

Also the percentage share of each component currency to be used as its weight is calculated by using the spot exchange rate.

The second approach expressly considers the total cost of deposits. For example, when a bank receives a dollar deposit for which it pays 7 percent interest rate and redeems part of the deposit in other currencies, it may incur additional cost should there be appreciation of the repayment currencies. If a repayment currency is to appreciate by, say, 1 percent, the bank may no longer be willing to pay 7 percent interest rate on the deposit of such a currency. Instead, it may pay 6 percent interest rate on the deposit and 1 percent additional cost in the form of a higher purchase price of the foreign currency in a forward contract in anticipation of payment obligations in foreign currencies.[10] This approach is known as the covered interest rate calculation, or Morgan formula, as shown in Table 4.9(b). For the depositor, there will be 6 percent interest rate and 1 percent exchange gain. In summary, the second approach takes the US dollar deposit rate as a reference rate and derives the remaining rates by making adjustment on the basis of a discount or premium. A discount (or premium) is an annualized percentage depreciation (or appreciation) of a foreign currency. Each weight is determined in the same manner as in the first method except that the dollar value of each currency is calculated with forward rates instead of spot rates.[11]

Although the second approach is more accurate in reflecting the total cost of funds on the SDR deposit rate, the first approach is preferred in practice because it is easier to calculate with readily available LIBORs. If interest rate parity holds, the two approaches would give the same result. Actually, the difference has been rather small, less than 0.125 percent.

Finally, the terminal repayment amount must be determined. Using the first method, we obtain the terminal value TV of the deposit in SDRs at the end of year as

$$TV = SDR\ 744{,}713 \times (1 + 0.07725) = SDR\ 802{,}242. \qquad (4.14)$$

With the new conversion rate of \$1.3289/SDR 1, given spot exchange rates at the time of deposit withdrawal (Table 4.8, column (5)), the terminal value in US dollars will be

$$SDR\ 802{,}242 \times (\$1.3289/SDR\ 1) = \$1{,}066{,}099. \qquad (4.15)$$

Depending on the contractual terms, the depositor can receive this amount in US dollars or in any other constituent currency whose amount can easily be determined by applying the appropriate spot rate prevailing at the time. Similarly, the depositor may get back the deposit in the multicurrencies prescribed in the value of the SDR.

Is this depositor better off by making the deposit in SDRs, compared with a straight dollar deposit? Obviously, this cannot be answered in advance since it depends on the future spot rates which will prevail at the time of deposit withdrawal. If the depositor had deposited in straight US dollars, she would have received a terminal value of \$1,070,000.

What is the condition needed for the depositor to get back the same principal amount? Let us refer to the exchange rates at the time of deposit and at the time of withdrawal, as given in Table 4.8. Japanese yen, for example, appreciated against the US dollar. Since the US dollar component remains unchanged in terms of the US dollar value, the remaining three currencies (deutsche mark, French franc, and pound sterling) jointly must have a net depreciation. More specifically, we have an initial conversion rate of \$1.3428 per SDR 1, of which the dollar component is \$0.572 and the Japanese yen component \$0.2301. At the time of withdrawal, the Japanese yen component becomes \$0.2313. Therefore, the remaining three currencies together must depreciate by \$0.0012 in order to maintain the same conversion rate.

Today, not only bank deposits are denominated in SDRs, but also syndicated credit, floating rate notes, and Eurobonds. Then, is investment in SDR financial assets really attractive for an investor seeking portfolio diversification on a global basis? Since the total yield on an international asset consists of exchange gain or loss (expressed in the annualized percentage) and the interest rate, the investor must consider the total yield and its variability. Because of the basket properties of the SDR, the exchange value of the SDR expressed in an individual component currency tends to be stable. Changes in the exchange value of each currency in the basket tend to be offset by opposite changes in the exchange values of some of the other currencies. In addition, since the exchange rate movements of the different currencies in the basket are not perfectly related, the standard deviation of the SDR's conversion rate in terms of a particular currency will be less than the weighted average of the five individual standard deviations of exchange rates in terms of that currency. This portfolio effect is somewhat less pronounced in the SDR interest rate, because interest rates in different countries tend to move in the same direction. Therefore, can the investor earn an appropriate total yield high enough while achieving such portfolio effect by investing in SDR assets? We will take up this question formally in Chapter 15.

The official European currency unit

The ECU has its roots back to 1950, when the European Payment Union, the predecessor of the European Economic Community (EEC), established the European unit of account (EUA) for use as its official accounting unit in settling intergovernmental transactions.

One unit of the EUA was set to be equivalent to the value of 0.888 67 gram of gold, which in turn was equal to one US dollar. The EUA was retained when the EEC was established by six founding countries (West Germany, France, Italy, the Netherlands, Belgium, and Luxembourg) in 1957. However, when the gold–dollar exchange system collapsed in the early 1970s, it became increasingly difficult to maintain that the value of the EUA be tied to the value of gold directly. As the SDR moved to the basket of currencies valuation method in 1974, the valuation method of the EUA was also changed by adopting eight-member-country currencies in the basket with each weight being determined by each country's GNP and share of world trade among the member countries. In December 1978, the European Council passed the so-called Brussels Resolution that established the European Monetary System (EMS) and a new unit of account, the ECU which was implemented in 1979 (Table 4.10). As a unit of account, the ECU was further revised in 1984 to include Greek currency and again in 1989 to include Spanish and Portuguese currencies.

Similar to the SDR, the official ECU functions almost as a full-fledged money in official transactions. However, some of its functions are more unique. One important function as a numeraire is that the ECU serves as a basis to indicate the degree of divergence in one exchange rate from the composite level (central rate) and to suggest the need for official intervention in the exchange markets.

Table 4.10 Currency composition of the ECU (in national currency units)

Country/currency	ERM[a]	Effective date						
		9/21/1989		9/17/1984		3/13/1979		6/28/1974
Germany/DM	Yes	0.6242	(30.1)[b]	0.719	(32.1)[b]	0.828	(33.0)[b]	(27.3)[b]
France/FFr	Yes	1.332	(19.0)	1.31	(19.1)	1.15	(19.8)	(19.5)
UK/£	Yes	0.08784	(13.0)	0.0878	(15.8)	0.0885	(13.3)	(17.5)
Netherlands/DF	Yes	0.2198	(9.4)	0.256	(10.2)	0.286	(10.5)	(9.0)
Italy/Lir	Yes	151.8	(10.15)	140.0	(9.2)	109.0	(9.5)	(14.0)
Belgium/BFr	Yes	3.301	(7.6)	3.71	(8.3)	–		
Denmark/DKr	Yes	0.1976	(2.45)	0.219	(2.7)	0.217	(3.1)	(3.0)
Ireland/I£	Yes	0.008552	(1.1)	0.00871	(1.2)	0.00759	(1.2)	(1.5)
Greece/Dr	No	1.44	(0.8)	1.15	(1.1)	–		
Luxembourg/LFr	Yes	0.13	(0.3)	0.14	(0.3)	–		
Belgium/BF– Luxembourg/LFr	–					3.80	(9.6)	(8.2)
Spain/Pta	Yes	6.885	(5.3)					
Portugal/Esc	No	1.393	(0.8)					

Sources: Bank for International Settlements (1979) 49th Annual Report, 145; Bevan, T. (1985) "The ECU – Europe's New Currency," Barclays Review, September: 82; HM Treasury (1989) Economic Progress Report No. 205, December; Ungerer, H. et al. (1990) The European Monetary System: Developments and Perspectives, Washington, DC: IMF, 61
Notes: [a] The countries participating in the Exchange Rate Mechanism as of December 31, 1991.
[b] Percentage.

The ECU account balances maintained at the European Monetary Cooperation Fund (EMCF) are reserve assets of participating countries. These reserve assets were created by the exchange of gold and dollars. When the central banks of participating countries made deposits of 20 percent of their gold and dollar reserves with the EMCF, an equivalent amount was credited to each participant's ECU account balance with the EMCF, which provides bookkeeping services, similar to the function of the IMF in relation to the SDR account. Recall that the official SDR allocation did not require any compensating payment. The SDR allocation was more like a unilateral gift from the IMF. Since the ECUs are reserve assets, participating governments can use them for official payment settlements.

Since the creation of the ECU was envisioned as a policy tool of the EMS for exchange rate stabilization, it is not only a means of payment but an intervention currency. In addition, the central banks participating in the Exchange Rate Mechanism (ERM) of the EMS arrange mutual very-short-term credit facilities (VSTF) in unlimited amount, which are used for the exchange market intervention. As at December 31, 1991, all EC member countries except Greece and Portugal participated in this ERM program.

The private European currency unit

Like the case of the SDR, the values of both the official ECU and the private ECU are fixed to the same basket of EC currencies. They differ, however, with respect to the way they are created, the way they can be used, and the return they offer. Although the EUA was first used in the private sector as a multicurrency composite instrument in 1975, it was only after the establishment of the EMS that the ECU market grew substantially. In private sector transactions, the ECU is used as a unit of account, for example for invoicing international trade transactions; it is used as a store of value, for example for making deposits; also it is partially acquiring the function of a means of payment, for example the redemption of ECU bonds may be made in ECUs directly instead of in specific national currencies.

The rapid growth of the ECU private market may be attributed to a number of factors. For many participants in the market, the ECU's total yield – exchange gain (or loss) and interest rate – has been viewed to be both stable and attractive. It is considered to be stable because of the exchange rate and economic policy commitment made by the ERM participant countries. There is no formal commitment by SDR participant countries to stabilize their currency value against the SDR. The ECU is attractive in borrowing for residents of certain countries (notably Italy and France) as its total cost of funds has turned out to be somewhat lower than the cost at home; at the same time the ECU is viewed as attractive in lending for residents of certain countries (notably the Netherlands and Germany) as its total yield is slightly higher than the available interest rate at home.

Another factor is that, for many operators involved with multicurrency operations in Europe, acquisition or issuance of ECU debt instruments reduces exposure in international asset and liability management. At the same time, this ready-made basket reduces transaction costs compared with costs involving separate transactions of individual component currencies. It is true that the use of the SDR as a hedging tool also reduces transaction costs, but it may not automatically serve as an asset–liability management tool for European regional operators.

On the other hand, until very recently there were some regulatory impediments to the private use of the ECU. All the governments of the EC countries treated the ECU *de facto* as a foreign currency subject to foreign exchange restrictions against capital outflows. For example, the German government regarded the ECU as a unit of account subject to its Currency Act which prohibited its residents from entering into indexed debts unless explicitly permitted to do so by its central bank. This meant that German residents could not incur ECU-denominated debts because ECU-debts were viewed as indexed debts. But this did not mean that they could not acquire ECU-denominated assets. This partial ban was lifted in 1987.

Currently, the ECU is increasingly used in bank deposit taking and lending, bond issues, and exchange market operations. For example, banks in the EC countries in 1987 reported assets and liabilities denominated in the ECU amounting to $78.5 billion and $69.4 billion respectively out of total foreign assets of $2,140.0 billion and total foreign liabilities of $2,171.0 billion. In the bond market in the same year, the total amount of issuance in foreign currencies was $175.6 billion, out of which 4.2 percent was in the ECU. The recent agreement by the Bank for International Settlements to operate a private-ECU clearing and settlement system and the plan for the total integration of the European Community in 1992 may give a further impetus for private uses of the ECU.

Other private artificial currency units

As pointed out earlier, the international monetary system abandoned the gold–dollar standard in the early 1970s, which in effect meant moving from a fixed exchange rate system to a floating rate system. With increased uncertainty in foreign exchange rates, many investors became reluctant to invest in foreign-currency-denominated debt instruments. Various banks tried to meet this concern by inventing new ACU-denominated debt instruments which would mitigate the impact of excessive exchange rate fluctuations. Among the private ACUs the following are some examples.

Eurco

The European composite unit (Eurco) was first introduced by a group of

European banks led by N. M. Rothschild & Sons in 1973. The European
Investment Bank was the first to borrow by issuing bonds denominated in
Eurcos. The Eurco is considered to be the first to base its value on a currency
basket. It consists of fixed amounts of the currencies of the nine EC member
countries. The amounts of the nine currencies are fixed permanently as
follows:

$$1 \text{ Eurco} = \text{DM0.90} + \text{FFr1.20} + \text{£0.075} + \text{Lit80} + \text{DF0.35}$$
$$+ \text{BFr4.50} + \text{DKr0.20} + \text{I£0.005} + \text{LFr0.50} \qquad (4.16)$$

The Eurco was not successful mainly because in the investors' eyes it contained too many weak currencies. This may imply that investors are as much
concerned with maximization of return on investment as with minimization
of foreign exchange risk.

Despite the less successful story of business in the Eurco, the currency
basket concept pioneered by the Eurco was subsequently applied to both the
new official SDR and the new official EUA in June 1974, as shown in Tables
4.7 and 4.10. In effect, the currency baskets of the Eurco and the official
EUA were then the same nine EC currencies; the only difference was the
weight assigned to each component currency.

Arcru

The Arab currency-related unit (Arcru) which was introduced by Hambros
Bank in 1974 was even less successful. It was hoped that the unit would
appeal to Arab investors and serve as a means of recycling surplus oil
revenues. The value of the Arcru was set to be equivalent to one US dollar
on June 28, 1974, and was based on the currencies of twelve Arab countries
(Algeria, Bahrain, Egypt, Iraq, Kuwait, Lebanon, Lybia, Oman, Qatar,
Saudi Arabia, Syria, and the United Arab Emirates). The two strongest and
the two weakest currencies measured against the US dollar were eliminated
and the middle eight currencies were used in calculating the value of the
Arcru with each currency having an equal weight of 12.5 percent. The
composition of the eight middle currencies would change over time as
the relative strength of each constituent currency changed. This obviously
created confusion in valuation and made the unit less attractive.

IFU

The International financial unit (IFU) was created by a French bank, Crédit
Lyonnais, in 1975 for use in its international banking operations (deposit
taking and bank lending). The value of the IFU was set to be equal to one
US dollar on April 1, 1974, and contained specific amounts of the currencies

of the Group of Ten countries as follows:

$$1 \text{ IFU} = \$0.210 + \text{DM}0.432 + £0.044 + ¥27.900 + \text{C}\$0.073 \\ + \text{Lit}46.700 + \text{DF}0.188 + \text{BFr}2.350 + \text{SKr}0.154. \tag{4.17}$$

One advantage of the IFU over the Eurco was that the IFC contained a broader spectrum of major currencies.

B-Unit

The B-Unit was created by Barclays Bank in 1974. The unit is simpler than the IFU. The value of the B-Unit is determined by five currencies, each having approximately the same weight of 20 percent, as follows:

$$1 \text{ B-Unit} = £1.00 + \text{DM}6.00 + \$2.40 + \text{FFr}11.50 + \text{SFr}7.00. \tag{4.18}$$

Neither the IFC nor the B-Unit have been successful.

As a matter of fact, the home-made ACUs have been far less successful than the private SDR and ECU. The former have some inherent disadvantages in marketing cost, the possibility of legal disputes, economies of scale, and official support.

THE OPTIMUM CURRENCY AREA

Related to the artificial currency unit is the topic of the optimum currency area.[12] A currency area is the area where a single common currency is used. However, in forming a currency area it is not a necessary condition to have a single common currency. Essentially the same effect of having a single currency can be achieved by fixing the exchange rates of the currencies within the area. Therefore the use of an ACU as a single currency represents the formation of a currency area consisting of countries whose currencies are the components of the ACU. The "optimum" currency area is the best grouping of regions or countries to achieve certain economic objectives such as smooth economic adjustment in response to changes in economic conditions.

How many currency areas in the world should we have? At one extreme there may be one international money in the whole world, and at the other extreme there may be as many different currencies as there are distinguishable economic organizations. In between, there are almost countless possibilities, with the most realistic alternatives being national or regional currency areas. Then, what makes a currency area optimal?

The optimality conditions may be examined from two different levels of analysis. At the microeconomic level, the optimum area is the area which assures a maximum efficiency in allocation of resources in the area. The formation of an optimum currency reduces transaction costs, eliminates uncertainty in exchange rate movements, and minimizes price instability within the area, all of which in turn contribute to an efficient allocation of resources.

More specifically, if a single currency is used in the entire region, there is no need to convert into another currency; thus transaction costs of conversion can be saved. Even if many currencies are used, transaction costs may still be reduced as long as they operate under a fixed exchange rate system. Recall the difference in the number of exchange rates under flexible and fixed exchange systems. Suppose there are a hundred countries each with its own currency. Under a flexible rate regime there will be 4,950 exchange rates, whereas under a fixed rate regime there will be ninety-nine. In between there are a number of possibilities. For example, suppose that a hundred countries are grouped into twenty regions each with five countries and that each region has a key currency plus four national currencies. The total number of possible exchange rates in the world then will be 270 (190 interregional rates and eighty intraregional rates (twenty regions each with four)). Thus, even under arrangements of many regional currency areas each with a small membership, such arrangements reduce the number of exchange rates substantially compared with the case of a flexible rate system. In addition, the permanently fixed rate system will enable the economic units in the region to concentrate more on production, trade and investment, thereby saving resources which might have been diverted to meet the exchange rate fluctuations. The price stability achieved by the fixed rate system would also discourage inefficient barter deals arising under more inflationary circumstances, thereby again enabling members to economize resources. Also the formation of such a region enables firms to view the entire region as a single market and to realize greater economies of scale. Therefore, from a microeconomic point of view, the optimum currency area is the area where the increasing marginal cost of administration of the currency area becomes equal to the decreasing marginal benefit of efficient resource allocation.

On the other hand, at a macroeconomic level, the optimum currency area is the area which maximizes the opportunity of economic adjustment processes.[13] To illustrate the point, suppose that there is a currency area which consists of two countries A and B, each of which produces one good, computers in A and cigarettes in B. Let us further assume that both A and B are in equilibrium with full employment of resources and a net zero trade balance. Now because of changes in consumer taste, the aggregate demand for computers increases, whereas the demand for cigarettes decreases, causing a trade surplus with inflationary pressure for A and a trade deficit with unemployment for B. How can these domestic and external disequilibrium conditions be corrected?

There are three possible ways to restore equilibrium.

1 Factors of production could move from B to A for employment in A, thus restoring the balance in trade between A and B, eliminating unemployment

in B and relieving cost-push inflationary pressure in A. In the real world factors are not perfectly mobile. Besides, not all that are mobile are easily adaptable to other uses.

2 If factors are not mobile, wages and prices must fall in B relative to A so that cigarettes become more attractive relative to computers. Again, in the real world downward adjustments of wages and prices are relatively sticky.

3 Yet another alternative is keeping prices in A and B constant and depreciating B's currency relative to A's, thereby *de facto* adopting a flexible exchange rate system.

Now we can see why the optimum currency area is characterized by the perfect mobility of factors of production and flexible price and wage adjustment. If these characteristics are satisfied, then a fixed exchange rate system is appropriate for countries A and B, enjoying all the benefits cited in microeconomic analysis. If not, a flexible rate system is appropriate. Thus, we can understand that the question of what the optimum currency area is, is reduced to those conditions that favor a fixed exchange regime versus a flexible exchange regime, a question first raised by Robert Mundell (1961).

THE MAASTRICHT TREATY ON THE EUROPEAN MONETARY UNION

Besides the theoretical inquiry, it is interesting to observe that a currency area consisting of the EMS member countries is about to become an approximation of a theoretical optimum currency area.

A series of actions taken by the European Community during the last few years provided the groundwork for a currency area. The Single European Act of 1986 essentially provided the freedom of movement of factors of production, that is, capital and human resources, in addition to free movement of goods and services. As noted earlier, free movement of factors of production is a prerequisite for creation of an optimum currency area. In addition, all the countries in the area have coordinated their monetary and fiscal policies, although to varying degrees, so that a possible misalignment of exchange rates among the member countries can be minimized when these exchange rates are permanently fixed. As pointed out earlier, fixing the exchange rates permanently with each other amounts to creation of a single common currency. With the establishment of a common central bank, the monetary union would become a reality.

The idea of creation of a monetary union in the European Community is not new. It first came to the fore in the Community in 1962, as recommended in the "EEC Action Programme of the Community for the Second Stage" without a fixed timetable. The idea was revived in a more concrete proposal in the Werner Report in 1970 in which it was proposed to complete the monetary union by 1980. The three-stage plan spelled out in the Delors Report in 1989 is the third major initiative to create the single currency area, known as the European Monetary Union (EMU). This plan is largely a revival of the proposal in the Werner Report.

The first stage of the Delors plan actually began on July 1, 1990, when the Community governments agreed to coordinate their monetary policy. Coordination of foreign exchange rate policy was already in force through the ERM of the EMS. A closer monetary policy coordination serves as a precursor to fulfil the so-called macroeconomic convergence requirements.

The Maastricht Treaty on the EMU signed by the heads of the twelve EC countries in Maastricht, the Netherlands, in December 1991 was intended to codify the implementation plan for the first stage as well as the second and third stages. According to the Treaty which requires unanimous ratification, each country must satisfy the convergence requirements to become an EMU member at the third stage. These convergence requirements are the strictly defined macroeconomic criteria, as noted below.[14]

1 The government deficit must be 3 percent or less of GDP.
2 The outstanding public debt must be no more than 60 percent of GDP.
3 The country's inflation rate must be no more than 1.5 percent above that of the three best performers in the Community.
4 The long-term government bond interest rate of a country must not exceed 2 percentage points of the average rate of the three lowest inflation countries in the Community.

The first two preconditions for entry are fiscal budgetary control requirements; the third is the inflation convergence requirement; and the last is the capital market integration requirement. In addition, each country must keep the value of its home currency within the narrow band of the ERM. Such exchange rate policy is interpreted as a signal of commitment to the EMU and to policies of price stability.

The second stage of the implementation plan begins on January 1, 1994. This is when tighter controls on foreign exchange rate fluctuations begin so that all the exchange rates can be brought to a converging level and further efforts are directed to meet the above convergence requirements. At the same time, on January 1, 1994, a European Monetary Institute will be created as a transitional organization, which will later be transformed into a central bank.

By the end of 1996 the Community governments must determine which countries have met the convergence criteria. If at least seven out of twelve qualify, the Community is deemed to have a "critical mass" already prepared for adoption of a single-currency area. The Community can then decide by a two-thirds majority to start the third stage by establishing a central bank and a single currency as early as January 1, 1997. The single currency will be known as the ecu, or European currency unit, whose value, as we discussed earlier, is determined on the basis of a basket of the EC member currencies. In view of possible future realignments, the exact composition of the currencies may not be the same as that presented in Table 4.10. Other than the question of the exact composition of the currencies, the crucial difference between the current ECU and the new ecu as a single currency is that the former's value relative to a member currency changes as any exchange rate changes, while the latter's value will be determined by fixing the exchange rates of all the member currencies irrevocably. Thus, the value of each currency is irrevocably fixed to the value of the ecu. It is perfectly conceivable that the ecu notes might say ecu on one side and pounds or marks on the other.

But even if seven or more countries do not qualify, the plan is set to move forward to the creation of a single currency by January 1, 1999, and a common central bank on July 1, 1998. In this case only countries qualifying by then join the EMU. Others may join later, as they become qualified. One exception is the case of the UK which retains an escape clause to opt out. That is, even if it becomes qualified, the UK can decide not to join, if it chooses to do so.

What are the likely effects of the creation of the EMU? One obvious advantage is that the monetary union will facilitate intra-community trade and commerce. In addition, when a realignment of a new single currency to an outside currency becomes necessary, the burden of the realignment is borne jointly by the member countries. Also, asymmetric burdens arising from exchange rate adjustments among member currencies will be eliminated. The current system of the ERM places asymmetric burdens between stronger and weaker currency countries. The burden of adjustment usually falls on the latter because a stronger currency country – mainly Germany – sets the policy orientation and exchange rate direction and the rest are to adjust accordingly, mostly using up their reserves. With the EMU, there will be no such thing as an internal exchange rate adjustment.

However, we cannot say that unified monetary policy pursued in the EMU will have no asymmetric effects on member countries. Moreover, a fundamental question is whether or not free factor movement and output market competition, as intended in the Single European Act and elsewhere, can be realized to the extent large enough to guarantee the workings of a single-currency system. Alternatively, is the EMU really necessary for the workings of a single European market? It may take some years before this question can be answered empirically. Nonetheless, creation of the EMU is an interesting transformation of the theoretical concept "optimum currency area" into a reality.

SUMMARY

In an open economy functions of money for international transactions are performed mainly by key national currencies, artificial currency units, and gold, with varying degrees of functional efficiency. A national currency with a higher level of general acceptability is a natural candidate for becoming a key currency. Greater acceptability of a currency in turn can be enhanced by its convertibility, stable value, and accessibility to major real and financial markets. Both deterministic and non-deterministic models of demand for a key currency are presented, showing that the optimum quantity of international money demanded changes proportionally less than changes in transaction size or variance in cash outflows. This chapter also outlined private uses of SDRs and ecus and showed a specific example of SDR deposit taking business.

At the macroeconomic level, changes in the value of a key currency can be measured, using an exchange rate index, the construction of which requires similar considerations as in the price index construction. The use of a particular national currency as international money raises the Nth currency issues and the optimum currency area. The optimum currency area can also be determined in terms of the composition of the artificial currency units, as demonstrated in the proposed formation of the EMU.

REVIEW PROBLEMS AND EXERCISES

1. According to Baumol's cash balance model, "the optimal cash balance does not have to increase in the same proportion as the size of total receipts increases." Explain why this is so.

2. Explain the precautionary cash balance model under uncertainty.

3. What do we mean by convertibility of a national currency?

4. What are the factors considered in choosing countries whose currencies are included in computing the US dollar exchange rate indexes?

5. Why should we use a multilateral weight instead of a bilateral weight in constructing the exchange rate index of a national currency?

6. Why is a geometric computational method preferred to an arithmetic method in construction of the foreign exchange index?

7. What is an artificial currency unit? To what extent does a particular ACU (for example, the SDR) perform the three functions of money?

8. How different are the official SDR and the private SDR?

9. Explain the following:
   (a) gold standard
   (b) gold bullion standard
   (c) gold–dollar standard

10. Why does a country which issues international money have an asymmetric advantage in conducting monetary policy?

11. How is the optimum currency area defined?

12. What are the convergence criteria, as predicated in the Maastricht Treaty?

13. One SDR is equivalent to a sum of the following (as of January 1, 1991):

$0.5720 (40%)   DM0.4530 (21%)   ¥31.800 (17%)
FFr0.8000 (11%)   £0.0812 (11%)

Suppose a prospective depositor has $1 million today, which he wishes to deposit in denomination of the SDR. The prevailing foreign exchange rates are as follows:

$1 = DM1.6631 = ¥122.63 = FFr5.4396 and £1 = $1.8243

(a) How much is the conversion rate between the SDR and the dollar?
(b) How much deposit is he making in SDRs?

14. Using the information given in Problem 13, calculate the interest rate on the SDR deposit. The deposit rates on component currencies at the time of deposit are as follows: $ deposit rate, 8 percent; DM deposit rate, 7 percent; ¥ deposit rate, 9 percent; FFr deposit rate, 7 percent; £ deposit rate, 10 percent.

15. Also at the time of deposit, one year forward exchange rates are as follows:

$1 = DM1.6440 = ¥124.40 = FFr5.4960 and £1 = $1.8600

(a) Find the premium or discount for each currency. (*Hint*: You have to use the spot rate quotations given in Problem 13, in addition to the forward rates above.)
(b) Find the covered interest rates (parity rates), given 8 percent on dollar deposits.

16. (a) How much will this depositor get back in US dollars one year later? The foreign exchange rates at the time of deposit withdrawal are as follows:

$1 = DM1.6493 = ¥124.54 = FFr5.4998 and £1 = $1.8660

(b) Is he better off by making the deposit in SDRs, as compared with a straight dollar deposit?

17. Suppose that the United States and the UK are under the gold standard as follows:

$450 = 1 oz   £300 = 1 oz
Gold transportation cost, $12 per ounce.

Further suppose that the currency exchange rate is $1.56 per pound. Will there be any international gold flow? If so, explain in which direction the flow will take place and why.

18. The following table shows a hypothetical trade table.

From/to	USA	UK	France	Japan
USA	–	20	50	10
UK	30	–	40	30
France	10	20	–	60
Japan	40	60	0	–

(a) Find the bilateral trade weight for the UK, France, and Japan.
(b) Find the multilateral trade weight for the UK, France, and Japan.

19. The following exchange rates are given for the base period and the subsequent period. Find the foreign exchange index for the US dollar for period 1.

Base period	$1.200/£1	$0.125/FFr1	$0.005/¥1
Period 1	$1.250/£1	$0.120/FFr1	$0.006/¥1

NOTES

1 For a proof, see, for example, Meyer (1970; 142–3).
2 For instance, Ott (1987: 5–14) and Artus and McGuirk (1981: 275–309) stress the importance of using capital flows as a basis for selecting an index component currency and for setting its weight.
3 The sketch of an exchange rate index below shows an asymmetric bias resulting from arithmetic computation. (The assumptions are that there are two foreign currencies with equal weight and that only one foreign exchange, rate changes, at a constant rate of 10 percent.)

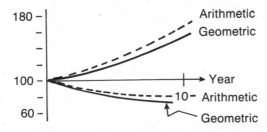

4 McKinnon (1979: 72–7) points out that 67.4 percent of exports and 25.7 percent of imports of Sweden in 1973 were invoiced in Swedish krona. A similar pattern was found in the Danish international trade.
5 The total stock of US dollar-denominated lending and borrowing as of the end of 1989 was $3,145.1 billion, accounting for 58.2 percent of the total outstanding

cross-border lending and borrowing of the Bank for International Settlements reporting banks. See Bank for International Settlements (1990: 134).

6 In a strict sense, a fixed exchange rate system is not identical with the existence of international money. See Kindleberger (1981: 9).

7 For an extensive coverage of the discussion, see Eichengreen (1985).

8 These include mostly official multilateral development banks and regional monetary funds.

9 Although the SDR interest rate is calculated weekly, interest is paid and charges are levied quarterly. The SDR interest rate is equal to a weighted average of domestic interest rates on certain short-term obligations in the five countries whose currencies are included in the SDR. See IMF (1981: 145; 1985: 145).

10 Another approach for the bank to hedge its liability position is simply to lend funds in SDRs.

11 The approach is also known as the "Morgan formula."

12 As presented in the latter part of this section, this topic was first introduced in the early 1960s in relation to exchange rate policy. See, for example, Mundell (1961: 657–665) and McKinnon (1963: 717–25).

13 This definition is given by Snider (1967: 13–14).

14 For details of the accord in Maastricht, see *New York Times* (December 10, 1991: A1, A6) and (December 12, 1991: A8). For a specific country (Spain) effort to meet the convergence criteria, see *Financial Times* (May 27, 1992: 14).

BASIC READING

Ascheim, J. and Park, Y. S. (1976) *Artificial Currency Units: The Formulation of Functional Currency Areas*, Princeton, N.J.: Princeton University.

Baumol, W. (1952) "The Transactions Demand for Cash: An Inventory Theoretic Approach," *Quarterly Journal of Economics*, 67 (4): 545–56.

Bryant, R. C. (1980) *Money and Monetary Policy in Interdependent Nations*, Washington, D.C.: Brookings Institution.

De Cecco, M. and Giovannini, A. (eds) (1989) *A European Central Bank? Perspectives on Monetary Unification after Ten Years of the EMS*, Cambridge: Cambridge University Press.

Eichengreen, B. (ed.) (1985) *The Gold Standard in Theory and History*, New York: Methuen.

Giavazzi, F. and Giovannini, A. (eds) (1989) *Limiting Exchange Rate Flexibility: The European Monetary System*, Cambridge, Mass.: MIT Press.

Gold, J. (1971) *The Fund's Concepts of Convertibility*, Washington, D.C.: IMF.

Harvey, J. L. and Straus, W. (1987) "New Dollar Indexes Are No Different from the Old Ones," *Federal Reserve Bank of Chicago Economic Perspectives*, July–August: 3–22.

IMF (1985) *The Role and Function of the International Monetary Fund*, Washington, D.C.: IMF.

Kindleberger, C. P. (1981) *International Money: A Collection of Essays*, London: Allen & Unwin.

Levich, R. M. and Simmariva, A. (1987) *The ECU Market*, Lexington, Mass.: D. C. Heath.

Masera, R. S. (1987) *An Increasing Role for the ECU: A Character in Search of a Script*, Princeton, N.J.: Princeton University.

McKinnon, R. I. (1979) *Money in International Exchange: The Convertible Currency System*, New York: Oxford University Press.

Miller, M. H. and Orr, D. (1966) "A Model of the Demand for Money by Firms," *Quarterly Journal of Economics*, 81 (3): 413–35.

Mundell, R. A. (1961) "A Theory of Optimum Currency Areas," *American Economic Review*, 50 (4): 657–65.

Ott, M. (1987) "The Dollar's Effective Exchange Rate: Assessing the Impact of Alternative Weighting Schemes," *Federal Reserve Bank of St. Louis Review*, February: 5–14.

Rosensweig, J. A. (1987) "Constructing and Using Exchange Rate Indexes," *Federal Reserve Bank of Atlanta Economic Review*, Summer: 4–16.

Snider, D. A. (1967) *Optimum Adjustment Processes and Currency Areas*, Essays in International Finance No. 62, Princeton, N.J.: Princeton University.

Sobol, D. M. (1981/2) "The SDR in Private International Finance," *Federal Reserve Bank of New York Quarterly Review*, Winter: 29–41.

FURTHER READING

Artus, J. R. and McGuirk, A. K. (1981) "A Revised Version of the Multilateral Exchange Rate Model," *IMF Staff Papers*, 28 (June): 275–309.

Bank for International Settlements (1990) *60th Annual Report*, 134.

Bevan, T. (1985) "The ECU – Europe's New Currency," *Barclays Review*, September: 82–6.

Cordero, R. (1990) *The Creation of a European Banking System*, New York: Peter Lang.

Johnson, H. G and Swoboda, A. K. (eds) (1976) *Conference on Optimum Currency Areas*, Cambridge, Mass.: Harvard University Press.

Keren, P. B. (1969) "The Theory of Optimum Currency Areas: An Eclectic View," in Mundell, R. A. and Swoboda, A. K. (eds) *Monetary Problems of the International Economy*, Chicago, Ill.: University of Chicago Press, 41–60.

IMF (1981) *Annual Report*, Washington, D.C.

Ingram, J. C. (1973) *The Case for European Monetary Integration*, Essays in International Finance No. 98, Princeton, N.J.: Princeton University Press.

Ishiyama, Y. (1975) "The Theory of Optimum Currency Area: A Survey," *IMF Staff Papers*, 22 (2): 344–84.

McKinnon, R. I. (1963) "Optimum Currency Areas," *American Economic Review*, 53 (4): 717–25.

Meyer, P. L. (1970) *Introductory Probability and Statistical Applications*, 2nd edn, Reading, Mass.: Addison-Wesley.

Ungerer, H., Hauvonen, J. J., Lopez-Claros, A. and Mayer, T. (1990) *The European Monetary System: Developments and Perspectives*, Washington, D.C.: IMF.

Willett, T. D. and Towers, E. (1976) *The Theory of Optimum Currency Areas and Exchange Rate Flexibility*, Special Papers in International Economics No. 11, Princeton, N.J.: Princeton University Press.

Chapter 5

Balance of international payments

INTRODUCTION

In this chapter, first, we examine the meaning of the balance of international payments statement and conventions used to prepare such a statement. In doing so, we study the classification of international transactions,
the concept of residency, and the double-entry bookkeeping system, as
applied to international transactions recording. We also examine various
categories of accounting balances in the balance of payments. We pay
attention to the fact that the balance of payments must be in balance in an
accounting sense, but this does not mean that the balance of payments is
in equilibrium.

Second, we will see the role of banks behind various types of international transactions. Banks are involved as facilitators or main players in
almost all types of international transactions.

Third, we will analyze the relationship between the current account in the
balance of payments and the national income account. Indeed, the balance
of payments is the transactions record of the window through which the
reporting country interacts with the rest of the world. Here, we start with
analysis of national income determination in an open economy. We then
proceed to examine the question of a dominant gap between the saving and
foreign exchange gaps, as a dominant constraint for economic development. Such an analysis is particularly relevant to international finance for
third-world country development. Finally, we see the relationship between
current account deficits and international indebtedness.

As the balance of payments reflects the supply of and demand for foreign
currencies, this chapter serves as an introduction to the next two chapters
on foreign exchange.

DEFINITIONS AND CONVENTIONS

The balance of international payments is a summary accounting statement
of international economic transactions between the residents of the

reporting country and those of the rest of the world during a given period of time.

Since it is a summary statement, it does not list every transaction individually. Instead, all the transactions are aggregated into a few major categories for presentation. Thus, each country may present its statement somewhat differently, depending on the significance it attaches to particular categories of transactions. For example, the US balance of payments is presented in greater detail for international capital flows, whereas the statements of primary commodity exporting countries usually give more detailed entries for their commodity exports.[1]

What kind of transactions, then, are to be included in the balance of payments? They must be economic transactions which involve exchanges of value, transferring something having economic value such as goods, services, and assets from one economic unit to another. They must be international transactions – transactions between residents of different countries. An international transaction does not necessarily involve a physical cross-border movement of goods or assets, but rather a change in ownership (or the right to use) between residents of different countries. For example, a purchase of a foreign firm does not result in bringing that firm to the home country. Even the ownership certificates (common shares) are almost always safe-kept in the foreign country. It is a change in the ownership which gives rise to recording in the balance of payments.

The reporting period is usually a year, but it varies depending on the categories of the balance of payments to be reported. For example, the reporting period for merchandise exports and imports is typically a calendar month, since the data for such transactions is easier to collect and in greater demand. On the other hand, the statements covering more comprehensive transactions are presented either on a quarterly basis or a yearly basis to coincide with national income and product accounts.

The information contained in the balance of payments is important for both public policy makers and private decision-makers. For public policy makers, the balance of payments position of the country serves as a key target as well as a key indicator in formulating and implementing monetary, fiscal, and commercial policies. For many private decision-makers, particularly for international bankers, investors, and traders, the balance of payments is one of the most reliable and readily available sources of information on international transactions, on which they frequently rely for their decision-making.

The balance of payments statement is important not merely because it is a major source of the country's international transactions data, but it also serves as a linkage between the country's national accounts and those of the rest of the world. Without it, for example, a country's input/output tables which show the flow of resources among the different industries within the economy would be incomplete, as each domestic industry is both a user and an intermediate supplier of foreign goods. The domestic flow-of-funds accounts that identify the sources and uses of financial resources must also include the foreign sector without which aggregate supply and demand cannot be balanced.

INTERNATIONAL TRANSACTIONS

Since international transactions covered in the balance of payments are those transactions between residents of different countries, it is necessary to determine who the residents of the reporting country are. In addition, as the balance of payments is constructed on the basis of double-entry book-keeping, each transaction gives rise to two entries: a credit entry and a debit entry of an equal amount. It is thus necessary to determine which entry is a credit item and which is a debit.

Determination of residence

In principle, residents of the reporting country are (a) individuals who reside in that country on a permanent basis, (b) corporations and nonprofit organizations which are located in that country, and (c) government agencies and establishments of the reporting country whether they are located at home or abroad. Residency is not always a clear-cut concept, however. In some instances, the residency must be determined using more than one criterion.

If a person resides in a country for one year or longer, the person is regarded to be a resident of that country. However, what if the person maintains her permanent legal domicile elsewhere? Basically, it is the economic residence, rather than the legal residence, which counts most. Then, what is economic residence? Individuals are engaged in three broad types of economic activities, namely the production of goods and services, their consumption, and the maintenance of residence, all in the same place or different places. When multiple places are involved, the residency is determined by the general center of interest, which is the place where both production and consumption are carried out substantially for one year or longer. If only one of them is carried out in a particular country, then the place of the remaining activity and the legal permanent domicile are considered as the general center of interest.

For example, a nurse from a Middle East country working in a hospital in a European country resides in the place where she works, yet she may maintain her legal permanent domicile in the country she came from. She participates in production and consumption of goods and services in the country where she is now. Thus, the European country of her work is her home country for balance of payments recording purposes. What about a commuter residing in one country and working in another within the EC?

Obviously, this commuter's center of interest lies in the country of residence, because that is the country in which he maintains his residence and carries out consumption activity. On the other hand, temporary visitors, students, seasonal workers, and commercial travelers coming from other countries are not regarded as the residents of the country of their location.[2]

Resident enterprises of a particular country are those located and engaged in business activities in that particular country. A subsidiary of a foreign corporation is a resident enterprise of a country where it is located. A branch of a foreign corporation is also a resident enterprise (unincorporated) of the country where the branch is located. All the transactions between a branch in one country and its parent in another are thus international transactions.[3]

In the case of government establishments, they are the residents of the home country regardless of their locations because of the recognition of the extraterritorial powers of the government. Thus, embassies, consulates, and foreign military establishments are residents of their home country, not the residents of the countries in which they are located even on a permanent basis.

Similarly, official international organizations such as the IMF, the World Bank, and the GATT are not residents of the host country because the host country government does not have control over such organizations.

Determination of debits and credits

As noted earlier, the balance of payments statement is constructed on the basis of a double-entry bookkeeping method. By this, each international economic transaction is posted twice, once as a debit item and once as a credit item in an equal amount. This method provides a built-in checking system to ensure that the sum of all debits equals the sum of all credits. The double-entry method also reflects the fact that, in exchange transactions, each transaction has its corresponding payment transaction (a *quid pro quo*), giving rise to two entries. We export something and in exchange receive payment for it, for example.

There are some instances where a corresponding transaction does not accompany a payment transaction, for example with gifts and SDR allocations. In such instances, entries that cannot be automatically paired are deliberately furnished.

Now, how can we decide which transaction is a debit entry and which transaction is a credit entry? Basically, all transactions which give rise to receiving foreign exchange by selling something are credit entries (+) and all transactions which give rise to paying foreign exchange by purchasing something are debit entries (−).

Consider a balance sheet of an economic entity. Table 5.1 regarding sources and uses of funds summarizes the changes in the balance sheet

Table 5.1 Sources and uses of funds

Changes in assets	Changes in liabilities	Effects on funds
Decrease in assets Decrease in claims	Increase in liabilities	Sources of funds (+)
Increase in assets Increase in claims	Decrease in liabilities	Uses of funds (−)

during a given period. Funds can be generated in two ways, namely by liquidating assets (or claims) or by borrowing. On the other hand, purchases of assets (or claims) or debt repayments are uses of funds.

The same idea is used to structure the debit and credit sides of the balance of payments by rotating Table 5.1 so that the sources and uses of funds are now sources and uses respectively of foreign exchange. More specifically, credits consist of selling goods and services (exports of goods and services), selling goodwill (unilateral transfers to the reporting country), and selling securities (capital inflows). Likewise, debits consist of buying goods and services (imports of goods and services), buying goodwill (unilateral transfers to foreigners), and buying securities (capital outflows).

ACCOUNTING BALANCES OF INTERNATIONAL TRANSACTIONS

Since the balance of payments is constructed on the basis of the double-entry bookkeeping system, the balance of payments always balances in an accounting sense, that is, total debits must be equal to total credits. We may also express this identity alternatively as

total credits − total debits = 0.   (5.1)

For the convenience of analysis, the components of the balance of payments are classified in a number of different ways. The broadest classification is to divide the components into two groups: the current account and the capital account. The net sum of each account is termed a balance, a partial balance, or a payments balance. A balance showing a net credit is termed a surplus and one showing a net debit is termed a deficit. Just as we may group international transactions into two accounts, we may draw a notional line and list all the current account items above the line and all the capital account items below the line. Then, the surplus or deficit of the current account is the sum of all items appearing above the line, while the surplus or deficit of the capital account is the sum of all items listed below the line:

$$\text{current account} + \text{capital account} = 0 \qquad (5.2a)$$

$$\text{current account} = -\text{capital account}. \qquad (5.2b)$$

The same procedure may be followed to divide the statement into more than two categories, in which case each additional notional line represents an additional category. Each balance is measured as the net sum of its components. Also a new balance can be created as the net cumulative sum of all items above the line.

Now, let us look at each major component of the balance of payments. Table 5.2 illustrates the structure of the US balance of payments in 1990. As shown in this table, the current account is subdivided into three categories: (a) exports and imports of goods, (b) exports and imports of services, and (c) unilateral transfers.

Selling goods abroad, which we call merchandise exports, causes a decrease in ownership of such goods, which in turn creates a source of foreign exchange. Similarly, buying goods from abroad, merchandise imports, causes an increase in ownership of such goods which in turn results in uses of foreign exchange. The net sum of exports of goods $(+)$ and imports of goods $(-)$ is a merchandise trade balance which is perhaps the most closely watched figure in the balance of payments because it is often regarded as an important indicator of competitiveness of the manufacturing sectors of the economy relative to the rest of the world. As presented in Table 5.2, the US merchandise trade balance was a deficit of $108.1 billion in 1990.

Services transactions are recorded in the same manner as merchandise transactions. The net sum of exports and imports of services is an invisible trade balance (or balance on services), which was a surplus of $38.3 billion in 1990. In services transactions, we include investment income (direct investment dividends, portfolio investment income, and interest income) and other services (military transactions, travel and passenger fares, shipping, royalties, license fees, educational services, financial services, insurance, telecommunications, and professional services). The net sum of the merchandise trade balance and the invisible trade balance is a balance on goods and services, which was $-$69.8 billion.

Unilateral transfers, also termed unrequited transfers, are the transactions which transfer economic value without compensating payments. They include government grants (such as foreign aid and contributions to international organizations) and private transfers (such as pension payments to foreign residents, remittances, private gifts including scholarships to foreign residents, and migrants' transfers of properties to their immigrating countries). If a US resident makes a gift to a foreign resident,

Table 5.2 Classification of 1990 US international transactions (in billions of US dollars)

Credit (+)	Debit (−)	Difference (net sum)
A Exports of goods	Imports of goods	Merchandise trade balance
389.6	497.7	− 108.1
B Exports of services Investment income 263.4	Imports of services Investment income 225.1	Balance on services 38.3
C = A + B		Balance on goods and services − 69.8
D Unilateral transfers to US residents	Unilateral transfers to foreigners	Net unilateral transfers − 22.3
E = C + D		Balance on current account − 92.1
F US government assets abroad other than reserve assets, net (increase (−))		
Repayments on US government loans Liquidation of assets abroad	US government credit Increase in other assets abroad	Net US government investment abroad 3.0
G US private assets abroad, net (increase (−))		
US divestment Liquidation of foreign securities Repayments on US loans	US direct investment Purchases of foreign securities US private loans	Net US private investment abroad − 58.5
H Foreign official assets in the United States, net (increase (+))		
Purchases of US government securities Purchases of other US assets	Liquidation of US government securities Liquidation of other US assets	Net foreign official investment in USA 32.4
I Foreign private assets in the United States, net (increase (+))		
Direct investment in USA Purchase of US securities Acquisition of other assets in USA	Divestiture in USA Liquidation of US securities Liquidation of other assets in USA	Net foreign private investment in USA 53.9
J Special drawing rights allocation (increase (+))		
Allocation received	Allocation withdrawn	SDR allocation 0.0
K Errors and omissions		Statistical discrepancy 63.5
L = F + G + H + I + J + K		Balance on capital account proper 94.3
M = E + L		Balance of payments 2.2
N US official reserve account, net (increase (−))		
Sales of gold Uses of SDRs Borrowing on reserve position in IMF Uses of foreign exchange	Purchases of gold Receipts of SDRs Repayments to IMF on reserve position Receipts of foreign exchange	Official settlement balance − 2.2

such a gift gives rise to a payment obligation. Thus it is recorded as a debit item. What is the corresponding entry in the balance of payments? It depends on how the gifts are made. If it is a gift of a good, then the corresponding entry will be an export, whereas if it is a cash payment, the entry will be an increase in foreign assets in the United States. The net amount of unilateral transfers was a deficit of $22.3 billion. This means that US transfer payments were greater than receipts.

The net sum of the above three subgroups of transactions is a balance of payments on current account, or simply the current account balance, which amounted to a deficit of $92.1 billion. This amount must be counterbalanced by the capital account. That is, the capital account must be a surplus of $92.1 billion, as the principle of double-entry bookkeeping requires.

The capital account items represent changes in ownership in the economy's foreign financial assets and liabilities.[4] As in transactions of goods and services, each capital account transaction involves two parties: one buying a financial asset and the other selling it. Thus, it is important to specify whose position we are referring to in recording capital account transactions. In the case of changes in ownership in assets abroad, the official and private investors' (buyers') positions of the reporting country are used as the reference. On the other hand, for assets in the reporting country, the foreign private and official investors' positions are used.

The capital account is subdivided by type of investment and by type of investor. The type of international investment includes direct foreign investment, long-term portfolio investment, short-term investment, and changes in official reserve holdings. As you recall, we studied the first three types of foreign investment in Chapter 2. The fourth type of transactions, changes in official reserve holdings, are changes in official gold holdings, SDRs, the reserve position in the IMF, and foreign exchange holdings.[5] Note that the total amount of official reserve holdings are stocks as of a certain date, whereas the changes in official reserves in the balance of payments are flows, which represent changes in stocks.

The capital account can also be subdivided by ownership groups, namely changes in the reporting country government assets abroad (usually government lending) (item F, $3.0 billion), changes in the reporting country private assets abroad (item G, −$58.5 billion), changes in the foreign official assets in the reporting country (item H, $32.4 billion), and changes in the foreign private assets in the reporting country (item I, $53.9 billion).

For the reporting country, an increase in assets abroad means an acquisition of financial assets abroad, giving rise to a debit (−), which is a capital outflow. For example, the negative amount of $58.5 billion of net US private investment is a net increase in foreign investment by US private investors. On the other hand, an increase in assets held by foreigners in the reporting country means borrowing by the reporting country, giving rise to a credit (+), which is a capital inflow.

SDRs, as we studied in Chapter 4, are international reserve assets created by the IMF and unilaterally transferred to member countries. The actual receipt of allocated SDRs is a debit item shown in the official reserve account (category N, Table 5.2), because it is an increase in assets abroad. The SDR allocation credit item in category J is a fictitious entry created to fulfill the principle of double-entry bookkeeping. There was no SDR allocation in 1990.

Errors and omissions are a balancing item (item K, $63.5 billion), classified as part of capital account with some justification. Even with the double-entry system of recording, substantial statistical discrepancies sometimes show up. Nonetheless, this figure is unusually high. These discrepancies are believed to originate usually from short-term capital movements, which include short-term speculative capital movements.

The final category in Table 5.2 is the official reserve account, which shows changes in official reserve asset holdings. From the identity (5.1), we can express the relationship between the official reserve account and the rest of the international transactions as

$$\underbrace{\underbrace{\text{current account} + \text{capital account proper}}_{\substack{(-92.1) \qquad\qquad (94.3)}}}_{\substack{\text{balance of payments}\\(2.2)}} = \underbrace{-\text{official settlement balance}}_{-(-2.2)} \qquad (5.3)$$

Thus, as the principle of double-entry bookkeeping requires, the sum of all component balances of international transactions is in balance, that is, zero.

BALANCE OF PAYMENTS EQUILIBRIUM

As long as the balance of payments is in balance in the accounting sense, will there be any difficulties for the country in meeting international payment obligations? The very reason that we listed the official reserve account last was that we wanted to separate this account from the rest. All other capital transactions and the current account transactions are termed as autonomous transactions because these transactions take place on the basis of independent motives other than balance of payments settlement considerations. On the other hand, transactions in the official reserve account are viewed as accommodating transactions, accommodating in the sense that they are used to meet the gap between autonomous payments and receipts. Therefore, if autonomous transactions create a persistent gap, then the economy is said to be in disequilibrium. The official reserve account cannot continue to be in deficit indefinitely. This is true even in the case of a surplus in the account.

Table 5.3 1990 US balance of international payments (in millions of US dollars)

Line	(Credit +: debits −)	1990	1991
1	Exports of goods, services, and income	652,936	676,496
2	Merchandise, adjusted, excluding military	389,550	416,517
3	Services	133,295	144,675
4	Transfers under US military agency sales contracts	9,899	10,429
5	Travel	40,579	45,551
6	Passenger fares	12,251	13,836
7	Other transportation	22,407	23,114
8	Royalties and license fees	15,291	16,330
9	Other private services	32,173	34,736
10	US government miscellaneous services	695	679
11	Income receipts on US assets abroad	130,091	115,306
12	Direct investment receipts	54,444	51,754
13	Other private receipts	65,702	56,011
14	US government receipts	9,945	7,541
15	Imports of goods, services, and income	−722,730	−704,842
16	Merchandise, adjusted, excluding military	−497,665	−490,103
17	Services	−106,919	−106,796
18	Direct defense expenditures	−17,119	−15,709
19	Travel	−38,671	−39,418
20	Passenger fares	−8,963	−9,289
21	Other transportation	−23,463	−23,467
22	Royalties and license fees	−2,644	−3,409
23	Other private services	−13,819	−15,030
24	US government miscellaneous services	−2,240	−2,474

(continued)

Table 5.3 Continued

Line	(Credit +: debits −)	1990	1991
25	Income payments on foreign assets in the United States	−118,146	−105,943
26	Direct investment payments	−1,782	−361
27	Other private payments	−78,494	−66,743
28	US government payments	−37,870	−38,839
29	Unilateral transfers, net	−22,329	19,728
30	US government grants	−17,486	25,111
31	US government pensions and other transfers	−2,947	−3,187
32	Private remittances and other transfers	−1,896	−2,196
33	US assets abroad, net (increase/capital outflow (−))	−57,706	−67,747
34	US official reserve assets, net	−2,158	5,763
35	Gold	−	−
36	Special drawing rights	−192	−177
37	Reserve position in the International Monetary Fund	731	−367
38	Foreign currencies	−2,697	6,307
39	US government assets, other than official reserve assets, net	2,976	3,572
40	US credits and other long-term assets	−7,319	−11,916
41	Repayments on US credits and other long-term assets	10,327	16,466
42	US foreign currency holdings and US short-term assets, net	−32	−979
43	US private assets, net	−58,524	−77,082
44	Direct investment	−33,437	−29,497
45	Foreign securities	−28,476	−46,215
46	US claims on unaffiliated foreigners reported by US nonbanking concerns	−1,944	n.a.
47	US claims reported by US banks, not included elsewhere	5,333	3,428
48	Foreign assets in the United States, net (increase/capital inflow (+))	86,303	79,503
49	Foreign official assets in the United States, net	32,425	20,585
50	US government securities	29,310	19,549
51	US Treasury securities	28,643	18,623
52	Other	667	926

53	Other US government liabilities	1,703	1,603
54	US liabilities reported by US banks, not included elsewhere	2,996	−1,856
55	Other foreign official assets	−1,586	1,289
56	Other foreign assets in the United States, net	53,879	58,918
57	Direct investment	37,213	22,197
58	US Treasury securities	1,131	16,861
59	US securities other than US Treasury securities	1,781	35,417
60	US liabilities to unaffiliated foreigners reported by US nonbanking concerns	3,779	n.a.
61	US liabilities reported by US banks, not included elsewhere	9,975	−15,046
62	Allocations of special drawing rights	–	–
63	Statistical discrepancy (sum of above items with sign reversed)	63,526	−3,139
63	a *Of which* seasonal adjustment discrepancy	–	–
	Memoranda:		
64	Balance on merchandise trade (lines 2 and 16)	−108,115	−73,586
65	Balance on services (lines 3 and 17)	26,376	35,879
66	Balance on investment income (lines 11 and 25)	11,945	9,363
67	Balance on goods, services, and income (lines 1 and 15 or lines 64, 65, and 66)	−69,794	−28,344
68	Unilateral transfers, net (line 29)	−22,329	19,728
69	Balance on current account (lines 1, 15, and 29 or lines 67 and 68)	−92,123	−8,616

Source: US Department of Commerce (1992) *Survey of Current Business*, March: 75.

However, the conceptual problem with autonomous transactions is twofold. First, the distinction between autonomous and accommodating transactions is an *ex ante* concept depending on motives which are difficult to identify by *ex post* transactions or transactors. Second, the government may restore other measures instead of using official reserves. Therefore, it is difficult to use the official settlement balance as an indicator of disequilibrium. For example, in the case of a potential decrease in official reserves, the government may take monetary policy action to increase the short-term interest rate in order to bolster private capital inflows, thereby lessening the need to use official reserves.

For such reasons, the US balance of payments published recently by the Department of Commerce does not list the official reserve account as the last category, as you may note from Table 5.3. The actual statement treats the official reserve account simply as one of many other accounts. Besides, under the flexible exchange rate system, the distinction between autonomous and accommodating transactions is less meaningful, because the balance of payment equilibrium is supposed to be reached automatically by market forces, that is, by market-determined exchange rates, without government intervention in final settlement.

THE ROLE OF COMMERCIAL BANKS

Commercial banks are involved in one way or another for almost every type of transaction reported in the balance of payments. Behind merchandise transactions, commercial banks provide trade financing, guarantee facilities, payment remittance and collection, foreign exchange services, and credit checking. They even provide international marketing information about potential buyers and sellers, sometimes through their specialized subsidiaries such as export trading companies. For services trade transactions, again banks provide an efficient international payment system, using global telecommunications networks such as the banking-industry-owned Society for Worldwide Interbank Financial Telecommunications (SWIFT). In addition, banks' own income earned abroad through international lending and other financial and information services is included in this category.

For capital account transactions, commercial banks play a primary role. They provide short- and medium-term international loans; they underwrite foreign-currency-denominated bonds and commercial paper and distribute them to their home country residents as well as to foreigners; they distribute home country securities to foreign residents. All of these cause capital outflows and inflows. They serve as portfolio asset managers or brokers and receive service fees. They receive deposits of foreign governments, which are known as official foreign exchange reserves of deposit making countries.

In addition, because international transactions involve residents of different countries, such transactions cause conversion of one currency into another in the foreign exchange markets. As we shall see in the next chapter, commercial banks are major participants in these exchange markets as traders as well as brokers.

THE RELATIONSHIP BETWEEN CURRENT ACCOUNT AND NATIONAL INCOME ACCOUNT

In order to examine the relationship between the current account and the national income account, first we examine the mechanics of national income determination in a closed economy and then we see how the income determination is modified as we add the current account balance in an open economy. Second, we study the current account balance as a measure of foreign saving needed to finance domestic investment, which in turn determines current and future aggregate income. The latter topic is particularly important for international lending to developing countries.

National income determination

In a closed economy, aggregate supply Y which represents the production side of the economy must be equal to aggregate demand which consists of consumption C, investment I, and government spending G:

$$Y = C + I + G. \tag{5.4}$$

Expression (5.4) is known as the income identity. Assuming that aggregate demand determines the amount of goods and services produced in the economy, let us examine the component functions of aggregate demand, starting with the consumption function. Aggregate consumption C of household units is basically a function of current disposable income Y_d, although aggregate consumption clearly depends on a host of other factors, such as wealth, expected future income, interest rates, and expected changes in prices:

$$C = a + bY_d \tag{5.5}$$

where a is a coefficient (constant) which represents a portion of consumption independent of disposable income and usually describes a subsistence level of consumption, and b is another coefficient representing the marginal propensity to consume which measures how much of one additional unit of money income is spent on consumption.

Disposable income is income available after tax T, which consists of proportional income tax tY and lump-sum tax V:

$$Y_d = Y - T \tag{5.6}$$

$$T = tY + V. \tag{5.7}$$

Proportional income tax thus depends on the tax rate t and income Y.

On the other hand, investment I which is decided by business units depends negatively on the interest rate i:

$$I = c - di. \tag{5.8}$$

Here, c and d are coefficients. Coefficient c describes the maximum investment capacity of the economy constrained by the available resources and the state of technology and d measures the sensitivity of investment with respect to changes in the interest rate.

Finally, government spending is assumed to be fixed. Then, we can rewrite the identity (5.4) in a functional form as follows:

$$Y = a + b(Y - tY - V) + c - di + G. \tag{5.9}$$

Solving for Y, we obtain the equilibrium level of income as

$$Y = \frac{1}{1 - b(1 - t)} (a - bV + c - di + G). \tag{5.10}$$

For example, if the coefficient a is equal to 80, b is 0.80, t is 0.15, c is 950, and d is 20; and if the variable V is 120, i is 10, and G is 1,000, then the equilibrium income Y will be

$$Y = (3.125)(1,734) = 5,419. \tag{5.11}$$

Now, let us consider the case of an open economy. The aggregate supply is the sum of domestic production and imports M. The aggregate demand is the sum of consumption, investment, and government spending plus a new component, exports X.

$$Y + M = C + I + G + X \tag{5.12}$$

which we can rewrite by consolidating the foreign sector as

$$Y = C + I + G + (X - M). \tag{5.13}$$

The term $X - M$ is net exports and corresponds to the current account balance.

Exports of goods and services are a function of the real exchange rate E^*:

$$X = e - hE^* \tag{5.14}$$

where e and h are coefficients. Coefficient e measures the maximum export capacity of the nation and h describes the sensitivity of exports with respect to changes in the real exchange rate. The real exchange rate can be defined as

$$E^* = \frac{FC/P_f}{\$/P_\$} = \frac{FC}{\$} \frac{P_\$}{P_f}. \tag{5.15}$$

Here, FC/\$ is the nominal exchange rate, which is expressed as the number of units of foreign currency FC per unit of home currency \$; $P_\$$ is the home price level; and P_f is the foreign price level. The exports function (5.15) states that exports will decrease as the nominal exchange rate increases or as the domestic price level rises faster than the foreign price level.

On the other hand, the imports function can be specified as

$$M = q + kE^* + mY. \tag{5.16}$$

Unlike the case of exports, imports depend not only on the real exchange rate but also on income. The coefficient q represents autonomous imports; k measures the sensitivity of imports with respect to changes in the real exchange rate; and m describes the marginal propensity to import. Then, the amount of net exports is

$$X - M = s - fE^* - mY \tag{5.17}$$

where $s = e - q$ and $f = h + k$.

The aggregate supply and demand equilibrium (5.13) for an open economy can be specified as

$$Y = a + b(Y - tY - V) + c - di + G + s - fE^* - mY \tag{5.18}$$

from which we derive the following equation which determines the equilibrium income:

$$Y = \frac{1}{1 - b(1 - t) + m} [(a + c + s) - bV - di + G - fE^*]. \tag{5.19}$$

From equation (5.19), we can see the direct effect of the foreign sector on the determination of national income. The foreign sector represented by the current account balance will contribute to changing national income, depending on the signs and values of s, f, E^*, and m. If the autonomous components of net exports are positive, obviously they will contribute to increasing income. A lower sensitivity coefficient f or a lower real exchange rate will also increase income. Likewise, a lower marginal propensity to import will increase income by increasing the magnitude of the trade multiplier $1/[1 - b(1 - t) + m]$.

For a numerical example, suppose that of the coefficients in the imports function e is equal to 660 and h is 30; of the exports function, q is 90, k is 20, and m is 0.1; of the common variables in both functions, FC/$ is 2/1 and $P_\$/P_f$ is 1.1/1; and all others are the same as in the case of the closed economy. We then obtain the equilibrium level of income:

$$Y = \frac{1}{1 - 0.8(1 - 0.15) + 0.1} \left[(100 + 950 + 570) - 0.8(120) - 20(10) \right.$$

$$\left. + 1,000 - 50 \frac{2}{1} \frac{1.1}{1} \right]$$

$$= (2.381)(2,214) = 5,272. \tag{5.20}$$

Likewise, we obtain the value of each aggregate expenditure category:

$$C = 100 + 0.8\,[5{,}272 - 0.15(5{,}272) - 120] = 3{,}589 \qquad (5.21a)$$

$$I = 950 - 20(10) = 750 \qquad (5.21b)$$

$$G = 1{,}000 \qquad (5.21c)$$

$$X = 660 - 30(2/1)(1.1/1) = 594 \qquad (5.21d)$$

$$M = 90 + 20(2/1)(1.1/1) + 0.1(5{,}272) = 661 \qquad (5.21e)$$

$$X - M = -67 \qquad (5.21f)$$

$$T = 0.15(5{,}272) + 120 = 911. \qquad (5.21g)$$

As we can see from the above analysis, the current account balance is an integral part of the national income account. Next, we examine a more specific relationship between the current account balance and the domestic saving gap.

Saving gap versus foreign exchange gap

For developing countries, a chronic problem is the shortage of domestic saving needed to finance the desired level of domestic investment. The income identity shows that such a gap between domestic investment and domestic saving is equal to the gap between imports and exports of goods and services (a current account deficit) of the nation. If this is the case, it does not matter which gap we choose to measure the need for foreign capital inflow. However, it has a greater policy significance to examine which gap is the more dominant so that the dominant gap is forcing the other to adjust toward the former.

Before examining the dominant gap, let us first specify the investment–saving gap. For this purpose, we specify the saving function. Since the aggregate output Y represents the value of final goods and services, an equal value of payments must be made as payments to factors of production, which is termed aggregate income. This aggregate income is split into three categories, namely tax payments T, consumption C, and private domestic saving S_p, as follows:

$$Y = C + S_p + T \qquad (5.22)$$

which is known as the national income identity. The domestic private saving function can be constructed by rearranging the income identity (5.22) and substituting equation (5.5) for consumption C:

$$\begin{aligned} S_p &= Y - tY - V - C \\ &= -a + (1 - b)(Y - tY - V). \end{aligned} \qquad (5.23)$$

For example, the equilibrium level of private domestic saving, based on the numerical figures presented in equation (5.16), will be

$$S_p = -100 + (1 - 0.8)[5{,}272 - 0.15(5{,}272) - 120] = 772. \qquad (5.24)$$

Now, let us specify the investment–saving gap in an open economy. By eliminating the common term C in equations (5.13) and (5.22), we obtain

$$I + G + (X - M) = S_p + T. \qquad (5.25)$$

We now wish to consolidate domestic sector variables on the left and foreign sector variables on the right:

$$I - S_p - (T - G) = M - X \qquad (5.26)$$

$$I - (S_p + S_g) = S_f \qquad (5.27)$$

where S_g is domestic government saving and S_f is foreign saving which is the current account deficit. Now, investment I is specifically to describe domestic investment. Equation (5.27) simply states that the domestic investment–saving gap must be met by foreign saving, which is the imports–exports gap, also referred to as the foreign exchange gap. Using previous numerical examples, we find that the saving gap is 67 since $I = 750$, $S_p = 772$, and $S_g = -89$. Obviously, the figure 67 can be directly derived from the current account deficit.

Now let us turn to the concept of the dominant gap. The data we obtain for the saving gap and the foreign exchange gap are the realized figures. And *ex post* the following condition must hold owing to the income identity, as we have pointed out earlier:

$$I - (S_p + S_g) = M - X. \qquad (5.28)$$

However, *ex ante*, which gap is the dominant gap so that the other one is forced to adjust to the former?

To answer this, we may decompose the realized values into two components:

$$I = I^* + I_u \qquad (5.29a)$$

$$S = S^* - S_u \qquad (5.29b)$$

$$M = M^* + M_u \qquad (5.29c)$$

$$X = X^* - X_u \qquad (5.29d)$$

where I^* is the minimum (politically) acceptable investment which depends on the desired growth rate and the state of technology; I_u is less productive investment undertaken because of forced adjustment; S^* represents the maximum potential saving; S_u is dissaving because of forced adjustment or negative incentives to save; M^* is the minimum necessary imports; M_u is less necessary imports due to forced adjustment; X^* is the maximum potential exports; and X_u is unrealized export potential because of forced adjustment or negative incentives to export.

The foreign exchange gap is said to be dominant if

$$I^* - S^* < M^* - X^*. \tag{5.30}$$

Then the adjustment would probably take place in the form

$$I^* + I_u - S^* = M^* - X^* \tag{5.31a}$$

or

$$I^* - (S^* - S_u) = M^* - X^*. \tag{5.31b}$$

That is, the adjustment would occur in the form either of undertaking additional investments which are less productive (5.31a) or of discouraging saving (5.31b). In this case, there is need for outward-looking policy. By this we mean that although initially the nation may concentrate on import substitution to reduce the exchange gap, it must focus on export promotion in order to reduce the exchange gap ultimately.

On the other hand, the saving gap is said to be dominant if

$$I^* - S^* > M^* - X^*. \tag{5.32}$$

This is the case in which the nation's inability to mobilize sufficient domestic saving forces an adjustment in the form of a greater current account deficit. That is, it is likely to increase unnecessary imports

$$I^* - S^* = M^* + M_u - X^* \tag{5.33a}$$

or to discourage realization of the maximum potential exports

$$I^* - S^* = M^* - (X^* - X_u). \tag{5.33b}$$

It is then necessary to focus economic policy on the development of well-functioning financial markets to promote domestic saving.

Current account deficit and international indebtedness

Now let us briefly look at the relationship between the current account balance and international indebtedness. The international indebtedness of a country is the total amount of external debt outstanding at a given time. Thus it is a stock concept. The current account deficit is an addition to the outstanding debt which existed at the beginning of the period. The current account deficit is thus a flow concept.

As we observed on pp. 100–4, the current account deficit is paid either by borrowing from abroad or by using up foreign asset holdings. Therefore, if there are no assets abroad to begin with, the current account deficit must be paid by borrowing from abroad. In this case, the international indebtedness of the country is the cumulative sum of current account deficits from the time of the opening of its economy to the rest of the world.

Table 5.4 shows the list of nineteen low- and middle-income countries whose international indebtedness exceeded $20 billion as of the end of 1987. These outstanding debts represent international borrowing largely from foreign commercial banks and to some extent from foreign governments and international financial organizations. Relatively large commercial banks were active during the 1970s and the early 1980s as financial intermediaries between the current account surplus countries and the current account deficit countries, as we examined in Chapter 3. The concentration of large international indebtedness in a few countries aggravated the international debt crisis, which we will examine in Chapter 17.

Table 5.4 International indebtedness of low- and middle-income countries (as of end of 1987 in millions of US dollars)

Per capita income ranking	Country	Debt outstanding
78	Brazil	123,932
74	Mexico	107,992
82	Argentina	56,813
36	Indonesia	52,581
21	India	46,370
76	Poland	42,135
65	Turkey	40,818
85	Korea	40,459
49	Egypt	40,264
88	Venezuela	36,519
18	China	30,227
46	Philippines	29,962
31	Nigeria	28,714
83	Yugoslavia	23,518
89	Greece	23,120
84	Algeria	22,881
67	Chile	21,239
55	Thailand	20,710
40	Morocco	20,706

Source: World Bank (1989) *World Development Report 1989*, Washington, D.C., 204–5
Note: Per capita income ranking: the World Bank member countries starting the lowest income country at 1.

SUMMARY

The extent to which economic transactions are carried out across national boundaries differs greatly among nations. The balance of international payments is a summary record of such transactions between residents of the reporting country and those of the rest of world. International banking activities are closely related to such transactions. Besides definitional questions, how to group and present economic transactions is an important question. Typically, these transactions are grouped into current account, capital account, and official reserve transactions account. Since a double-entry method is used for recording each economic transaction, it is posted once as a debit item representing a use of foreign exchange and once as a credit item representing a source of foreign exchange. Therefore, the balance of payments must balance in an accounting sense. However, this does not guarantee the equilibrium condition in each account.

Since the current account is a summary of goods and services transactions with outsiders, it acts as a window for GNP through which its component expenditures in the foreign sector are recorded. Comparing the *ex ante* gap between exports and imports with that between domestic investment and domestic saving, we can determine the dominant gap, which is important for policy prescription. Also, this chapter examined the outstanding international indebtedness of a country as a cumulative result of its balance of payments deficits.

REVIEW PROBLEMS AND EXERCISES

1. For balance of payments recording purposes, how is an individual person's residence determined?

2. Is a transaction between a French bank at home and its foreign branch an international transaction or a domestic transaction? Why?

3. Prepare a list as detailed as possible of services which are included in the exports and imports of services in the balance of payments.

4. What are the major problems in trying to differentiate between accommodating transactions and autonomous transactions?

5. What is the relationship between the current account balance and international indebtedness?

6. When we say that the balance of payments must balance in an accounting sense, what does this mean?

7. Using an income determination model in an open economy, explain how the current account balance affects the equilibrium level of income.

8. If the foreign exchange gap is a dominant gap, what does this mean in relation to the saving gap?

9. Record the following transactions in the US balance of payments, using the double-entry system. Also indicate which category of transactions they are with reference to Table 5.2.
   (a) A British manufacturer purchases $400,000 of computer chips from an American company. Payment is made by a check drawn against a US bank in New York.
   (b) American tourists traveling in Korea spend $3,000. They obtain the needed Korean won by cashing dollar-denominated travelers' checks at Korean banks. These banks deposit the travelers' checks with banks in San Francisco.
   (c) A US company purchases a majority of the shares of a foreign corporation by paying $10 million. The sellers of the shares are foreigners, who deposit their proceeds in a bank in New York.
   (d) A US resident sends a bank draft of $500 to her relative in Mexico.
   (e) A US corporation transfers its deposit of $1,000,000 from a bank in Chicago to a bank in London.
   (f) The Federal Reserve Bank of New York borrows DM600 million from the German Central Bank in exchange for US Treasury bills. The applicable exchange rate is $1.00 = DM1.50.
   On the basis of the above transactions, is the US balance of payments in deficit or in surplus?
   If the remaining balance is to be offset by changes in official reserve holdings, are such changes debit items or credit items?

10. Balance of payments information is given as follows:

    Exports of goods, 1,000   Exports of services, 1,200
    Imports of goods, 1,300   Imports of services, 800
    Unilateral transfers, − 250 US assets abroad, − 560
    Foreign assets in the
    United States, 740

    (a) Find the merchandise balance.
    (b) Find the current account balance.
    (c) Find the official reserve transaction balance.
    (d) In this case, are the official reserves increasing or decreasing?

11. The following information is given about a closed economy:

    $$C = 100 + 0.8Y_d \qquad I = 800 \qquad G = 900$$
    $$T = 0.2Y + 100.$$

    (a) Find the equilibrium level of Y.
    (b) Find the equilibrium level of private saving.
    (c) Does the equilibrium condition $(I + G = S_p + T)$ hold?

12. The above economy became an open economy with the following changes:

$$X - M = -150.$$

(a) Find the new equilibrium level of Y.
(b) Find the new total saving S (domestic private, government, and foreign).

NOTES

1 For a comprehensive guide for preparation of the balance of payments, see the IMF *Balance of Payments Manual* (1977).
2 Although students may stay in countries of their study longer than one year, they are basically engaged in consumption activities only, while maintaining their permanent domicile elsewhere. Therefore they are not classified as residents of countries in which they study. However, determination of residence is not strictly based on the application of the above criteria, but rather by enumeration. It is designed to ensure consistency with the concepts used in the United Nation's *A System of National Accounts*.
3 For tax purposes, however, the definition of residence may be different. For example, according to the US Internal Revenue Code, US branches abroad are regarded as US residents, part of their home parents, subject to US taxation immediately, whereas foreign subsidiaries are treated as foreign residents subject to US taxation only when they remit dividends to their US parents.
4 Although there may be changes in ownership in real assets such as land and ships between residents of different countries, such changes in ownership are considered as changes in financial assets, which are construed to represent the real assets. Therefore, real assets are deemed as always being owned by the residents of the economy in which such assets are located.
5 The reserve position in the IMF is equivalent to one-fourth of the member country quota which can be withdrawn by a member country for its use.

BASIC READING

Balassa, B. A. and Williamson, J. (eds) (1990) *Adjusting to Success: Balance of Payments Policy in the East Asian NICs*, Washington, D.C.: Institute for International Economics.
Badger, D. G. (1951) "The Balance of Payments: A Tool of Economic Analysis," *IMF Staff Papers*, 2 (1): 86–197.
Chenery, H. B. and Strout, A. M. (1966) "Foreign Assistance and Economic Development," *American Economic Review*, 56 (4). Reprinted in Chenery, H. (1979) *Structural Change and Development Policy*, New York: Oxford University Press, 382–455.
Cohen, B. J. (1981) *Banks and the Balance of Payments: Private Lending in the International Adjustment Process*, London: Croom Helm.
De Vries, M. G. (1987) *Balance of Payments Adjustment, 1945 to 1986: The IMF Experience*, Washington, D.C.: IMF.

Fair, E. D. and De Boissieu, C. (eds) (1989) *The International Adjustment Process: New Perspectives, Recent Experience, and Future Challenges for the Financial System*, Boston, Mass.: Kluwer Academic.

Hooper, P. and Mann, C. L. (1989) *The Emergence and Persistence of the U.S. External Imbalance, 1980–87*, Princeton Studies in International Finance, Princeton, N.J.: Princeton University Press.

Host-Madsen, P. (1967) *Balance of Payments: Its Meanings and Uses*, Washington, D.C.: IMF.

IMF (1977) *Balance of Payments Manual*, 4th edn, Washington, DC: IMF.

Meier, G. M. (1989) *Leading Issues in Economic Development*, 5th edn, New York: Oxford University Press, Chapter 8.

Mookerjee, A. and Cash, J. (1990) *Global Electronic Wholesale Banking*, London: Graham & Trotman.

Nawaz, S. (1987) "Why the World Current Account Does Not Balance," *Finance and Development*, September: 43–5.

World Bank (1989) *World Development Report 1989*, New York: Oxford University Press, 1–144.

FURTHER READING

Cohen, R. (1989) *World Trade and Payments Cycles: The Advance and Retreatment of the Postwar Order*, New York: Praeger.

Golub, S. S. (1986) *The Current-Account Balance and the Dollar, 1977–78 and 1983–84*, Princeton Studies in International Finance, Princeton, N.J.: Princeton University Press.

Kindleberger, C. P. (1969) "Measuring Equilibrium in the Balance of Payments," *Journal of Political Economy*, 77: 873–91.

Kubarych, R. M. (1984) "Financing the U.S. Current Account Balance Deficit," *Federal Reserve Bank of New York Quarterly Review*, 24–31.

Meade, J. (1951) *The Balance of Payments*, London: Oxford University Press.

Stern, R. M. (1973) *The Balance of Payments: Theory and Economic Policy*, Chicago, Ill.: Aldine.

US Bureau of the Budget, Review Committee for Balance of Payments Statistics (1965) *The Balance of Payments of the United States*, Washington, D.C.: US Government Printing Office.

US Department of Commerce, *Survey of Current Business*, various issues.

Part II

International money and exchange markets

Chapter 6

Foreign exchange market structure

INTRODUCTION

The foreign exchange market in one country is a market where foreign currency is traded in exchange for the home currency or for currencies of other countries. Although foreign exchange is a means of payment of another country, this does not mean that the entire stock of that country's currency is foreign exchange. Rather it is only part of the money stock, which becomes foreign exchange when it is traded in exchange for another currency or when it is held by residents of countries other than the country of the currency.

Foreign exchange consists of paper money, coins, and transaction balances at banks, all denominated in foreign currency units. In addition, foreign exchange includes other financial instruments arising from international transactions and nearing maturity, such as near-maturity foreign drafts or bankers' acceptances which can readily be converted into foreign means of payment.

The foreign exchange market basically performs four major functions. First, it converts the purchasing power which can only be exercised within a national boundary of one country to that of other countries. Such conversions often result in transfer of purchasing power from residents of one country to those of others. Second, it functions as a clearing house for foreign exchange demanded and supplied in the course of international transactions by residents of various countries. Without this, buyers and sellers themselves must find their prospective counterpart sellers and buyers. Third, it provides facilities for hedging foreign exchange risks. This function has become increasingly important since the IMF-sponsored international monetary system abandoned the fixed exchange rate regime in 1973. Fourth, the exchange market provides credit for international trade, particularly as it functions as a secondary market for international trade finance instruments. Note that there is a spectrum of differences in maturity of traded foreign exchange, ranging from zero to a relatively short period. If the maturity is zero, the foreign exchange market functions strictly as an

Table 6.1 Average daily turnover in foreign exchange markets (during April 1989 in billions of US dollars)

| Country | Gross turnover | Net turnover | | | Via brokers (%) |
		Total	Interbank	Nonbank customers	
UK	241	187	161	26	38.0
USA	174	129	116	10	44.0
Japan	145	115	78	34	35.0
Switzerland	68	57	47	9	19.0
Singapore	63	55	49	6	–
Hong Kong	60	49	44	5	35.0
Australia	37	30	22	6	33.0
France	32	26	21	5	42.0
Canada	18	15	10	4	40.0
Netherlands	16	13	11	2	41.0
Italy	15	14	12	2	22.0
Belgium	12	10	7	1	37.0
Others	55	48	40	4	
Total	936	748	618	114	

Source: Banca D'Italia (1990) *Economic Bulletin*, February: 52
Note: "Net turnover" is net of double counting arising from local interbank business. Further adjustments (for cross-border double counting, −204, and for estimated gaps in reporting, +100) yield a final net turnover of about $644 billion. The estimated gaps were largely to cover the German market, which was not surveyed because of legal restrictions. "Others" include Denmark, Sweden, Bahrain, Finland, Greece, Ireland, Norway, Portugal, and Spain.

exchange market. If the maturity is other than zero, it functions as a credit market.

Besides its functions, the significance of the market is manifested in its sheer size. A survey of the central banks of twenty-one countries in the course of the month of April in 1989 shows that an average of $936 billion was traded daily in their respective exchange markets, as shown in Table 6.1. Among the participating countries, the UK led the volume accounting for 25.7 percent, followed by the United States with 18.6 percent, and Japan with 15.5 percent. The data on the German market were not available.

PHYSICAL CHARACTERISTICS OF THE MARKETS

The foreign exchange transactions (buying and selling) may be carried out anywhere. However, such transactions require identification of prospective buyers and sellers. Without an efficient market, the identification of prospective market participants would be a costly search process. This process can be shortened by formation of a readily identifiable group of market-makers who are willing to trade in both ways, that is, to buy and to sell, at their pronounced prices, which are in turn determined by the prevailing overall market supply and demand conditions.

Then, the prospective market-takers, who are to take the prices set by market-makers as given, will be able to reduce search costs in finding their counterpart dealers. Since foreign exchange itself is a rather standardized product, it does not require a personal inspection of the product by visitation. Thus, a telephone or telex method would be by far the quickest and most inexpensive method of search and execution of transactions.

For such reasons, the foreign exchange market in the United States, for instance, consists of an electronic network of commercial banks, located largely in New York City and to a lesser extent in other major cities such as Chicago, San Francisco, Los Angeles, and Miami, which buy and sell foreign currency, the bulk of which constitutes checking deposits. These banks communicate directly with each other as well as with brokers and other market participants by telephone, telex, or computer. Therefore there is no fixed place of exchange – all the buyers and sellers who are scattered around the country but connected by telecommunications systems and assisted by brokers constitute the exchange market. Obviously, they are further connected by market participants in other countries as well.

The three-tier markets

The New York foreign exchange market may be conveniently described as a three-tier market according to the type of participants. The first-tier market is the retail market where the transactions between the banks and their customers who are ultimate users and suppliers of foreign exchange take place. The second-tier market is the wholesale market where domestic interbank transactions take place. The third-tier market is also an integral part of the wholesale market, but the transactions are between banks in New York and those abroad. Let us look at these markets more closely.

The first-tier market

In this retail market, banks' typical customers include international trading companies, multinational corporations, individuals remitting or receiving funds abroad, nonbank financial institutions involved in international transactions, and foreign government agencies.

A bank may deal in this market in two different ways: (a) on a customer's account basis or (b) on the bank's own account basis. The first method is also known as "on best effort basis," by which the bank takes an order from the customer and goes into the market on behalf of the customer to purchase or to sell foreign exchange. Thus, the bank is acting as a broker.

On the other hand, according to the second method, the bank takes profit or loss by purchasing and selling foreign exchange directly. Although any bank can deal on a customer's account basis, there are a relatively small number of banks, on the order of a hundred, in New York which actively trade on their own account basis. These banks trade not only in response to their customers' needs but also for hedging as well as speculative purposes. Which method a bank should use in foreign exchange transactions may depend on several factors, such as the size of foreign exchange transactions, the bank's overall involvement in foreign exchange business, the frequency with which a particular foreign exchange is traded by the bank, and the volatility of exchange rate movements.

The second-tier market

In this market, banks deal with other banks for foreign exchange sales and purchases for a large size, usually a minimum of $250,000 equivalent. The overwhelming bulk of all foreign exchange transactions occurs in this wholesale market, also known as the interbank exchange market, where banks seek to adjust their exchange positions either for hedging or for speculation. The need for hedging usually arises when a bank buys or sells foreign exchange in response to meeting the needs of its customers. In effect, it has been estimated that banks normally require four to six transactions in this market to cover each customer's order executed in the retail market, as shown in Table 6.1.

In addition to the hundred or so banks which are actively engaged in foreign exchange trading, there are about a score of foreign exchange brokerage houses in this market, mainly matching buyers and sellers and receiving a commission which is customarily paid by the selling bank. The advantage of using a brokerage house is that it functions as an information clearinghouse, which reduces the search cost and enables both transacting parties to maintain anonymity until a transaction is arranged. Anonymity reduces the chances of one party being forced to a less advantageous position. These brokerage houses are doing business not only with banks in the home market but also with brokers and banks abroad.

In addition, currency futures trading was introduced in this market by the Chicago Mercantile Exchange through the establishment of the International Monetary Market (IMM), which has catered to individuals, business firms, and financial institutions which find the interbank market inaccessible or unsuitable for their needs. Thus, the IMM now functions in a way as a bridge between the retail market and the interbank market. In London, a function similar to that of the IMM is performed by the London International Financial Futures Exchange (LIFFE).

The Federal Reserve and the Exchange Stabilization Fund of the Treasury Department from time to time intervene in this market through foreign exchange open market operations to stabilize exchange rates. The Exchange Stabilization Fund (equivalent to the Exchange Equalization Account in the UK) was originally established in the 1930s for the purpose of stabilizing exchange rates under the fixed rate system. Today, its functions are mainly to serve as the window of the government to transact with foreign monetary authorities and international financial institutions such as the IMF, while the Federal Reserve has assumed a greater role in stabilizing foreign exchange rates. [1]

The third-tier market

The third-tier market, or the international correspondent banking market, is the market where home banks interact with banks abroad for foreign exchange dealings. When banks in New York find it difficult to adjust their positions in the home interbank market, they seek to purchase or sell foreign exchange to foreign banks which are located in the country where the foreign exchange is their home currency. The New York banks are increasingly dealing directly with their own branches abroad, as well as with exchange brokers abroad.

In addition, foreign central banks and exchange authorities are important participants in this market and often they may jointly turn out to be the single most important player in the market. As in the case of the EMS, at times several foreign central banks simultaneously intervene in the exchange market in their respective countries, enhancing their influence further in the exchange markets.

In this type of market, the New York and London foreign exchange markets have the closest relationship, complementing each other's functions. Since the New York market over the longer period tends to be a net buyer of the British pound (a net seller of the dollar), while the London market is a net buyer of the dollar (a net seller of the pound), each market's shortage is covered by the other market. Furthermore, New York banks look to London for their purchases of various European, African, and Middle Eastern currencies which are heavily traded in the London market, while London banks often obtain Canadian, Latin American, and Far Eastern currencies in the New York market. Thus, these two exchange markets are functioning as international centers through which each center is reaching out to the other's satellite exchange markets.

Figure 6.1. shows the above three-tier markets with a case where bank A's customer sells British pounds to her bank and it shows the subsequent flows of pounds to the ultimate buyer, who is selling US dollars in exchange.

The time-zone structure

One important physical characteristic of the exchange market is the fact

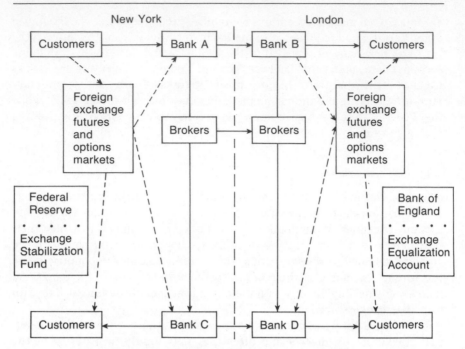

Figure 6.1 Foreign exchange market structure: →, a possible flow of the pound sold by bank A's customer; in London the direction of flows may become less clear, possibly, in either direction; – – →, an alternative flow going through futures and options markets

that market-makers are scattered around the world, operating in different time zones; this has some operational implications.

Although major banks operate on the twenty-four-hour basis, the active trading hours tend to be confined to the hours in which both markets are formally open. For example, both New York and London exchange markets overlap for their business hours between 8 : 00 and 11 : 30 a.m. in New York time. It is during this overlapping period that major pound–dollar transactions are carried out. Thus, transactions during the period other than the overlapping period tend to be those for marginal adjustments in their foreign exchange inventories. Also marginal adjustments take place in peripheral markets in different locations with different time zones. In this way, the foreign exchange market continues to function twenty-four hours a day.

As shown in Figure 6.2, the London and Frankfurt markets have their business hours overlapping with New York, inheriting the market conditions on that day from the former. Since San Francisco has only a half hour overlap with London, its market conditions are by and large determined by interactions with the New York market. By the time the US

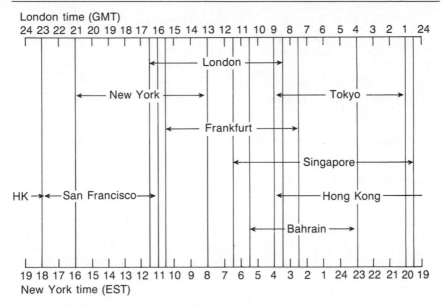

Figure 6.2 Foreign exchange market time zones
Source: Adapted from *Euromoney* (April 1979), 14–15

market closes, Hong Kong is up, followed by Singapore and Tokyo. Among these three Asian markets, the Singapore market stretches out its business hours to eleven and a half, thereby providing a safe bridge between the US and European markets.

Since the bulk of dollar–pound transactions take place during the overlapping business hours between New York and London, the exchange rates during these hours tend to be more competitive. That is, the buying and selling rates quoted by market-makers are more responsive to the underlying supply and demand conditions, and the spread between the buying and selling rates becomes narrower. On the other hand, the spread in the foreign exchange markets elsewhere tends to be wider because of lack of depth of the market.

EXCHANGE TRANSACTION METHODS

When the amount of a transaction is relatively small as in the case of a tourist buying a foreign currency, paper monies are typically exchanged simultaneously. However, when the size of a transaction becomes larger, say £5 million, the foreign exchange transaction usually takes the form of transferring the said amount from the seller's account to the buyer's account. For example, suppose that Citibank is selling £5 million to IBM from the former's account maintained with Barclays Bank in London and in turn Citibank receives $7.5 million from IBM for payment. The execution of such transactions is recorded as changes in the balance sheets of the buying and selling banks.

Citibank		Barclays Bank	
Assets	Liabilities	Assets	Liabilities
£100 million deposits at Barclays			£100 million deposits at Citibank
− £5 million			− £5 million
+ $7.5 million			+ £5 million deposits of IBM

Then, how does Citibank instruct Barclays Bank to transfer its account to the IBM account? The method of instruction to make payment is often referred to as the method of payment. The selling bank can provide three different ways to instruct the transfer, depending on the customer's needs. In most instances, the selling bank sends a transfer instruction via telex to the bank where the former maintains its foreign currency account. However, the actual transfer will not take place until the predetermined future date.

The second method is that the bank sends the transfer instruction via air-mail. In this case, how soon Barclays Bank executes the transfer depends on the postal service, which takes a longer time than telex. When the customer makes her purchase payment at the time of contract and receives foreign exchange later, the customer is effectively lending money to the bank free of interest. The amount of money the bank uses free of interest payment because of the time lag between the payment and the receipt is termed a bank float in the foreign exchange market. The foreign exchange rate should reflect this bank float.

The third method is that the bank may simply hand out a formalized instruction (known as a bank draft) to the customer, who in turn takes it to London and presents it to Barclays Bank for claim. In this case, again there is a time gap between the customer's payment and the availability of foreign exchange to the customer.

FOREIGN EXCHANGE MARKET PRODUCTS

Spot exchange

Spot foreign exchange is foreign currency which is to be delivered within two business days from the contract date. Although it is possible to arrange the delivery on the next day or even on the same day, it is a convention to make a delivery two eligible business days later from the date of contract. We call this delivery date the spot value date.

Although it would no longer be necessary in the current state of communications technology, the requirement of two eligible business days in major foreign exchange markets such as London, New York, Frankfurt, and Paris is designed to provide reasonable time for transmitting instructions to the overseas location where the foreign currency is paid or received and for ensuring the settlement according to the *valeur compensée* principle. By this, we mean that both parties to a contract are required to deliver their respective currencies for exchange simultaneously so that fairness can be assured. For example, if a contract to exchange US dollars for British pounds is made on Friday, the settlement date will be the following Tuesday as long as markets are open for business in both countries. Otherwise, one party would be presenting her currency without receiving an equivalent value in another currency.

In some instances, it is possible to set two different dates, one for delivery of one currency and another for delivery of the other currency. Suppose, for example, that a foreign exchange buyer delivers US dollars four days earlier than he is receiving British pounds. According to the *valeur compensée* principle, the foreign exchange rate should reflect the free-loan nature of this advance payment, which we defined as bank float earlier. Suppose that the foreign exchange rate is $1.60/£1 and the interest rate in the US market is 10 percent; the equilibrium exchange rate per pound is the present value of $1.60 equivalent to be received four days later, as shown below:

$$\$1.6/\left[1 + 0.10(4/360)\right].\tag{6.1}$$

Forward exchange

A forward exchange contract is a contract between two parties whereby both parties commit themselves to deliver a fixed amount of one currency in exchange for another at a specified future date or during a predetermined period. In either case the delivery date will be later than two business days from the date of contract. Since a fixed amount of one currency will be exchanged for a fixed amount of another currency in the future, the foreign exchange rate applied for the delivery of the currencies is fixed at the time of the contract, regardless of the exchange rate movements between the time of contract and the time of settlement.

The common maturity for forward exchange ranges between thirty and 180 days. For example, if it is a thirty-day forward (contract), it is to be delivered on the eligible business day which is the spot value date plus thirty days. If this is not an eligible date, it must move forward until the first eligible date is found without moving into the following month. In such an instance, it must move backward until the first eligible date is found. With such an arrangement, the last day of a month tends to be a clearing day for foreign exchange transactions.

Since the participants' risk (that is, their possible loss due to exchange rate fluctuations) increases as maturity becomes longer, fewer forward contracts are committed beyond six months. Furthermore, contracts with maturity longer than one year are rare even for currencies having a well-developed spot market, thus requiring special negotiations. The situation can be readily seen by examining Figure 6.3. The full lines represent market-makers' bid (buying) and offer (selling) curves and the broken lines represent market-takers' bid and offer curves, which are not actually revealed. Both market-makers and market-takers will only be willing to commit themselves to selling foreign exchange (pounds sterling) at higher prices as the maturity becomes longer. Likewise, both of them will only be willing to contract to buy foreign exchange at lower prices as the maturity becomes longer. The exchange market exists only when the potential bid rates (reservation prices) of market-takers are higher than the offer rates of market-makers or when the potential supply rates of the former are lower than the bid rates of the latter. In Figure 6.3, such conditions are satisfied until maturity becomes m^*, beyond which no forward market exists. We may also note that the spread between market-makers' bid and offer rates widens to accommodate the greater potential rate fluctuations as maturity becomes longer.

Currency swaps

A currency swap transaction is a special case of repurchase agreements, by which one party sells a given amount of foreign exchange at a given exchange rate with a promise to buy back the foreign exchange at a predetermined rate at a later date. For the other party in the contract, this is a reverse repurchase agreement. In swap transactions, the amount of sale of a foreign currency always equals the amount of repurchase. However, in terms of the home currency units, the amount of payment and the amount of receipt will usually be different. This difference per unit of foreign currency is termed the swap rate. In the next section, we shall study the meaning of swap rates in more detail.

We may also consider a swap as a combination of a spot exchange transaction and a forward exchange transaction. An example of a swap is a combination of a spot sale of pounds against dollars which is to be settled two business days later and a forward purchase of pounds against dollars. If the parties for both transactions are the same, we call the two combined transactions a pure swap. If the party from which the purchase is made is not the same person to whom the sale was made, the combined transactions

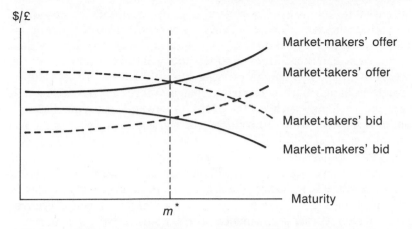

Figure 6.3 Buying and selling rates with varying maturities

are termed an engineered swap. In this case each transaction is an outright sale or purchase transaction. Swap transactions reduce transaction costs including search costs and serve as a convenient tool for hedging purposes.

Foreign exchange futures

A foreign exchange futures contract or simply a foreign exchange futures is a standardized form of a forward contract. Therefore, by such a futures contract one party is committing to buy and the other party to sell a standardized amount of a particular foreign currency. As shown in Table 6.2, each contract size is fixed according to the traded currencies.

Table 6.2 Foreign exchange futures contracts (International Monetary Market)

Currency	Contract size	Futures market quotes ($)	1 point equals ($)	Minimum rate fluctuation ($)	Maximum daily fluctuation ($)
DM	125,000	0.6154	0.0001	0.0001	0.0100
¥	12,500,000	0.6670	0.0001	0.0001	0.0100
£	62,500	1.8117	0.0001	0.0002	0.0200
SFr	125,000	0.7449	0.0001	0.0001	0.0150
C$	100,000	0.8668	0.0001	0.0001	0.0075
A$	100,000	0.7846	0.0001	0.0001	0.0075

Sources: International Monetary Market (1977) *Understanding Futures in Foreign Exchange*, Chicago, Ill.: IMM; *Wall Street Journal* (July 26, 1990), C10
Note: In the forward exchange market, the Japanese yen is quoted on a per-yen basis, whereas in the foreign exchange futures market it is quoted on a per-100-yen basis.

In addition to the size of a contract, some important standardized features include the delivery date, which is fixed on the third Wednesday of the month for all currency futures delivery months. Since the delivery date is fixed, someone entering futures contracts today and again tomorrow, for instance, is in effect entering contracts having different maturities. Unlike the forward exchange market, foreign exchange futures are traded through an organized exchange such as the IMM, a subsidiary of the Chicago Mercantile Exchange, which introduced the foreign exchange futures for the first time in 1972.

Furthermore, unlike the case of forward contracts, a gain or loss from a futures contract is posted daily as if the settlement were to take place daily. This practice is known as "marked to the market daily." This is important to protect the exchange clearing house which acts as the ultimate guarantor of the contract performance. For administrative convenience, a minimum rate fluctuation is established. For pound sterling, it is $0.0002 per pound or $12.50 per contract. Also, the maximum daily fluctuation is set. This is intended to mitigate the risk arising from unexpected large fluctuations in the exchange rates.

For example, suppose that Thunderbird Bank enters a British pound futures sale whereby its sale price is fixed at $1.7957. Then the subsequent exchange rate movements affect the purchase price by this bank. Assume the rates have moved as shown in Table 6.3. A rise in the value of the British pound against the US dollar by 160 points at the end of the first day means that this seller must purchase her contract at a $1,000 higher price if she were to meet her contractual obligation at the end of this day. Thus, a rise in the exchange rate results in a loss to the futures seller and a gain to the futures buyer. This gain or loss is posted to each participant's margin account each day.

In order to prevent performance default, buyers and sellers must satisfy the margin requirement by depositing the required margin money with their respective brokers. Initially, a buyer or seller deposits the so-called initial

Table 6.3 An example of "marked-to-the-market daily" (one British pound futures contract)

Date	Settlement rate per pound ($)	Rate fluctuation (points)	Marked-to-the-market daily	
			Seller's account ($)	Buyer's account ($)
1st day	1.8117	+ 160	− 1,000	+ 1,000
2nd day	1.8037	− 80	+ 500	− 500
3rd day	1.8137	+ 100	− 625	+ 625
Cumulative	+ 0.0180	+ 180	− 1,125	+ 1,125

margin ($3,000 in the case of the British pound contract) to which the daily loss (or gain) is debited (or credited). If the margin account balance exceeds $3,000, the customer may withdraw the exceeding portion from her account. On the other hand, if the balance drops below the maintenance margin ($2,000 in the case of the British pound), it must be replenished up to the initial margin level. If Thunderbird Bank is to get out of the futures market, it must enter a purchase contract having the same delivery date to offset the previous sale contract.

In this market, not only banks but also retail market participants deal directly with each other through the exchange. Many individuals participating in this market do so for speculative purposes, partly evidenced by the fact that only a small portion of total futures contracts are actually delivered.

Currency options

A currency option is a contract that gives the option holder the right to buy or sell a specified amount of a particular foreign currency at a contractual price within a specific period (American option) or on a specific date (European option). A call option gives the right to buy, whereas a put option gives the right to sell. Just like currency futures, currency options traded on exchanges are standardized contracts.

Currency options were first introduced on the Philadelphia Exchange in 1982 and are now traded on other exchanges in Chicago, London, Montreal, and elsewhere. The standardized currency options contract sizes traded on the Philadelphia Exchange are half the sizes of respective currency futures contracts traded on the IMM, as shown in Table 6.4.

An option contract involves a buyer, a seller, their respective brokers who bring them together, and the exchange where the option is traded. The buyer of an option pays the fee (known as premium) to the seller (or writer)

Table 6.4 Contract sizes of currency options (Philadelphia Exchange)

Currency	Contract size	American style	European style
£	31,250	Yes	
C$	50,000	Yes	Yes
DM	62,500	Yes	
¥	6,250,000	Yes	
SFr	62,500	Yes	
A$	50,000	Yes	Yes

Source: Wall Street Journal (July 26, 1990), C10

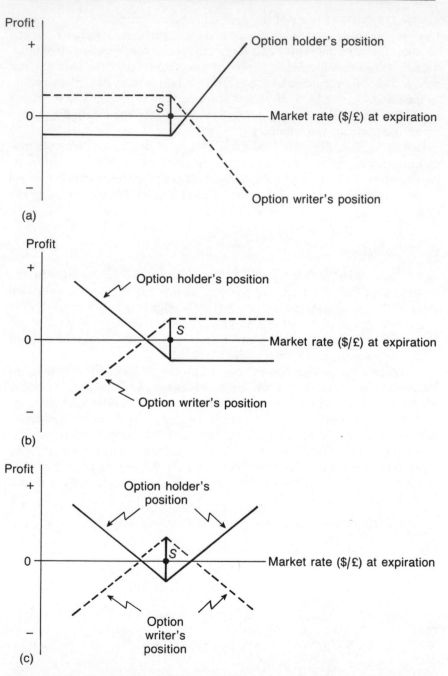

Figure 6.4 Currency options (*S*, exercise price): (a) call option; (b) put option; (c) straddle option

for the right. The premium depends on (1) the relationship between the exercise price and the current spot exchange rate, (2) the volatility of exchange rate movements, and (3) the maturity.

Now let us examine a call option on British pounds (contract size of £31,250). Suppose that the purchase of this option costs $0.04 per pound and the exercise price is $1.4000. The option expires in one month. Then the option buyer pays $1,250 for the right to buy £31,250 at a price of $1.4000 per pound any time within one month.

When the option holder exercises the right to purchase, she has to pay the exercise price (also known as strike price) S in addition to the premium π which she has already paid. Since the foreign currency purchased through the options can be sold at the market price P, profit Φ is determined as follows:

$$\Phi = P - (S + \pi) \tag{6.2}$$

The option holder faces three alternative situations in terms of profitability of her call option.

1 If $P \leqslant S$, the loss is equal to or greater than the premium. Thus the loss can be limited to the amount of the premium by not exercising the option.
2 If $S < P < S + \pi$, the loss can be minimized by exercising the option.
3 If $P \geqslant S + \pi$, the profit will be non-negative if the option is exercised.

An option that would be profitable (not necessarily positive in profit) to exercise at the current market rate is said to be "in the money," like cases 2 and 3 above. An option whose exercise price is the same as the current market price is said to be "on the money." An option that would not be profitable to exercise at the current price is then said to be "out of the money."

Figure 6.4 illustrates the relationship between the profitability of an option and the current market price. Figure 6.4(a) shows the profit for a call option with exercise price S. The full line represents the option buyer's profit position, whereas the broken line represents the option writer's position. Similarly, Figure 6.4(b) illustrates the case of a put option. Figure 6.4(c) exhibits the profit position of the option holder with a simultaneous purchase of a put and a call at the same exercise price (known as a straddle option) as well as the option writer's position.

Now let us examine how an option premium can be set. The option premium is determined in the competitive marketplace, depending on a number of factors: (1) the location of the expected exchange rate, (2) the location of the exercise price relative to the expected exchange rate, (3) the volatility of exchange rate movement manifested by its standard deviation, and (4) the profit goal set by the dealer.

Figure 6.5 illustrates the relationship between the premium and the above factors. Suppose that the probability of the market rate ($/£) is distributed

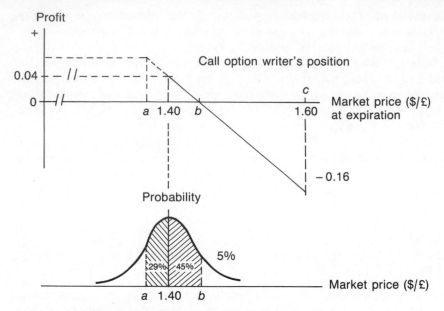

Figure 6.5 Determination of currency options premium: $a = \$1.38$, the price at 0.8σ below the exercise price; $b = \$1.44$, the price at 1.6σ above the exercise price

normally around an expected rate of $1.40 with a standard deviation of $0.025. It is unlikely that the market rate moves up beyond $1.60 from a practical point of view. Suppose further that the bank plans to write a call option with the exercise price of $1.40 and hopes to have positive profit 95 percent of the time. What premium should the bank charge? And what is the expected profit, given the above premium? The premium then must be equivalent to the distance between the exercise price and point b in Figure 6.5 which is 1.6 from the exercise price in terms of a standardized z distribution, below which the cumulative probability is 45 percent (or 95 percent from the origin). Therefore,

$$premium = 1.6 \times \$0.025 = \$0.04. \tag{6.3}$$

The expected value of this option contract per pound may be roughly calculated as follows:[2]

$$\$0.04 \times 0.50 + \$0.04 \times (1/2) \times 0.45 - \$0.16 \times (1/2) \times 0.05$$
$$= \$0.025. \tag{6.4}$$

The first term represents the expected value when the range of the market price is equal to or less than the exercise price, and the second term represents the expected value when the market price is between the exercise price and the breakeven price; and the third term is the value when the market price is above the breakeven price.

If the exercise price is now set at $1.3800 by request of the customer, then what should the new premium be? If the bank dealer's objective is still to have a 95 percent chance of a profit, she should set the premium at $0.0600. On the other hand, if the bank's objective is to have the same level of expected profit, which is $0.0294, then the premium should be about $0.0574.[3]

FOREIGN EXCHANGE RATE QUOTATIONS

Price quotation method and volume quotation method

The methods of foreign exchange rate quotations used in the marketplace are an example of the institutionalization of market behavior and give good insight into the inner workings of the marketplace. The foreign exchange rate is expressed as a number of units of one currency per unit of another currency. For example, suppose that $1.0000 is equal to DM1.6000 in New York. We may express this relationship in two different ratios:

1 $1.0000/DM1.6000 = $0.6250/DM1
2 DM1.6000/$1.

The first ratio treats the deutsche mark as a special commodity whose value is expressed as a number of units of US dollars. On the other hand, the second ratio treats the US dollar as a special commodity. Alternatively, we can think of this second ratio as expressing how many units one US dollar can command of a special commodity which is the foreign currency.

When the value of one unit of a foreign currency is expressed as a number of units of the home currency just like any prices in goods markets, the exchange rate is said to be in the form of a price quotation. On the other hand, when the value of the home currency is expressed as a number of units of a foreign currency, the method is known as a volume quotation method. In New York, the rate $0.6250/DM1 is in the form of a price quotation. However, in Frankfurt, the same expression constitutes a volume quotation. Similarly, the exchange rate DM1.6000/$1 is a volume quotation in New York, while it is a price quotation in Frankfurt.

Obviously, it is important to identify which way the foreign exchange rate is quoted. Conceptually the price quotation method provides a convenient analogy which can be found in goods markets. On the other hand, the volume quotation method provides a means of ready comparison for many foreign currencies simultaneously. For example, the London market may quote the rates for the US dollar, deutsche mark, Japanese yen and Korean won as follows:

$1.6245/£1;   DM2.7703/£1;   ¥249.85/£1;   W1,137.96/£1.

Then we immediately find that all the numerator currency values are equal:

$1.6245 = DM2.7703 = ¥249.85 = W1,137.96.

The price quotation method is common practice in major foreign exchange markets except for the London and New York markets. In London, the volume quotation method is used. This is due to the tradition of treating the pound sterling as the central currency to which other currencies are referred. In New York, the volume quotation method was adopted in 1978 mainly to create a direct mirror image of rates quoted in foreign markets so as to make a rate comparison easier. However, rates for certain currencies such as the Australian dollar, British pound, Irish pound, New Zealand dollar, and South African rand are quoted by the price quotation method in New York, reflecting the fact that in the home market of these currencies the volume quotation method is used.

Bid and offer rates

Since banks act as market-makers for foreign exchange dealings, they quote both bid rate (buying price) and offer rate (selling price) simultaneously. The first price is always the bid and the second price the offer. Quotations usually include the fourth decimal place digit (known as points or 1/10,000 currency units). The difference between the offer and the bid is a spread which represents the profit margin in foreign exchange dealings. A dealer bank is said to be efficient if it consistently quotes its offer rate lower than the market rate and its bid rate higher than the market rate and its spread narrower than the market spread. As you may recall, the spread is a function of maturity. As the maturity becomes longer, the spread tends to become larger, reflecting greater exchange rate risk with longer maturity.

In the retail market, bid and offer rates are typically quoted outright, meaning without omitting any digits. For example,

	Bid	Offer
Spot	$1.6540/1.6543 (per pound)
1-month forward	1.6551/1.6560
3-month forward	1.6437/1.6448

On the other hand, in the wholesale market dealers may quote rates in a simplified way by quoting only the last two digits in the case of a spot offer and quoting by points in the case of forward bids and offers. By point quotations, we mean that the forward rates are quoted as the difference between the outright forward rate (r_{0j}) and its respective spot rate (r_{00}). For example, the above outright rates may be quoted as:

	Bid	Offer
Spot	$1.6540/43	
1-month forward	11/17 (points premium)	
3-month forward	103/95 (points discount)	

Instead of quoting 11/17 points premium or 103/95 points discount, the dealer may simply quote 11/17 and 103/95.

It is understood that if the value of the first figure is less than that of the second, it is a premium. If the first figure is greater than the second one in absolute terms, it is a discount.[4] Note that the basic principle of rate quotations is to provide accurate information in an efficient way. Rate quotations other than outright quotations are designed to enhance efficiency, which is important when many rates are quoted simultaneously. Nonetheless, accuracy is always the foremost important consideration. Therefore, if it is necessary, "big figures" as a reminder may be included in rate quotations in addition to the last two digits.

Similar to the point quotation are the swap rates, which are also the difference between the forward and spot rates. However, in this case, they are based on actual swap transactions. There are two swap rates:

1 the bid rate $p_{0j} - s_{00}$ means "sell the near date and buy the far date";
2 the offer rate $s_{0j} - p_{00}$ means "buy the near date and sell the far date."

Therefore, a bid or an offer is with reference to the far date.

For example, one-month swap rates may be computed as

$$1.6551 - 1.6543 = 0.0008$$
$$1.6560 - 1.6540 = 0.0020.$$

Then the swap rates in conjunction with the spot rates may be quoted as

Spot	1.6540/43
1-month swap	8/20
3-month swap	106/92

A forward rate may also be expressed in terms of the rate of annualized changes, which provides a convenient basis of comparison with interest rates. For example, let us use the one-month forward bid rate whose annualized percentage change from the spot rate is

$$\left(\frac{p_{01} - p_{00}}{p_{00}}\right) \frac{365}{30} = \left(\frac{1.6551 - 1.6540}{1.6540}\right) \frac{365}{30}$$

$$= 0.008092 \qquad \text{(or } 0.8092\%)$$

Under the price quotation method, the positive value of the annualized rate of change means a premium, representing appreciation of the foreign currency, whereas a negative value means a discount. We also note that an annualized rate of 0.8092 percent means that, if the rate of monthly change during the next eleven months is exactly the same as in the first month, then the annual rate of change will be 0.8092 percent. Obviously, there is no guarantee that the next eleven months will witness exactly the same rate of monthly change.

Information content of rate quotations

Suppose that a particular dealer calls you and quotes her bid and offer. Depending on the level of rates quoted by this particular dealer in comparison with the market rates which are in effect the average rates quoted by most dealers, we can draw a certain inference with respect to (1) this particular dealer's intention about trying to sell or to buy, (2) this dealer's anticipation on the rate movement, and (3) eventual market supply and demand conditions.

Case I

The dealer quotes both bid and offer rates (expressed in price quotations) above their corresponding market rates. Then her intention is to purchase and not to sell foreign exchange. She may also be anticipating upward movements of the rate. If other dealers have a similar intention, the market demand curve shifts outward from D to D' and the market supply curve shifts inward from S to S' as shown in Figure 6.6. Eventually, the market exchange rate will settle at a higher level.

Case II

The dealer quotes both bid and offer below their corresponding market rates. This time, her intention is to sell and not to buy foreign exchange. She may be anticipating a lower rate. For the market as a whole, the supply will increase and the demand will decrease, causing the market rate to decrease.

Case III

The dealer quotes the bid rate higher and the offer rate lower than their corresponding market rates. Her intention is to increase the volume of transactions, that is, both buying and selling. Whether she wishes to increase or decrease her foreign exchange inventory depends on the relative deviations of her rates from the respective market rates. She may be anticipating that the rate movements will be stable so that the rate will

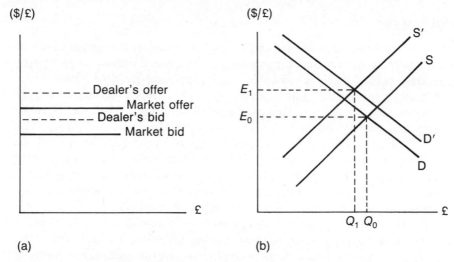

Figure 6.6 Dealer's rate quotations: (a) individual dealer's bid and offer;
(b) market supply and demand

stabilize at the current level with reduced fluctuations. If a majority of dealers behave in a similar way, both supply and demand will increase. Where the equilibrium level of the exchange rate will settle depends on the relative changes in supply and demand.

Case IV

The dealer may quote bid and offer rates at the same level as their respective market rates. In this case, she may be content with the current level of business, while she may not be anticipating any discernible rate movements but rate fluctuations to be greater than in case III.

Case V

The dealer quotes the bid lower and the offer higher than their respective market rates. Her intention is not to do business. The mean value of the market rates may be at the current level but the rate fluctuations are anticipated to be greater than in Case IV. For the market as a whole, both supply and demand may decrease, thinning the market. Such may be the case on a Friday afternoon, a day before a holiday break, when the dealers have already built up an optimal inventory to ride through uncertainty and do not want to change it.

In the next chapter, we will study the determination of foreign exchange rates and opportunities in foreign exchange markets.

SUMMARY

The foreign exchange market is the market where means of payments of foreign countries are traded. Such means of payment include foreign paper money, coins, checking balances, and near-maturity debt instruments. According to market participants, the structure of foreign exchange markets may be characterized as the retail (first-tier), wholesale (second-tier), and correspondent (third-tier) markets. Modes of operations, rate quotation methods, and the extent of the use of brokers are different in the different markets. It is also useful to characterize the market by product line, such as spot exchange, forward exchange, exchange futures, currency swaps, and currency options. In the next chapter, we will study arbitrage opportunities among the sub-markets of these products.

Partly for efficiency reasons and partly for different usage needs, a variety of exchange rate quotation methods are used, such as bid and offer rates, price and volume quotations, point and swap rate quotations, and discount and premium. As an example of effective use of price information, it is shown that by comparing the bid and offer rates quoted by a market-maker with the respective market rates, we could infer the purported intention of this dealer and the likely direction of rate movements anticipated by this person.

REVIEW PROBLEMS AND EXERCISES

1. Elaborate on major functions of the foreign exchange market.

2. When we say foreign exchange, what do we mean by this exactly?

3. Why is the structure of the foreign exchange market the way it is?

4. Why do banks still often use brokers in the foreign exchange market, instead of dealing directly with each other?

5. What is the structural relationship between the New York and London foreign exchange markets?

6. If you are to conduct foreign exchange transactions during formal business hours on a twenty-four-hour continuous basis, which markets would you go into to do so?

7. How will the existence of overlapping business hours for two or more exchange markets probably affect the terms and conditions of exchange transactions?

8. When a bank sells foreign exchange, how does the bank transfer foreign exchange to the buying customer?

9. (a) How are the spot value date and the forward value date determined?
   (b) Suppose that a separate one-month forward pound was sold on the following dates: March 23, 1992 (Monday); April 25, 1992 (Tuesday). Find the respective forward value date.

10. What are major differences between the following paired instruments?
    (a) Spot and forward exchange
    (b) Forward exchange and currency futures
    (c) Currency futures and foreign exchange options

11. From the level of bid and offer rates that a particular dealer quotes, we can make certain inference regarding her intention and her anticipation of rate movements. Explain five different cases.

12. A DM futures sale contract was committed by Phoenix Bank at $0.6150 on the IMM exchange. Subsequently, the following futures prices prevailed:

1st day settlement price	$0.6155
2nd day settlement price	0.6125
3rd day purchase price	0.6160

    (a) Find the "marked to the market daily" amount for each day.
    (b) What is the amount of profit (or loss) from this contract should the bank decide to get out of the futures contract on the third day?
    (c) What is the amount that the bank receives (or pays) on the third day as the settlement payment in order to get out of this contract? Is it the "marked to the market" amount on the third day or the cumulative profit (or loss) amount?

13. The pound options market conditions on the Philadelphia Exchange are as follows.

    Call options: premium, $0.04 per £; exercise price, $1.5000
    Put options: premium, $0.02 per £; exercise price, $1.5000

    (a) Should a call option holder exercise the option right if the market rate is $1.502 at expiration? Why?
    (b) What about a put option holder if the market rate is $1.4500 at expiration?
    (c) Show the range of the exchange rate within which a straddle option holder loses money.

14. Thunderbird Bank offers foreign exchange call options. It wants to make sure that it would not lose money with a 95 percent confidence interval, which is still a competitive pricing range. The expected exchange rate during the options maturity is $1.6500 with a standard deviation of $0.0400.
    (a) If the exercise price is to be set at the expected rate level, how much premium should the bank charge?
    (b) If the exercise price is to be set at $1.5500, how much premium should the bank then charge?

15. The following information is given:

> Spot rate $1.6034/38 per £
> 1-month   10/14
> 2-month   6/3
> 3-month   12/16

   (a) Convert the above into outright quotations.
   (b) Using the average of bid and offer rates for each maturity, compute the premium or discount per annum for each forward maturity.

16. Given the following, find the swap rate for each forward maturity.

> Spot $0.4500/0.4501 per DM
> 1-month   0.4496/0.4498
> 3-month   0.4502/0.4508

17. The following rates are quoted by foreign exchange traders who are market-makers.

> German mark trader   DM1.5285/1.5295 per $
> French franc trader   FFr5.8525/5.8575 per $

   (a) Find the cross rate for purchasing French francs against German marks.
   (b) Find the cross rate for purchasing German marks against French francs.

NOTES

1 For a concise yet comprehensive survey of market intervention by the Exchange Stabilization Fund and the Federal Reserve for the period from 1958 to 1990, see Pauls (1990).
2 We can use the following equations to calculate the expected value in a more precise way. First, the profit function Φ is

$$\Phi = 0.04 \qquad\qquad \text{for } x \leqslant 1.40$$
$$= S + \pi - x = 1.44 - x \qquad \text{for } 1.40 < x \leqslant 1.60$$

and the expected profit function $E(\Phi)$ is then

$$E(\Phi) = 0.04 \int_{0}^{1.40} \frac{1}{\sigma(2\pi)^{1/2}} \exp\left(-\frac{1}{2}\right)\left(\frac{x-S}{\sigma}\right)^2 dx +$$

$$\int_{1.40}^{1.60} (1.44 - x) \frac{1}{\sigma(2\pi)^{1/2}} \exp\left(-\frac{1}{2}\right)\left(\frac{x-S}{\sigma}\right)^2 dx$$

$$\approx 0.0294$$

where x is the market price, S is the exercise price (1.40), and σ is the standard deviation (0.025).

3 Using equation (6.4), we may now let x be the premium which is to be solved for.

$$x(0.2119) + x(1/2)(0.2881 + 0.45) - (0.16)(1/2)(0.05)$$
$$= 0.0294.$$

Therefore, $x = 0.0574$.

4 This is true if the spread for forward is greater than that of spot. Suppose that the spot spread is k and the forward spread is q which is greater than k by d. Then, whether foreign currency is appreciating (a case of premium) or depreciating (a case of discount), we have the following relationship:

$$s_{00} - p_{00} = k$$
$$s_{0j} - p_{0j} = q = k + d$$

where s_{00} and p_{00} are spot offer and bid rates and s_{0j} and p_{0j} are forward offer and bid rates. The first subscript represents the time of contract commitment and the second subscript the time of settlement. Then we have

$$(s_{0j} - p_{0j}) - (s_{00} - p_{00}) = d.$$

By rearranging, we now have

$$(s_{0j} - s_{00}) - d = (p_{0j} - p_{00}).$$

If $d = 0$, then $p_{0j} - p_{00}$ equals $s_{0j} - s_{00}$. For $d > 0$, $s_{0j} - s_{00} > 0$, and $p_{0j} - p_{00} > 0$; then $s_{0j} - s_{00}$ must be greater than $p_{0j} - p_{00}$. On the other hand, for $d > 0$, $s_{0j} - s_{00} < 0$, and $p_{0j} - p_{00} < 0$; then the absolute value of $p_{0j} - p_{00}$ will be greater than that of $s_{0j} - s_{00}$ by d.

BASIC READING

Banca D'Italia (1990) "Turnover on the Foreign Exchange Market," *Economic Bulletin*, February: 51–5.

Bodurtha, N., Jr and Courtadon, G. R. (1987) *The Pricing of Foreign Currency Options*, Monograph Series in Finance and Economics 1987–4/5, New York: New York University Press.

Chrystal, K. A. (1984) "Guide to Foreign Exchange Markets," *Federal Reserve Bank of St. Louis Review*, March: 5–18.

Einzig, P. (1970) *A Textbook on Foreign Exchange*, 2nd edn, London: Macmillan.

Giddy, I. H. (1983) "Foreign Exchange Options," *Journal of Futures Markets*, Summer: 143–66.

International Monetary Market (1977) *Understanding Futures in Foreign Exchange*, Chicago, Ill.: IMM.

Kubarych, R. M. (1983) *Foreign Exchange Markets in the United States*, New York: Federal Reserve Bank of New York.

McKinnon, R. I. (1979) *Money in International Exchange*, New York: Oxford University Press, 21–6.

Pauls, B. D. (1990) "U.S. Exchange Rate Policy: Bretton Woods to Present," *Federal Reserve Bulletin*, November: 891–908.

Revey, P. A. (1981) "Evolution and Growth of the United States Foreign Exchange Market," *Federal Reserve Bank of New York Quarterly Review*, Autumn: 32–44.

Riehl, H. and Rodriguez, R. M. (1983) *Foreign Exchange and Money Markets*, New York: McGraw-Hill.

Ritchken, P. (1987) *Options: Theory, Strategy, and Applications*, Glenview, Ill.: Scott, Foresman, 366–81.

FURTHER READING

Black, F. and Scholes, M. (1973) "The Pricing of Options and Corporate Liabilities," *Journal of Political Economy*, May–June: 637–54.

Den Dunnen, E. (1985) *Instruments of Money Market and Foreign Exchange Market Policy in the Netherlands*, Hingham, Mass.: Kluwer Academic.

Goedhuys, D. (ed.) (1985) *The Foreign Exchange Market in the 1980s: The Views of Market Participants*, New York: Group of Thirty.

Leuthold, R. M., Junkus, J. C. and Cordier, J. E. (1989) *The Theory and Practice of Futures Markets*, Lexington, Mass.: D.C. Heath.

Rothstein, N. H. and Little J. M. (1984) *The Handbook of Financial Futures*, New York: McGraw-Hill.

Siegal, D. R. and Siegel, D. F. (1990) *Futures Markets*, Chicago, Ill.: Dryden Press.

Wonnacott, P. (1982) *U.S. Intervention in the Exchange Market for DM. 1977–80*, Princeton Studies in International Finance, Princeton, N.J.: Princeton University Press.

Chapter 7

Foreign exchange rate and arbitrage

INTRODUCTION

Having studied the foreign exchange market structure in the previous chapter, we now turn our attention to the determination of foreign exchange rates by analyzing foreign exchange supply and demand. Unlike supply functions of goods and services, the supply of a currency depends on not only its price (exchange rate) but also the quantity of goods demanded at that price, causing a peculiar possibility of market instability. We then study how the exchange rates are determined in the long run, applying the purchasing power parity theory and its extension – a monetary approach.

Next, we examine arbitrage opportunities arising from exchange rate movements, including interest rate arbitrage, spatial arbitrage, term arbitrage, and arbitrage between futures and ·options. Within the context of arbitrage behavior, we examine how a bank, as market-maker, may respond to foreign exchange needs of customers and at the same time minimize its own risks, using a variety of market tools. We evaluate three cases, namely, a case of using forward market tools, a second case of using money market tools combined with exchange market tools, and a third case involving swap arrangements.

Finally, we take a look at kinds of foreign exchange services that banks typically provide for different types of customers.

FOREIGN EXCHANGE RATE DETERMINATION

Supply and demand for a currency

Since 1973, most major currencies have been under the flexible exchange rate system. Thus, exchange rates of these major currencies are basically determined by supply and demand. What then, are the factors determining supply and demand? The underlying factors are primarily those transaction items listed in the balance of payments of the country.

Basically, debit items such as imports of goods and services, transfer payments, and capital outflows cause supply of the home currency and demand for foreign currencies. We should note that debit transactions cause supply of the home currency whether the payment is eventually made in a foreign currency or in the home currency. More specifically, if the payment is invoiced in a foreign currency, home residents would supply their home currency in order to obtain the foreign currency. If the payment is to be made in the home currency, obviously home residents would then directly supply their home currency. Similarly, credit items such as exports of goods and services, transfer receipts, and foreign capital inflows cause demand for the home currency and supply of foreign currencies, regardless of which currency is received.

Now let us derive supply and demand for a currency for international transactions. Let us illustrate a case involving two countries, America and Britain. For an illustrative purpose, we will use the supply and demand for British pounds, which will be the home currency for Britain but a foreign currency for America. Suppose that Britain imports wheat. The price of wheat, say $4 per bushel, is determined by the worldwide market supply and demand and it is given for Britain. Alternatively, we may consider that the supply of wheat to Britain is infinitely elastic so that wheat can be supplied at a constant price of $4 per bushel from America. The import price of wheat in pounds P_m is:

$$P_m = P_w/r = \$4/r \tag{7.1}$$

where P_w is the worldwide price in dollars and r is the exchange rate ($/£). The demand for wheat in Britain Q_m depends on the pound price of wheat, which in turn depends on the foreign exchange rate:

$$Q_m = Q_m(P_m) = Q_m(P_w/r). \tag{7.2}$$

The total expenditure for British imports is the total supply of pounds $S_£(r)$, which is

$$S_£(r) = \frac{P_w}{r} Q_m\left(\frac{P_w}{r}\right). \tag{7.3}$$

We note that when a currency supply curve is drawn, the amount of pounds supplied is shown on the horizontal axis and the price of a currency, given by the exchange rate, on the vertical axis. Unlike the case of the supply curve for a good, the quantity of a currency supplied is the total expenditure which depends on both the quantity of a good bought and the price at which it is bought, as shown in equation (7.3).

Now let us return to the case of the demand for pounds. Suppose this time that Britain exports cloth. The export price of cloth P_c is determined by the production cost in Britain which is a world leader in textiles and

Britain can supply cloth at that price, say £1.50 per yard, as much as demanded. The export price in dollars P_x is then

$$P_x = rP_c = r \times £1.50. \tag{7.4}$$

Since demand for cloth in America Q_x depends on the dollar price, it can be expressed as

$$Q_x = Q_x(rp_c). \tag{7.5}$$

Then, the demand for British pounds is

$$D_£(r) = \frac{P_x Q_x}{r} = \frac{rP_c Q_x(rP_c)}{r} = P_c Q_x(rP_c). \tag{7.6}$$

The equilibrium exchange rate can thus be found by solving for r where the excess demand for pounds is zero:

$$D_£(r) - S_£(r) = 0. \tag{7.7}$$

For illustration, suppose that Britain's demand for imports from America (7.2) and America's demand for imports from Britain (7.5) are both linear functions of the exchange rate, and parameters are given, for example, as below:

$$Q_m = a - b(P_w/r) = 120 - 22(P_w/r) \tag{7.8}$$

$$Q_x = c - d(rP_c) = 200 - 40(rP_c). \tag{7.9}$$

The equilibrium in the balance of payments of Britain requires

$$\frac{4}{r}\left(120 - 22\frac{4}{r}\right) - 1.5[200 - 40(r \times 1.5)] = 0 \tag{7.10}$$

from which we find that $r = \$1.517/£1$ and $S_£(r) = D_£(r) \approx £163.46$.

Stability of foreign exchange markets

Since the supply curve of a currency is a locus of points, each representing total payment at a given exchange rate, it may not always exhibit a smooth monotonic upward-sloping curve. Whether there is an increase or a decrease in total payment due to a decrease in the price of the imported good depends on the price elasticity of demand for the good imported. For example, if the percentage increase in the quantity of a good demanded is greater than the percentage decrease in the price of the good, the total expenditure will increase as the price decreases. In general, the price elasticity of demand is measured by the percentage change in quantity of a good demanded divided by the percentage change in the price of the good. If this ratio is greater than unity in absolute value, the demand is said to be elastic and the total expenditure will increase as the price drops. On the other hand, if this ratio is less than unity, the demand is said to be inelastic and the total expenditure will decrease as a result of the price fall. If the ratio is unity, the demand is said to be unitary elastic and the total expenditure will remain constant as the price changes.

Let us look at a more specific example in Table 7.1. If the exchange rate is to rise from $1.30 to $1.40 per pound, the import price for Britain will then decrease from £3.08 to £2.86. As a result, the quantity of a good imported will increase from 52.31 to 57.14. With these changes, the computed elasticity will be 1.29. Since the demand is price elastic, a greater payment for imports will result from a decrease in the price of the imported good.

As we can see from column (5) in Table 7.1, the total payment which is the supply of pounds increases until the exchange rate reaches $1.500/£1. Thereafter, the total payment decreases. This is shown by a backward-bending portion of the currency supply curve in Figure 7.1(a). We can also draw the same inference by looking at the elasticity coefficients in column (4). It is entirely possible that only the backward-bending portion is within the practical range of exchange rate movements. Then the supply curve will be a downward-sloping curve as shown in Figures 7.1(b) and 7.1(c).

Now let us briefly look at the demand curve for pounds, which can be derived from the value of exports from Britain, as we noted earlier. In terms of dollar payment for Britain's exports, a similar pattern as that discussed

Table 7.1 Supply and demand for a currency

	Supply of a currency (£)				Demand for a currency (£)			
$r(\$/\pounds)$ (1)	P_m (2)	Q_m (3)	$-\varepsilon_\mu$ (4)	P_mQ_m (5)	P_x (6)	Q_x (7)	$-\varepsilon_x$ (8)	$(1/r)P_xQ_x$ (9)
2.00	2.00	76.00	0.63	152.00	3.00	80	–	120.00
1.90	2.11	73.68	0.69	155.12	2.85	86	1.50	129.00
1.80	2.22	71.11	0.76	158.02	2.70	92	1.33	138.00
1.70	2.35	68.24	0.85	160.55	2.55	98	1.17	147.00
1.60	2.50	65.00	0.96	162.50	2.40	104	1.04	156.00
1.517	2.64	61.99	0.96	163.46	2.28	109	0.92	163.47
1.50	2.67	61.33	1.10	163.56	2.25	110	0.92	165.00
1.40	2.86	57.14	1.29	163.27	2.10	116	0.82	174.00
1.30	3.08	52.31	1.57	160.95	1.95	122	0.72	183.00
1.20	3.33	46.67	2.00	155.56	1.80	128	0.64	192.00
1.10	3.64	40.00	–	145.45	1.65	134	0.56	201.00

Notes: The following numerical parameters are used for the above computation: $P_m = 4/r$; $P_x = r \times 1.50$; $Q_m = 120 - 22P_m$; $Q_x = 200 - 40P_x$.
The price elasticity coefficient between two exchange rates is calculated by moving from a higher price to a lower one. For example, ε_m shown at $1.40/£1 is
→ $[(57.14 - 52.31)/52.31] / [(2.86 - 3.08)/3.08] = 1.29$.

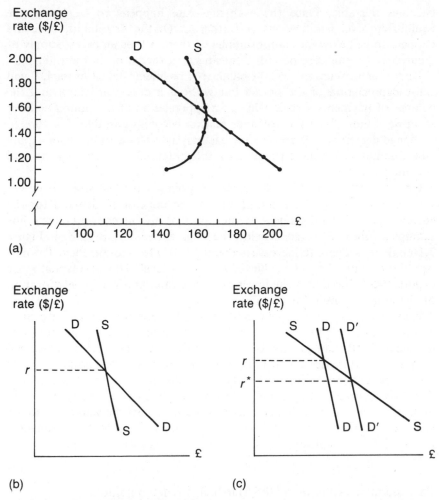

Figure 7.1 Supply and demand functions of a currency (£): (a) supply and demand for a currency (£); (b) stable market; (c) unstable market

above emerges. However, as can be seen from equation (7.6), the demand for pounds, which is the flip-side of the supply of dollars, depends solely on the quantity of the exported good, because the pound price of the exported good is constant.

What sort of implications can we draw when the supply and demand curves are both inelastic but one of them is less inelastic than the other? Suppose the demand curve is less inelastic than the supply curve, as shown in Figure 7.1(b). The exchange market will then still be stable. However, if the supply curve is less inelastic, as shown in Figure 7.1(c), the market becomes unstable. Once the exchange rate happens to be above the equilibrium level, it will be pushed further up. On the other hand, if the rate happens to be below the equilibrium level, there will be an excess supply of a currency (in this case pounds), causing a further drop in the rate.

Under such circumstances, the balance of payments deficit of the UK will cause depreciation of the pound but without a downward limit and the balance of payments surplus will cause appreciation of the pound without an upward limit. Thus the exchange market becomes unstable. For foreign exchange dealers it will become increasingly important to estimate supply and demand functions correctly, as the potential loss for dealers will become unlimited.

On the other hand, if it is desirable for policy makers to stop the downward spiral, this can be accomplished by an increase in demand for the currency (exports) or by a decrease in supply of the currency (imports). For example, if the market rate is below the original equilibrium rate r in Figure 7.1(c), there is a need to increase demand (D'D') for the currency. The new equilibrium rate r^* may be achieved at a lower level. This means that more exports will be needed at the lower exchange rate, implying a deterioration of the terms of trade for Britain.

Now, what is the precise condition needed for the foreign exchange market to be stable? Intuitively, if the pound depreciates, the import price in pounds for Britain goes up; this should discourage imports; the effect will be greater as the price elasticity ε_x of UK imports is greater. Similarly, the same pound depreciation will reduce the dollar price for US imports, thereby encouraging UK exports. The higher the price elasticity ε_m of US imports is, the more US import payment is. If at least the sum (in absolute value) of these two elasticities is greater than unity, the balance of payments for the UK will improve and the exchange market will be stable:

$$| -\varepsilon_x | + | -\varepsilon_m | > 1. \tag{7.11}$$

This condition is known as the Marshall–Lerner condition.[1]

Purchasing power parity theory

In the previous section we stated in simple terms that the foreign exchange rate is determined by supply and demand and that supply factors are the credit items in the balance of payments and demand factors are the debit items. Alternatively, we can classify these factors according to the predictability and immediacy of their impact on foreign exchange rate movements, namely as random factors, shocks (unexpected events), seasonal and cyclical factors, and long-term factors. Certain market participants such as daily exchange dealers may be more interested in random factors or shocks which would influence their daily profit more heavily, whereas seasonal exporters or importers may be more concerned about seasonal factors which would determine their receipts or payments in their currency. However, if they are repeat international market participants, they would be interested in the long-term factors in addition to their particularly relevant factors, since the long-term factors provide an overall frame of exchange rate movements. And that is a major concern of economic policy makers. Therefore we will focus our attention on the long-term factors.

One of the most enduring theories to explain exchange rate behavior is the purchasing power parity (PPP) theory, which focuses on the long-term relationship between the relative inflation rates of two given countries and the exchange rate of their currencies. It holds that currencies are valued for what they will buy and that the exchange rate between two currencies is determined by their internal purchasing powers as measured by the ratio of the general price levels in the two countries in question. Therefore, any changes in relative national price levels are expected to cause changes in the exchange rate.

In essence, the PPP theory is a theory of nominal exchange rate determination and its movements in long-run equilibrium under the assumptions that underlying real factors are constant and the trade balance is in equilibrium. Let us look at the case of two countries, say the United States (home country) and the UK (foreign country). The equilibrium exchange rate satisfies the following condition, which represents the fact that the trade account is in balance:

$$P_\$Q_x = P_£Q_m r \qquad (7.12)$$

where $P_\$$ is the home currency price of home country exportables, $P_£$ is the foreign currency price of imports from the foreign country, Q_x is the physical quantity of exports of the home country, Q_m is the physical quantity of imports from the foreign country, and $r(\$/£)$ is the exchange rate in terms of the number of home currency units per foreign currency unit. The equilibrium exchange rate is then

$$r = \frac{Q_x}{Q_m} \frac{P_\$}{P_£}. \qquad (7.13)$$

The first term Q_x/Q_m represents the real terms of trade, that is, the number of physical units of exports to be given up in exchange for a unit of imports. The ratio is determined by the underlying real factors such as factor endowment and production technology.

Expression (7.13) is known as the absolute PPP theory which states that the equilibrium exchange rate will be equal to the ratio of domestic to foreign price levels ($P_\$/P_£$), given the real factors expressed by Q_x/Q_m. The absolute PPP theory may be expanded to incorporate additional factors such as (1) transportation costs and (2) differences between the domestic general price level and the export price. The first may be incorporated by writing

$$P_\$(1 + t_\$)Q_x = P_£(1 + t_£)Q_m r \qquad (7.14)$$

where $t_\$$ represents the export transportation cost as a percentage of $P_\$$ and $t_£$ the import transportation cost as a percentage of $P_£$. Next, the second factor can be incorporated using the ratio α of the export price to the home country general price level and the ratio β of the foreign currency import price to the foreign country general price level . Then,

$$\alpha P_\$(1 + t_\$)Q_x = \beta P_£(1 + t_£)Q_m r. \qquad (7.15)$$

The equilibrium exchange rate will be

$$r = \frac{Q_x}{Q_m} \frac{1 + t_\$}{1 + t_£} \frac{\alpha}{\beta} \frac{P_\$}{P_£}. \qquad (7.16)$$

Equation (7.16) is known as the Bresciani-Turroni version of the PPP theory. Despite its comprehensiveness, the Bresciani-Turroni version is not significantly different from the absolute PPP theory represented by equation (7.13) as long as underlying real factors are reasonably stable.

Because of the weak empirical evidence supporting the absolute PPP theory, the relative PPP theory has been advanced. It states that the rate of change in the equilibrium exchange rate is determined by the difference between the rate of price changes in home and foreign countries. With a suitable choice of units of measurement, we can set $Q_x/Q_m = 1$. Then we can rewrite equation (7.13) as

$$r = P_\$/P_£ \qquad (7.17a)$$

or

$$P_\$ = P_£ r. \qquad (7.17b)$$

For the PPP as expressed in equation (7.17b) to continue to hold at the end of one period, it is necessary to have the following relationship:

$$P_\$(1 + p) = P_£(1 + p^*)r(1 + \hat{e}) \qquad (7.18)$$

where p, p^*, and $\hat{e}$ are the expected rates of change in the home price, the foreign price, and the exchange rate respectively. The rate of change compared with the previous period may be expressed as the ratio of (7.18) to (7.17b) so that we have

$$1 + p = (1 + p^*)(1 + \hat{e}) \qquad (7.19)$$

or

$$\hat{e} = \frac{p - p^*}{1 + p^*}. \qquad (7.20a)$$

As an approximation we have

$$\hat{e} = p - p^*. \tag{7.20b}$$

That is, the rate of change in the foreign exchange rate is the difference in the rates of inflation in the domestic and foreign economies. Note that if the exchange rate is expressed as a number of units of foreign currency per home currency, the rate of change in the exchange rate must be this difference, $p^* - p$, and not the difference shown in equation (7.20b).

Then, what is the major cause for the price level changes? According to a monetary approach, the cause can be found in the disequilibrium between the demand for and supply of money. When the nominal supply of money, M_s, is equal to the nominal demand for money, M_d, the money sector is said to be in equilibrium:

$$M_s = M_d. \tag{7.21}$$

In equilibrium, the real supply of money must also be equal to the real demand for money, since we are simply dividing both sides by the same price level:

$$\frac{M_s}{P} = \frac{M_d}{P}. \tag{7.22a}$$

When conditions in the money sector are other than equation (7.21) or (7.22a), the money sector is in disequilibrium, causing the price level to change.

The nominal money supply is determined by the central bank, whereas the real demand for money is determined by the economic units in the economy depending on the interest rate and real income. The real demand for money for liquidity preference purposes is affected by the opportunity cost of holding money, that is, the interest rate i, while the real demand for money for transactions purposes largely depends on real aggregate income Y. Then,

$$M_s/P = L(i, Y) \tag{7.22b}$$

where $L(i, Y) = M_d/P$. The real demand for money will increase as the interest rate falls or as real income increases. On the other hand, the real demand for money will fall as the interest rate rises or as real income falls. Now, let us look at the effect of a nominal money supply change on the price level. An increase in money supply will cause a rise in the price level. On the other hand, the real demand for money may also rise if the interest rate falls and real income increases as a result of the increase in money supply:

$$P = M_s/L(i, Y). \tag{7.23}$$

In order to see the effects of such changes on the foreign exchange rate, let us return to equation (7.13). Substituting each country's equation (7.23) for its respective price level, we have

$$r = \text{(scalar)} \, \frac{P_\$}{P_\pounds}$$

$$= \text{(scalar)} \, \frac{M_{s\$}/ L_\$(i_\$, Y_{US})}{M_{s\pounds}/ L_\pounds(i_\pounds, Y_{UK})}$$

$$= \text{(scalar)} \, \frac{M_{s\$}}{M_{s\pounds}} \frac{L_\pounds(i_\pounds, Y_{UK})}{L_\$(i_\$, Y_{US})}. \tag{7.24}$$

We can now easily see how each variable affects the exchange rate movement. A rise in $M_{s\$}$, $i_\$$, or Y_{UK} will cause a rise in the exchange rate. On the other hand, a rise in $M_{s\pounds}$, $i_\pounds$, or Y_{US} will cause a fall in the exchange rate.

FOREIGN EXCHANGE MARKET ARBITRAGE

An arbitrage is economic behavior which involves purchase of a good in one market and sale of the good in another for profit. Arbitrage brings about temporarily segmented markets into one single market, and thereby the law of one price prevails. In the foreign exchange markets, we frequently observe such arbitrage behavior. In order to have profitable arbitrage, there must be differences in the price of one currency in terms of another in different markets. Unexpected events such as central bank interventions, political shocks, or unexpected economic news cause a temporary shift in supply and demand conditions, creating momentary opportunities for profit until a new equilibrium point is reached.

Interest rate arbitrage

In Chapter 2, we studied interest rate arbitrage as a motivation for short-term international capital movement. Interest rate arbitrage takes advantage of interest rate differentials in different national markets by borrowing in a market where the cost of funds is cheaper and investing in a market where the rate of return is higher, after taking exchange rate movements into consideration. We noted that there were three possible cases:

1 If $(1/r_{00})(1 + i_f)r_{01} > 1 + i_d$, $\qquad\qquad$ (7.25a)

then invest abroad.

2 If $(1/r_{00})(1 + i_f)r_{01} < 1 + i_d,$ (7.25b)

then invest at home.
3 If $(1/r_{00})(1 + i_f)r_{01} = (1 + i_d),$ (7.25c)

it does not matter where investment takes place.

In the case of foreign investment, the process starts with conversion of the home currency into the foreign currency at the spot rate r_{00}, investment in foreign financial assets which yield at the interest rate i_f and finally conversion of the terminal value of investment back into the home currency at the future exchange rate r_{01}. This foreign investment opportunity is compared with the domestic investment opportunity which is yielding the rate of return i_d. The arbitrage involves choosing the higher return route as investment and the lower return route as borrowing. If an arrangement has been made through a forward contract to convert foreign currency back into the home currency at the end of the investment period, the arbitrage is said to be a covered arbitrage and the exchange rate r_{01} represents the forward rate. If no forward contract has been arranged as part of the arbitrage process, the arbitrage is said to be an uncovered arbitrage and the exchange rate at the end of the period is the spot rate prevailing then.

How does the interest rate arbitrage bring about integrated domestic and foreign money markets? In order to see the relationship between the interest rate differential between the home and foreign money markets and the exchange rate differential between the spot and forward markets, we use the annualized premium $(+)$ or discount $(-)$, as defined as below:

$$R = (r_{01} - r_{00})/r_{00}.$$ (7.26a)

We then rewrite the one-year forward rate r_{01} as

$$r_{01} = (1 + R)r_{00}.$$ (7.26b)

Substituting equation (7.26b) for r_{01} in equation (7.25c) and rearranging, we obtain the following equilibrium condition in the money markets and exchange markets simultaneously:

$$R + i_f R = -(i_f - i_d).$$ (7.27a)

If the second term on the left side $i_f R$ is relatively small, we may then discard this term and obtain the following as an approximation of the equilibrium condition:

$$R = -(i_f - i_d).$$ (7.27b)

Figure 7.2 illustrates the relationship between the discount (or premium) and the interest rate differential, using numerical examples. We call the line

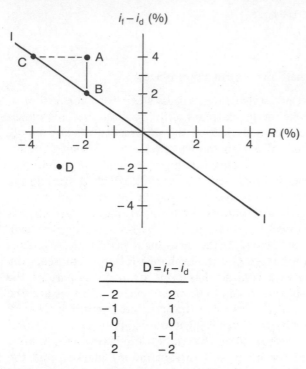

R	$D = i_f - i_d$
−2	2
−1	1
0	0
1	−1
2	−2

Figure 7.2 Interest rate parity diagram

II in Figure 7.2 the interest rate parity line, which is the locus of points each of which represents the equilibrium condition achieved jointly by the money markets and exchange markets. A diagram depicting the interest rate parity line is known as the interest parity diagram.

The market adjustment process

Suppose that the current market condition can be represented by point A in Figure 7.2, which means that the foreign interest rate is higher than the domestic interest rate by 4 percentage points but the value of the foreign investment assets will decrease by 2 percentage points one year later. Then the net gain from investing abroad is 2 percent. Therefore there will be a capital outflow. This capital outflow will cause the domestic interest rate to rise and the foreign interest rate to fall, causing the market condition to change from point A to point B.

At the same time, the investment in foreign financial assets will increase demand for foreign currency, causing the spot rate to rise, and the anticipated sale of foreign assets later will cause the forward rate to fall, causing point A to move toward point C. Once the market conditions reach point B or point C, there will be no force to make further movements. In effect, any point between C and B inclusive is a possible new equilibrium point. Exactly where the equilibrium point is going to settle depends primarily on the relative size of the money markets and exchange markets. Since the money market size is relatively larger, there is a tendency for the markets to settle near point C. Suppose now that the market conditions are represented by point D. Obviously, investment in the domestic market is more attractive, resulting in a capital inflow.

What happens when the market conditions can be represented by a point near the parity line but not on the line? If the transaction cost is positive, a minor deviation (about one-eighth of 1 percent) from the interest parity line may not cause capital movements. In such instances, we may consider the interest parity line as a band whose width represents the transaction costs.

Variants of the interest rate parity diagram

One variant of interest rate parity is the international Fisher condition which states that the expected interest rate differential between the domestic and foreign markets is determined by the difference between the expected rates of domestic inflation and foreign inflation. This is an extension of the Fisher effect which states that the nominal interest rate is approximately the sum of the real interest rate and the expected rate of inflation. This can be shown as follows:

$$1 + i_d = (1 + \tau)(1 + p) \tag{7.28a}$$
$$= 1 + \tau + p + \tau p$$

$$i_d \approx \tau + p \tag{7.28b}$$

where τ is the real interest rate and p is the expected rate of inflation.

Similarly, we find the foreign interest rate as the sum of the real interest rate and the expected rate of inflation p^* in the foreign country:

$$i_f \approx \tau + p^*. \tag{7.28c}$$

We then have the expected interest rate differential as the difference between the expected rates of inflation in the foreign and home economies, assuming that the real rates in the two economies are the same:

$$i_f - i_d = p^* - p \tag{7.29a}$$

which we may use to relabel the vertical axis.

Equation (7.29a) is known as the international Fisher effect or Fisher-open effect, which can be rewritten as

$$i_d = i_f + (p - p^*). \tag{7.29b}$$

That is, the expected domestic nominal interest rate is equal to the expected foreign nominal interest rate plus the difference in the expected rates of inflation between the domestic and foreign economies.

The second variant of interest rate parity is the relative PPP *ex ante*:

$$R = (r_{11} - r_{00})/r_{00} = \hat{e} = p - p^{*}. \tag{7.30}$$

In this case we label the horizontal axis by the expected discount or premium, which is computed by using a future expected rate in place of a forward rate. Obviously, if the forward rate is the unbiased expected future rate, then the numerical result will be the same between the relative PPP rate and the forward discount or premium.

Spatial arbitrage

Spatial arbitrage takes advantage of differences in exchange rates in different markets by buying foreign currency in a cheaper market and selling it in a dearer market simultaneously. In effect we may consider this as a special case of interest rate arbitrage where the duration of holding foreign exchange is so short that the interest rate terms are zero. Then, from equations (7.25a), (7.25b), and (7.25c) we have the following three possible conditions:

$$(r_{0j}/r_{00})(1 + 0) - (1 + 0) \lessgtr 0 \tag{7.31}$$

where r_{00} is the buying price and r_{0j} is the selling price. The ratio of r_{0j}/r_{00} must be greater than unity for the spatial arbitrage to be profitable. If only two currencies are involved in spatial arbitrage, we call it a bilateral arbitrage.

However, if more than two currencies are involved, the outcome is not obvious. Suppose the foreign exchange rates are as follows: New York, $\$/\pounds = 1.4252$, $DM/\$ = 1.6016$; London, $\$/\pounds = 1.4259$, $DM/\pounds = 2.2804$; Frankfurt, $DM/\$ = 1.6004$, $DM/\pounds = 2.2824$. Then how should we proceed? With three currencies, there are six alternative ways to proceed in arbitrage. An arbitrageur may start with any currency and follow the direction either clockwise or counterclockwise. If the arbitrageur carries out a $1 million arbitrage in one direction (clockwise, say), she might first purchase pounds in London, deutsche marks in Frankfurt, and finally dollars in Frankfurt, making a profit of $662:

$$\$1,000,000(\pounds1/\$1.4252)(DM2.2824/\pounds1)(\$1/DM1.6004) = \$1,000,662$$

On the other hand, if the arbitrageur operates in the opposite direction (counterclockwise), she will make $1,457:

$$\$1,000,000(DM1.6016/\$1)(\pounds1/DM2.2804)(DM1.4259/\pounds1) = \$1,001,457.$$

As long as the bid and offer rates are the same, it does not make any difference which currency one begins with. The rate of return for the clockwise movement will be 0.000 662 and for the counterclockwise movement 0.001 457. Therefore the counterclockwise process should be chosen.

Term arbitrage

A term arbitrage is an arbitrage which takes advantage of inconsistency in the term structure of exchange rates along with the term structure of interest rates. Figure 7.3 shows the case of a two-period investment horizon. Alternatively we may consider that this is the case where our basic interest rate arbitrage module is expanded into two modules.

We want to measure the profitability at point C. To reach point C which represents the terminal value in denomination of the home currency ($) at the end of period 2, there are four possible alternative routes.

1 Invest at home for the entire two periods:

$$(1 + i_{d1})(1 + i_{d2}).$$ (7.32a)

2 Invest at home in period 1 and invest abroad in period 2:

$$(1 + i_{d1})(1/r_{01})(1 + i_{f2})r_{02}.$$ (7.32b)

3 Invest abroad in period 1 and invest at home in period 2:

$$(1/r_{00})(1 + i_{f1})r_{01}(1 + i_{d2}).$$ (7.32c)

4 Invest abroad for the entire two periods:

$$(1/r_{00})(1 + i_{f1})(1 + i_{f2})r_{02}.$$ (7.32d)

If there is at least one distinctive alternative which gives a higher return than the others, the arbitrage process will continue until the term structure of interest rates and the exchange rate structures become consistent so that no route is better than the others.

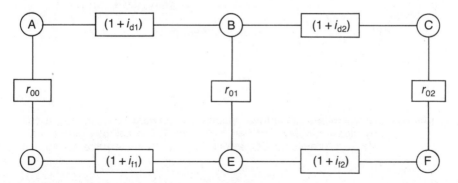

Figure 7.3 A two-period term arbitrage mechanism

Arbitrage between currency options and currency futures

Although currency options and forward contracts are distinctive financial instruments, a suitable combination of call and put options mimics a forward (or futures) contract. Thus, if there is any difference between the cost of combined options and the forward price, arbitrage will take place between options and forward (futures) markets.

Suppose that a bank is planning to sell pounds forward and it is looking for a hedging tool. The bank needs to buy pounds forward or its alternative. As we noted from Figures 6.4(a) and 6.4(b), if the bank buys a call and sells a put at the same exercise price simultaneously, this combination of two options will have the same effect on the contractual right and obligation as a forward purchase contract. If the market price is higher than the exercise price, the bank will exercise its option because of positive profit. If the market price is below the exercise price, the bank will be forced to buy the foreign exchange from the put buyer. In either case, the bank must purchase the foreign exchange at the exercise price. This is exactly what happens in the case of the forward purchase contract. The bank must buy the foreign exchange whether the market price is higher or lower than the forward rate.

In Figure 7.4, curve AA represents the combination of a call buy and a put sale without costs; curve BB represents the same combination with costs; curve CC represents a forward purchase. For example, the strike price S is \$1.40; π_{cb}, the premium paid for a call buy, is \$0.04; π_{ps}, the premium received for a put sale, is \$0.02; the borrowing interest rate i

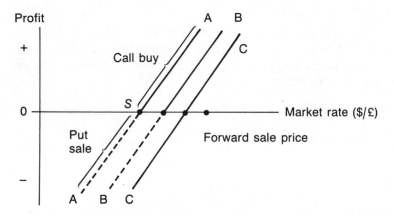

Figure 7.4 Equivalence of combined options and forward contract: AA, a call buy plus a put sale (without premium); BB, a call buy plus a put sale (with premium); CC, a forward buy; S, strike price

is 10 percent; and the maturity n is 90 days. The total cost of using a combination of options in lieu of a forward purchase is

$$
\begin{aligned}
\text{cost} &= S + (\pi_{cb} - \pi_{ps})[1 + i(90/360)] \\
&= \$1.40 + (\$0.04 - \$0.02)[1 + 0.10(90/360)] \\
&= \$1.4205.
\end{aligned} \tag{7.33}
$$

Therefore, if the forward purchase rate is higher than the above cost of combined options, the bank may simply substitute the options for the available forward. Such activities would continue until the options costs and the forward rate become the same. At the same time, if the forward sale price is higher than the options costs, the bank may profit simply by purchasing the foreign currency to be delivered in the future through the combination of a call buy and a put sale and selling the forward.

Furthermore, from equation (7.33), we may generalize the equilibrium condition between options and forward contracts as

$$
r_{0n} = S + (\pi_{cb} - \pi_{ps})[1 + i(n/360)] . \tag{7.34a}
$$

Therefore,

$$
\pi_{cb} - \pi_{ps} = \frac{r_{0n} - S}{1 + i(n/360)} \tag{7.34b}
$$

which is known as the put–call parity equation.[2]

Now, let us take a look at more practical aspects of foreign exchange dealings by banks.

FOREIGN EXCHANGE DEALING MECHANICS FOR BANKS

In general, the main objective of a bank in foreign exchange dealings is to maximize profit, given risks. There are several sources of risks in exchange dealings. Perhaps the most common type of risk is the foreign exchange rate risk, which is a possible loss due to foreign exchange rate fluctuations. This risk can be minimized by exchange position limits and hedging. The second type of risk is the liquidity risk, a possible loss due to the bank's inability to meet short-term payment obligations. This can be minimized by a borrowing arrangement. The third type of risk is credit risk which is a possible loss due to performance default of counterpart dealers. This may be minimized by credit analysis and trading limits. In this section, we will confine our attention to the minimization of two types of risk, exchange rate risk and liquidity risk.

Foreign exchange positions

Let us first look at the definition of exchange positions and then examine the method of establishing exchange position limits.

Definition of exchange positions

Suppose that the following T-account shows the commitments of a bank to buy and sell foreign exchange at different maturities:

	Inflows (+)		Pounds	Outflows (−)	
Period 0	P_{00}	£20 million		S_{00}	£20 million
1	P_{01}	25		S_{01}	15
3	P_{03}	30		S_{03}	5
	$\Sigma P_{0i} =$	£75 million		$\Sigma S_{0j} =$	£40 million

P_{0i} is the amount of purchase and S_{0j} the amount of sale, both contracted at time 0 and to be settled at times i and j respectively. We may then define the bank's foreign exchange positions as follows.

1 The bank is said to have no net position if

$$\Sigma P_{0i} = \Sigma S_{0j}$$

which may be divided into two subcategories:
(a) a square position which is the position where $P_{0i} = S_{0i}$ for every maturity i, and
(b) a gap position which is the one where $P_{0i} \neq S_{0i}$ for at least two maturities.
2 The bank is said to have a net position or to have an exposure if

$$\Sigma P_{0i} \neq \Sigma S_{0j}$$

which again may be subdivided into two subcategories:
(a) a long (or overbought) position if $\Sigma P_{0i} > \Sigma S_{0j}$, and
(b) a short (or oversold) position if $\Sigma P_{0i} \neq \Sigma S_{0j}$.

The numerical example in the above T-account shows that this bank has a long position. Such an open position may have been created as a result of a deliberate effort of the bank on the basis of its expectation that the exchange rate ($/£) would move upward. In this case the bank is said to have an outright speculative position. Or the bank may have created such a position simply by responding to the needs of customers. Then, the bank is said to have a passive speculative position.

Position limits

In either case, US banks are required by bank regulations to establish their own guidelines on foreign exchange operations, which must include exchange position limits consistent with sound and prudent banking practices. Dependence on the position limits as a key regulatory tool results from recognition of the difficulty and administrative costs associated with using alternative regulatory tools, such as restricting specific uses of forward contracts or imposing on banks the costs of regulating forward and futures contracts. How should a bank determine its position limits as the core of its own guidelines?

Suppose we can assume that the relationship between bank income and capital is fairly stable, say 15 percent per year in terms of the rate of return on bank equity. Then it would be reasonable to establish position limits with reference to the size of capital in order to hold down potential losses so that the bank capital would not be impaired excessively. Commercial banks can set several alternative limits:

1 With a total position limit the sum of the long and short positions is limited to a designated proportion of bank capital K:

$$\Sigma P_{ij} + \Sigma S_{ij} \leqslant aK. \tag{7.35a}$$

2 With a gross position limit the greater of the bank's long or short position is limited to a designated proportion of bank capital:

$$\max(\Sigma P_{ij}, \Sigma S_{ij}) \leqslant bK. \tag{7.35b}$$

3 With a net position limit the difference between the bank's aggregate long and short positions must not exceed a designated proportion of capital:

$$|\Sigma P_{ij} - \Sigma S_{ij}| \leqslant cK. \tag{7.35c}$$

4 With a gap position limit the difference between the bank's long and short positions for each maturity must not exceed a certain proportion of capital:

$$|P_j - S_j| \leqslant c_j K. \tag{7.35d}$$

For the first three cases, it is easy to see that the following relationship holds: $a > b > c$. In the case of the gap position, as the maturity becomes longer, the position limit becomes more restrictive so that $c_1 > c_2 > \cdots > c_n$.

Setting a position limit is essentially a trade-off between (a) restrictive limits that would reasonably assure that potential losses would be confined to within the acceptable range and (b) higher ceilings that would allow banks to enjoy greater trading flexibility but with greater risk. Now let us see how a position limit can be established. Since the rate of return on equity ϕ is the ratio of earnings after tax (EAT) to capital K, we can express EAT with reference to capital as $\text{EAT} = \phi K$. The permissible loss from exchange dealings is a management decision variable, which can be set as a certain percentage, say α of EAT. Then,

permissible loss $= \alpha \text{EAT} = \alpha \phi K$.

Meanwhile, the range of daily rate fluctuations in terms of the standard deviation σ can be measured from the daily experience data. On the basis of the estimated σ, the bank can set a certain confidence interval as a management decision, say a one-tail 95 percent interval in the case of a net position limit. With this, the bank would not face, for more than 5 percent of the time, exchange losses that exceeded the amount $\alpha \phi K$ from either a rise or a fall in the exchange rate. The daily net position limit X can then be established from the following relationship:

$$1.645\sigma X \leqslant \alpha \phi K. \tag{7.36a}$$

Thus,

$$X \leqslant (1/1.645\sigma)\alpha \phi K. \tag{7.36b}$$

For example, a bank has \$500 million capital, its rate of return on capital is 15 percent and it faces a standard deviation of exchange rate fluctuations to 2 percent around the average rate. The bank management wishes to keep potential loss from exchange loss limited to 10 percent of earnings with a one-tail 95 percent confidence interval. Then the net exposure should be limited to \$228 million, which is about 45.6 percent of capital. Obviously, if a bank puts more emphasis on foreign exchange trading business, it may reduce its confidence interval and increase the loss limit, thereby raising position limits.

Alternative solutions in exchange dealings

Suppose that a bank is selling three-month £1 million forward in response to a customer's demand. The bank immediately faces exchange rate risk and possibly liquidity risk. In order to remove these risks, the bank may use (a) a forward market solution, (b) a money market solution, or (c) a swap solution. A solution is meant to maximize profit while removing risks. Assume that this bank is a market-maker facing the following market conditions:

spot, \$1.5000/1.5005 per pound
3-month forward, 1.4800/1.4860   3-month swap rate, 205/140
US interest rate, 10.0%/11.0%   UK rate, 12.2%/12.8%.

Forward market solution

The simplest approach is to use the forward market. As shown in Figure 7.5(a), this involves (1) a forward sale of £1 million, which will yield dollar proceeds in the amount of \$1,486,000, represented by (1′). However, this forward sale will immediately create exchange rate risk. In order to offset this risk, the bank may purchase forward exchange in the amount of £1 million

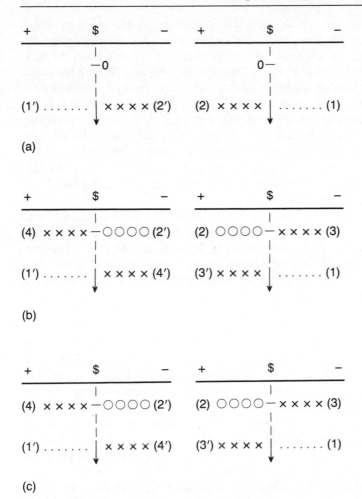

Figure 7.5 Foreign exchange dealing mechanics: (a) forward market solution;
(b) money market solution; (c) swap market solution. The center
line of each T-account represents the time vintage running from
the present time at the upper level to the future at lower level(s)

represented by (2), and it pays dollars in the amount of $1,480,000, as shown
by (2′). The difference between (1′) and (2′), $6,000, is the profit. This
forward solution is equivalent to a spatial arbitrage which involves buying
forward exchange in the wholesale market and selling it in the retail market.

Money market solution

This is the case in which the money markets for both currencies are used by borrowing one currency in one market and lending the other currency in the other market. By doing so, both exchange rate and liquidity risks are removed. Instead of national money markets, often the Eurocurrency markets are tapped for this purpose. Transactions (1) and (1') are the same as in the forward market solution. In order to hedge the short position, this time the bank buys spot exchange which is in turn to be loaned out. How much forward exchange the bank should purchase depends on the lending rate. Since the bank must have £1 million three months later, the amount that the bank must purchase now is the present value of £1 million, which will be £968,992. This is represented by transaction (2). Equal to (2), transaction (3) represents the amount of lending, which three months later becomes £1 million, as shown by (3').

On the other hand, when we look at the dollar transactions, the amount of dollars to be spent to purchase £968,992 is $1,453,488, represented by (2'), which the bank needs to borrow (4). The amount $1,489,825 shown by (4') is the principal and interest to be paid three months later. This solution results in a loss of $3,825. This is the result of an inadequate pricing of the forward contract.

Swap solution

The use of the swap market starts with a forward sale of £1 million (1) and spot purchase of £1 million (2). As we studied in Chapter 6, such a combination is termed an engineered swap in which the counterpart dealer of each transaction is different. For a swap solution, the bank sells the spot-purchased £1 million (3) with a promise of repurchase (3'). Meanwhile, on the dollar account, the engineered swap ((1') + (2')) results in a loss of $14,000 and the swap transaction ((4) + (4')) in a gain of $20,500. Thus the swap solution gives a net gain of $6,500.

In summary, the simplest solution is a forward solution and the next a swap solution. A market solution becomes attractive when the maturity becomes longer and the amount larger.

FOREIGN EXCHANGE SERVICES FOR CUSTOMERS

For exporters

If an American exporter sells goods abroad and receives a credit in foreign currency in the form of a check or draft denominated in a foreign currency, she can arrange with a foreign exchange dealer bank to sell this claim at the quoted rate for exchange of the home currency or some other currency. If the exporter has received the foreign currency in the form of a bank balance at a bank abroad, the exporter again can sell this claim to the bank which in turn will credit the dollar amount in the exporter's account for her disposal.

If the exporter knows that she is to receive a certain amount of foreign currency at a fixed future date, she may contract to sell the foreign exchange for future delivery at a predetermined rate, which is forward exchange. The rate at which she is willing to sell may depend on her expectations on the future rate. If she believes there is a possibility that the dollar value of the foreign currency will depreciate below the currently available forward rate, she is likely to sell her foreign exchange forward.[3] In the event that the dollar value does depreciate, the exporter benefits from the fixed rate which was established by a forward contract. If the dollar value does not change, the exporter at least benefits from the removal of uncertainty. Obviously, if the rate goes up, the exporter cannot take advantage of a higher rate. If the exporter is overtly concerned about this type of advantage, she may purchase a currency put option instead of a forward sale.

For importers

An American importer will receive invoices in foreign currency billed to him by his overseas suppliers. The importer usually pays in US dollars to the bank, the dollar amount being determined by the spot rate. The bank then makes payment on behalf of the importer to the foreign exporters through their banks abroad. If the payment is instead to be made in the future, the importer may purchase foreign exchange forward so that the amount of foreign currency payment can be fixed in advance. However, if the importer wants to hedge against the rising exchange rate and at the same time to take advantage of foreign currency depreciation, he may purchase currency call options.

For international investors

Many corporations are engaged in overseas operations requiring investments. These may be projects, branches, or subsidiaries, all of which may require transfer of working capital abroad and the subsequent repatriation of profit. As a result, banks can provide a wide variety of foreign exchange services. Banks provide not only trade and investment financing in foreign currencies, but also currency swaps and multicurrency loans. A currency swap provides a convenient tool for an investor who wants to enter a foreign market for short-term investment and needs the assurance that his investment can be converted back to home currency at a predetermined rate.

Foreign exchange risk management service

Within foreign exchange services, foreign exchange risk management has become an important function of large commercial banks. It typically starts with the identification and measurement of foreign exchange risks: transaction exposure risk, accounting risk (also known as translation risk), and economic risk.

The degree to which the value of future cash transactions is affected by exchange rate fluctuations is termed the transaction exposure risk. The value of cash inflows in various currencies will be affected by the respective exchange rates by which these foreign currency values are converted into the home currency value or some other designated currency value. Similarly, the value of a firm's cash outflows depends on their respective exchange rates. Once the degree of risk is identified and measured, then cost–benefit analysis is needed to determine whether or not to hedge and which tool to use in the case of hedging.

On the other hand, the translation risk is the degree of variation in the value of the multinational corporation's consolidated financial statements which depends on foreign exchange rate fluctuations. In measuring the translation risk, one first needs to determine which currency to use as the unit of account for financial statements of foreign operations. The currency used to denominate the financial statements is called the functional currency. The choice of such a currency depends on the extent of relevance of the economic environment represented by the currency without excessive distortion caused by other factors such as a high rate of inflation.

The next step is the translation of these financial statements into the home currency value or some other designated currency value for consolidation of the financial statements or for comparison of performance. One needs to adopt certain accounting principles by which accounting items are classified so that certain items are translated by the current exchange rate and the remaining items by the historical rates. Therefore changes in exchange rates between the functional currency and the home currency (or some other designated currency) cause the translation risk.[4] A loss or gain caused by the translation is a paper loss or gain. However, if one attempts to reduce such paper loss or gain and uses hedging tools, there will be real costs.

The economic exposure risk is a broader measure. It is the degree to which the present value of entire future cash flows can be influenced by rate fluctuations. We can find an analogy for this problem at a macroeconomic level. It is the measure of the possible effect of depreciation or appreciation of foreign exchange on the entire balance of payments. Likewise, possible changes in the present value of entire cash flows for individual firms depend on a host of factors such as changes in export sales, local sales, the import content of input for production, asset valuation, and overall competitiveness, all of which are affected by exchange rate movements.

As pointed out earlier, the final step in foreign exchange risk management is the employment of appropriate tools to reduce risks, known as hedging tools. They include foreign exchange forward contracts, currency futures, currency options, and currency swaps. Banks employ these tools, not only for customers, but to hedge their own positions and transactions.

SUMMARY

The major factors determining the foreign exchange rate in the short-run and long-run are separated. In the short-run, the exchange rate is determined simply by supply and demand for foreign exchange. However, the supply curve of foreign exchange which is based on exports may not necessarily be a usual upward sloping curve. Instead it may turn out to be a backward bending curve, suggesting the potential instability in the exchange rate determination. For the long-run exchange rate determination, the purchasing power parity (PPP) theory may be used. The theory asserts that under the balance of payments equilibrium, the exchange rate is determined by the relative purchasing powers of two countries. A monetary approach is a natural extension of the PPP, arguing that the relative price levels are in turn determined by the relative changes in the money supply in the two countries or relative changes between the nominal supply and the real demand for money.

Once expected exchange rates are given along with interest rates in the markets, dealers can then determine whether or not arbitrage opportunities exist. Such opportunities are not confined to traditional interest rate, spatial, and term arbitrage, but also arbitrage between currency options and futures. This chapter also examined foreign exchange dealing mechanisms for banks, which purport both maximization of return and minimization of risks. The part of minimization of risks involves establishment of foreign exchange exposure position limits. How banks provide foreign exchange services for their customers is also mentioned.

REVIEW PROBLEMS AND EXERCISES

1. Discuss the case in which depreciation of the home currency may not improve the balance of payments deficit.

2. What assumptions are needed for the Marshall–Lerner condition to hold?

3. Differentiate between the absolute PPP theory and the relative PPP theory.

4. What sort of modifications are incorporated in the Bresciani-Turroni version of the PPP theory?

5. Why can you say that spatial arbitrage is a special case of interest rate arbitrage?

6. Show the equivalence between a forward buy and a combination of a call buy and a put sale. What about a forward sale and a combination of a put buy and a call sale?

7. Explain the following:
   (a) transaction exposure
   (b) translation exposure
   (c) economic exposure

8. (a) Draw the interest parity diagram.
   (b) Differentiate the interest parity line from the international Fisher's line and from the purchasing power parity line.

9. Suppose the current market conditions are characterized by the following:

   $$I_f - i_d = 3\% \qquad R = -2\%.$$

   (a) In which direction will capital flow?
   (b) How will the market equilibrium be restored?

10. Explain how a foreign exchange position limit can be established in relation to a bank's capital.

11. Suppose that America is importing goods (Q_m) from and exporting goods (Q_x) to Britain with the following functional relationships:

   $$Q_m = 120 - 18P_\$$$
   $$Q_x = 150 - 30P_\pounds$$
   $$P_\$ = \pounds 3 \times r \qquad P_\pounds = \$4/r$$

   where the exchange rate r is expressed in a price quotation method.
   (a) Find the equilibrium exchange rate which maintains the balance of payments in equilibrium.
   (b) Fill in the blanks in the following table.

Exchange rate	Price of imports ($)	Q_m	Elasticity	Supply of dollars
$1.80	_____	____	_____	_____
$1.60	_____	____	_____	_____
$1.40	_____	____	_____	_____
$1.20	_____	____		_____

   (c) Is the change in the total expenditure in dollars due to the change in the exchange rate from $1.40 to $1.60 consistent with the value of the elasticity?

12. The following information is given:

    Spot   SFr2.24/$1
    One-year forward   SFr1.900/$1
    US interest rate   10%
    Switzerland rate   3.7%

    (a) In which direction will international money flow?
    (b) If the Swiss central bank wishes to stop the international money
         flow (into or from Switzerland), at what level should it set the
         domestic interest rate?

13. The following information is given:

    New York $1.1180/£1   FFr8.1647/$1
    London $1.1178/£1   FFr9.3963/£1
    Paris   FFr8.1125/$1 FFr9.3890/£1

    (a) What are six possible alternative routes for arbitrage?
    (b) Find the best solution.

14. The following market information is given:

    spot rate, $1.2000/£1
    1-year note rate in the United States, 11.00%; in the UK, 13.00%
    2-year note rate in the United States, 10.00%; in the UK, 12.50%

    (a) Find the one-year equilibrium forward rate.
    (b) Find the two-year equilibrium forward rate.
    (c) If your expected one-year exchange rate is $1.2500/£1, will you
         buy or sell the one-year forward? Assume you are risk neutral.
    (d) If your expected two-year rate is $1.1800/£1, will you buy or sell
         the two-year forward?
    (e) Now the investor's time horizon is two years. The investor wishes
         to maximize the return in two years. Find the best route.

15. Suppose XYZ bank has created a short forward position by selling a
    six-month £1 million forward. Assume this bank is a market-maker with
    the following market conditions:

    spot rate $1.100/1.1050
    6-month forward   1.0700/1.0770
    US interest rate   10.0%/10.5%
    UK interest rate   13.0%/13.3%
    swap rates   40/30

    Evaluate the following possible solutions:
    (a) forward market solution
    (b) money market solution
    (c) swap solution.

NOTES

1 For the derivation of the result in (7.11), let us start with the balance of payments equilibrium condition where the excess demand for pounds is zero:

$$B(r) = D_£(r) - S_£(r) = 0$$

where $B(r)$ is the balance of payments. Differentiating $D_£(r)$ in (7.6) with respect to r, we obtain

$$\frac{dD_£(r)}{dr} = P_c \frac{dQ_x}{d(rP_c)} P_c$$

$$= \frac{P_cQ_x}{r} \left[\frac{rP_c}{Q_x} \frac{dQ_x}{d(rP_c)}\right]$$

$$= (D_£(r)/r)(\varepsilon_x).$$

Likewise, differentiating $S_£(r)$ in (7.3) with respect to r, we obtain

$$\frac{dS_£(r)}{dr} = \frac{P_w}{r} \frac{dQ_m}{d(P_w/r)} \frac{(-P_w)}{r^2} + \frac{Q_m(-P_w)}{r^2}$$

$$= \frac{-1}{r} \frac{P_wQ_m}{r} \left[\frac{P_w/r}{Q_m} \frac{dQ_m}{d(P_w/r)} + 1\right]$$

$$= -(S_£(r)/r)(\varepsilon_m + 1).$$

Thus the following condition must hold so that depreciation of pounds will improve the balance of payments of Britain. Note that in equilibrium $D_£ = S_£$ and that an increase in r means appreciation of pounds as r is expressed in number of dollar units per pound.

$$\frac{dB(r)}{dr} = \frac{dD_£}{dr} - \frac{dS_£}{dr} = \frac{S_£(r)}{r(\varepsilon_x + \varepsilon_m + 1)} < 0.$$

Therefore,

$$|-\varepsilon_x| + |-\varepsilon_m| > 1.$$

2 In the case of a forward sale, the equilibrium condition will be

$$r_{0n}^* = S - (\pi_{pb} - \pi_{cs})(1 + in/360)$$

where r_{0n}^* is the forward offer rate, π_{pb} is the put buy premium paid, and π_{cs} is the call sale premium received. Therefore we shall have the following put–call parity equation similar to equation (7.30b):

$$\pi_{cs} - \pi_{pb} = \frac{r_{0n}^* - S}{1 + in/360}.$$

3 In a strict analysis, we may rephrase the preceding statement as follows: If the exporter's expected utility due to possible depreciation of the foreign currency is lower than the utility derived from the fixed rate through a forward contract, then the exporter will contract to sell forward exchange.

4 The accounting principle currently used to classify accounting items is the current rate method. See Financial Accounting Standards Board (1981) for general guidelines for the preparation of financial statements of US multinationals' foreign

operations in a functional currency, translation of the statements in the reporting currency, and consolidation of the statements.

BASIC READING

Bresciani-Turroni, C. (1934) "The Purchasing Power Parity Doctrine," *L'Egypte Contemporaine*, 25 May: 433–64. Reprinted in his *Saggi di Economia*, Milan: Giuffre, 1961.

Chrystal, K. A. (1984) "Guide to Foreign Exchange Markets," *Federal Reserve Bank of St. Louis Review*, March: 5–18.

Clinton, K. (1988) "Transaction Costs and Covered Interest Arbitrage: Theory and Evidence," *Journal of Political Economy*, 96 (2): 356–70.

Dornbusch, R. (1987) "Purchasing Power Parity," in *The New Palgrave: A Dictionary of Economics*, New York: Stockton Press, vol. 3, pp. 1075–85.

Fieleke, N. S. (1985) "The Rise of Foreign Currency Futures Market," *New England Economic Review*, March–April 38–47.

Financial Accounting Standards Board (1981) *Statement of Financial Accounting Standards No. 52: Foreign Currency Translation*, Stamford, Conn.: FASB, December.

Humphrey, T. M. (1979) "The Purchasing Power Parity Doctrine," *Federal Reserve Bank of Richmond Economic Review*, May–June: 3–13.

Krueger, A. O. (1983) *Exchange-Rate Determination*, Cambridge: Cambridge University Press.

Revey, P. A. (1981) "Evolution and Growth of the United States Foreign Exchange Market," *Federal Reserve Bank of New York Quarterly Review*, Autumn: 32–44.

Riehl, H. and Rodriguez, R. M. (1983) *Foreign Exchange and Money Markets*, New York: McGraw-Hill.

Stockman, A. C. (1987) "The Equilibrium Approach to Exchange Rates," *Federal Reserve Bank of Richmond Economic Review*, March–April: 12–30.

Wolkowitz, B., Lloyd-Davies, P. Gendreau, B. C., Hanweck, G. A. and Golgberg, M. A. (1982) *Below the Bottom Line*, Staff Studies No. 113, Washington, D.C.: Board of Governors of the Federal Reserve System.

FURTHER READING

Callier, P. (1981) "One-Way Arbitrage and Its Implications for the Foreign Exchange Markets," *Journal of Political Economy*, December: 1177–86.

Frenkel, J. A. and Johnson, H. G. (eds) (1978) *The Economics of Exchange Rates*, Reading, Mass.: Addison-Wesley.

Frenkel, J. A. and Levich, R. M. (1975) "Covered Interest Arbitrage: Unexploited Profit?" *Journal of Political Economy*, 73 (2): 325–37.

Gilbert, R. A. (1992) "Implications of Netting Arrangements for Bank Risk in Foreign Exchange Transactions," *Federal Reserve Bank of St. Louis Review*, January–February: 3–16.

Grubel, H. G. (1966) *Forward Exchange, Speculation, and the International Flow of Capital*, Stanford, Calif.: Stanford University Press.

Hudson, N. R. L. (1979) *Money and Exchange Dealing in International Banking*, New York: Wiley.

International Monetary Market (1979) *Understanding Futures in Foreign Exchange*, Chicago, Ill.: IMM.

Jacque, L. L. (1978) *Management of Foreign Exchange Risk*, Lexington, Mass.: D.C. Heath.

Officer, L. (1976) "The Purchasing-Power-Parity Theory of Exchange Rates: A Review Article," *IMF Staff Papers*, 23 (1): 1–60.

Thornton, D. L. (1989) "Tests of Interest Rate Parity," *Federal Reserve Bank of St. Louis Review*, July–August: 55–66.

Chapter 8

Eurocurrency markets

THE DEFINITION AND STRUCTURE OF THE MARKET

In this chapter we start with the definition of the Eurodollar market and more generally the Eurocurrency market. The definition will become clearer when we visualize the Eurodollar market consisting of three submarkets. We then study two main alternative approaches to explaining the growth of the Eurocurrency market, namely the balance of payments approach and the regulatory difference approach. Next, we examine the type of instruments traded in this market. We then discuss characteristics of international banking centers where the Eurocurrency market flourishes. We include US international banking facilities (IBFs) in our study, as they artificially mimic bookkeeping functions of banks in the Eurocurrency market. Finally, we examine the question of whether the Eurocurrency market is inflationary or not. This question brings us back to reexamine the fundamental nature of the workings of the Eurocurrency market.

The definition of the Eurodollar and Eurocurrency markets

The Eurocurrency market is made by banks which accept deposits and extend credit in currencies other than the currency of the country in which they are located. In other words, the Eurocurrency market is a banking market where banks carry out their deposit taking and lending activities in foreign currencies, that is, currencies other than that of the country in which the bank is located. The deposit received in the Eurocurrency market is thus known as a Eurocurrency deposit and the credit provided in that market is known as a Eurocurrency credit. Therefore, for example, a sterling deposit received by a foreign bank in London is not a Eurocurrency deposit. Likewise, a sterling deposit received by any bank in London from a foreign depositor is not a Eurocurrency deposit either. On the other hand, a dollar deposit received by any bank in London, whether a UK bank or a US bank subsidiary, from a resident of any country is a Eurodollar deposit. Therefore, what matters here is the country of the bank location and the country of the currency in question.[1]

A number of currencies are used in the Eurocurrency market. Among them, the US dollar is still the most important currency. Formally, Eurodollar deposits may be defined as those dollar-denominated deposits placed with banks outside the United States, whereas Eurodollar credit is dollar-denominated credit extended by banks outside the United States.

The deposits taken in the Eurocurrency market are typically time deposits, and loans provided in the Eurocurrency market are primarily bank loans, although nonbank loans such as Euro-commercial paper are increasingly gaining importance. Compared with other financial markets, the Eurocurrency market is essentially a short-term financial intermediation market. It is different from the long-term direct finance markets such as the Eurobond market or the Euroequity market. Also, it is different from the foreign exchange market in which the means of payment of one country is exchanged for that of another country simultaneously, as we studied in Chapter 6.

Although banks have accepted non-resident currency accounts since the earlier days of banking, the name Eurodollar account came into use in the 1950s. The name Eurodollar is derived from "Eurobank," which is the international cable code of the Banque Commerciale pour l'Europe du Nord, S.A., the Paris affiliate of the State Bank of the then Union of Soviet Socialist Republics.[2] In the early 1950s, many Eastern European governments decided to transfer their dollar accounts from banks in New York to non-US banks in Europe, partly because of their fear that their accounts might be frozen by the US government or attached by US claimants during the heightened Cold War. At the same time, they wanted to establish lines of dollar credit outside the United States. The cable code Eurobank became associated with transactions in these dollars, and these dollars that were on deposit outside the United States became known as Eurodollars or Eurodollar deposits. Today, such deposit-taking banks are located not only in Europe but also in other financial centers throughout the world, including Hong Kong, Singapore, Bahrain, and the Cayman Islands. As a consequence, offshore dollar deposits regardless of specific location are termed Eurodollar deposits.

Now let us take a look at the criteria needed to define the term "Eurodollar deposits" in a more systematic way. There are three basic criteria that we must consider for the definition of deposits in a closed economy, namely the type of financial institutions taking deposits, the type of deposits, and the type of depositors. In an open economy, each factor will have an added international dimension. Therefore we are faced with six factors: (1) the type of financial institutions taking deposits, (2) the location of the institutions, (3) the type of deposits (or any other liabilities), (4) the currency denomination of the deposits, (5) the type of depositors, and (6) the residence of the depositors.

As pointed out earlier, a common definition of Eurodollar deposits is that they are those deposits, denominated in dollars, with banks outside the United States. It therefore does not refer to whether depositors are individuals or financial institutions, nor whether depositors are residents or non-residents of the country of the currency. On the other hand, a definition used to determine the US monetary aggregate M2, for example, is different from the above. It includes only those dollar-denominated deposits held by nonbank US residents at overseas branches of US banks. The reason for excluding deposits of non-US residents is based on an assumption that US residents are more likely to spend the dollar deposits in the near term, whereas foreign residents are more likely to hold them as a store of value. On the other hand, to count only those deposits held at US branches abroad, rather than at any foreign banking institution, has no analytic basis. It is simply based on an administrative convenience, that is, on which deposit data are readily available in a timely fashion to the Federal Reserve.

Structure of the Eurocurrency market

As shown in Figure 8.1, the Eurocurrency market may be conveniently subdivided into three submarkets: (1) the Eurocurrency deposit market where banks outside the country of the currency take deposits from non-bank depositors, (2) the Eurocurrency interbank market where banks place their deposits with each other, and (3) the Eurocurrency credit market where banks make Eurocurrency loans to nonbank borrowers.

The interest rate charged in the interbank market, in London, for example, is known as the London Interbank Offered Rate (LIBOR). The

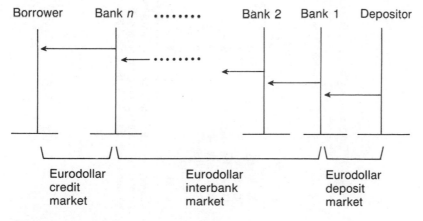

Figure 8.1 Eurodollar market structure

Table 8.1 Eurocurrency composition of the positions of Bank for International Settlements reporting banks (in billions of US dollars)

Currencies	Changes				Stocks at end-1988			
	Assets		Liabilities		Assets		Liabilities	
	1987	1988	1987	1988		(%)		(%)
US dollar	184.3	93.6	193.4	161.0	1,328.3	(59.1)	1,535.5	(60.1)
Others	101.4	115.6	130.8	123.3	920.2	(40.9)	1,018.4	(39.9)
Deutsche mark	31.9	31.2	41.5	41.5	293.0	(13.0)	340.2	(13.3)
Japanese yen	30.8	14.0	23.8	7.5	159.3	(7.1)	141.3	(5.5)
Swiss franc	−1.5	−4.8	10.5	−16.1	113.9	(5.1)	138.8	(5.4)
Sterling	5.2	22.8	13.9	21.7	69.1	(3.1)	86.3	(3.4)
ECU	8.4	16.1	5.9	17.2	85.0	(3.8)	76.9	(3.0)

Source: Bank for International Settlements (1989) *59th Annual Report*, 116
Note: The data cover only positions of banks in industrial countries reporting to the BIS. In addition, non-dollar Eurocurrency positions do not include those of banks in the United States. For a list of the BIS reporting countries, see Table 8.2.

second bank in Figure 8.1 may say that "we were offered to take a substantial amount of deposit of a certain maturity on or about 11 : 00 a.m. at a certain rate." That certain rate is a LIBOR, which may vary from one bank to another depending on the individual bank's credit standing in the market.

This interbank market performs at least three important functions: (1) it enables banks to adjust their fund positions efficiently, (2) it effectively provides interest rate arbitrage tools by letting banks borrow and lend in different currencies, and (3) it constitutes an efficient search process linking surplus economic units and deficit economic units. Thus, when the market is tight, such a search may not require a long process and the interbank market is likely to shrink. Conversely, when the market is loose, interbank intermediation tends to expand. Also, an expansion or contraction of the interbank market is easily influenced by the changing perception of risk in the market. A perceived increase in default risk of market participants would easily cause a temporary contraction of the market.

Besides Eurodollars, there are several Eurocurrencies such as Euromarks, Euroyen, Euro-Swiss francs, Eurosterling, and Euro-French francs among others. However, as is shown in Table 8.1, the Eurodollar still dominates, accounting for approximately 60 percent of Eurocurrency bank assets as well as bank liabilities in 1988. Deutsche marks (with 13 percent) and Japanese yen (with 7 percent) and other currencies make up the rest.

DEVELOPMENT OF THE EURODOLLAR MARKET

What has caused the development of the Eurocurrency market and particularly the Eurodollar market? There are two basic ways of looking at the development of the Eurodollar market, namely a US balance of payments approach and a regulatory difference approach. We will also discuss some variants of these two. Let us look at the balance of payments approach first.

Balance of payments approach

Immediately after the Second World War, the US dollar became the most preferred currency in international transactions because of its desirable characteristics, namely its direct access to huge goods and services markets, the stable value of its purchasing power, and overall confidence, all of which we examined in Chapter 4. During these years, the demand for dollars exceeded the supply of dollars, the situation known as the "dollar shortage." The difference was satisfied by the US balance of payments deficit which was primarily incurred by US aid to the European recovery. As Europe recovered from the war destruction and became again capable of producing goods and services for its consumption as well as exports, this dollar shortage was gradually reversed and replaced by the "dollar glut."

The dollar shortage abroad encouraged people to keep dollars as a pool of funds outside the United States and the dollar glut added funds to the pool. Also the balance of payments policies of Western European countries and the United States helped to foster the development of the Eurodollar market. For example, the return of convertibility of Western Europe's currencies in 1958 brought about a major increase in international banking transactions. At the same time, the measures taken by the US government to restrict outflows of capital, for example the Interest Equalization Tax (IET) in 1963, the mandatory Foreign Investment Restraint Program (FIRP) in 1965, and the voluntary Foreign Credit Restraint Program (FCRP) in 1966, had the opposite result. By taxing the difference in the cost of funds between the US market and elsewhere, the IET practically removed the advantage of raising long-term funds in the US capital market. However, as a result of this, foreign borrowers tried to seek a new market where they could raise dollar funds. This gave an added impetus to the development of the Eurodollar market. The mandatory FIRP was intended primarily to restrict the outflow of direct investment capital, which was regarded as exporting jobs from the United States, as we studied in Chapter 2. Likewise, the voluntary FCRP was to restrict bank lending to foreign residents including foreign subsidiaries of US-based multinational corporations. Although both the FIRP and the FCRP reduced outflows of capital from the United States, the problem was that once capital had flown, it remained abroad, providing additional permanent sources of funds abroad. Realizing that such hodgepodge measures were a futile exercise in trying to prevent capital outflows and relieving the dollar devaluation pressure, the US government terminated all such programs in 1971.

Between 1971 and 1981 the US current account balance was almost even on average with a cumulative surplus of only $3 billion. This might suggest that the size of the Eurodollar market would remain relatively unchanged. However, during the same period, the market size increased from slightly below $100 billion to over $600 billion. It became difficult to link the market growth to the US balance of payments position. How can we account for this rapid growth of the market?

To answer such a puzzle, Hogan and Pearce (1982), for example, argue that a US balance of payments deficit is not a necessary condition for growth of the Eurodollar market. They contend that the growth of the Eurodollar market is caused by the growth of the Eurodollar debt. Their contention implies two things. First, debt may be incurred by any country, not necessarily by the United States. So long as there are some countries which remain persistently as debtors, while others are creditors, then debt will accumulate, causing growth of the Eurodollar market. Therefore there is no need to have a direct relationship between the growth of the Eurodollar market and the growth of the US balance of payments deficit. Because much of the debt is denominated in US dollars, it has appeared as if the underlying cause is the US deficit. The second point is that what we are measuring is not the Eurodollar money stock but the Eurodollar debt. Recall Figure 8.1 which shows the three subsets of the Eurodollar market. One end of this whole Eurodollar market is the Eurodollar deposit market where banks predominantly receive time deposits rather than checkable deposits. That is, these banks are issuing debt instruments, not direct means of payment. Using this fact, Hogan and Pearce argue that an increase in the Eurodollar deposit market is not a result of the deposit expansion process but rather a result of a persistent surplus in some countries. Likewise, the increase in the Eurodollar credit market where borrowers issue debt instruments is a result of a persistent deficit of some other countries. Therefore the growth of the Eurodollar market is a result of a simultaneous growth of both ends of the market and that is what we are measuring.

Conversely, if debts were regularly paid off so that debtors were sometimes creditors and creditors were sometimes debtors, then there would be little accumulation of debts but a high velocity of transactions, causing little growth of the Eurocurrency market. This point will become clearer on pp. 192–7 when we examine the changes (or lack of changes) in the balance sheet of the US banking system in the Eurodollar expansion process.

Regulatory difference approach

On the other hand, Aliber (1976) and Dufey and Giddy (1978) argue that the primary cause of development of the Eurodollar was the regulatory differences between the home country and overseas banking centers. We may note that regulatory differences include cost differences as well as constraint differences. However, their focus was more on regulatory cost differences. Now, how do regulatory cost differences affect the deposit and lending rates and eventually the size of Eurodollar intermediation? Let us examine the determination of Eurodollar interest rates first.

Determination of the equilibrium interest rate

Using the asset–liability T-account (Figure 8.2(a)), compare the situations faced by two banks, one receiving a loan application and the other receiving deposits. When a bank receives a large-sized loan application, it will go into the interbank market to raise the needed funds immediately. Thus, the bank's demand for funds is the derived demand for funds. Likewise, a bank receiving deposits from a customer may wish to place such funds in the interbank market unless it can find a suitable nonbank borrower. Therefore, placing the deposit funds in the interbank market is the derived supply.

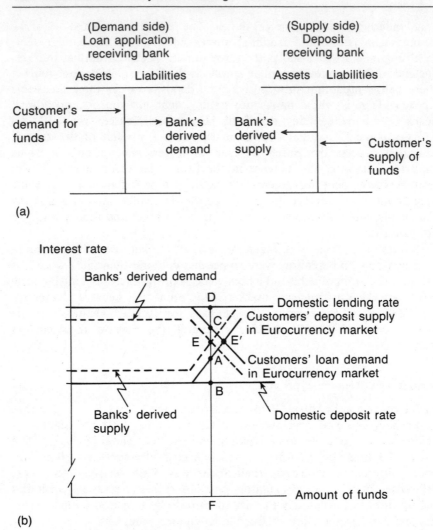

Figure 8.2 Determination of Eurodollar interest rates: (a) individual bank's
supply of and demand for funds; (b) determination of equilibrium
deposit and lending rates (E, equilibrium point with intermediation
fees (markup); E', equilibrium point without intermediation fees)

Figure 8.2(b) shows the equilibrium condition in the interbank market.
Since the Eurodollar market is an extension of the US domestic banking
market, its deposit floor-rate and lending ceiling-rate are determined by the
domestic deposit and lending rates respectively. Point E represents the interbank equilibrium point determined by the derived supply and demand
curves. Without bank intermediation fees, the equilibrium point would be

at E'. The vertical distance between the corresponding straight and broken lines represents the intermediation fee, which is the interest rate spread. Under the interbank equilibrium condition, the difference between points A and B represents the regulatory differences on deposits. Similarly, the distance between C and D measures those regulatory differences on the bank assets side. In general, the nominal rate of Eurodollar deposits is higher than the domestic deposit rate. Likewise, the nominal rate of Eurodollar credit is lower than the domestic lending rate. As long as regulatory costs are lower abroad, then there is a reason for the existence of the Eurodollar market. Such lower costs would provide windfalls for market participants. Now let us look at the regulatory cost arbitrage process.

Inward and outward arbitrage

To minimize the cost of funds, US banks may seek funds from the domestic market or from the Eurodollar market. We may classify their arbitrage activities as outward or inward arbitrage depending on the direction of flow of funds in response to interest rate incentives. Outward arbitrage occurs when the domestic effective interest rate is lower, while inward arbitrage occurs when the Eurodollar interbank market rate is lower.

Suppose that the nominal domestic time deposit rate i is 10 percent; the deposit insurance premium rate ϕ is 0.195 percent; and the required reserve ratio rr is 3 percent. Then the effective cost of funds at home can be calculated as

$$\frac{i + \phi}{1 - rr} = \frac{10\% + 0.195\%}{1 - 0.03} = 10.510\% \tag{8.1}$$

of which 0.510 percent is the regulatory cost. Banks outside the United States which are not subject to the bank regulation can afford to pay up to 10.510 percent on their deposits. If offshore banks have to pay a higher rate than this, there will be an outward arbitrage. On the other hand, if banks have to pay a nominal rate higher than 10 percent at home while they pay 10.510 percent or less in the offshore market, an inward arbitrage will take place, provided that such funds are not subject to reserve requirements and insurance premiums.

Now, let us go back to our basic question of the existence and growth of the Eurocurrency market. Suppose that regulatory cost differences no longer exist between the domestic money markets and the Eurocurrency market. Would the Eurocurrency market disappear? Most probably it would not, according to McKinnon (1977). Unlike the regulatory cost difference argument, he contends that the growth of the Eurocurrency market is caused in large part by useful additional functions that it performs.

For example, the Eurocurrency market functions to rechannel home-currency-denominated funds back to home country borrowers, as was the case during the US monetary crunch in 1969. It also provides an efficient international capital transfer mechanism between savers and borrowers of different countries, as demonstrated in the petro-dollar recycling in the mid-1970s, immediately following the formation of the OPEC oil cartel. This point is strikingly similar to the Hogan–Pearce argument. In addition, with the advent of the floating exchange rate system in the mid-1970s, the need for traders to hedge against exchange rate risk has markedly increased. By trading with each other in the Eurocurrency market in the form of multi-currency intermediation (borrowing in one currency and lending in another), banks can more conveniently cover their customers' hedging needs.

In summary, on the growth of the Eurocurrency market, the McKinnon view implicitly emphasizes the importance of regulatory constraint differences which favor non-resident banks and enable them to exercise greater flexibility. This flexibility in turn has enabled the market to respond to the changing needs of financial services. However, as domestic markets are also acquiring such flexibility through deregulation at home, the Eurocurrency market may become less necessary, unless its advantage stems from more than asymmetric bank regulations. A corollary to this is that in the future there might be a less distinctive demarcation line between the Eurocurrency market and the domestic money markets in their ability to meet changing needs of financial services.

INSTRUMENTS OF THE EURODOLLAR MARKET

The bulk of money held in the Eurodollar market is fixed rate time deposits. The maturities of Eurodollar time deposits range from overnight to several years. A main shortcoming of time deposits is obviously lack of liquidity. Negotiable certificates of deposit (CDs) for which a secondary market exists enhance liquidity. Regardless of the original maturity, an efficient secondary market would enable investors to convert their investment instruments into means of payment within a short period of time and with relatively small capital loss and transaction cost.

Following a successful introduction of domestic dollar CDs in the US money market in 1961, Eurodollar CDs were introduced in London in 1966. There are two types of CDs. One type is issued to tap available funds in the market. Accordingly, the size of such CDs, known as tap CDs, are tailored to the availability of funds, usually ranging from $250,000 to $5 million. The second type of CDs are similar to bonds. These are issued in aggregate amounts of $10 million to $30 million each time, depending on the need of the issuing bank. The total issue is partitioned into a number of $10,000 certificates each having the same terms and conditions (such as interest rate, maturity, interest payment dates, and place of payment). This type of instrument is convenient when a bank is faced with the need to raise a large amount of funds at short notice.

When the maturity of deposits becomes longer, depositors will be concerned to insure a fair return on their deposits which will reflect changing market conditions, particularly when the market trend seems upward. Eurodollar floating rate CDs (FRCDs) which were introduced in the late 1970s were designed to satisfy such needs. A typical maturity of FRCDs ranges from one and a half to five years and their interest rates are adjusted every three months or six months on the basis of the current LIBOR.[3] For longer term funds, banks usually issue, in lieu of sub-ordinated debentures, Eurodollar floating rate notes (FRNs), whose maturity is a bit longer than those of FRCDs, ranging typically between five to seven years. But unlike FRCDs, FRNs can also be issued by nonbank firms.

On the other hand, financial instruments typically used in the Eurodollar credit market include Eurodollar bank loans, Euro-commercial paper, FRNs, and note issuance facilities (NIFs). An NIF is a medium-term line of credit arrangement under which a borrower can issue short-term paper, known as Euro-notes, and underwriting banks are committed either to purchase any notes which the borrower is unable to sell or to provide standby credit. The maturity of the line of credit arrangement is five to seven years, whereas borrowers issue their own name notes with maturities of three to six months. The Euro-notes issued by borrowing banks are usually short-term CDs, whereas those notes issued by nonbank borrowers are promissory notes. When unsold notes are bought by an underwriting bank, such notes pay at a predetermined spread relative to a certain reference rate such as the LIBOR.

In this market as well as in other financial markets, new innovative debt instruments have been prolifically introduced in recent years to meet the needs of both borrowers and investors. We will examine financial innova-tions more in Chapter 9. Now, let us take a look at general characteristics of international banking centers.

INTERNATIONAL BANKING CENTERS

International banking centers are places where a substantial cluster (or critical mass) of banks are located and engaged not only in Eurocurrency transactions but also in home currency transactions to external parties. One measure of size of international banking centers is the size of external positions of banks in the respective centers. Table 8.2 shows the size of external assets and liabilities of banks in countries where major inter-national banking centers are located. In terms of gross assets, the UK (represented mainly by London) is still the leader, followed by Japan and then the United States.

Table 8.2 International banking centers by country (in billions of US dollars)

External positions of banks in	Changes in gross assets		Changes in net assets		Stocks at end-1988		
	1987	1988	1987	1988	Gross assets		Net assets
UK	89.1	34.0	−6.2	−27.7	883.6	(19.7)[a]	−78.4
France	37.9	23.3	1.6	−9.9	275.9	(6.2)	−16.3
Germany	17.0	17.4	4.1	8.8	206.0	(4.6)	76.2
Luxembourg	19.0	19.5	1.1	4.6	188.6	(4.2)	17.1
Belgium	16.5	1.3	−2.7	−2.6	142.8	(3.2)	−24.7
Netherlands	12.5	15.1	0.9	2.9	122.3	(2.7)	8.2
Switzerland	16.4	0.0	4.7	−3.8	117.0	(2.6)	37.2
Italy	−1.5	2.7	−5.1	−7.5	62.8	(1.4)	−35.2
Austria	1.6	−0.6	−1.9	−1.3	50.3	(1.1)	−11.0
Others[b]	9.2	3.1	−18.7	−19.2	78.6	(1.8)	−74.8
Total European reporting countries	217.6	115.7	−21.9	−55.8	2,128.0	(47.4)	−97.0
USA	31.4	46.5	−48.0	−13.5	555.8	(12.4)	−34.5
of which IBFs	31.5	32.0	−18.8	1.3	309.4	(6.9)	−26.5
Japan	166.5	166.7	−24.5	−23.2	733.7	(16.4)	−38.7
of which JOM[c]	89.9	138.5	−0.2	2.7	311.0	(7.4)	3.0
Canada	−0.4	−6.5	−2.7	−3.2	48.0	(1.1)	−23.3
Asian centers[d]	135.7	88.7	9.2	8.1	598.3	(13.3)	43.1
Caribbean centers	46.7	8.3	−1.1	−3.6	421.4	(9.4)	15.2
Total	597.5	419.4	−89.0	−91.3	4,485.3	(100.0)	−135.2

Source: Bank for International Settlements (1989) 59th Annual Report, 115
Notes: [a] Percentage. [b] Other reporting countries include Spain, Denmark, Sweden, Finland, Ireland and Norway. [c] Japan offshore market similar to IBFs in the United States. [d] Asian centers include Bahrain.
Net (external) assets = gross (external) assets − gross (external) liabilities.

As for international banking centers, there are two types: functional centers and offshore centers. Functional centers are those where full banking services are provided, for example London, New York, Frankfurt, Paris, and Tokyo, whereas offshore centers are those whose functions are primarily limited to Eurocurrency transactions or bookkeeping. The latter type of centers are, in many instances, the results of deliberate governmental efforts to attract banking business there. There are twenty or so such places including Anguilla, the Bahamas, Bahrain, the Cayman Islands, Hong Kong, Jersey, Luxembourg, the Netherlands Antilles, and Singapore. Of course, some of these centers do have substantial domestic banking markets side by side.

In order to attract offshore banking business, the host government may provide a number of incentives such as (1) low regulatory costs — low capital requirements (which must be held in the form of onshore assets), low or no license fees, easy entry, and low or no local tax on profit; (2) efficient telecommunications facilities; and (3) a sufficient number of skilled workers.

What, then, are the benefits of establishing such centers? The host countries benefit by increased employment, government revenue, and easier access to the international banking market should they need it. On the other hand, there are also direct as well as indirect costs to the host countries. The direct cost includes upgrading of communications systems, training of workers, and the cost of regulatory supervision. Indirect cost includes diminution in autonomy in conducting monetary policy, increased potential for tax evasion, capital flight, and a deleterious competitive effect on local banks.

In addition, one major issue involving offshore centers is their effect on other international banking markets. In order to equalize the regulatory environment of each center, regulatory harmonization is needed to ensure that no center may have competitive advantage compared with others in attracting business. Since regulatory harmonization is difficult to achieve, center-based countries tend to engage in regulatory competition, that is, they competitively reduce regulatory burdens.

Finally, since the City of London plays a dominant role as an international banking center, we will discuss London-specific issues in Chapter 11.

US INTERNATIONAL BANKING FACILITIES

US IBFs are in effect, as pointed out in Chapter 3, booking facilities established within the United States under the special regulatory framework which mimic offshore centers.

Since 1981, US banking organizations (bank holding companies, banks, Edge Act corporations, and Agreement corporations) and branches and agencies of foreign banks in the United States have been permitted to establish IBFs which are exempt from reserve requirements, deposit insurance, and interest rate ceilings.

IBFs can take deposits from two groups of depositors. One group consists of interbank market participants (such as the IBF's parent, other IBFs, and foreign banks), whereas the other group consists of nonbank foreign residents. They can take time deposits with a size of $100,000 or more. For the first group, the minimum maturity is overnight because these IBFs are effectively competing against other offshore centers where the minimum maturity is also overnight, whereas deposits from the second group require a two-day advance notice. In turn all such deposit money can be loaned out to the IBF parent, or other IBFs, or any foreign residents whether they are banks or nonbank residents. When the parent receives deposits from its IBF, such deposits are no longer exempt from the regulatory requirements.

Usually terms and conditions of deposits are negotiated by the head office, and instead of booking such deposits abroad they are booked with IBFs, thereby saving communications expenses and at the same time reducing regulatory costs. As shown in Table 8.2, the total IBF deposit stock at the end of 1988 was $309 billion. This implies that the regulatory saving for the US banking industry as a whole amounts to approximately $1.6 billion on the basis of the regulatory cost figure of 0.51 percent when the CD rate is 10 percent and given regulatory costs.

Why, then, have IBFs not replaced all offshore booking facilities? There still remain some important differences between depositing with IBFs and depositing with offshore facilities. First, there are possible differences in federal and local income tax implications depending on organizational forms and home office locations of banks; second, the degree of banking secrecy which can be enforced at home and abroad may be different; third, the perceived political risk on deposits with IBFs may be higher than that of offshore deposits for residents of some countries which are regarded as unfriendly to the United States. Besides, the IBF deposit money cannot be loaned to domestic customers. Therefore IBFs are not perfect substitutes for offshore deposit facilities. This supports the McKinnon view on the importance of regulatory constraint differences which we discussed earlier.

Having examined the institutional aspects of international banking centers and IBFs, we now turn our attention to the macroeconomic role of banks in such centers.

IS THE EUROCURRENCY MARKET INFLATIONARY?

Another important issue involving the Eurocurrency market is whether or not the market is a potential major source of worldwide inflation. The answer largely depends on the magnitude of the credit multiplier within the market. This issue is particularly important since no monetary authorities are in direct control over the market to restrain monetary expansion. In addition, this issue brings us back to reexamining the fundamental nature of the workings of the Eurocurrency market.

Let us look at how the Eurodollar multiplier is determined. Suppose that a US import firm has a deposit of $1,000 with a US bank whose T-account is as follows:

US bank	
$1,000 cash	$1,000 deposit of US firm

This US firm imports goods from an export firm in the UK and pays $1,000 in a check drawn against its US bank. Assume that the UK export firm does not foresee an immediate use of dollars but that it will need them in ninety days. So it deposits this $1,000 check to open a three-month time deposit. The UK bank receiving the check will send it to the US bank for collection. The T-accounts of the US bank and the UK bank may then appear as follows:

US bank		UK bank	
$1,000 cash	− $1,000 deposit of US importer	+ $1,000 deposit at US bank	+ $1,000 deposit of UK exporter
	+ $1,000 deposit of UK bank		

Now, this UK bank keeps 10 percent of its deposit for its reserves and lends the remaining 90 percent to a British import firm.

US bank		UK bank	
$1,000 cash	$100 deposit of UK bank	$100 deposit at US bank	$1,000 deposit of UK exporter
	− $900 deposit of UK bank	− $900 deposit at US bank	
	+ $900 deposit of UK importer	+ $900 loan to UK importer	

The British importer uses $900 of the borrowed money to pay its import bill to a French exporter, which in turn makes a three-month time deposit with a French bank. Like the UK bank above, this French bank keeps 10 percent of the deposited amount for its reserves and lends out the remainder to a French importer.

US bank		French bank	
$1,000 cash	$100 deposit of UK bank	+ $90 deposit at US bank	+ $900 deposit of French exporter
	− $900 deposit of UK importer	+ $810 loan of French importer	
	+ $90 deposit of French bank		
	+ $810 deposit of French importer		

If such a deposit (as well as credit) expansion process continues, the final state of the T-accounts of the US bank and consolidated Eurobanks appear as shown below. The US bank has the same total amount of $1,000 of deposits on its liabilities side as it started with, but it has an array of different depositors consisting of Eurobanks. Meanwhile, the Eurobanking system as a whole has a total amount of $10,000, ten times the original deposit, on its liabilities side and the sum of $1,000 as bank reserves and $9,000 as bank loans on its assets side. The bank reserves are maintained with the US bank (or US banking system).

US bank		Eurobank system	
$1,000 cash	Reserves of Eurobanks	Reserves at US bank	Deposits of customers
	$100 UK bank	$100 UK bank	$1,000 UK exporter
	$90 French bank	$90 French bank	$900 French exporter
	$81 3rd Eurobank	$81 3rd Eurobank	$810 3rd exporter
	⋮	⋮	⋮
	$1,000	$1,000	
		Credit to customers	
		$900 UK importer	
		$810 French importer	
		$729 3rd importer	
		⋮	
		$9,000	$10,000

Since the original Eurodollar deposit of $1,000 has caused a chain expansion of deposits totaling $10,000, we may state that the original deposit multiplied ten times. Likewise, the original bank credit of $900 has multiplied again ten times to become a total credit expansion of $9,000.

deposit multiplier = total expanded deposits/original deposit   (8.2)

credit multiplier = total expanded credit/original credit.   (8.3)

Now, we can express the above process in algebraic form. Suppose the initial Eurodollar deposit amount is T, the reserve ratio is r, and the marginal propensity to lend is b, which is $1 - r$. Then the total amount of the Eurodollar deposits D can be expressed as

$$D = T + bT + b^2 T + \cdots + b^n T.$$ (8.4)

That is, the first bank receives an amount T of deposit, the second bank an amount bT, the third bank $b(bT)$ and so forth. In order to simplify the above equation, we multiply both sides of the equation by b; then we have

$$bD = bT + b^2 T + b^3 T + \cdots + b^{n+1} T.$$ (8.5)

Subtracting equation (8.5) from equation (8.4), we have

$$(1 - b)D = T - b^{n+1} T.$$ (8.6)

Therefore the total expansion of the Eurodollar deposits within the Eurobank system will be

$$D = \frac{1}{1 - b} T$$ (8.7)

because the term $b^{n+1} T$ approaches zero as n approaches infinity. The term $1/(1 - b)$ is known as the Eurodollar deposit multiplier,[4] and is also equal to the Eurodollar credit multiplier which is the ratio of total expanded credit to the original credit. Using our numerical figures, we have

total deposits = $[1/(1 - 0.9)]\,1,000 = 10,000$ (8.8)

total credit = $[1/(1 - 0.9)]\,900 = 9,000$.   (8.9)

Then, what is the actual magnitude of the Eurodollar deposit multiplier? Estimates of the value of the multiplier vary. Friedman (1969), for example, argued that there was no basic difference between the domestic market and the Eurodollar market in generating credit expansion. However, the actual value of the Eurodollar deposit multiplier would be substantially larger than the domestic multiplier because the Eurobanks held less reserves to their deposit liabilities. This is in part due to the fact that there were no regulatory reserve requirements; there was less need to hold precautionary reserves because of less volatile deposit liabilities; and it was easier to have access to the interbank market if Eurobanks needed liquidity. Basically, Friedman was looking at the expansion process in our Eurobank system.

On the other hand, Klopstock (1968), Hewson and Sakakibara (1974) and Lee (1973) estimated that the Eurodollar multiplier was relatively small, ranging between 0.5 and 1.51.[5] Unlike Friedman, Hewson and Sakakibara were essentially looking at the unchanging liabilities of our US banking system above. Their estimates were based on the notion that, unlike domestic banks which have the ability to create demand deposits which become part of the money stock, the Eurobanks do not have such ability, but act instead as match-makers between nonbank depositors and borrowers without engaging in size and maturity intermediation. This is because Eurodollar deposits are mainly time deposits. As such, the banks are not capable of expanding deposit money. This incapacity of Eurobanks to expand deposit money is akin to that of old savings and loan associations in the United States or that of old building societies in the UK when they did not have demand or checkable deposit taking powers. Thus, nonbank borrowers of Eurodollars are likely to spend the borrowed dollars immediately in the United States, instead of going through many rounds of chain payments, as shown in our example in the Eurobank system. The leakage back to the United States is so rapid that the multiplier is about 1.0.

Using this line of argument, we may see the possibility of different values of the multiplier. If the leakage is complete at the second round, then the multiplier will be

$$(1,000 + 900)/1,000 = 1.9. \tag{8.10}$$

If the leakage back to the United States is complete at the third round, the multiplier will be

$$(1,000 + 900 + 810)/1,000 = 2.71. \tag{8.11}$$

Besides, there is another source of variation which is the speed of the deposit and credit expansion process. Even if the expansion process is supposedly to continue to the end without leakage, the maximum multiplier value may not be realized if the original depositor withdraws its deposit in the middle of the expansion process.

In sum, the fact that estimated money and credit multipliers are generally low, close to unity, implies that in practice there is no inflationary effect arising from transactions in the Eurocurrency market. A relatively low multiplier is consistent with the argument that Eurocurrency transactions mainly involve debt instruments (time deposits) and not direct means of payment (demand or checkable deposits).

SUMMARY

The Eurocurrency market is basically a multi-facet banking market consisting of deposit, interbank, and credit markets where deposits and credit are denominated in currencies other than that of the country in which banks are located. Despite the proliferation of other currency markets, the Eurodollar market is still the largest one, having about 60 percent of the Eurocurrency market share.

Earlier, the phenomenal growth of the Eurodollar market in 1960s and 1970s was attributed to the US balance of payments deficit plus unintended side effects of US tax and foreign investment control policy measures. However, later studies point out that the regulatory cost and constraint differences were major causes of the market growth. Furthermore, a number of international banking centers have been fostered deliberately by countries such as Bahrain and Cayman Islands through reduced regulations. IBFs, bookkeeping facilities located within the United States, mimic the regulatory environment of the Eurocurrency market.

The existence of the Eurocurrency market, which operates outside the purview of any monetary authorities, was feared to be inflationary for the world economy. However, empirical studies show that the Eurocurrency credit multipliers are relatively low, largely because Eurocurrency deposits are debt instruments (time deposits) and not means of payment (demand deposits).

REVIEW PROBLEMS AND EXERCISES

1. Explain the differences between the commonly defined Eurodollar deposits and those included in the US monetary aggregate M2.

2. Show how the Eurodollar interbank equilibrium rate is determined, using supply and demand curves.

3. Explain how the US capital outflow restraint programs in the 1960s helped develop the Eurodollar market.

4. How different is the Hogan–Pearce argument from the traditional balance of payments approach in explaining the growth of the Eurodollar market?

5. Would the Eurocurrency market disappear if regulatory cost differences no longer existed between the Eurocurrency market and domestic money markets? Use the McKinnon argument.

6. What are the costs and benefits of establishing offshore banking centers for a host country?

7. Describe the characteristics of IBFs. Can IBFs completely mimic offshore bookkeeping banking facilities?

8. Give a main reason why each of the following might open a Eurodollar deposit account: (a) a UK-based firm; (b) the government of Iraq; (c) a US-based firm.

9. Suppose that a US-based company IBM makes a $1 million deposit with Barclays Bank in London by transferring its account from Citibank in New York. Show the transactions, using T-accounts. Do these affect the US monetary aggregate?

10. Now IBM wants to convert its dollar account into a sterling sight account. To meet this need Barclays sells its dollar account with Citibank to a French bank which in turn uses its sterling account with Barclays to make its payment. Show these transactions, using T-accounts. Do these affect the total size of Eurodollar deposits?

11. Since dollars are used more extensively in invoicing international sales, is the Eurodollar multiplier likely to be larger than those of other Eurocurrencies?

12. What are the main problems in estimating the Eurodollar multiplier?

13. The following information is given:

> domestic CD rate, 9.50%   Eurodollar CD rate, 10.25%
> Deposit insurance premium, 0.12%
> Reserve requirement, 3% on domestic deposits

Is there an outward arbitrage incentive in this case? Show why.

NOTES

1 Johnston (1983: 1–7), for example, clearly differentiates Eurocurrency lending (as foreign currency lending to any residents) from international lending (as lending to foreign residents in any currencies).
2 See Kvasnicka (1969: 10).
3 In the FRCD underwriting contract as in other types of instruments, an agent bank is designated. This bank receives the interest rate information from the so-called reference banks – generally London offices of major international banks two business days prior to the commencement of the next interest period. The reported rates are then averaged to arrive at the reference LIBOR. Therefore, which banks are included in the reference bank group makes a difference in determining a reference LIBOR.
4 Obviously, this is the simplest form of the multiplier. Probably the most comprehensive multiplier can be found in Brunner (1973: 127–66).
5 More specifically, the estimates of the value of the Eurodollar multiplier vary as follows:

Klopstock (1968)	0.50–0.90
Klopstock (1970)	1.05–1.09
Hewson and Sakakibara (1974)	1.00
Lee (1973)	1.51
Makin (1972)	10.31–18.45
Friedman (1969)	large

BASIC READING

Aliber, R. Z. (1976) *The International Money Game*, 2nd edn, New York: Basic Books.
Bank for International Settlements, *Annual Report*, various issues.
Brunner, K. (1973) "Money Supply Process and Monetary Policy in an Open Economy," in Connolly, M. B. and Swoboda, A. K. (eds) *International Trade and Money*, Toronto: University of Toronto Press, 127–66.
Bryant, R. C. (1980) *Money and Monetary Policy in Interdependent Nations,* Washington, D.C.: Brookings Institution, Chapter 3.
Dufey, G. and Giddy, I. H. (1978) *The International Money Market*, Englewood Cliffs, NJ: Prentice Hall, Part III.
Friedman, M. (1969) "The Eurodollar Market: Some First Principles," *Morgan Guaranty Survey*, October: 13–22. Reprinted with clarifications in *Federal Reserve Bank of St Louis Review* (1971) July: 16–24.
Goodfriend, M. (1986) "Eurodollars," in *Instruments of the Money Market*, Federal Reserve Bank of Richmond, 53–64.
Hewson, J. and Sakakibara, E. (1974) "The Eurodollar Multiplier: A Portfolio Approach," *IMF Staff Papers*, 307–28.
Hogan, W. P. and Pearce, I. F. (1982) *The Incredible Eurodollar*, London: Allen & Unwin.
Johnston, R. B. (1983) *The Economics of the Euro-Market: History, Theory and Policy*, New York: St Martin's Press.
Klopstock, F. K. (1968) *The Euro-dollar Market: Some Unsolved Issues*, Essays in International Finance No. 65, Princeton, N.J.: Princeton University Press.
—— (1970) "Money Creation in the Eurodollar Market – A Note on Professor Friedman's View," *Federal Reserve Bank of New York Monthly Review*, January: 12–15.
Kreicher, L. (1982) "Eurodollar Arbitrage," *Federal Reserve Bank of New York Quarterly Review*, Summer: 10–21.
Kvasnicka, J. G. (1969) "Eurodollars – An Important Source of Funds for American Banks," *Federal Reserve Bank of Chicago Business Conditions*, June: 10.
Lee, B. E. (1973) "The Eurodollar Multiplier," *Journal of Finance*, September: 867–74.
McKenzie, G. W. (1976) *The Economics of the Euro-Currency System*, New York: Wiley.
McKinnon, R. I. (1977) *The Eurocurrency Market*, Essays in International Finance No. 125, Princeton, N.J.: Princeton University Press.
Makin, J. H. (1972) "Demand and Supply Functions for Stocks of Eurodollar Deposits: An Empirical Study," *Review of Economics and Statistics*, 54(2): 381–91.
Swanson, P. (1988) "Interrelationships Among Domestic and Eurocurrency Deposit Yields: A Focus on the US Dollar," *Financial Review*, February: 81–94.

FURTHER READING

Balbach, A. B. and Reslter, D. H. (1980) "Eurodollars and US Money Supply," *Federal Reserve Bank of St. Louis Review*, June/July: 2–12.
Corrigan, E. G. (1987) "Coping with Globally Integrated Financial Markets," *Federal Reserve Bank of New York Quarterly Review*, Winter: 1–5.

Hallwood, P. and MacDonald, R. (1986) *International Money: Theory, Evidence and Institutions*, Oxford: Blackwell, Chapter 10.

Hodjera, Z. (1978) "Asian Currency Market: Singapore as a Regional Financial Center," *IMF Staff Papers*, 25(2): 221–53.

Mayer, H. W. (1976) "The BIS Concept of the Eurocurrency Market," *Euromoney*, May: 60–6.

Wellons, P. A. (1977) *Borrowing by Developing Countries on the Euro-Currency Market*, Paris: OECD.

Chapter 9

International financial innovations

CONCEPTUAL FRAMEWORK FOR FINANCIAL INNOVATIONS

Financial innovation has been an on-going phenomenon in financial markets over the last 150 years, having given rise to modern banking and other financial systems. However, the pace of financial innovations has accelerated in the past two decades, causing some (for instance, Finnerty 1988; Miller 1986) to call it revolutionary.

The term "financial innovation" differs from just plain improvement or marginal improvement which goes on always. Financial innovation may be defined basically as unforecastable drastic improvements in the form of a new financial product, or a new delivery system, or a new organizational setup to provide financial services. It is unpredictable because the incidence and timing of the underlying forces cannot be identified in advance. Although financial innovations may take place in a variety of ways, we will focus our study in this chapter on financial product innovations and their effect on the international financial markets.

As shown in Table 9.1, financial instruments may be characterized by a number of their attributes from the point of view of the economic deficit unit (DU) as well as that of the surplus unit (SU). Although most attributes may be regarded as major characteristics by both sides, there are some subtle differences in emphasis by each side. Moreover, the desirable directions of improvement may not always coincide. Major attributes may include (1) costs of funds (or returns on investment), (2) credit risk, (3) market risks (interest rate, exchange rate, and inflation risks), (4) maturity, and (5) other implicit attributes (management control, delivery system, and so forth).

Whether financial innovation is to create an entirely new product or a modified one, it is either to enhance desirable attributes or to reduce undesirable ones, or to reallocate risks.

Table 9.1 Attributes of financial instruments and supply–demand for financial innovations

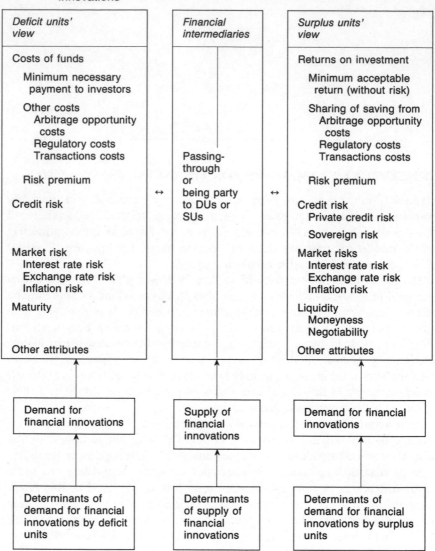

Demand for financial innovations

Demand for financial innovations by the deficit units

For the DUs, any improvement in reducing costs of funds will be desirable. As shown in Table 9.1, the costs of funds consist of several components:

(a) a minimum necessary payment to the investor for a given maturity and other implicit attributes, (b) broadly defined transactions costs, and (c) a risk premium. The broadly defined transactions costs in turn include market arbitrage opportunity costs, regulatory costs, and narrowly defined transactions costs such as agency, marketing, and dealing costs. With an increased awareness of differences in costs of funds in many different markets, DUs have sought to take advantage of arbitrage opportunities, and this has resulted in a surge in demand for new financial instruments and techniques which would enable them to do so. We can term such a movement a market integration process.

The DUs are also concerned about their own credit risk as perceived by potential creditors, since the perceived credit risk will affect the risk premium they must pay. Similarly, they are concerned about market risks such as interest rate, exchange rate, and inflation risks, as they affect their respective risk premiums. There is a trade-off for the DUs either to assume risks, thereby not paying risk premiums, or to transfer risks, thereby paying premiums. In either case, the DUs are interested in seeking new ways to reduce risk premiums.

Demand for innovations by the surplus units

For the SUs, it is desirable to have higher returns on investment, given liquidity and other implicit attributes. The returns for SUs can be increased by sharing gains from market arbitrage or reduced regulatory and transactions costs. In order to share such gains and cost savings, SUs became more willing to go beyond the traditional boundary of investment. In addition, the SUs became concerned about drastic rises in virtually all types of market risks as well as credit risk, looking for new hedging tools which could be used to transfer risks at low costs.

Thus, we may classify the demand for financial innovations by motivation as follows: (1) innovations that reduce costs of funds (or enhance returns on investment); (2) innovations that transfer credit risk; (3) innovations that transfer market risks (interest rate, exchange rate, inflation risks); and (4) innovations that enhance liquidity. As costs-of-funds reducing (or returns-on-investment enhancing) innovations would broaden the access for DUs to the previously inaccessible financial market, we may call such innovations also credit-generating innovations.[1]

The underlying forces for demand for innovations

Then, what are the underlying factors which caused an unprecedented surge in financial innovations in both domestic and international financial markets in recent years, particularly the 1980s? According to a Bank for International Settlements study (1986), several important forces may be identified.

First, drastically increased volatility of both interest rates and exchange rates has increased rate risks for both DUs and SUs. The central bank in the United States in 1979 and those in other countries later changed the mode of monetary policy by switching the policy target from the interest rates to the money stock, causing greater fluctuations in interest rate movements. Likewise, the Bretton Woods arrangement of a fixed exchange rate system was superseded by a floating rate system in 1973, permitting greater fluctuations in exchange rates. In addition, a higher inflation rate in the 1970s after the 1973 oil shock kept interest rates at an unusually high level. All these created the needs for efficient risk-transferring tools.

Second, the early 1980s witnessed an abnormal deterioration in creditworthiness in many sectors, partly as a result of the severe recession. However, collapses of the energy sector and the Third World country debt crisis led to a more than proportional impact on the creditworthiness of the banking industry. Potential depositors began investing in capital-market-type instruments instead of deposit instruments. An increased use of capital-market-type instruments was further fueled by the discovery by DUs that direct financing was often a less costly avenue of financing. However, for SUs to invest more and more in such capital market instruments inevitably increased illiquidity in their investment portfolio, which in turn increased the demand for liquidity-enhancing innovations.

Third, in the 1980s there was an abnormal increase in demand for credit because of demographic changes, government deficits, and changes in corporate finance. Creating the crowding-out effect, a drastic increase in government deficit in the United States in the 1980s forced private sector borrowers to seek alternative sources of credit. As larger firms broadened their sources of funds to include the Eurobonds market in the early 1980s, the second-tier firms were also forced to seek new low-cost sources of funds in order to remain competitive. Another cause for the increased demand for credit came from large financing needs for mergers and acquisitions which surged as a result of relaxed governmental attitudes.

Fourth, because of advances in information technology, it became easier for both DUs and SUs to identify and take advantage of arbitrage opportunities in different markets on a global basis. Indeed, advances in technology are also one of the major causes of the supply of financial innovations, which we discuss below.

Supply of financial innovations

Now let us look at the supply side of financial innovations. Financial intermediaries, particularly commercial banks and investment banks, are major suppliers of financial innovations. In general, financial intermediaries may simply match the needs of DUs to those of SUs, providing pass-through services. If the needs of the two sides cannot be matched, financial intermediaries step in and become parties to DUs or to SUs, satisfying their needs by creating new financial instruments or techniques. In fact, this is precisely the process of structuring a "complete market," in which everyone is able to find what he or she wants to buy or sell.[2]

Determinants of the supply of financial innovations

There are at least three major underlying causes for the supply of financial innovations in recent years. First, because of advances in telecommunications, information processing, and computing, the cost of processing information has been substantially reduced. This has resulted in the linking of markets worldwide and at the same time a reduction in the arbitrage margin in standard product transactions. Therefore, banks were forced to look for new products with larger margins. The advances in technology in turn made it easier to design new rather complex instruments and to monitor them in the market. Thus, advances in technology have diminished old opportunities but at the same time have created new ones for banks.

Second, regulatory cost or constraint differences create new opportunities for regulatory arbitrage. In the 1960s and 1970s, US banks produced new products to avoid reserve requirements, interest rate ceilings, and deposit insurance premiums. As a successful result, banks were able to share regulatory cost savings with their customers. When the interest rate ceilings were removed in the earlier 1980s in the United States, banks were able to offer deposits at freely determined rates so that returns on deposits could be linked with any market. However, since the mid-1980s, the imposition of bank capital requirements has resulted in changes in the way banks do business, moving away from asset-based to fee-based activities. This switch gave greater motivation for financial innovations.

Third, the competition in the banking market has increased among depository institutions partly owing to the deregulation trend which started in the early 1980s in the United States and in the mid-1980s in the EC countries as well as in Japan. It was spurred on even between banks and non-financial firms, the more so by advances in information technology. Such advances enabled any firm with a customer base to provide generic versions of financial services (such as loans, deposits, credit cards, and limited insurance). Therefore, any commercial firm having a larger customer base could enjoy economies of scale in such generic services. Banks had to seek new approaches, either "boutique-type" customized services or new product innovations. At the same time changes in the attitudes within the banking industry toward more entrepreneurial approaches provided the corporate culture needed for financial innovations.

Fourth, an earlier stage of financial innovations during the 1970s provided basic tools such as Eurocurrency products, repurchase agreements, syndicated loans, standby letters of credit, and floating rate notes

(FRNs). These basic tools became foundations for the next take-off of financial innovations in the 1980s. Without previous innovations, next generation innovations would have come more slowly.

In summary, with advances in information technology, changes in bank regulations, and heightened competition, banks became more willing to supply financial innovations, sometimes producing excessive innovations without significant value.[3]

An example of innovation as a process of removing regulatory constraints

Recall that regulatory constraint differences were one of the major growth factors for the Eurocurrency market, which we studied in Chapter 4. Let us examine a case of financial innovation which is largely directed at removing regulatory constraints. More specifically, suppose that a bank is faced with the following linear programming constraint.[4]

Maximize profit (net interest income) subject to

1 a total funds F constraint[5] $S + L + R \leqslant F$,
2 a reserve requirements constraint $S + L \leqslant F - R$,
3 a liquidity constraint $S \geqslant aL$, and
4 a loan balance constraint $L \geqslant C$,

where S is securities investment, L is the loan portfolio, R is the reserve assets (regulatory variable), a is the minimum proportion of securities to loans ($0 < a < 1$) (management decision variable), and C is the minimum loan amount (management decision variable).

The above problem is represented in Figure 9.1. Moving from C to D reduces regulatory constraints which affect the liability side of the bank balance sheet. Such a move can be accomplished by offering Eurodollar deposits. Moving from D to F is a return-biased (return-increasing) innovation. Instead of mortgage loans, banks may purchase mortgage-backed securities, which in turn can be stripped and sold to investors. Without increasing risk measurably, transactions on stripped mortgage-backed securities could increase return. Similarly, moving from D to E is a liquidity-biased (liquidity-enhancing) innovation. This may be accomplished by reverse repurchase agreements by banks, which in turn can be financed through repurchase agreements. Again, without innovation of financial instruments such as repurchase agreements, a movement from D to E could enhance liquidity but only at the expense of a substantially lower return.

Therefore, it is convenient to look at a financial product as a composite of utility-bearing attributes or characteristics, and the value of the product is represented by a weighted sum of the values of these attributes. The equilibrium price of a financial product as a composite unit is determined

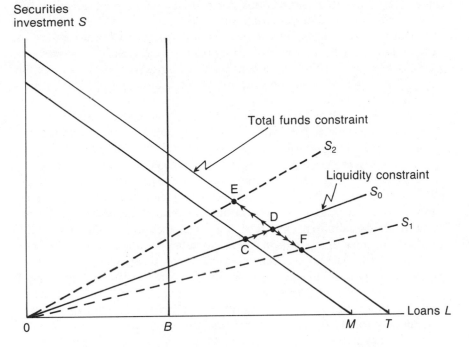

Securities
investment S

Figure 9.1 Financial innovation as a process of removing production
constraints: a, proportion $(0 < a < 1)$ (management decision
variable); B, given amount of loan balance (management decision
variable); L, loan portfolio; M, reserve constraint $(T - R)$ (regulatory
variable); S, securities investment; T, total resource constraint

jointly by its supply and demand. The supply side is essentially determined
by the production cost with given constraints and the demand side by
investor taste.[6]

INTERRELATIONSHIP BETWEEN CHANGES IN FINANCIAL ATTRIBUTES

As already suggested, the underlying motives for financial innovations are
mainly intended to enhance desirable attributes of financial products on the
one hand and reduce undesirable attributes on the other, or to reallocate
these attributes to market participants.

We note that categories of motivation for financial innovation are not
necessarily mutually exclusive, but rather are interrelated. For example, one
way to increase the rate of return is (a) to take advantage of regulatory and
tax differences, or (b) to create product differentiation, thereby creating a
monopolistic market, or (c) to standardize products, thereby reducing

advertising and other transactions costs. Also the purpose of increasing marketability is to reduce transactions costs.

In addition, certain changes in the attributes cause a reallocation of risks, either by reducing the overall risks or by transferring such risks between the participating parties. Finally, enhancement of liquidity is desirable for one party, but it may increase uncertainty to some other parties, and it may cause transactions costs to rise.

Thus we can make a more general statement about the above categories of motives for financial innovation. That is, opportunities to create new products exist because of market imperfection or because of mildly segmented markets. Such imperfection is created by tax or regulatory differences, or differences in technological advances. In a broader sense, differences in overall financial market environments provide incentives for innovations. Thus, financial innovations are created and used as arbitrage tools to bridge different markets. Through such a process, segmented markets are integrated, reducing arbitrage opportunities, and at the same time integrated markets are segmented, as financial innovations themselves create monopolistic markets, resulting in a small-scale Schumpeterian neighborhood of equilibrium at a microeconomic level.[7] In the process, financial innovations repackage utility-bearing characteristics of financial instruments traded in different markets, thus blurring the uniqueness of each instrument.

Since it is relatively easy to imitate financial innovations, the inventor institutions tend to internalize their new products, as they do the value of other intangible assets. For example, when it is difficult to control the transfer of a particular piece of financial technology, it would be easier for the inventor institution to embody such technology in its own final products or to tie it in with other products. Such customized services hinder the diffusion of technology and make marketing more expensive but prolong monopolistic profit opportunities.

Generally, however, when a new financial product is standardized, market integration is speedier and more effective and the development of the secondary market is easier. Besides, inventor institutions are not without benefits with standardization. Frequent innovations enhance the "reputation" or "credibility" of the inventor institution, and this in turn reduces the marketing cost of the institution.[8]

TYPES OF MARKET INTEGRATION TOOLS AND IMPLICATIONS FOR MARKET PARTICIPANTS

Figure 9.2 shows examples of financial innovations as market arbitrage tools which facilitate market integration. According to differences in market conditions, markets are divided into domestic and foreign markets. Domestic markets are further segmented into money markets, capital

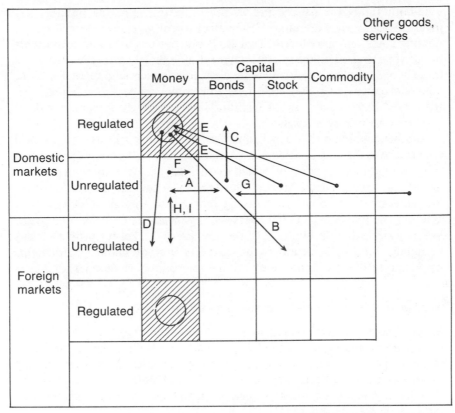

Figure 9.2 Financial innovation as a process of market integration: A, interest
rate swaps; B, debt–equity swaps; C, stripped securities;
D, Eurodollar deposits; E, market index deposits; F, caps,
corridors, and collars; G, price-level-adjusted mortgages (PLAMs);
H, SDR deposits; I, ECUs; shaded circle, banking market;
→ direction of market integration

markets (bonds and stock), commodity markets, and other goods and
services markets. Each market is also subdivided into regulated and
unregulated markets. The same classification method applies to foreign
markets.

Money and capital market integration tools

Interest rate swaps integrate the money market and the capital market by
allowing two participants into a different market where each has comparative advantage in borrowing so that the joint borrowing cost for them can
be reduced. Puttable bonds which are bonds with put options provide

long-term funds for issuers and at the same time provide liquidity for investors. Since they are almost equivalent to roll-over commercial paper, floating costs can be reduced. That is, if put options attached to puttable bonds are exercised on the interest payment date shortly after their issuance, these bonds are then essentially equivalent to commercial paper. If options are not exercised, then they are similar to commercial paper having rollover features. Furthermore, such substitutability effectively integrates capital markets into money markets.

Another case in point is debt–equity swaps. A bank sells its Third World country loans (usually problem loans) at a discount in the secondary market to a multinational corporation which in turn sells the debt instrument to the debtor country for local currency. This local currency is then used for direct investment, linking domestic banking markets to foreign stock markets. Without the secondary market, debt–equity swaps can hardly take place. We may argue that the existence of the secondary market for problem loans is mainly due to the heterogeneous expectations of market participants about the future performance of the debtor country economies.

Regulated and unregulated market integration tools

Stripped securities are created by separating (stripping) the principal and interest payments from an underlying debt instrument and selling the claims to the payment streams as new and separate securities. They were initially created as tools to take tax arbitrage in the United States as well as in Japan, thus linking regulated markets (heavily taxed markets) and unregulated markets (less taxed markets).

A better known example is the case of Eurodollar deposits, as we studied in Chapter 8. The growth of Eurodollar deposits has been prompted by regulatory differences such as differences in reserve requirements, deposit insurance requirements, interest rate ceilings on deposits, and portfolio regulation.

Banking and stock (or commodity) market integration tools

Instead of making a direct investment in stock, gold, or other commodities, an investor may mimic such investment by making deposits with a bank which pays interest which is linked to the performance of indexes of stocks or to the commodity prices. Such deposits are known as market index deposits. Thus, investors can save transaction costs and yet have the same or a similar benefit of investing in other assets.

Money and exchange market integration tools

Currency swaps and currency futures provide a mechanism linking domestic and foreign exchange markets. SDR deposits and ECU deposits are also tools integrating domestic and foreign money markets and exchange markets.

Financial market and real sector integration tools

Recently introduced price-level-adjusted mortgages (PLAMs) are mortgages with monthly payments that change as the price level changes so that the real value of these payments remains constant. Thus these tools are indeed directly linking the capital market to the real sector.

Summary

The data on the magnitude of these instruments are sketchy: interest rate swaps, $170 billion, 1986; debt—equity swaps, $28.3 billion, 1985—8; Treasury strips outstanding, $48.3 billion, 1988; ECU accounts outstanding, $204.8 billion, 1987; and Eurodollar deposits outstanding, $1,377.9 billion, 1987.[9] These magnitudes except for the Eurodollar deposits and interest rate swaps are relatively small in relation to their respective cash market size. However, since they are newcomers in the market, their influence is exerted at the margin. Thus, their relative influence may be greater than their relative proportion in the market indicates. An OECD-sponsored study by Fukuda and Hanazaki (1986) suggests that financial innovations result in market integration in terms of convergence of real interest rates among financially open economies.

NEW FINANCIAL TOOLS FOR REALLOCATION OF RISKS

As shown in Table 9.2, a number of new instruments have been invented to reallocate credit as well as market risks.

As credit risk reallocation tools, for example, Eurocurrency-syndicated loans, note issuance facilities (NIFs) with standby letters of credit, and forfaiting are available. Each Eurocurrency-syndicated loan usually has more than a hundred participating lenders, thereby effectively distributing credit risk to many. An NIF with a standby letter of credit is a medium-term facility under which a borrower can issue short-term paper (often known as Euro-notes) in its own name but underwriting banks provide payment guarantee. Thus, credit risk is transferred to underwriting banks from Euro-notes investors. Forfaiting is a promissory note issued by an importer with a bank guarantee.

For the reallocation of interest rate risk, financial futures and forward rate arrangements are available. Financial futures or interest rate futures are standardized contracts, traded on exchanges, which commit parties to purchase or to sell specified financial securities in the future at given prices (price indexes), which in turn fix the corresponding interest rates in advance. A forward rate agreement is a contract by which the seller of the

Table 9.2 Examples of financial innovations

Products	Value[a]	Regulatory causes
Market integration and transactions-costs-reduction tools		
Interest rate swaps	A, Y, IR	
Market index deposits (MID)	A, Y, T	
Variable rate preferred stock	A, Y	
Debt–equity swaps	A, Y	1983 ILSA[b]
Eurocurrency instruments	A, Y, RC	Rate ceiling/reserve requirement
Zero coupon bonds (in Japan)	A, Y, RC	Preferential tax
Parallel loans	A, Y, RC	Exchange control
Standby letters of credit	A, Y, RC	Bank capital requirements
Mandatory convertible notes	RC	Bank capital requirements
Credit risk reallocation tools		
Eurocurrency syndicated loans	CR, T	
NIFs with standby letters of credit	CR, T	
Forfaiting	CR	
Market risk reallocation tools		
Caps, floors, collars	IR	
Forward rate agreements with LIBOR	IR	
Three-month Eurodollar deposit futures	IR	
NIFs with full underwriting commitment	IR, T, CR	
Foreign exchange swaps	ER, T	
Cross-currency swaps	ER, IR, T	Exchange control
Foreign currency options	ER	
Multicurrency (SDR, ECU, etc.) deposits, bonds loans	ER, T	
Price-indexed UK government bonds	PR	
Liquidity-enhancement tools		
Puttable bonds	L, T	
Eurocurrency floating rate notes	L, T	

Notes: [a] A, market arbitrage; ER, exchange rate risk reallocation; IR, interest rate risk reallocation; L, liquidity enhancement; PR, inflation risk reallocation; RC, regulatory cost reduction; T, transactions-costs reduction; Y, yield reallocation.
[b] US International Lending Supervision Act of 1983.

contract promises to buy debt instruments issued by the buyer of the contract at a predetermined price in case the issuer is unable to sell her new securities at or above the predetermined price. Therefore, this effectively sets the maximum cost of funds for the buyer of this contract.

In addition, caps, corridors, and collars are also available. A cap is a contract which promises, for a fee, that the buyer of the contract will be reimbursed if the market rate rises above the ceiling rate. Unlike the case of fixed rate borrowing, it has the feature of an option, since the buyer of the cap can benefit when the market rate falls below the ceiling rate (cap) at the time of actual borrowing. In this case it is equivalent to not exercising the option contract. As shown in Figure 9.3, until the market interest rate goes up to 10 percent, the cap buyer can enjoy the lower rate and it does not trigger the cap contract. A corridor is a contract which limits the range of hedge that the corridor seller provides. Figure 9.3(b) shows the case of a 4 percent limit. A collar is a contract which has a ceiling rate as well as a floor rate to protect both the buyer and the seller of the collar contract. When the market rate falls below the floor rate, the buyer will reimburse the seller the difference between the floor rate and the market rate. On the other hand, if the market rate is above the ceiling rate, the contract functions in exactly the same way as a cap. A variation of a collar is a forward rate agreement in which the ceiling and the floor rates are the same. Therefore, if the reference rate (often LIBOR) turns out to be above the predetermined rate on the settlement date, the contract buyer receives the difference. If it turns out to be below, the contract writer receives the difference. Thus, a forward rate agreement is in effect an over-the-counter financial futures contract. In addition, interest rate swaps are increasingly used as interest rate risk transfer tools.

For the reallocation of foreign exchange rate risk, hedgers as well as speculators may use foreign currency futures, or foreign exchange options, or traditional forward contracts, as we studied in Chapter 6. In addition, foreign exchange swaps and cross-currency swaps are in use. The former is a transaction in which one currency is sold against another for one delivery date with a simultaneous agreement to reverse the transaction at a future date. The latter is a transaction in which two counterparties exchange specific amounts of two different currencies at the outset and repay in a form of installments over time.

On the other hand, the PLAM plan is an example of protecting mortgage lenders from erosion of their purchasing power. Likewise, price-indexed UK and Italian government bonds serve a similar purpose.

Obviously, whether to assume or to transfer market risks depends on the decision-maker's utility function which in turn depends on the trade-off between return and risk. Hedging is in essence to transfer risk, whereas speculation is to assume risk. As pointed out earlier, hedging and speculative activities have increased since the implementation of the floating exchange rate system in 1973 and the change in the Federal Reserve monetary policy target from the interest rate to the money stock in 1979, coupled with the acceleration of inflation in the late 1970s and early 1980s.

Several other chapters also deal with a variety of financial innovations in more detail. For example, as you recall, SDR and ECU deposits are

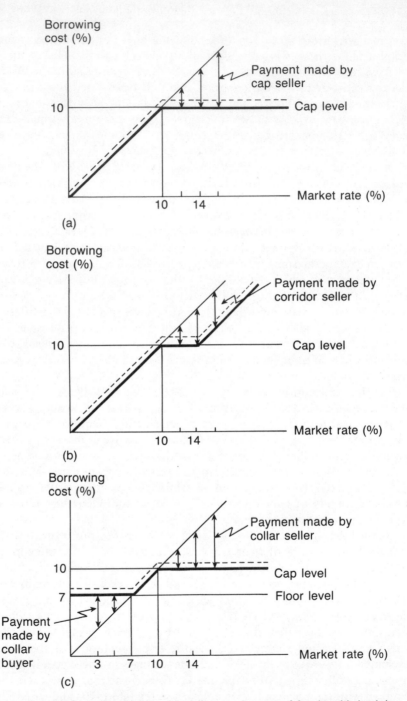

Figure 9.3 (a) Cap; (b) corridor; (c) collar: ———, cost of funds with hedging contract (without premium); – – –, cost of funds with hedging contract (with premium)

discussed in Chapter 4; foreign exchange options and futures in Chapters 6 and 7; Eurodollar certificates of deposit, their variants, FRNs, NIFs and other Eurocurrency-related instruments in Chapter 8. In addition, forfaiting and other trade-finance-related new instruments are presented in Chapter 15. Finally, in Chapter 17, we discuss market-oriented debt reduction instruments such as debt–equity swaps, debt–debt swaps, and buybacks, among others.

IMPLICATIONS OF FINANCIAL INNOVATION FOR MACROECONOMIC POLICY[10]

The rapid development of financial innovation has raised concern for the implementation of macroeconomic policy, particularly monetary policy. There are two major sources of concern. First, financial innovation creates confusion; second, it enables a low-cost transformation between money and near-money (or any other financial assets), resulting in destabilization of the economy.

Confusion is due to the practical difficulty of identifying monetary assets and measuring their degree of moneyness.[11] One measure to determine the degree of moneyness is a measure of turnover in purchasing final output (GNP).[12] Another approach is to regress aggregate expenditures on the size of each instrument and to use the estimated coefficient as a basis for the measurement of significance. Probably the most appealing approach is to use the relative yield for the weighting scheme.

The weighting method, proposed by Barnett (1980), is based on the proposition that financial assets that provide medium of exchange services are distributed on a continuum with pure medium of exchange assets at one end and pure store of value assets at the other. The pure medium of exchange assets earn no interest and are used only as a medium of exchange, whereas the pure store of value assets (BBB-rated bonds) earn a market interest rate but are not directly useful as a medium of exchange. Therefore, as shown in equation (9.1), the relative yield ratio of the former is zero, resulting in the highest weight of "one." Likewise, the relative yield ratio of the latter is one, resulting in a zero weight. Between these two extremes, there are a range of financial assets receiving a weight between zero and one.[13]

$$\text{weight} = 1 - \frac{\text{rate of instrument in question}}{\text{BBB bond rate}} \tag{9.1}$$

According to this approach, it has been suggested that the monetary aggregate should include medium of exchange assets (currency, travelers' checks, demand deposits, other checkable savings deposits, share draft accounts, money market deposit accounts, money market mutual funds, savings deposits with automatic transfer service (ATS)) and non-medium of exchange assets (savings deposits without ATS, small time deposits, repurchase agreements, Eurodollar deposits, large time deposits, US savings bonds, short-term Treasury securities, commercial paper, and bankers' acceptances), each with a varying weight.

Since financial innovations are improvements relative to the existing financial instruments, some of the instruments, such as puttable bonds, excluded from the above list may in fact qualify for inclusion. In addition, there is a tendency to enhance the liquidity of each instrument; the aggregation weight may understate the moneyness. Errors in underestimation cause a deviation from the optimal money supply. Thus, there is welfare loss. Also the existence of possible estimation error in the money stock suggests that the interest rate target might be a better one. The lower transformation cost and the similarity between money and other financial assets make money one of a wide spectrum of Gurley–Shaw financial assets, thereby increasing substitution between these assets. This implies that the slope of the LM curve becomes flatter, making monetary policy less effective.[14]

In an open economy, we may use the Argy–Porter (1972) type model to evaluate the effect of financial innovation. The model has four sectors, namely the real sector, foreign sector (current account), domestic money sector, and foreign money sector. The real sector equilibrium is achieved when the aggregate supply is equal to the aggregate demand, which is an increasing function of the spot exchange rate (expressed in terms of home currency units per foreign currency). The foreign sector is in equilibrium when the current account is zero. The exports are an increasing function of the spot exchange rate, whereas the imports are a decreasing function of the spot rate and an increasing function of real income. The current account thus has a positive relationship with the spot exchange rate. The third sector is the domestic money market and the fourth sector the foreign money market. Through arbitrage, these two markets will be in equilibrium jointly when the following holds:

$$i_d = i_f + \frac{r_{0j} - r_{00}}{r_{00}} \tag{9.2}$$

or

$$r_{00} = \frac{r_{0j}}{1 + (i_d - i_f)} \tag{9.3}$$

where i_d is the domestic interest rate, i_f is the foreign interest rate, r_{00} is the spot exchange rate (home currency units per foreign currency), and r_{0j} is the forward exchange rate. We note that equations (9.2) and (9.3) are variations of (2.12). Then an increase in real income causes a rise in the demand for real money, resulting in a higher domestic interest rate, which in turn reduces the spot rate, provided that the forward rate is stable. This equilibrium relationship between the spot rate and real income can be

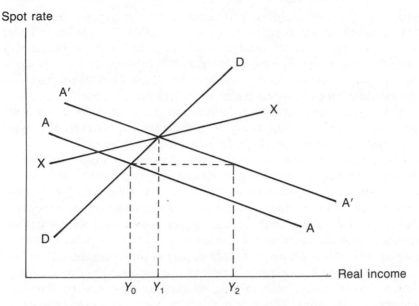

Figure 9.4 Equilibrium in international financial asset markets, real goods and service markets, and balance of payments account: AA, foreign and domestic money market equilibrium line; A'A', shift in AA; DD, real sector equilibrium line; XX, balance of payments equilibrium line

shown by line AA in Figure 9.4. Similarly, the real sector equilibrium is represented by DD, and the current account sector by XX. The effect of financial innovation is to flatten the demand curve for real money and consequently the curve AA.

As in the case of the flatter LM curve in a closed economy, the flatter portfolio investment equilibrium curve AA implies that monetary policy will be less effective. In such instances, fiscal policy might be more effective when used in conjunction with foreign exchange policy.

IMPLICATIONS FOR THE INTERNATIONAL MONETARY FUND

In addition to the macroeconomic implications, we can draw several interesting implications for the operations of the IMF, which shapes the international monetary system. These implications have direct bearings in many countries which are attempting to liberalize their financial markets.

International reserve assets: concept and measurement

"International reserves" were defined by the Ossola Report (Group of Ten 1965) as "those assets of monetary authorities that can be used, directly or through assured convertibility into other assets, to support its rate of exchange when its external payments are in deficit."[15] Obviously, this definition was based on the fixed exchange rate regime. However, it also implies that the role of international reserves is to serve as a buffer stock to accommodate fluctuations in external transactions. For this purpose, not only traditional reserve assets (such as the reserve position in the IMF, official SDRs, foreign exchange holdings, and gold) but also the country's short-term borrowing ability should be included in the reserves. Our main interest here is what to include in foreign exchange holdings.

In the case of the domestic monetary aggregate, as noted earlier, the inclusion of particular component assets is determined by the likelihood of the conversion of such assets for spending. On the other hand, in the case of international reserves, the inclusion of particular claims on non-residents is determined by the availability of such assets to monetary authorities for discharging external payment obligations.

Nonetheless, it is desirable to include as part of the international reserves not only medium of exchange claims but also non-medium of exchange claims on non-residents with varying weights, as suggested by Barnett's monetary services index. This is particularly so when such assets can easily be used as collateral for external borrowing, and when financial innovation is blurring the line between medium of exchange claims and non-medium of exchange claims. Otherwise, a country's ability to meet short-term payment obligations would be underestimated.

Currency convertibility at the theoretical maximum

The operation of Article VIII and Article XIV of the IMF's Agreement clearly depends on the definition of "currency convertibility." One major objective of the IMF is to foster a multilateral system of payments for current transactions and to contribute to the balanced growth of world trade through the elimination of exchange restrictions. The principles to achieve this objective are embodied in Article VIII, which obligates member countries to avoid exchange restrictions, and in Article XIV, which on the other hand allows a transitional period for member countries to be exempt from such obligations.

Currency convertibility has meant different things at different times, as we studied in Chapter 4. The current IMF rule stipulates that member countries are free to place controls on capital movements as long as current payments or transfers are not restricted. With continuous financial innovations through which world financial markets are integrated, such a provision for restrictions is becoming redundant. Instead, the IMF should seek currency convertibility at the theoretical maximum should it desire to increase worldwide efficiency not only through trade but also through international capital markets.

Harmonization of surveillance on exchange restrictions and financial market restrictions

Because of a closer linkage between the foreign exchange market and the financial market through financial innovations, even if a country keeps a clean hand in the foreign exchange market, a dirty hand, i.e., government meddling, in the financial market will have a similar effect to a dirty hand in the former.

Thus, limiting surveillance to the foreign exchange market only is incomplete. The need for harmonization of surveillance on both markets in the broad sense seems to have been recognized in a report prepared in 1972 by the IMF Executive Directors and in the 1986 Tokyo Economic Declaration. The latter requires the examination of mutual compatibility of broad economic policies. However, surveillance on the exchange market without a similar surveillance on financial markets would be less complete.

Moving from an Article XIV to an Article VIII status country

Financial innovation also has some implications for a country planning to move from an Article XIV status to an Article VIII status. Such a move involves the process of liberalization of its economy. Market integration by financial innovations may have reduced the importance of the debate on the order of liberalization.

It is argued that the very source of government control is fiscal deficits, which force policy makers to search for second-best solutions, resulting in more and more controls. More specifically, fiscal deficits require inflation-tax financing, which in turn pushes the price level up, leading to governmental control over domestic prices, domestic financial markets (interest rates), foreign exchange markets (exchange transactions and exchange rates), international trade, and international capital movements. Therefore, when the government decides to reverse the process, it may be desirable to liberalize the economy starting from the root of restrictions. Nonetheless, under the condition of greatly integrated markets through financial innovation, the question of which market is first to be liberalized and which one next becomes less important.

A central clearinghouse for special drawing rights

Among financial innovations, the taking of SDR deposits by commercial banks has a direct bearing on the operations of the IMF. Recently, some effort has been exerted by the IMF to make the private SDR more acceptable. Such efforts include a simplification in 1981 of the number of component currencies from sixteen to five, and the daily announcement of exchange rates applicable for determination of the conversion rate between the dollar and the SDR. However, the private use of the SDR remains mainly as a unit of account and not so much as a medium of exchange, whereas the ECU has gained broader acceptance as a means of payment. With the Bank for International Settlements accepting the role of clearing-house for private ECU transactions in 1986 and with the integration of the EC in 1992, the use of the ECU is expected to increase substantially as a means of payment settlement.

Contrary to the case of the ECU, the SDR lacks official support. As Kenen (1983) points out, if the SDR is to be used as a full-fledged reserve asset, there must be a direct link between the official SDR and the private SDR. For this purpose, there is a need to establish a clearinghouse which can be used to clear private payments – a clearing house to be sponsored by the IMF similar to Coats's proposal (1982). The clearinghouse may function like the Interdistrict Settlement Fund in the United States, while the central bank of each country may function like each district Federal Reserve Bank in serving its customer banks. Under such a plan, whenever a bank in one country makes an SDR payment to a bank in another country, official SDRs are transferred automatically from the central bank of the payer country to the central bank of the payee country. A full integration of private and official SDRs requires removal of "the official acceptance limit" and "designation." Then, the SDR may become a full-fledged international reserve asset. With the international SDR clearing system available, a wider use of the private SDR can be expected; a wider use of the private SDR in turn may create a money multiplier effect, generating additional private SDRs.

SUMMARY

A financial instrument can be conveniently viewed as a composite product having multiple attributes such as costs of funds (or rates of return), credit risk, market risks (such as interest rate risk, exchange rate risk, and infla-tion risk), maturity, and liquidity among others. A financial innovation is an unexpected sudden improvement to enhance desirable attributes and to reduce undesirable ones. As the traditional banking business areas became more standardized and competitive, banks seeking higher profit margin have become more entrepreneurial, willing to provide more innovative products to meet the needs of customers. On the other hand, customers facing more volatile market conditions have sought to mitigate such con-ditions with more innovative financial instruments. Market participants have been able to take monopolistic profit arising from the market segmen-tation by using such tools as interest rate swaps and Eurodollar deposits. Also innovations have produced more efficient risk allocation tools such as cross-currency swaps, NIFs with standby letters of credit, syndicated bankers' acceptances, and collars, among others.

However, at the macroeconomic level, financial innovations make it more difficult for monetary authorities to control the money stock because of the blurred line between money and other financial assets. Likewise, financial innovations cause underestimation of the international reserves, and make it more difficult for the IMF to conduct surveillance on the exchange market intervention by member governments because the exchange market and the financial market are now so integrated.

REVIEW PROBLEMS AND EXERCISES

1. What were the major causes of the demand and supply of financial innovations in recent years?

2. What are typical attributes of a financial instrument and how are these attributes related to each other?

3. Explain financial innovation as a process of removing regulatory constraints.

4. What are the major causes of financial innovations in recent years?

5. Give specific examples of regulatory causes and their effect on producing certain new financial products.

6. Explain which markets the financial instruments listed as market integration tools in Table 9.2 are likely to bridge.

7. Give examples of financial innovations transferring the following type of risk:
   (a) credit risk
   (b) interest rate risk
   (c) foreign exchange rate risk
   (d) inflation risk

8. Why can we say that caps, corridors, and collars have a characteristic similar to that of options?

9. Why is it difficult to conduct monetary policy under continual financial innovations?

10. Why does the current IMF definition of international reserves probably underestimate the size of reserves?

11. What is the problem in using the IMF definition of convertibility of currency?

NOTES

1 See Bank for International Settlements (1986: 177–89) for a credit-generating view.

2 For a more detailed discussion of this concept of a complete market, see Flood (1991: 32–57).

3 For instance, Desia and Low (1987: 112–40) attempt to differentiate between a trivial innovation and an important innovation by measuring the distance of the new product and existing ones in a commodity space.

4 For the use of a linear programming method for bank asset and liability management, see, for instance, Cohen and Hammer (1967: 147–65).

5 Technically, this first constraint is redundant. However, when the second constraint is removed, the first one becomes an effective constraint.

6 For an analysis of the relationship between the price of a final product and the amount of a certain attribute, see Rosen (1974: 34–55).

7 See Schumpeter (1939: 207–9).

8 For a general discussion of credibility built on useful services consistently provided by a firm, see Sobel (1985: 557–73). Ross (1989: 541–56) uses a theory of repeat buying to demonstrate a source of reducing marketing costs.

9 For the market size of interest rate swaps, see Felgran (1987: 28); for debt–equity swaps, see US Treasury Department (1989); for Treasury strips, see Becketti (1988: 24); for ECU and Eurodollar figures, see Bank for International Settlements (1988: 119–20).

10 This section and the following were adapted mainly from Kim (1990).

11 Theoretically, these two issues are the same. It is possible to include everything in monetary assets first and then sort out each component on the basis of the degree of moneyness.

12 For a detailed discussion, see Spindt (1985: 175–204). For a comparative analysis of alternative weighting schemes, see Batten and Thornton (1985: 29–40).

13 Graphically, we can show hypothetical weights as shown below (A, currency; B, savings deposits; C, small time deposits; Z, BBB-rated bonds (most liquid non-medium of exchange asset)).

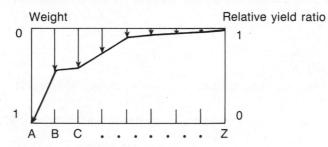

14 See Simpson and Parkinson (1984: 12–19) for the reason why monetary policy may be ineffective.

15 See Group of Ten (1965).

BASIC READING

Argy, V. and Porter, M. G. (1972) "The Forward Exchange Market and Effects of Domestic and External Disturbances under Alternative Exchange Rate Systems," *IMF Staff Papers*, 19 (November): 503–28.

Bank for International Settlements (1986) *Recent Innovations in International Banking*, Prepared by a Study Group established by the Central Banks of the Group of Ten Countries, Basle: BIS.

—— (1988) *58th Annual Report*, Basle: BIS.

Batten, D. S. and Thornton, D. L. (1985) "Lag-Length Selection and Tests of Granger Causality between Money and Income," *Journal of Money, Credit, and Banking*, 17 (June–July): 29–40.

Becketti, S. (1988) "The Role of Stripped Securities in Portfolio Management," *Federal Reserve Bank of Kansas City Economic Review*, May: 20–31.

Coats, W. L. (1982) "The SDR as a Means of Payment," *IMF Staff Papers*, 29 (3): 422–36.

Desia, M. and Low, W. (1987) "Measuring the Opportunity for Product Innovation," in De Cecco, M. (ed.) *Changing Money: Financial Innovation in Developed Countries*, Oxford: Blackwell, 112–40.

Finnerty, J. D. (1988) "Financial Engineering in Corporate Finance: An Overview," *Financial Management*, Winter: 14–33.

Flood, M. D. (1991) "An Introduction to Complete Markets," *Federal Reserve Bank of St. Louis Review*, March–April: 32–57.

Ganitsky, J. and Lema, G. (1988) "Foreign Investment through Debt–Equity Swaps," *Sloan Management Review*, Winter: 21–9.

Gold, J. (1971) "The Fund's Concepts of Convertibility," Pamphlet Series No. 14, Washington, D.C.: IMF.

IMF (1978) *Articles of Agreement* (effective 1 April 1978), Washington, D.C.: IMF.

—— (1985) *The Role and Function of the International Monetary Fund*, Washington, D.C.: IMF.

Kenen, P. B. (1983) "Use of the SDR to Supplement or Substitute for Other Means of Finance," in G. M. von Furstenburg (ed.) *International Money and Credit: The Policy Roles*, Washington, D.C.: IMF, 327–360.

Kim, T. (1990) "Dynamics of Financial Innovation and Its Implications for the IMF," in SOAC Publication Committee (ed.) *Toward One World Beyond All Barriers*, vol. III, *A Better World Economic Order*, Seoul: Poong Nam, 151–82.

Mayer, T. (1982) "Financial Innovation – Conflict Between Micro and Macro Optimality," *American Economic Review*, 72 (2): 29–33.

Miller, M. H. (1986) "Financial Innovation: The Last Twenty Years and the Next," *Journal of Financial and Quantitative Analysis*, 21 (4): 450–71.

Rosen, S. (1974) "Hedonic Prices and Implicit Markets: Product Differentiation in Pure Competition," *Journal of Political Economy*, 82 (1): 34–55.

Ross, S. A. (1989) "Institutional Markets, Financial Markets and Financial Innovation," *Journal of Finance*, 44 (3): 541–56.

Schumpeter, J. A. (1939) *Business Cycle*, New York: McGraw-Hill, 207–9.

Simpson, T. D. and Parkinson, P. (1984) "Some Implications of Financial Innovation in the United States," Staff Studies, Board of Governors of the Federal Reserve System, September: 12–19.

Spindt, P. A. (1985) "Money is What Money Does: Monetary Aggregation and the Equation of Exchange," *Journal of Political Economy*, 93 (1): 175–204.

Van Horne, J. (1985) "Of Financial Innovations and Excesses," *Journal of Finance*, 40 (3): 621–31.

FURTHER READING

Barnett, W. A. (1980) "Economic Monetary Aggregation: An Application of Index Number and Aggregation Theory," *Journal of Econometrics*, 14 (1): 11–48.

Bicksler, J. and Chen, A. H. (1986) "An Economic Analysis of Interest Rate Swaps," *Journal of Finance*, 41 (3): 645–55.

Cohen, K. J. and Hammer, F. S. (1967) "Linear Programming and Optimal Bank Asset Management Decisions," *Journal of Finance*, 22 (2): 147–65.

Errunza, V. and Moreau, A. F. (1989) "Debt-for-Equity Swaps under a Rational Expectations Equilibrium," *Journal of Finance*, 44 (3): 663–80.

Felgran, S. D. (1987) "Interest Rate Swaps: Use, Risk, and Prices," *New England Economic Review*, November–December: 22–32.

Fukuda, M. and Hanazaki, M. (1986) "Internationalization of Financial Markets: Some Implications for Macroeconomic Policy and for the Allocation of Capital," *Working Papers 37*, OECD Department of Economics and Statistics, November.

Group of Ten (1965) *Report of the Study Group on the Creation of Reserve Assets* (Ossola Report), Washington, D.C.: IMF.

King, S. R. and Remolona, E. M. (1987) "The Pricing and Hedging of Market Index Deposits," *Federal Reserve Bank of New York Quarterly Review*, Summer: 9–20.

Masera, R. S. (1987) *An Increasing Role for the ECU: A Character in Search of a Script*, Essays in International Finance No. 167, Princeton, N.J.: Princeton University Press.

Silber, W. L. (1983) "The Process of Financial Innovation," *American Economic Review*, 73 (2): 89–95.

Sobel, J. (1985) "A Theory of Credibility," *Review of Economic Studies*, 52: 557–73.

US Department of the Treasury (1989) *Interim Report to Congress Concerning International Discussions on an International Debt Management Authority*, March.

Chapter 10

The US money and banking markets

INTRODUCTION

This chapter provides a concise overview of the US money and banking markets. For the student who is interested in comparative analysis of money and banking markets in other countries, this chapter, together with the next one on the UK markets, may serve as a convenient reference point for such analysis. We first examine (1) characteristics of the overall banking industry structure in terms of the size distribution and the rather unique dual banking system in the United States, and (2) types of banking organizational forms typically used to conduct banking business in the United States.

Second, we review the changing regulatory environments which have shaped the scope and nature of banking activities. Since the current state of regulatory environments is the cumulative result of past legislative actions, a review of the important points of several major banking acts will be helpful in understanding often seemingly conflicting regulatory rules. We then discuss the current regulatory agency structure and regulatory issues. The current regulatory issues include policy problems of deposit insurance, the separation of commercial banking from investment banking, interstate banking, and risk-based capital requirements.

Our attention is then turned to the role of banks in the money sector. The importance of the role of banks in the economy has well been recognized, as they not only provide the payment settlement system but also serve as a crucial part of the money supply process which determines the amount of money in the economy. Therefore, we will examine how the money stock is determined, how a change in the money stock affects the economy, and how banks play a crucial part in the process. Finally, we will look at characteristics of money market instruments which are either part or close substitutes of monetary assets.

THE COMMERCIAL BANKING MARKET STRUCTURE

An overview of the structure of the commercial banking industry

The structure of the US banking system is unique in comparison with those of other countries around the world. The banking structure is often characterized by size distribution or by type of banks in the industry. As of the end of 1990, there were 12,672 insured US commercial banks operating in the United States, while in other countries a far smaller number of banks dominate in their domestic markets.

For example, in the UK six nationwide retail banks, together with seven regional retail banks, operate more than 12,000 branches throughout the country, dominating the domestic retail banking market. Similarly only eleven domestically chartered banks in Canada are major players in the domestic market, with over 7,000 branches nationwide. In Japan, there are seventy-five commercial banks which dominate retail and corporate banking markets. Out of this total number, eleven banks are so-called "city" banks having nationwide branches and the remaining sixty-four are "regional" banks.

As we can see from Table 10.1, many US commercial banks are rather small. As of the end of 1987 about 6,400 US banking organizations (almost two-thirds of the total) had an asset size of less than $50 million. These banks as a whole held about 5.9 percent of the total banking assets of $2,597 billion then. Meanwhile, there were only 262 banking organizations which had an asset size of over $1 billion and they together held about

Table 10.1 Size structure of banking organizations (as of end of 1987)

Asset size range (millions of US dollars)	Number of banks	Percentage of total	Total amount of assets (in billions of US dollars)	Percentage of total
Less than 50	6,389	62.2	152.0	5.9
51–100	2.071	20.1	143.9	5.5
101–1,000	1,557	15.1	358.9	13.8
1,001–5,000	173	1.7	401.9	15.5
5,001–25,000	72	0.7	822.1	31.7
Greater than 25,000	17	0.2	718.5	27.7
Total	10,279	100.0	2,597.3	100.0

Source: Amel, D. F. and Jacowski, M. J. (1989) "Trends in Banking Structure since the Mid-1970s," *Federal Reserve Bulletin*, March: 125
Note: The data reported here are based on the consolidated banking organizations, not individual banks. The assets reported here do not include foreign assets.

75 percent of total assets in the banking industry. Even among these relatively large banks, the size variation was substantial, ranging from $1 billion to over $200 billion. Does this mean that there is no optimal size of a bank? We will return to this question in the next section.

Another unique aspect of the US banking industry is the so-called dual banking system. By this we mean that there are two parallel regulatory structures in chartering, supervising, and examining banks in the United States. [1]One side of the regulatory structure consists of the state regulatory agencies and their regulatory systems and the other side consists of three federal agencies, namely the Office of the Comptroller of the Currency (OCC), the Federal Reserve System, and the Federal Deposit Insurance Corporation (FDIC), and their respective regulatory systems. Therefore, in the United States there is a certain amount of built-in competition between the state and federal regulatory agencies. That is, in principle a bank can choose its own regulatory master. The Federal Reserve System is the central bank system in the United States, consisting of the policy-making Federal Reserve Board of Governors and its instrumentalities, Federal Reserve Banks. It is also called the Federal Reserve, or the System, or simply the Fed.

As shown in Table 10.2, we may classify banks on the basis of three criteria, namely charter, Federal Reserve membership, and FDIC membership. First, under the dual system, a bank may be chartered by either a state or a federal agency. If it is chartered by a state agency, it is classified as a state bank. If it is chartered by a federal agency, the Office of the Comptroller of the Currency, it is a national bank. National banks must bear "national" in their names, indicating their national charter. With regard to Federal Reserve membership, all national banks are automatically members of the Federal Reserve System. However, Federal Reserve membership is not mandatory for state-chartered banks. Those state banks which join the System, subject to the approval of the Federal Reserve, are called state member banks, whereas those state banks which remain outside the System are termed state nonmember banks. The membership does not imply that these member banks directly participate in the central bank policy-making decisions but rather that they serve as loose instrumentalities of policy implementation. There are certain benefits of membership in the System such as (1) borrowing privilege from the Federal Reserve when a member bank is temporarily in need of liquidity, (2) use of the Federal Reserve facilities for collecting checks, settling clearing balances, and electronic funds transfers, (3) use of currency services, (4) use of information services, and (5) participation in electing six of the nine directors of the Federal Reserve Bank in their district. However, since 1980 all nonmember banks which are subject to the Federal Reserve reserve requirements have also been accorded an equal access to the Federal Reserve services (items (1) through (4) above). There is therefore practically no

Table 10.2 Regulatory classification of commercial banks (as of December of 1980, 1987, 1990)

Source of charter	Classification of banks	Federal Reserve System members	FDIC members	Number of banks		
				1980	1987	1990
Office of Comptroller of the Currency	National banks			4,425	4,572	3,990 (27,396)
State bank regulatory agencies	State banks	State member banks		997	1,091	1,057 (5,908)
		State nonmember banks	State nonmember insured banks	9,013	7,853	7,347 (17,827)
			State nonmember noninsured banks	328	290	278 (111)
Total number of banks				14,763	13,516	12,672 (51,242)

Sources: FDIC (1981) 1980 Annual Report of the Federal Deposit Insurance Corporation, Washington, DC, 222; Board of Governors of the Federal Reserve System (1991) The Annual Report 1990.
Note: Figures in parentheses are the number of branches and additional offices as of December 31, 1990.

difference between member and nonmember banks in terms of receiving Federal Reserve services. However, the main difference today lies in the regulatory jurisdictions. As for the third criterion, FDIC membership, all national banks and state member banks are automatically required to become members of the FDIC. On the other hand, state nonmember banks are not required to join the system. However, as shown in Table 10.2, a majority of state nonmember banks have membership in the FDIC. Such banks are classified as state nonmember insured banks. Therefore, the remainder of state banks constitute state nonmember noninsured banks. Although their deposits are not insured by the FDIC, many of them are covered by state insurance funds.

The organizational structure of banking

Banks conduct their banking business through a variety of organizational forms such as branches, bank holding companies, special organizations, and correspondent banking networks.

Branch versus unit banks

It has been pointed out that some two centuries ago there were fundamental differences in political philosophy between two schools of thought, namely Jeffersonian and Hamiltonian, which gave rise to the basis of argument for branch versus unit banking.[2] Envisioning the American economy as evolving essentially into an agrarian economy, the Jeffersonian school advocated a decentralized government and unit banking, functioning as a community bank. The Hamiltonian school foresaw that the American economy would become an industrial economy and that, in order to support such an economy, it would be essential to have a centralized government and a branch banking system. The latter would be important in particular for mobilizing and reallocating financial resources on a nationwide basis.

Currently, branch banking is advocated on two major grounds. First, it provides economies of scale and an efficient channel through which available funds are reallocated. Second, it also provides a risk reduction mechanism in the form of geographical diversification of banking activities. For multi-product firms, like banks, overall economies of scale occur if total costs increase proportionally less than output when there is a simultaneous and equal percentage increase in each of the firm's products. For example, such simultaneous increases may occur when branches offering similar services are multiplied. There is some evidence that economies of scale are operative in the banking industry only up to a certain size – banks with a deposit size up to about $100 million.[3] This implies that a local bank with a deposit size of $100 million can effectively compete against any large banks including large money-center banks having a nationwide branch network.

Ironically, the efficient reallocation of financial resources is a major point of contention by the Jeffersonian school against nationwide branching. They argue that funds raised in a particular community should remain there and should be used in that community instead of being channeled elsewhere where the demand is highest. A branch network would support such reallocation too easily.

According to a recent Federal Reserve survey (Amel and Jacowski 1989), the branch banking restrictions may be classified into four categories based on the degree of restrictiveness in geographical coverage, namely (1) unit banking, (2) limited branching, (3) statewide branching, and (4) interstate branching. Note that it is the state law which precedes the federal law in defining the boundary of branch expansion.

According to the unit banking rule, no branch banking is permitted. All banking transactions are therefore carried out in the head office. Any national bank operating in such a state must follow the same restriction. Traditionally, Midwestern farm states, which were heavily influenced by the ideas of the Jeffersonian school, were characterized by this unit banking system. As of the end of 1987 there were four states practicing unit banking. [4]

On the other hand, the limited branching rule permits establishment of branches within well-defined geographical areas such as city limits or county limits or over several counties. In the latter case, it is usual to include the county in which the head office is located plus contiguous counties. Or the state law may simply set the number of counties in which a bank can establish its branches. As of the end of 1987, eleven states were practicing the limited branching rule.

Meanwhile, Western states as well as Atlantic coastal states traditionally provided statewide branching early on. Recently, more and more states are permitting statewide branching, reaching a total number of thirty-five by the end of 1987.

Unlike the case of branching within a given state, interstate branching was uniformly prohibited until the state of Maine permitted interstate branching for the first time in the 1970s. Such prohibition came from individual state legislations as well as two federal laws. At the federal level, the McFadden Act of 1927 first became the law prohibiting interstate banking, although the original intention of the Act was to equalize the branching power of national banks to the extent enjoyed by state banks. However, the problem was that no state then permitted its state-chartered banks to expand their branch network into other states. In addition, the Douglas Amendment to the Bank Holding Company Act of 1956 prohibited bank holding companies from acquiring out-of-home state banks. Nonetheless, in recent years there has been a discernible trend towards relaxing the restrictions on interstate branching through state initiatives. As of the beginning of 1991, twenty-five states (plus the District of Columbia) permitted nationwide branching. We will return to branching issues later.

Bank holding companies

A bank holding company is a company which holds at least one bank. The term "holding" means that (1) the company owns at least 25 percent of voting shares of a bank, or (2) the company has the controlling influence in electing a majority of bank directors. There are rebuttable cases when the ownership of voting shares is greater than 5 percent but less than 25 percent. In such instances, the Federal Reserve determines the applicability of the definition case by case. In 1987, there were 4,919 one-bank holding companies and 985 multi-bank holdings. Their combined market share in terms of banking assets was 91 percent then. There were 4,375 banks which did not have a bank holding company structure.

The advantages of having a bank holding company are several. First, the bank holding company device has been used to overcome regulatory restrictions, such as branch banking restrictions, interest rate ceilings, and reserve requirements. A bank holding company which owns multiple banks is effectively creating a branch system with one of the banks serving as a flagship bank. To avoid interest rate ceilings on deposits, particularly during the 1970s, bank holding companies issued commercial paper in place of subsidiary bank certificates of deposit. Similarly, in order to avoid reserve requirements on travelers' checks issued by banks, bank holding companies created travelers' check issuance subsidiaries.

A bank holding company setup permits opportunities not only for the economies of scale but also for economies of scope. There are two types of economies of scope. For a given product mix and a given scale of production for each product, if the total costs from joint production of all products in the product mix are less than the sum of the costs of producing each product independently, then there exist global economies of scope. Likewise, if the cost of producing a particular good jointly with other products is less than the cost of producing it independently, then we say that there exist product-specific economies of scope. Often cited sources of economies of scale and scope include the availability of specialized labor, computer and telecommunications technology, and information, all essential to the banking industry.[5]

Another advantage often cited for the formation of a bank holding company is that it can enter into nonbank activities which have the effect of risk diversification. However, some opponents of bank holding company expansion argue that nonbanking activities are inherently riskier than traditional banking, therefore, diversification into such activities does not necessarily reduce the overall risk but rather increases it.

The Federal Reserve, the regulator of bank holding company matters, appears to have taken a cautious approach to regulating bank holding companies yet steadily permitting new activities (such as underwriting of municipal revenue bond and commercial paper) to provide competitive powers for the banking organizations. In addition, a bank holding company serves as a managerial control center.

Bank mergers and acquisitions

Two banks may be merged into an entirely new entity (merger), or one of them may be acquired by the other (acquisition), and the acquired bank usually becomes a branch of the acquiring bank or a subsidiary of the bank holding company. During the five-year period from 1983 to 1987, 1,973 banks were either converted into branches or absorbed into other forms.

By mergers and acquisitions, a banking organization can expand its facilities where it was previously not permissible. In either case, an approval from a federal regulatory agency is required. If the resulting (surviving) bank is a national bank, approval must come from the Office of the Comptroller of the Currency. For a state member bank, it must come from the Federal Reserve; and for a state nonmember insured bank from the FDIC. In addition, the US Justice Department may challenge such an approval on the basis of the anti-competitive effect.

What are the criteria for merger approval? Although several factors such as (1) the financial resources of the acquiring banking organization, (2) its managerial resources, and (3) the convenience and needs of the community are considered, the main focus has been on (4) the probable impact on competition. If the merger is to lead to monopoly, most likely the proposed merger will not be approved. If it is to reduce competition "substantially," it is unlikely that the merger will be approved. Then, what do we mean by reducing competition "substantially"? In the landmark decision of 1963 on a merger case involving two Philadelphia banks, the Supreme Court decided that 30 percent or more of the market share is substantial.[6] More recently, in order to determine the probable anti-competitive effect, the Department of Justice issued merger guidelines which use the Herfindahl–Hirschman index (HHI) to measure the market structure. The HHI is the sum of the squares of market shares (measured in percentages) of each bank in the relevant market. For example, if there are only two banks with an equal market share, the HHI will be 5,000 ($= 50^2 + 50^2$). As shown in Table 10.3, whether or not the Justice Department is likely to challenge depends on the degree of concentration of the existing market and the extent of an increase in the HHI index as a result of the merger.

Because of global competition, it is more likely that mergers and acquisitions in the US banking industry will accelerate in coming years until the number of banks is reduced substantially.

Other organizational forms

As we studied in Chapter 3, organizational forms are employed to conduct

Table 10.3 Bank mergers guideline

Post-merger market concentration	Increase in HHI	Department responses
Highly concentrated (HHI ≥ 1,800)	Less than 50 points Greater than 100 points Between 50 and 100 points	Unlikely to challenge Likely to challenge Possible challenge
Moderately concentrated (1,000 ≤ HHI < 1,800)	Less than 100 points Greater than 100 points	Unlikely to challenge Possible challenge
Unconcentrated (HHI < 1,000)	Not relevant	Unlikely to challenge

Source: Di Clemente, J. J. and Fortier, D. A. (1984) "Bank Mergers Today: New Guidelines, Changing Markets," *Federal Reserve Bank of Chicago Economic Perspectives*, May–June: 4.

banking services fully or partly. Banking organizations limited to international transactions include Edge Act corporations and Agreement corporations. In addition, so-called "nonbank banks" which do not meet the dual criteria of charter and activity perform almost the same full-service banking. Yet, they are free to operate on a nationwide basis. Also, many functions of full-service banking have been unbundled and assigned to financial subsidiaries of bank holding companies. Therefore they may jointly perform the same banking services. For example, for consumer banking, they operate consumer finance companies, credit card companies and travelers' checks companies. For commercial lending, they employ commercial finance companies, leasing companies, and factoring companies. They also conduct limited investment banking business, using merchant banks and joint venture capital companies. Furthermore, a number of thrift institutions have been added as part of banking organizations through acquisitions by bank holding companies.

Foreign banks in the United States

Foreign banks grew most rapidly in the United States during the 1970s prior to the enactment of the International Banking Act of 1978. Since then, the pace of growth has slowed. However, the significance of their presence in the US market has been manifested in many ways. For example, by the end of 1987, a total of 246 foreign banks had presence in the US market with 689 offices in a variety of organizational forms such as branches, agencies, Edge Act corporations, and US bank subsidiaries. They posted total assets of $642.6 billion, which was equivalent to 22.6 percent of total assets of all commercial banks in the United States. We will return to their organizational structure in Chapter 13.

Correspondent banking networks

In addition, banks have correspondent banking networks, through which they may provide a whole spectrum of banking services to other banks. Correspondent banking is banking services provided by one bank to others. Usually money-center banks function as correspondent banks, whereas regional banks function as respondent banks. Respondent banks purchase services from correspondent banks in a wholesale fashion and sell them to their customers in the retail market. The reason why respondent banks buy services from other banks instead of producing by themselves is simple. It is because doing so is cheaper.

CHANGING REGULATORY ENVIRONMENTS

The regulatory environments in the US banking industry have changed considerably over the last several decades. New major banking laws have been enacted each time a new problem reached crisis level. Therefore, there were some elements of overreaction in legislation which themselves in turn became sources of problems in later years. Here, we briefly examine highlights of major banking laws enacted between 1913 and now.

Highlights of major Banking Acts

Federal Reserve Act of 1913

This Act established the Federal Reserve System with the aim of providing liquidity to commercial banks in order to prevent the recurring collapse of the banking system in the United States. Nationwide bank panics largely due to the illiquidity of banks had become a regular occurrence (1873, 1884, 1893, and 1907). The panic of 1907 finally led to the establishment of the Federal Reserve System despite the public fear of potential concentration of economic power in one system.

Banking Act of 1933

This Act which is also commonly known as the Glass–Steagall Act was enacted during the banking crisis of the depression period. During the four-year period from December 1929 to December 1933, the number of banks dropped from 24,633 to 15,015. Understandably, the major aim of the Act was to maintain soundness of the banking system, even at the expense of competition. Major provisions of the Act include (1) the separation of commercial banking from investment banking and the prohibition of commercial banks from investment banking business, (2) the establishment of the FDIC to provide deposit insurance for banks, (3) the imposition of interest rate ceilings on deposits (particularly demand deposits) to reduce undue competition among banks for funds, (4) the establishment of the per-borrower lending limit at 10 percent of the bank's capital in order to force diversification of lending risk, and (5) the establishment of the margin requirement (mr), expressed in terms of the percentage of the market value of securities, which is the minimum payment that must be made by the buyer of securities from his own funds.

Let us look more closely at several important provisions among the above, first the provision governing the separation of commercial banking from investment banking. Indeed, because of the importance attached to the required separation of commercial banking from investment banking, the Banking Act of 1933 is often identified as the law separating these two fields of banking. Massive bank failures following the stock market crash in 1929 were largely due to the fact that banks were ill prepared to assume the price risks associated with investment banking. This Act forced banks to choose either commercial banking or investment banking. Today, however, many banks which chose commercial banking as their line of commerce find their scope of business too restrictive for competing effectively against investment banks.

Next, although partly helped by the improved economic conditions, the establishment of the FDIC greatly reduced the number of bank failures in subsequent years. It was hailed as one of the most successful government programs. From 1934 through 1981, the number of insured banks that closed due to financial difficulties totaled 586, averaging only about twelve banks a year. However, more recent experience indicates that deposit insurance alone cannot prevent bank failures. From 1982 through 1987 the total number of bank failures reached 611, averaging about 102 banks a year.

The establishment of the margin requirement was designed for the Federal Reserve to control the temperature of the capital market by adjusting the availability of credit in the market through changes in the margin requirement. The difference between unity and the margin requirement, $1 - mr$, is thus the maximum percentage that banks can lend to securities buyers. The current margin requirement was set at 50 percent in 1974. Since then, the Federal Reserve has not changed the percentage, implying that it has not used the margin requirement as a policy tool for adjustment of economic conditions, but rather as a tool for bank safety. Since it is a selective policy tool, the effect can be more direct but at the same time there will be greater distortion in resource allocations.

As pointed out earlier, all the above major provisions and the per-borrower lending limit were intended to maintain the soundness of the banking system even at the expense of competition.

The International Banking Act of 1978

Prior to the enactment of this comprehensive federal law in 1978, foreign banks in the United States were regulated primarily by state laws. Congressional as well as Federal Reserve studies then indicated that all in all foreign banks had competitive advantage in the US market because of the lack of a unified law. This Act roughly equalizes competitive banking powers between US domestic banks and foreign banks in the US market. We will study this Act in more detail in Chapter 13.

The Depository Institutions Deregulation and Monetary Control Act of 1980

By 1980, the restrictive effects of the Banking Act of 1933 became apparent. Banks were no longer happy to be surrounded by the regulatory wall within which they faced little competition until early 1970s. In the mid-1970s nondepository institutions such as money market mutual funds began offering high yield investment opportunities for potential depositors with large deposit size, directly disintermediating funds from the depository institutions. Banks were unable to compete against them because of the interest rate ceilings on their deposits. Thus, a new rationale was established. Soundness of the banking system cannot be achieved by simply restricting competition but it can be achieved by promoting competition and making the banking industry profitable.

According to the Act, deregulation was aimed at removing the interest rate ceilings on deposits in an orderly manner within six years so that depository institutions could compete against nondepository institutions. Also, competition was to be promoted among depository institutions (banks, savings and loan associations (S&Ls), mutual savings banks, and credit unions). For this purpose, two approaches were used. One was to impose an equal reserve requirement burden on all depository institutions according to their size. Another approach was to grant all depository institutions the power to offer checking account services.

The uniform reserve requirements were also intended to provide the Federal Reserve System with a more effective monetary control system. However, it was later determined that the imposition of reserve requirements on small institutions would create an excessive administrative burden while not materially improving the effectiveness in money supply control. Therefore a certain amount of deposits ($3.6 million in 1992) was exempted from the reserve requirements. In this way small institutions are practically exempted from reserve requirements. The exemption level is annually adjusted according to a predetermined formula with reference to the growth in transactions accounts.

With checkable savings deposits, competitive powers of nonbank depository institutions were to be brought up approximately to the level of commercial banks. In addition, S&Ls were given new consumer and commercial lending powers, although such powers were limited to 20 percent of their total assets. This new power was also meant to provide S&Ls with the ability to match the maturity of assets to that of liabilities to some extent. Because of the very nature of S&Ls' mortgage lending business, they were facing rising short-term interest costs while their lending rates were locked in at a lower level for a longer term. Such risk was partly mitigated by using futures contracts in the government-guaranteed GNMA certificates, which were introduced in the Chicago Board of Trade in 1975.

Garn–St Germain Depository Institutions Act of 1982

Within two years from the time of enactment of the Depository Institutions Deregulation and Monetary Control Act, a new major financial institutions Act had be enacted because of the rapidly deteriorating conditions of the S&Ls and also of commercial banks to some extent. S&Ls were granted a greater flexibility to adjust their positions by permitting them to provide short-term consumer and commercial loans up to 40 percent of their total assets. However, this flexibility became a source of abuse later, as many S&Ls used up their permissible commercial lending limit by purchasing high-yield junk bonds which proved to be very risky.

Second, a number of direct assistance measures were provided. These were aimed at giving prompt aid to problem institutions by the Federal Savings and Loan Insurance Corporation (FSLIC) or by the FDIC, depending on whether they were S&Ls or banks. In addition, in the case of bank failures involving a total asset size of $500 million or more, out-of-state deposit taking institutions were permitted to acquire the bank. This signaled a relaxation of restrictions on out-of-state acquisitions for the first time in thirty years.

However, other provisions with good intention may have worsened the plight of problem institutions. The FDIC and FSLIC insurance coverage was increased to $100,000 per depositor from $40,000 in order to allow a larger safety net for depositors. However, it soon became apparent that depositors were willing to make larger deposits (often in excess of the coverage) with high-interest-paying depository institutions, regardless of the institutions' financial conditions, since they knew their deposits would be protected. High-interest-paying depository institutions must seek high-yield investments. Many of them wound up investing in junk bonds or commercial real estate. The collapse of the junk bond market and the real estate market in recent years caused the demise of many depository institutions, particularly S&Ls.

The Garn–St Germain Act also increased the per-borrower lending limit for national banks from 10 percent of bank capital to 25 percent to bring it to the level permitted for state-chartered banks in many states. However, this lending limit increase also caused concentration of lending to fewer borrowers, defeating diversification requirements.

Financial Institutions Reform, Recovery and Enforcement Act of 1989

The patchwork was no longer working. A drastic reform was needed. This new Act was designed to restructure the regulatory agencies to handle massive failures of S&Ls and banks. According to this Act, the FDIC now has two separate insurance funds: (1) the Bank Insurance Fund (BIF) to insure bank deposits, and (2) the Savings Association Insurance Fund (SAIF) to insure S&L deposits. In addition, the FDIC has management responsibility for a newly created liquidation agency, the Resolution Trust Corporation (RTC), whose main responsibility is to dispose of failed S&Ls and banks.

The FSLIC which provided deposit insurance for S&Ls was dissolved because of its poor monitoring record, and its insurance functions were transferred to the SAIF. Similarly, the Federal Home Loan Bank Board (FHLBB) which was the regulatory policy-making body for federal S&Ls was also resolved because of its poor supervisory performance. Its S&L supervisory function was transferred to a newly created agency, the Office of Thrift Supervision, under the Department of the Treasury. In addition to the regulatory function, the FHLBB had two additional primary responsibilities, namely setting housing finance policy and supervising the district Federal Home Loan Banks, which provide liquidity to financial institutions in home loan business. These two functions were assumed by the newly created Federal Housing Finance Board.

The RTC was partly financed by government general revenue with an initial funding of $50 billion and in the future it is to be financed by increased deposit insurance premiums. Where is the money spent? As long as the value of the assets of a failed institution is less than the value of the FDIC-insured liabilities, the difference constitutes the cost to the RTC.

Furthermore, the new law basically requires that S&Ls go back to the original function of housing finance. They must hold at least 70 percent of their total assets in housing-related mortgage. They can no longer hold junk bonds. Their commercial real estate loans must be held down, not to exceed four times their capital.

Current regulatory agency structure

Currently, commercial banks in the United States are regulated in a number of different ways including (1) bank chartering, (2) by approval of organizational changes (domestic branches, foreign branches, mergers), (3) by bank supervision and examination of banking activities (including compliance of assets, liabilities, off-balance-sheet, and capital requirements), (4) by providing deposit insurance, (5) by implementing monetary control (reserve requirements, credit control) and providing bank liquidity, when needed, and (6) by consumer credit protection.

The regulatory powers are shared by federal agencies (OCC, FRS, and FDIC) and state agencies, depending on the categories of regulation. As shown in Table 10.4, in principle the Office of the Comptroller of the Currency is responsible primarily for supervision and examination of national banks; the Federal Reserve is responsible for monetary control through controlling the required reserves of all depository institutions and providing liquidity, when needed; and the FDIC is responsible for the insurability of insured banks and S&Ls. However, the regulatory powers of the federal agencies overlap with those of state agencies, mainly because the Fed also has regulatory responsibility over the state member banks and the FDIC over the state nonmember insured banks.

Multiple regulatory agency versus single regulatory agency

Some economists argue that a multiple regulatory agency system promotes competition among regulatory agencies, as they will be more innovative in regulating banks and at the same time they will be less excessive in imposing regulatory rules. On the other hand, the multiple system creates conflicting rules and too much overlapping, causing inefficiency. The Federal Financial Institutions Examination Council was established in order to minimize confusion and conflicts and to establish better coordination. This five-member council (representatives from the Fed, the OCC, the FDIC, the FHLBB (now the OTS), and the National Credit Union Administration) has been working on the development of more uniform regulation and regulatory procedures. A recent legislative proposal, the Financial Institutions Safety and Consumer Choice Act of 1991, submitted by the Treasury Department to Congress proposes a consolidation of regulatory functions to the two agencies under the Treasury Department. Now let us look at summary functions of individual federal regulatory agencies for commercial banks.

The Office of the Comptroller of the Currency

The OCC was established by the National Currency Act (later renamed the

Table 10.4 Bank regulatory structures in the United States

Category of regulation	OCC	FRS	FDIC	State agency
National banks				
Bank charter	x			
Domestic branch license	x			
Foreign branch license[a]		x		
Merger	x			
Supervision and examination	x			
Deposit insurance			x	
Monetary control and liquidity		x		
Consumer credit protection		x		
State member banks				
Bank charter				x
FRS membership		x		
Domestic branch license[a]		x		x
Foreign branch license[a]		x		
Merger		x		x
Supervision and examination		x		x
Deposit insurance			x	
Monetary control and liquidity		x		
Consumer credit protection		x		
State nonmember insured banks				
Bank charter				x
Domestic branch license[a]			x	x
Foreign branch license[a]			x	
Merger			x	x
Supervision and examination			x	x
Deposit insurance			x	
Monetary control and liquidity		x		
Consumer credit protection		x		
Bank holding companies				
National		x		
State		x		x
Edge corporations		x		
Agreement corporations		x		x

Note: [a] Indicates prior consent from the respective federal agency.

National Banking Act) of 1863. It issues charters for new national banks; issues licenses for branches and trust powers of national banks; approves bank mergers, if the resulting bank is a national bank; and regulates and examines all national banks.

The Federal Reserve System

It is the central bank of the United States and conducts monetary policy to control the growth of the money stock and credit in the banking and other financial markets; imposes reserve requirements on all depository institutions including foreign banks in the United States; and sets the discount rates and provides liquidity to all depository institutions including foreign banks operating in the United States. In addition to the monetary control functions, the FRS performs regulatory functions. It gives prior consent for the establishment of a domestic branch by a state member bank; also gives prior consent for the establishment of a foreign branch by any FRS member bank; and approves mergers if the resulting bank is a state member bank. The Federal Reserve is also responsible for overseeing a variety of consumer credit protection laws (such as the Truth in Lending Act, the Fair Credit Reporting Act, etc.). Furthermore, the Federal Reserve has the overall supervisory responsibility over bank holding companies, Edge Act corporations and Agreement corporations.

Federal Deposit Insurance Corporation

It insures deposits of banks and S&Ls up to $100,000 per depositor account; manages the RTC which acts as receiver for all national banks placed in receivership and for state insured banks when requested by the state agencies; and requires all insured banks to submit reports on their financial conditions. In addition to the deposit insurance related functions, the FDIC is responsible for the supervision and examination of all state nonmember insured banks; gives prior consent for the establishment of a domestic or foreign branch of state nonmember insured banks; and approves bank mergers, if the resulting bank is a state nonmember insured bank.

The bank regulatory agency in each state

It issues charters for new state banks; regulates and examines all state-chartered banks usually in cooperation with the respective federal agencies; issues licenses for branches and trust powers of state banks; and approves state bank mergers, the formation of state bank holding companies, and the acquisition of state bank subsidiaries, as required by state laws.

Current bank regulatory issues

Bank failures and deposit insurance

Causes for recent bank failures are manifold: (1) increased interest rate risk, (2) interest rate deregulation causing high costs of funds, (3) deterioration of the quality of assets due to the collapse in bank lending markets such as the real estate market at home and the sovereign credit market abroad, and (4) a deposit insurance system which encourages banks to hold risky assets.

In particular, under the current regulatory structure, depositors do not have incentives to impose market discipline on the uses of their deposit funds by banks, because their deposits are insured, creating a moral hazard. That is, the deposit insurance may have the effect of altering the behavior of banks to engage in more risky investment. A high insurance premium does not ensure adequacy of the deposit insurance funds under the FDIC. Other more fundamental solutions must be found. Issues surrounding the deposit insurance are (1) whether or not to reduce the *de jure* and *de facto* coverage amount from the current level of $100,000, (2) whether or not to link the insurance premium to the adequacy of risk-based capital or certain market signals (use of puttable subordinated debts to be issued by banks), and (3) whether or not to give more authority on the methods of resolution of failed banks to the Treasury Department which is directly accountable to taxpayers.

When a bank fails, the FDIC steps in in the capacity of receiver and the FDIC faces the cost of resolving the failed bank. The most frequently used method of resolution during the period 1987–9 was the purchase and assumption method, followed by the insured deposit transfer method and the payoff method. For instance, in 1989, out of 206 failed banks, 174 banks were disposed of under the purchase and assumption method, in which the FDIC pays a healthy bank to take over all the failed bank's deposits (both insured and uninsured) and some or all of the assets. The difference between the deposit value and the asset value is what the FDIC pays. On the other hand, an insured deposit transfer is a case in which the acquiring bank takes over the insured deposits only. The cost for the FDIC is the amount equivalent to the value of the deposits less any intrinsic value (goodwill) that the buyer attaches to the deposit accounts. Finally, in a payoff case, the FDIC pays the bank's insured depositors immediately and shares the proceeds from the bank's assets with uninsured depositors. The major difference between the three methods is that the purchase and assumption method protects the uninsured depositors 100 percent. Although uninsured depositors may incur loss, their recovery rate in recent years has been about 80 percent.[7] Which method to choose? The FDIC (through the RTC) must choose the least costly method. But other considerations such as the needs of the community and the probable impact on the financial community are taken into consideration.

Separation of commercial banking and investment banking

As pointed out earlier, the Glass–Steagall Act prohibits commercial banks from engaging in investment banking. However, this does not mean that they are totally prohibited. They may underwrite federal government securities and municipal general bonds; they may arrange private placement of private securities; and they may also operate bank-sponsored mutual funds as their trust activities.

Recently, banks have broadened their investment banking powers through permissions of bank regulatory agencies or court decisions so that they can now underwrite municipal revenue bonds and commercial paper, in addition to mortgage-backed securities. Municipal revenue bonds are those issued to undertake specific revenue-generating projects such as toll highways, toll bridges, and fee-paying recreational facilities. Accordingly, their repayments are backed by the revenue generated from the earmarked projects, whereas general bonds are those whose repayments are backed by the general tax revenue. Also a subsidiary of a bank holding company may engage in investment banking as long as such a subsidiary is "firewalled" from the affiliate bank, and its revenue does not exceed 5 percent of the total banking organization revenue. "Firewalled" means that strict quantitative limits are applied on loans from the affiliate bank to the investment bank and all business deals between them must be at arm's length. These commercial banks are likely to intensify their inroads into investment banking.

Interstate banking

The main rationale for interstate banking is that nationwide banking organizations will be less vulnerable to regional economic conditions because such organizations will be able to offset losses in depressed regions by profits in prosperous regions. Second, although empirical evidence does not totally support this, some economies of scale can be realized.[8] Third, as the banking industry is globalized, there is greater pressure from foreign regulatory agencies for reciprocal treatment. For instance, the European Community requires the reciprocity rule so that if US banks are to enjoy the European Community as a single banking market, the United States must provide its whole regions as a single market. As shown in Table 10.5, twenty-eight states in 1993 permit nationwide branching. Out of the twenty-eight, seventeen states require reciprocal treatment whereas eleven states do not attach any strings. It is likely that more interstate branching will be realized in the near future. This may cause further consolidation of banks.

Risk-based capital adequacy requirement

Before 1985, banks were not formally required to hold an explicit capital −assets ratio, known as the capital ratio.[9] However, by 1985 three regulatory agencies (OCC, Fed, and FDIC) agreed to impose a minimum capital−assets ratio of 6 percent. During the 1980s the asset composition of banks shifted from less risky to more risky; risk has increased even within the same category of assets, as evidenced by increased charge-offs on loan

Table 10.5 Interstate banking legislation (as of February 1, 1989)

A   No entry from other states (5 states)
     Hawaii, Kansas, Iowa, Montana, North Dakota
B   Regional with reciprocity requirement (18 states)
     Alabama, Arkansas, Connecticut, Florida, Georgia, Indiana (6/1/92 to
     become national and reciprocal), Maryland, Massachusetts, Minnesota,
     Mississippi, Missouri, New Hampshire, North Carolina, South Carolina,
     Tennessee, Virginia, Washington, Wisconsin
C   National with reciprocity requirement (16 states)
     California (1/1/91), Colorado (1/1/91), Delaware (6/30/90), Illinois
     (12/1/90), Kentucky, Louisiana, Michigan, Nebraska (1/1/91), New
     Jersey, New York, Ohio, Pennsylvania (3/4/90), Rhode Island, Vermont
     (2/1/90), Washington, West Virginia
D   National with no reciprocity requirement (11 states and District of
     Columbia)
     Alaska, Arizona, District of Columbia, Idaho, Maine, Nevada, New
     Mexico (1/1/90), Oklahoma, Oregon (7/1/89), Texas, Utah, Wyoming

Source: Adapted from King, F., Tschinkel, S. L. and Whitehead, D. D. (1989) "Interstate
Banking Development in the 1980s," *Federal Reserve Bank of Atlanta Economic Review*,
May–June: 35–7
Note: The dates in parentheses are effective dates.

assets, for instance; and banks increased their off-balance-sheet commitments such as standby letters of credit. Faced with these problems, the three regulatory agencies began to consider risk-based capital requirements. At the same time the Federal Reserve and the Bank of England jointly developed a common set of risk-based capital requirements in 1987. Other countries joined subsequently. After further negotiations, a final agreement was reached in 1988 by the Basle Committee, a group of twelve industrial countries meeting under the auspices of the Bank for International Settlements. This final agreement also became the foundation for the minimum capital requirements for the European Community minimum regulatory harmonization program, which we will study in Chapter 14.

According to the new risk-asset requirements, bank assets are classified into four categories according to the degree of credit risk. The dollar amount of each item in a particular category is weighted by the risk weight for its category (0, 20, 50, or 100 percent). The sum of risk-adjusted assets and off-balance-sheet exposures is the total risk-based assets, for which banks have to hold the minimum capital. By the end of 1992, banks had to have total capital equal to at least 8 percent of risk-adjusted assets. In addition, banks must have met the leverage requirement which is the minimum ratio of capital to total assets.

What are the potential impacts of the new capital requirements on banks? As of June 1989, about 700 banks out of about 12,900 would fail to meet the new requirements and about 300 banks are relatively large banks with an average asset size of $3.04 billion.[10] This implies that there might be some slowdown in risk-asset-based activities. The problem with the risk-asset requirements is that they are based solely on credit risk and do not take into account other risks such as interest rate and exchange rate risks.

MONETARY POLICY AND THE ROLE OF COMMERCIAL BANKS

Recall the monetary approach we studied in Chapter 7 which attempts to explain how the foreign exchange rate is determined as the nominal money supply is changed, given the real demand for money. Such a nominal money supply change can also cause changes in the interest rate and real income at home. Since the late 1970s, the control of money supply growth has become the major task of the Federal Reserve.

The importance attached to achieving an optimal quantity of money supply is that only such a quantity provides monetary environments conducive for the economy to achieve (1) a steady high economic growth rate, (2) a low unemployment rate, (3) a stable price level, and (4) an equilibrium balance of payments.[11]

The Federal Reserve provides an important ingredient for the money supply, that is, the base money. The base money is basically the monetary liabilities of the Federal Reserve System, consisting of the bank reserves and the currency in circulation. Any increase in the assets of the Federal Reserve Banks is the source of base money, while any increase in the other liabilities of the Banks is a use of the base. The Federal Reserve is capable of changing the monetary base, as it can change its asset or liability items. It uses three general quantitative tools to change the base money: (1) open market operations, that is, buying and selling of government securities in the open market; (2) the provision of short-term liquidity adjustment credit and some extended-term credit to commercial banks and other depository institutions through the discount window of the Federal Reserve Banks; and (3) changes in reserve requirements.

Changes in the base money cause changes in the money stock in a multiple fashion, as shown in Figure 1.1 (Chapter 1). The ratio of the money stock to the base money is termed the money multiplier, which is determined jointly by the banking system, nonbank public, and the Federal Reserve. The M1 money multiplier as of the end of 1991 was about 2.73.

Once the money stock is determined, how does it affect the real output and the price level? An increase in money stock creates an excess supply of money, causing the interest rate to drop. On the one hand, the lower interest rate stimulates investment which in turn increases aggregate income. Increased income then increases the transaction demand for money. On the other hand, the lowered interest rate also increases the demand for money, this time the speculative demand for money. Thus eventually an equilibrium condition in the monetary sector is restored after an influence has been exerted in the real sector. Whether the lowered interest rate can be maintained or not depends on the absence of income and price anticipation effects.[12]

Now let us turn our attention from the macroeconomic role of commercial banks in the money supply process to their microeconomic role in the market where money market instruments are traded.

DOMESTIC MONEY MARKET AND THE ROLE OF COMMERCIAL BANKS

The money market refers to the market where short-term high-quality credit instruments are traded. Such instruments include Treasury bills, commercial paper, bankers' acceptances, negotiable certificates of deposit, loans to security dealers, repurchase agreements, and federal funds. Banks are active participants in this market as investors, dealers, and guarantors.

Treasury bills

A Treasury bill is a short-term obligation of the US government. Ranked by the amount outstanding and the trading volume, Treasury bills are the most important money market instruments. Their original maturity ranges from 91 to 364 days. They are attractive as investment instruments for a number of reasons: there is no default risk; they are highly liquid, as there is a well-developed secondary market; and interest income from Treasury bills is exempt from state and local income taxes. Banks invest in Treasury bills extensively as their secondary reserve assets. Some large banks are also Treasury bill dealers, trading often with a margin of 0.5 basis points.

Certificates of deposit

Negotiable certificates of deposit (CDs) are perhaps the second most important money market instruments today. They were first introduced only in 1961 with the formation of a secondary market. With the secondary market CDs became very liquid, regardless of the original maturity. Negotiable CDs are issued in large denominations with a minimum of $100,000. Typically, the maturity ranges from seven days to one year. In the domestic market they are sold on an add-on basis, that is, a principal plus interest basis, whereas in the Eurodollar market they are often sold on a discount basis. Default risk can be eliminated if the amount is $100,000 or less, as they are then insured at home. Although the CD secondary market is well developed, it does not have the same depth as the Treasury bills market. The rates for prime-name bank CDs are several basis points higher than the Treasury bill rates, and those for lesser-name bank CDs are about 25 basis points or more higher.

Banks needing a relatively large amount of funds at short notice can raise such funds by issuing CDs and selling them to CD dealers, who in turn distribute them to investors. Such a process is similar to commercial paper issuance. CDs issued by US branches of foreign banks within the United States fall under the category of Yankee CDs, as opposed to Eurodollar CDs which are those issued by any bank outside the United States.

Commercial paper

Commercial paper is the unsecured promissory note of a nationally known company with an initial maturity of 270 days or less. A maturity longer than 270 days would be treated the same as bonds which require registration with the Securities and Exchange Commission. The minimum denomination is $5,000 and they are sold at a discount. They are used as substitutes for bank loans. The name commercial paper came from the fact that originally commercial paper was issued by commercial finance companies engaged in inventory and accounts receivable financing. Today, banks participate in this market as guarantors as well as underwriters. These guarantee facilities have helped smaller firms, which could not have access to this market in the past, issue their paper now.

Bankers' acceptances

A draft drawn by an exporter and accepted by a bank (usually the letter of credit issuing bank) for a future payment becomes a bankers' acceptance. Bankers' acceptances may also be created as financial paper without underlying transactions. Banks are creators, investors, and dealers of bankers' acceptances. We will study this topic in more detail in Chapter 16.

Federal funds

These are commercial bank deposits at Federal Reserve Banks which are loaned to other banks. Maturity is usually overnight to one week. The empirical data indicate that money-center banks are usually net borrowers of funds.

SUMMARY

This chapter gave an overview of the US money and banking markets. The US banking system is somewhat unique in terms of industry structure and the regulatory structure. There are over 12,000 commercial banks in the United States with capitalization ranging from one million dollars to over five billion dollars. Such variations raise the question of the optimum size of a bank. Some empirical studies indicate that economies of scale and scope are operative for up to about $100 million asset banks.

Under the dual banking system, commercial banks are chartered and regulated primarily either by the state regulatory system or by the federal system. Within the federal system, the Office of Comptroller of the Currency, the Federal Reserve, and the FDIC share regulatory responsibilities ranging from charter and bank supervision to monetary control and bank holding company supervision to deposit insurance. The current regulatory issues include interstate banking expansion, relaxation of Glass–Steagall Act on investment banking, adequacy of deposit insurance in preventing moral hazard, and resolution of failed banks and thrift institutions.

Aside from providing credit and payment settlement mechanisms for the economy, commercial banks are major participants in the money supply process, which determines the overall economic conditions of the nation. In addition, commercial banks are borrowers, lenders, and dealers in the money market, where short-term high-quality credit instruments such as Treasury bills, commercial paper, certificates of deposits, federal funds, and repurchase agreements are traded.

REVIEW PROBLEMS AND EXERCISES

1. What is meant by the dual banking system in the United States?

2. What are the pros and cons of branch banking?

3. Explain the emerging trends in interstate branching.

4. If you were the bank regulator, how would you determine whether or not to grant a bank merger application?

5. What are the advantages of using a bank holding company?

6. Did the Garn–St Germain Act of 1982 help or hurt savings and loan associations? Why?

7. Briefly explain the following banking laws:
   (a) National Banking Act
   (b) Federal Reserve Act
   (c) McFadden Act
   (d) Glass–Steagall Act
   (e) Depository Institutions Deregulation and Monetary Control Act
   (f) Financial Institutions Reform, Recovery, and Enforcement Act

8. Which federal regulatory agency is responsible for the supervision and examination of the following depository institutions?
   (a) federal savings and loan associations
   (b) national banks
   (c) state member banks
   (d) state nonmember insured banks.

9. What are the issues in the current deposit insurance system?

10. How does the FDIC resolve failed banks? Can you say which method is the best?

11. How is the monetary aggregate determined? What is the role of the commercial banks?

12. What are the factors which might influence the currency ratio?

13. Explain the characteristics of the following money market instruments:
    (a) Treasury bills
    (b) Certificates of deposit
    (c) Commercial paper

NOTES

1 This dual system originates from different interpretations of the US Constitution. A strict interpretation of the Tenth Amendment to the Constitution accords only those powers listed in the Constitution to the federal government, giving the residual powers to the state governments. Bank chartering is not listed. Thus the state governments have inherent powers of bank chartering, while the National Banking Act of 1863 anyway empowered a federal agency to issue charters. See Perkins (1984: 831).
2 For more detailed debate, see Perkins (1984: 831–40).
3 See Clark (1988: 16–33).
4 See Amel and Jacowski (1989: 121).
5 Clark (1988: 18–19).
6 Bank deposits were used as a proxy to represent the size of banking activities. The geographical area was defined by the existing state branch banking limits rather than the metropolitan economic area.
7 See Keeton (1991: 5).
8 Clark (1988: 18–19).
9 See Keeton (1989: 41).
10 Keeton (1989: 49).
11 The first three policy objectives were stated in the Employment Act of 1946, and the Federal Reserve added the "reasonable balance in transactions with foreign countries" in its statement of purposes in 1974. These objectives were further articulated in the Full Employment and Balanced Growth Act of 1978.
12 Friedman (1968: 378–94).

BASIC READING

Amel, D. F. and Jacowski, M. J. (1989) "Trends in Banking Structure since the Mid-1970s," *Federal Reserve Bulletin*, March: 120–33.
Brewer, E. III (1989) "Full-Blown Crisis, Half-Measure Cure," *Federal Reserve Bank of Chicago Economic Perspectives*, November–December: 2–17.
Clark, J. A. (1988) "Economies of Scale and Scope at Depository Financial Institutions: A Review of the Literature," *Federal Reserve Bank of Kansas City Economic Review*, September–October: 16–33.

Di Clemente, J. J. and Fortier, D. A. (1984) "Bank Mergers Today: New Guideline, Changing Markets," *Federal Reserve Bank of Chicago Economic Perspectives*, May–June: 3–14.

Federal Reserve Bank of Minneapolis (1988) "A Case for Reforming Federal Deposit Insurance," *1988 Annual Report*, 3–16.

Garcia, G., Baer, H., Brewer, E., Allardice, D. R., Cargill, F. T., Dobra, J., Kaufman, G. G., Conczy, A. M. L., Laurent, R. D. and Mote, L. R. (1983) "The Garn–St Germain Depository Institutions Act of 1982," *Federal Reserve Bank of Chicago Economic Perspectives*, March–April: 3–30.

Hunter, W. C. and Wall, L. D. (1989) "Bank Merger Motivations: A Review of the Evidence and an Examination of Key Target Bank Characteristics," *Federal Reserve Bank of Atlanta Economic Review*, September–October: 2–19.

Keeley, M. (1990) "Deposit Insurance, Risk, and Market Power in Banking," *American Economic Review*, 80(5): 1183–200.

Keeton, W. R. (1989) "The New Risk-Based Capital Plan for Commercial Banks," *Federal Reserve Bank of Kansas City Economic Review*, December: 40–60.

—— (1991) "The Treasury Plan for Banking Reform," *Federal Reserve Bank of Kansas City Economic Review*, May–June: 5–24.

King, B. F., Tschinkel, S. L. and Whitehead, D. D. (1989) "Interstate Banking Update," *Federal Reserve Bank of Atlanta Economic Review*, May–June: 32–51.

Perkins, E. J. (1984) "Monetary Policy," in Green, J. (ed.) *Encyclopedia of American Political History: Studies of the Principal Movements and Ideals*, New York: Charles Scribner's Sons, vol. 2: 831–40.

FURTHER READING

Banaian, K., Laney, L. O. and Willett, T. D. (1983) "Central Bank Independence: An International Comparison," *Federal Reserve Bank of Dallas Economic Review*, March: 1–13.

Brunner, A. D., Hancock, D. and McLaughlin, M. M. (1992) "Recent Developments Affecting the Profitability and Practices of Commercial Banks," *Federal Reserve Bulletin*, July: 459–83.

Burke, J. (1984) *Antitrust Laws, Justice Department Guidelines, and the Limits of Concentration in Local Banking Markets*, Staff Studies No. 138, Washington, D.C.: Board of Governors of the Federal Reserve System.

Calomiris, C. W. (1989) "Deposit Insurance: Lessons from the Record," *Federal Reserve Bank of Chicago Economic Perspectives*, May–June: 10–31.

Evanoff, D. D. (ed.) (1985) "Financial Industry Deregulation in 1980s," *Federal Reserve Bank of Chicago Economic Perspectives*, September–October: 3–79.

Friedman, M. (1968) "Factors Affecting the Level of Interest Rates," in *Proceedings of the 1968 Conference on Savings and Residential Financing*. Reprinted in Havrilesky, T. M. and Boorman, J. T. (eds) (1980) *Current Issues in Monetary Theory and Policy*, 2nd edn, Arlington Heights, Ill.: AHM Publishing, 378–94.

Thorton, D. (1988) "The Effect of Monetary Policy on Short-Term Interest Rates," *Federal Reserve Bank of St. Louis Economic Perspectives*, May–June: 53–72.

Chapter 11

The UK money and banking markets

THE UK BANKING MARKET

The banking and money markets in the UK, like their respective markets in the United States, are not two distinctive mutually exclusive markets. Rather, they overlap each other substantially. We define the banking market in terms of major market participants – banks in this case – whereas we define the money market in terms of financial instruments traded. Since banks are also important dealers of money market instruments, it is natural that the two markets overlap.

First we examine the characteristics of the British banking market, focusing our attention on the type of banks and their major activities. We will also point out the mode of operation should it be significantly different from those in other markets.

The British banking market structure

Banks in the UK are a diverse group of financial institutions which are characterized by the fact that on the liabilities side they take deposits with relatively short maturity and that on the assets side they make loans for a variety of purposes with longer maturity, longer than the deposit maturity. In addition, many banks provide ancillary services, such as payment guarantee facilities, corporate financial advice, and investment management.

At present, banks in the UK are classified into eight groups for statistical reporting purposes: (1) retail banks, (2) British merchant banks, (3) other British banks, (4) American banks, (5) Japanese banks, (6) other overseas banks, (7) other (quarterly reporting small) banks, and (8) discount houses. Except for the first group of banks, all others are by and large engaged in wholesale banking, which involves relatively large-sum deposit taking and lending with narrow interest rate margins.

This classification of banks, as announced in August 1989 by the Bank of England, is based partly on functions, partly on ownership and partly on data-gathering convenience. Therefore each group does not necessarily

represent banks with distinctive functions. Rather, many different groups
of banks perform similar functions. As Gurley and Shaw (1960) noted, the
major function of financial intermediaries is to acquire "illiquid primary
securities" while issuing "liquid indirect securities" to the nonfinancial
sector. It is therefore easy for each type of financial institutions, particularly larger ones, to extend their services into areas previously specific to a
particular type of banks, thereby blurring the grouping boundaries. In
effect, as early as 1959, such possibilities were clearly noted in the Radcliffe
Report because of the similarity of liabilities of financial institutions.[1]

Table 11.1 shows major changes in the classification of banks in recent
years. Prior to the enactment of the Banking Act 1979, financial institutions

Table 11.1 Changing UK banking sector

UK banking sector (12/31/1978)		Institutions forming the monetary sector (11/16/1983)		Institutions included within UK banks (12/31/1990)	
London clearing banks	6	Retail banks	19	Retail banks	21
Scottish clearing banks	3				
Northern Ireland banks	4				
Accepting houses	35	Accepting houses	35	British merchant banks	36
Other British banks	70	Other British banks	241	Other British banks	150
Overseas banks	201	American banks	63	American banks	42
		Japanese banks	25	Japanese banks	31
		Other overseas banks	227	Other overseas banks	277
Consortium banks	29	Consortium banks	23		
Bank of England Banking Department	1				
Discount houses	18	Discount houses	10	Discount houses	8
	367		644		557

Sources: Committee to Review the Functioning of Financial Institutions (1980)
Appendices, London: HMSO, June: 394; Bank of England, *Quarterly Bulletin* (1981),
December: 533–7; (1983), December: 564–8; (February 1991), "Notes and definitions to
the tables"

recognized as banks were the so-called "listed banks," which were under the Bank of England credit control scheme and submitted their returns to the Bank. In a sense, at that time banks were defined by the regulatory relationship with the Bank of England rather than by a formal charter. These banks were collectively known as the "UK banking sector." But there were a number of banks falling outside the Bank's control, yet performing similar functions to those of the listed banks.

After the enactment of the Banking Act 1979, all recognized banks and licensed deposit-takers were brought under the control of the Bank of England so that the reported number of banks increased substantially.[2] In addition, some banks established by special legislation, known as Schedule 1 banks, were also brought under the new retail banks group largely on the basis of their retail banking functions. Since the liabilities of these banks constituted a bulk of certain monetary aggregates (M1, M2, and M3), the name "banking sector" was replaced by the term "monetary sector."[3]

However, in 1989 the conversion of a large building society into bank status brought about a major break in monetary aggregate data series, making the use of the term monetary sector inappropriate. There are two reasons for this. First, since the main components of M1, M3, and M3c are the liabilities of banks and such components do not include those of building societies, any conversion between a building society and a bank will cause a break in the data series.[4] As a consequence, the monetary aggregate statistics (M1, M3, M3c) sensitive to such switching will no longer be published. Second, the remaining monetary aggregates will thus be M2, M4 (plus possibly M4c), and M5.[5] However, the liabilities of banks in these remaining monetary aggregates are no longer so predominant as to call the group of banks the monetary sector. Therefore, the institutions in the monetary sector were renamed "banks in the United Kingdom."

As shown in Tables 11.1 and 11.2, as of the end of 1990 there were 557 banks with total assets of £1,258.5 billion. The market share of the foreign banks as a whole in terms of asset size was 56.4 percent, while that of the retail banks was 33.1 percent. Therefore the combined share of all other banks was only 10.5 percent. Now let us take a brief look at individual groups of banks.

Retail banks (21)

Included in this group are (a) London clearing banks (National Westminster Bank, Lloyds Bank, Barclays Bank, Midland Bank, Coutts & Co.), (b) Scottish clearing banks (Bank of Scotland, Clydesdale Bank, Royal Bank of Scotland), (c) Northern Ireland banks (Allied Irish Banks, Bank of Ireland, Northern Bank, Ulster Bank), (d) Trustee Savings Banks (TSB Bank, TSB Northern Ireland, TSB Bank Scotland), (e) Girobank, (f) other retail banks (Co-operative Bank, Abbey National, Abbey National

Table 11.2 British banking market structure (as of December 31, 1990) (in billions of pounds)

Type of banks	Liabilities and capital		Assets		Total liabilities/ total assets
	Sterling (1)	Foreign currencies (2)	Sterling (3)	Foreign currencies (4)	(5)
Retail banks	364.8	61.3 (14.4)[a]	355.0	71.1 (16.7)[a]	426.1 (33.1)[b]
Merchant banks	42.6	16.8 (28.3)	40.8	18.6 (31.3)	59.4 (4.6)
Other British banks	48.9	7.6 (13.5)	46.1	10.4 (18.5)	56.5 (4.4)
American banks	21.3	89.0 (80.7)	20.2	90.1 (81.7)	110.3 (8.6)
Japanese banks	43.1	211.4 (83.1)	40.5	214.0 (84.1)	254.5 (19.8)
Other foreign banks	108.2	251.4 (69.9)	109.3	250.3 (69.6)	339.6 (28.0)
Other banks	2.5	1.7 (33.3)	2.3	1.9 (36.4)	4.2 (0.3)
Discount houses	14.7	0.5 (3.2)	14.7	0.5 (3.2)	15.2 (1.2)
Total					1,285.8 (100.0)

Source: Bank of England (1991) *Quarterly Bulletin*, June: 3.2–3.8, 4
Notes: Banks included in retail, merchant, other British banks, American banks, Japanese banks, and other foreign banks are monthly reporting banks generally with a total balance sheet of £100 million or more, or eligible liabilities of £10 million or more.
"Other banks" are quarterly reporting small banks.
[a] Percentage of total liabilities and capital or of total assets.
[b] Percentage of the industry total.

Treasury Services, Yorkshire Bank), and (g) the Bank of England Banking Department. All of the above are involved in retail deposit-taking business and have access to their local clearing system. In order to conduct retail deposit-taking business, they maintain extensive branch networks. In 1985, the branch networks of the clearing banks alone totaled approximately 12,800.[6]

As their names imply, Scottish clearing banks and Northern Ireland banks are regional clearing banks. On the other hand, the London clearing banks, particularly the so-called "big four" (Barclays, Lloyds, Midland, and National Westminster) have dominated in retail banking business throughout the UK either directly or through their regional subsidiary clearing banks. One of the basic functions of the clearing banks is the provision of the payment mechanism, namely the cheque clearing system and the electronic funds transfer system. Their two other fundamental functions are deposit taking and lending. They take retail deposits as well as wholesale deposits. Retail deposit facilities are offered to individuals and organizations primarily through branch networks. They include current accounts (equivalent to demand deposits), interest-bearing sight deposits (similar to checkable savings deposits), and regular savings deposits. Wholesale deposits are large interest-bearing deposits (usually at least £50,000) on which the interest rate is closely linked to money market instruments. They include time deposits and negotiable certificates of deposit. On the lending side, clearing banks provide credit to both personal customers and companies. Lending facilities offered to personal customers include overdrafts, personal loans, mortgage loans, credit card finance, and professional business loans, while those offered to corporate customers include overdrafts, term loans, syndicated loans, leasing, and factoring.

Trustee Savings Banks (TSBs) started out as unincorporated thrift institutions (similar to mutual savings banks in the United States) in the early nineteenth century to provide savings facilities for small savers. In the name of protecting small depositors, they were heavily regulated and their business was confined to taking savings-type deposits and investing received deposit money in public sector debt.

By the end of 1978, there were eighteen TSBs with over 1,600 branches. Each had its own clearly defined business region. Now the number has decreased to three, one covering Northern Ireland, another Scotland, and the third England and Wales. Meanwhile, their asset-based activities have been expanded to a full range of personal credit facilities including personal loans, overdrafts, credit cards, mortgage loans, and small business loans. Although they still aim their business predominantly at personal customers, they are today full-fledged retail banks.

Girobank was established in 1968, after years of debate in response to the recommendation of the Radcliffe Report (1959), to provide an inexpensive, convenient, speedy money remittance service and cashing facilities for consumers through over 20,000 post offices. As additional services were added subsequently, such as a payments service for government units to the personal sector and therefrom, personal loans, and a remittance service for business, the bank has slowly transformed into a full-fledged retail bank. Meanwhile, it became a fully operational member of the London Clearing House in 1983.

Other retail banks include the Co-operative Bank, Yorkshire Bank and the recently converted Abbey National. The Co-operative Bank serves customers through a national network of branches and outlets of the co-operative societies. It receives deposits from individuals, various co-operative societies, trade unions, and local authorities. It provides loans to individuals and co-operative societies as well as to non-co-operative societies. The Yorkshire Bank operates as a retail bank in the North of England and the Midlands. Abbey National was a building society and became a bank in 1989. Its total assets then were £32 billion, compared with £190 billion for all building societies and £340 billion for banks' total sterling assets. Even without making their conversion into the status of banks, building societies have already been in direct competition with banks in savings deposit business. The conversion of such a large society is expected to create greater competitive environments in the banking and money markets.

As noted earlier, also included in the retail banks is the Bank of England Banking Department. Why? The Bank of England has two major departments, the Issue Department and the Banking Department. The Issue Department is responsible for issuance of bank notes. As such, it is treated as part of the government for national accounting purposes. The Banking Department is the banker to government, to banks, as well as to a small number of certain individuals. To serve as the banker to the government, it maintains banking accounts for the Exchequer, Paymaster General, and other government departments. It makes short-term funds available to the government in exchange for government securities. Such funding needs often arise, as government payments and receipts are not perfectly synchronized. Just like individuals maintaining their accounts with banks to settle their payments, London Clearing House member banks maintain their clearing balances with the Banking Department to settle payments of their own as well as on behalf of other nonmember banks. In addition, the Banking Department receives or supplies bank notes, depending on the demand for till money by banks. If the Department needs more bank notes than it has in stock, it in a sense buys them from the Issue Department in exchange for government securities. In addition, the Banking Department also serves a small number of private customers who have maintained their accounts dating from prenationalization days and Bank of England staff members. Thus, the business of the Banking Department resembles that of any retail bank except that customers are substantially different. The Department is a member of the London Bankers' Clearing House.

As shown in Table 11.2, the retail banks as a group had total assets of £426.1 billion as of December 1990, 33.1 percent of the total assets of the British banking industry. The major sources of funds for the retail banks were deposits taken from the nonbank UK private sector such as households and firms, comprising about 51 percent of total sources of funds. On the assets side, the retail banks as a group contributed about 55 percent of the total assets for advances to the UK private sector.

In lending, the retail banks have been guided by the real bills doctrine, which argues that, in trust of public money, clearing banks should lend only short-term loans based on real bills. These loans have the characteristics of being short term, productive, and self-liquidating in nature. That is, money is loaned to borrowers to enable them to purchase inventories; then, inventories are sold on credit terms (thus creating accounts receivable); when payment is made, accounts receivable are retired into cash which is now ready for use for the loan repayment.

By and large following this doctrine, clearing banks, when faced with nontraditional business opportunities such as term loan lending or loan syndications in the 1960s and 1970s, opted to conduct such business through their subsidiaries. In this way, the clearing banks would be insulated from new unfamiliar risks. However, when a number of secondary banks, many of which were subsidiaries of clearing banks, got into financial difficulties in the early 1970s, it proved to be unwise to insulate in such a way. As a consequence, clearing banks started entering nontraditional markets more directly.

British merchant banks (38)

Many British merchant banks originated as merchants in the nineteenth century, developing banking services as an adjunct to their merchanting business. Since the main thrust of their banking services was the business of accepting bills, they acquired the name "accepting houses." Their knowledge about their trading areas gave them a distinctive advantage in evaluating the creditworthiness of potential borrowers abroad in the early days. With diversification in business over the years, today they deal primarily with the corporate sector and engage in wholesale banking. Their primary sources of funds are time deposits and certificates of deposit (CDs), whereas on the assets side they mainly concentrate on medium-term lending. Unlike commercial banks, early on they were engaged in longer-term financing such as development financing. For example, for the development of the Americas, British colonies, and other developing territories, which were supported by some £3.6 billion between 1870 and 1913, about 40 percent of loans were raised by London accepting houses.[7] Reflecting their heavy engagement in international banking, their foreign-currency-denominated assets are about 30 percent of total assets, twice as large as the proportion for retail banks.

Nonetheless, their major contribution to corporate finance comes from their investment banking activities, underwriting not only sterling securities but also Eurocurrency bonds and equity. For the last few decades, they have diversified their activities in a number of directions including investment fund management, merger and acquisition service, factoring, leasing, as well as the formation of alliances with stockbroking and stockjobbing firms.

Other British banks (150)

Included in this group are subsidiaries of the clearing banks specializing in international, merchant, and wholesale banking. Also included are finance houses, now authorized as banks, and British overseas banks such as Standard Chartered Bank. In addition, among the offshore banking institutions in the Isle of Man and the Channel Islands (such as Jersey and Guernsey), those British institutions which opted to submit their returns to the Bank of England are included. Despite the large number of banks, their market share in the banking industry is relatively small, only 4.4 percent.

Subsidiaries of the clearing banks and finance houses depend heavily on interbank and CD markets for their funding needs. Funds are used for medium-term loans, installment loans, mortgage loans, international loans, etc., depending on their specialized field. British overseas banks are those which have their head offices in London but their branches located outside the UK, mainly in the UK's old colonies. They acted as efficient allocators of financial resources between different geographical locations and functioned as central banks of British colonies in the past.

Overseas banks (350)

As of December 1990, there were 350 foreign banks operating in London. Their total market share measured by assets was about 57 percent. About 75 percent of their assets as well as liabilities were in foreign currencies. Among the foreign banks, the market share of the Japanese bank group (thirty-one banks) was the highest with 19.7 percent, followed by that of the American bank group (forty-two banks) with 8.6 percent. Under the Banking Act 1979, foreign banks as well as British banks have to be authorized by the Bank of England in order to take deposits either as recognized banks or as licensed deposit-takers. The majority of foreign banks operating in London are recognized banks. And they are engaged in wholesale banking business.

In earlier classifications of banks, a separate grouping was provided for consortium banks. These were banks established by several parent banks to carry out specialty business in international banking areas. None of these parent banks held more than 50 percent of the shares of the consortium bank, and at least one of them was a foreign bank. Their principal activities were the provision of term loans in foreign currency to corporate customers and public customers and they were active in the loan syndication business. These banks are now lumped into the group of "other overseas banks."

Discount houses (8)

Discount houses originally started their staple trade in the discounting of inland bills presented by "country banks." As international trade grew, discounting foreign bills of exchange became more important until the First World War. Then their business shifted toward underwriting Treasury bills and making the secondary market for such Treasury bills and later for the short-end of gilt-edged securities. During the last three decades they have gradually increased their activities in the local authority securities and certificates of deposit markets and more recently in the commercial paper market.

Overall, discount houses are financial institutions unique to the London money markets, performing several different functions. First, discount houses make the market for bank liquidity. Their function is similar to the federal funds market in the United States in which US banks typically adjust their liquidity positions through borrowing and lending funds which are held by commercial banks at the Federal Reserve. In the UK this is done through discount houses. That is, when banks have excess liquidity, they place such funds with discount houses on call or at short notice. When banks are in need of liquidity, they call in their money or borrow directly from discount houses. Second, with a blessing from the Bank of England, discount houses act as the discount window of the central bank for banks. In addition, they are for the Bank of England the "market feeler" that is an essential ingredient needed for the conduct of monetary policy. Third, discount houses are investment companies, investing in short-term money market instruments with the borrowed money. The difference between the rate of return on investment and the cost of funds is the source of profit. The money market instruments in which discount houses usually invest include Treasury bills, gilt-edged stocks, local authority securities, commercial bills, certificates of deposit, and more recently commercial paper. Fourth, discount houses are securities dealers, generating profit by buying securities at lower prices and selling them at higher prices. Investment requires a minimum period of holding, usually at least overnight, in order to earn interest income, whereas dealing does not require such a minimum period of holding.

The UK bank regulatory framework

Unlike the case of the United States, the Bank of England is the *de facto* singular bank regulatory agency, although the Treasury has the final say on the matters of bank regulation and monetary control. The Bank of England was originally founded in 1694 to finance the war against France. The note-issuing power of the Bank was reaffirmed by the Bank Charter Act of 1844. In 1946 the Bank was nationalized to become officially the central bank of the UK under the Bank of England Act, by which the Treasury was given power to give directions to the Bank from time to time.

Largely in the capacity of the central bank in the UK, the Bank of England exercised prudential controls over the banks informally prior to the enactment of the Banking Act of 1979.

1971 Competition and credit control

In 1971 the Bank of England introduced a new system of monetary regulation and control which was aimed at improving the competitive environment within the banking system and resorting to the price mechanism instead of credit rationing for credit allocation, while ensuring overall credit control to check inflationary pressure. For these purposes, new reserve requirements were imposed uniformly on all banks; the quantitative ceiling on credit allocation was removed; and the interest rate target was replaced by the money stock target in implementing monetary policy, which prompted banks to anticipate greater fluctuations in interest rates. All these changes forced clearing banks to abandon almost all of their interest rate agreements (known as "cartels") and standard service fee agreements (known as "standard tariffs").

Prudential regulation prior to 1979

Since clearing banks were the ones which predominantly carried out domestic banking business, the Bank of England monitored their operations closely. There were a number of banks outside the clearing system, however, which played important specialist roles, for example as accepting houses and discount houses. In addition, many banks classified today as other British banks were outside the supervision of the Bank of England. For such a financial institution to be regarded as a bank, it had to take a number of steps, starting at very basic banking services with no recognition at all. That is, such an institution might start as a money lender with a money lending license or with exemption of the license, as provided by the Money Lenders Acts 1900–27. Then, it must be recognized as a bank by the UK Inland Revenue to receive or pay interest gross of tax. Next, to hold non-disclosed reserves or to deal in transactions in foreign exchange it must obtain an authorization from the Bank of England. With such a set of minimum authorizations, a financial institution was expected to evolve eventually into a bank, while earning recognitions from the banking community. In sum, a financial institution wishing to become a bank had to go through multiple steps of apprenticeship.

The Banking Act 1979

For the first time, with the Banking Act 1979 the Bank of England was formally empowered to regulate all banks in the UK, replacing the informal supervision imposed over a limited number of banks, so-called listed banks. There were two major reasons which prompted this legislation. First, since the secondary banks were operating outside listed-bank supervision, the 1973–5 banking crisis (with twenty-four banks involved) in the secondary money market was initially viewed as outside the purview of the Bank of England. However, the seriousness of the problem and the connection between clearing banks and financially troubled secondary banks raised the concern of the Bank of England, forcing the Bank eventually to render direct assistance. This event suggested that closer supervision would be necessary for all banks, not just the listed banks. Second, it became necessary to streamline bank supervisory functions in line with the First Banking Directive of the European Community issued in 1977, which required that member countries provide minimum regulatory policy harmonization.

Following the Banking Act 1979, depository institutions were classified as either "recognized banks" or "licensed deposit-takers." The minimum conditions that a bank had to fulfill in order to gain the recognized status were that

1 it had enjoyed a high reputation and standing in the financial community for a reasonable period of time;
2 it provided either a wide range of services or a highly specialized service covering (a) deposit taking, (b) overdrafts or other forms of lending, (c) foreign exchange services, (d) the financing of foreign trade and medium-term loans, or (e) financial advice, investment management services, and securities-transactions-related credit;
3 business was performed with integrity and prudence;
4 it was under direction of at least two individuals;
5 it met the minimum net asset requirements.

Meanwhile, licensed deposit-takers had to satisfy the same conditions 3–5. Instead of enjoying a high reputation and standing, their officers had to be "fit and proper." Note that licensed deposit-takers are the type of institutions, as described earlier, that must go through a number of steps and wait for years before the full honor of being a recognized bank is accorded. There were also some banks which were outside the purview of these two categories. These were special banks established by special legislation, known as Schedule 1 banks, such as Trustee Savings Banks and building societies.

The Banking Act also established the Deposit Protection Fund, similar to the FDIC in the United States. The Fund is administered by the Deposit Protection Board under the Bank of England. The idea of deposit insurance was initially opposed by the clearing banks because of potential moral hazard. They contended that the existence of a deposit protection scheme might actually make it easier for an imprudent bank to flourish, as such a bank might take on far riskier investment.[8] In addition, it was argued that the deposit insurance was a simple subsidy to less sound banks supported at the expense of prudent banks. A scaled-down version of the scheme was finally adopted. A major difference in the deposit insurance program was that in the UK the coverage was limited to 75 percent of the first £10,000. Here, a co-insurance element is incorporated, whereas in the United States 100 percent of the first $100,000 is insured, creating moral hazard, as we studied in the last chapter.

In addition, the minimum net assets requirement was imposed; sufficient liquidity holding was required; and individual banks had to establish their foreign exchange exposure management program.

The Banking Act 1987

This new legislation augmented the regulatory powers of the Bank of England. Banks are no longer classified into two categories. A single category of authorization was established and all depository institutions must satisfy the "fit and proper" test. The single classification became necessary largely for two reasons. First, under the 1979 Act, when banks were classified into recognized banks and licensed deposit-takers, immediately the latter were perceived as less creditworthy banks, pushing their costs of funds up. Second, a failure of a recognized bank in 1984, instead of a licensed deposit-taker, undermined the rationale for maintaining a distinction between the two groups, leaving the impression that the classification was by and large arbitrary. Meanwhile, the insurance coverage was increased to £20,000 with 75 percent payoff. As a member country of the Basle Committee, the UK imposes risk-based bank capital requirements similar to the US requirements.

THE UK MONEY MARKETS

Now let us look at instruments traded in the British money market. Similar to the US money market, the UK money market is the market where high-quality short-term financial instruments are traded. However, the UK money market seemed well divided into two markets, namely the traditional market on the one hand and the parallel (or secondary) market on the other, during the period from the time the secondary market appeared in the 1950s to the time it faced its major crisis in the early 1970s.

The traditional money market

The discount houses, clearing banks, and the Bank of England are major participants in this market. Of these three groups, the discount houses play a central role. They make markets, that is, they quote buying and selling prices of short-term high-quality instruments at which they are prepared to deal. As noted earlier, the type of instruments traded in this market are commercial bills, Treasury bills, and short-ends of gilt-edged stocks. In addition, discount houses receive deposit money in the form of call money.

Call money is short-term deposits received by discount houses mainly from clearing banks and payable upon call. Call money accounts are secured by assets of discount houses in most instances. Depending on maturity, there are several types of call money: (a) overnight money which is payable automatically the next day; (b) day-to-day money which has no fixed maturity and is payable upon call; (c) notice money, which requires an advance notice, either two days or seven days; and (d) time money, which has a fixed maturity.

Commercial bills have been used since the seventeenth century as a means of raising short-term funds in the UK. Today bills are one of the most convenient instruments of financing for commercial firms and at the same time serve as investment instruments for many. A bill of exchange is an unconditional order drawn by one person (usually the seller) to another (usually the buyer) demanding payment of a certain amount at a fixed future time (usually three- to six-month maturity). Bills are used for financing international and inland trade as well as for accommodation finance. The quality of a bill as an investment instrument depends on the creditworthiness of the accepting bank and the discount bank. For example, a bill which is accepted by a well-recognized bank and discounted by a discount house would be regarded as a highest quality instrument. In addition to sterling bills of exchange, foreign currency bills are also traded in this market.

Treasury bills have provided for the British government an important method of raising the short-term funds it needs and at the same time a means of controlling the money stock by selling or buying them. Bills are practically riskless and very liquid. Their risk is low because they are obligations of the Treasury and as such repayment is guaranteed by the UK government. Their liquidity is high because there is a well-developed secondary market where, regardless of the remaining maturity, holders of Treasury bills can sell them at the going market rates at any time they wish. Treasury bills are issued with maturities of ninety-one days or thereabouts in denominations ranging from £5,000 up to £1,000,000 and sold at a discount. For example, if the yield on a discount basis is 11 percent, the selling price can be found by solving the following for P:

$$\frac{100 - P}{100} \frac{365}{91} = 0.1100. \tag{11.1}$$

Thus, $P = 97.2553$. This means that for every £100 face value the buyer of the Treasury bill pays £97.2553. Note that the effective yield will then be higher than 11 percent, as we replace the denominator term 100 by 97.2553.

Next, for investors short-dated gilt-edged stocks are an attractive alternative to Treasury bills. The term "gilt-edged" refers to British government obligations or government guaranteed securities. Note that the term stocks are used in place of bonds, as they are traded on the London Stock Exchange. Although they are basically capital market instruments, their "shorts," which are those having a maturity of five years or less, are actively traded by discount houses and clearing banks as money market instruments.

The parallel market

Different from the traditional money market, the so-called parallel market was developed at the fringe of the traditional market by other market participants such as banks in the "other British banks" category and foreign banks. Major instruments traded in this market include local authority securities, CDs, commercial paper, and interbank loans.

Local authorities borrow money by issuing local authority bills, deposits, and short-term bonds (yearlings, for instance). Local authority bills are also known as revenue bills, money bills, or local government promissory notes, which are issued, with maturities of less than six months, by local authorities under the Local Government Act of 1972. The interest rates on local authority bills are slightly higher than those on Treasury bills. Local authority bills are negotiable instruments, whereas local authority deposits (deposit receipts) are nonnegotiable. Local authority bonds are usually issued as yearlings which mature in a year and six days.

Eurodollar certificates of deposit were introduced in London in 1966, and sterling CDs were made available two years later. A sterling CD is a negotiable receipt issued by a UK bank or a foreign bank as evidence of a deposit of sterling for a stated period at a stated interest rate. It is issued at par on the interest-to-maturity basis. It is a bearer instrument and fully negotiable. For banks, CDs are convenient tools for raising a relatively large sum of funds within a short span of time, as banks can sell their CDs to CD dealers. Therefore, banks may go into the CD market to raise funds with amount and maturity equivalent to loan applications, thereby easily matching asset and liability maturities. Although sterling CDs are issued up to five years, the bulk of them have a maturity of three to six months. Foreign currency

CDs are also actively traded in the parallel market. In fact, part of the parallel market constitutes the Eurocurrency market.

Commercial paper was formally introduced in the money market in 1986. It is a promissory note issued by a well-known corporation. Commercial paper is different from commercial bills, however, in that the former usually does not have underlying transactions and is a one-name paper. Only qualified corporations can issue commercial paper in the UK, whereas there is no such restriction in the United States.

Traditionally, clearing banks in the UK avoided borrowing from other banks unless they had major liquidity problems of their own, partly because clearing banks each had a large number of branches that made the law of large numbers operative in estimating the needed funds. In addition, they relied on liquidity provided by the discount houses. Thus, their philosophy was not to rely on the interbank market. However, banks operating on the fringe of the parallel market had to depend on the interbank market for their short-term funds. This practice was facilitated by the increasing demand for foreign exchange which the traditional discount market was less well prepared to provide.

Despite our attempt to explain the traditional money market and the parallel money market separately, it will be difficult to maintain the segmented market view. This is partly because participants in each market are moving into the other market. Recent banking legislation makes the separation of participants in these two markets less meaningful.

LONDON AS AN INTERNATIONAL FINANCIAL CENTER

In Chapter 8 we studied the advantages and disadvantages of having an international banking center and some major factors for becoming such a center. Let us look at the case of London. London has achieved its position as *the* international financial center partly as the cumulative result of historical incidents such as the accumulation of national wealth through industrial revolution, the financing of the British Empire, the traditional philosophy of openness, and its position as a historical gateway between the old and the new world.

In more recent years, the British government and the Bank of England have made more deliberate efforts to maintain London as the international financial center. Such efforts include encouragement for the development of Eurocurrency markets in London, maintaining a stable monetary and financial environment, steady deregulation of the financial sector, and the transformation of unwritten regulations into written ones which are more helpful for newcomers in the market. In addition, the banking business in London has traditionally emphasized the financing of international trade and investment, which is one of the major attractions encouraging foreign banks to locate in London. The existence of an adequate banking infrastructure and expertise is another contributing factor. The infrastructure includes telecommunications and transportation facilities, office facilities, support services (such as printing, accounting, and legal services), the language spoken, and established banking practices.

However, London may not sustain its position as *the* international financial center in the future, but may become one of several. As Table 11.3 shows, New York and Tokyo which each have their own larger economic base may be real contenders in the areas of international bank lending, foreign exchange dealing, and securities transactions. In addition, the implementation of the 1986 single market legislation of the European Community may provide proportionally greater advantages for Paris, Luxembourg, and Frankfurt, simply because they are positioned on the European continent. In addition, the location of the new EMU central bank in the near future will affect the position of London markedly.

From the habitat institutions' point of view, why should they locate in London? More fundamentally, what is the centralizing force which pulls financial institutions toward one location? One answer is that such a location provides an economic environment which enables the resident institutions to take advantage of externalities or to realize economies of scope. For example, a worldwide telecommunications system may disseminate information instantaneously to anyone located anywhere. However, it does so only when the information is registered with the system. Otherwise, there

Table 11.3 Comparison of market size among the three largest centers

Type of business	Ranking		
	1st	2nd	3rd
International bank loans outstanding as percentage share of total market ($2,390 billion) (end of 1988)	Japan 20.6	UK 20.5	USA 10.0
Foreign exchange turnover (net, billions of US dollars) (April 1989)	London 187	New York 129	Tokyo 115
Futures and options exchanges as percentage share of total traded lots (547 million contracts) (1988)	Chicago 80.7	London 6.6	Tokyo 3.9
Stock exchanges (1988) Market value of domestic securities (billions of US dollars)	Tokyo 3,840	New York 2,722	London 711
Number of listed domestic companies Number of listed foreign companies	1,571 122	7,387 349	2,054 526

Sources: Bank of England (1989) *Quarterly Bulletin*, November: 516–28; Bank for International Settlements (1989) *59th Annual Report*, 106

is no need for financiers to be located at a centralized location. Tips and ideas obtained from personal contacts at a center generate externalities of information which put those at the center in a distinctively advantageous position. Likewise, if the infrastructure is well developed, it is more likely that the resident institutions may realize economies of scope or economies of scale. In addition, direct cost reduction measures such as low taxes, low rentals, and low regulatory costs are conducive to attracting financial firms. In Chapter 3, we used the term "host-country-specific advantages" encompassing a whole set of comparatively favorable conditions in a host location.

Now let us take a look at the position of a center. Why should any locality be nurtured to become an international financial center? Obviously, there are both benefits and costs of maintaining a particular locality as a center. For London, such benefits include contributions to the balance of payments, employment, and tax revenue. For example, in 1988 the net balance of payments surplus of the UK financial sector was £7.0 billion, the bulk of which was generated in London. Insurance earnings were the largest, amounting to £3.8 billion; banking earnings were £0.9 billion; and the rest such as investment funds management, securities dealings and brokerage, and others accounted for £2.6 billion. In terms of employment contribution, the banking sector in London had 198,000 employees as of September 1987, which was 6 percent of the total employment in the UK industries and services. Furthermore, the financial sector as a whole in the UK produced 19.5 percent of GDP in 1988, which provides an indirect measure of tax revenue.[9] In addition, British domestic corporations enjoy an easy access to worldwide financial markets as well as trade and corporate finance services. Also, the steady inflow of foreign financial institutions to London has stimulated competition within the UK financial markets.

On the other hand, the disadvantages of London being an international financial center include higher local rents, increased regional disparity between London and other areas, overdependence on a single sector, and greater difficulty in conducting monetary policy.

SUMMARY

In this chapter, characteristics of the UK banking system were examined, emphasizing types of banks and their activities. At present, banks in the United Kingdom are classified into eight groups for statistical reporting purposes, namely retail banks, British merchant banks, other British banks (such as British overseas banks and parallel market banks), American banks, Japanese banks, other overseas banks, quarterly reporting small banks, and discount houses. The retail banks group includes London and other regional clearing banks, Trustee Savings Banks, and Girobank among others, all of which provide payment settlement services. Except for the first group banks, other group banks are by and large engaged in wholesale banking business.

With the Banking Act, 1979 the Bank of England was formally empowered to regulate all the banks in the UK for the first time, replacing the informal supervision imposed over a limited number of banks, so-called listed banks. The Banking Act, 1987 further strengthened the supervisory powers of the Bank of England, requiring that all the banks which conduct banking business must be "authorized."

The last part of this chapter raised the question whether or not London could remain as *the* international financial center. London faces competition not only from New York and Tokyo but also from European regional centers such as Frankfurt, Paris and Luxembourg.

REVIEW PROBLEMS AND EXERCISES

1. Explain the main characteristics of the following groups of banks:
   (a) retail banks
   (b) British merchant banks
   (c) overseas banks
   (d) consortium banks
   (e) Girobank
   (f) Trustee Savings Banks
   (g) discount houses
   (h) British overseas banks

2. What is the rationale for the inclusion of the Banking Department of the Bank of England in the category of retail banks?

3. If you were an adviser on the statistical reports prepared by the Bank of England, would you suggest some other grouping of banks, other than the current classification?

4. Define the following banks:
   (a) recognized banks
   (b) licensed deposit-takers
   (c) Schedule 1 banks

5. According to the Banking Act 1987, what are the factors considered by the Bank of England to authorize the establishment of a bank?

6. How would a money lending company over the years evolve into a full-fledged bank in the UK?

7. How different is the UK deposit insurance program compared with the US system? Is the UK system more likely to reduce moral hazard?

8. How different are the traditional and parallel money markets?

9. Suppose that the UK Treasury bill rate on a discount basis is 8.125 percent. What is the market value of the bill per £100 par value?

10. Briefly explain the following financial instruments:
    (a) gilt-edged stocks
    (b) commercial bills
    (c) local authority securities
    (d) sterling certificates of deposit
    (e) commercial paper
    (f) call money

11. Evaluate the advantages and disadvantages of locating your banking office in London.

NOTES

1 In order to have an effective monetary policy, first there must be a well-defined monetary aggregate under control of the Bank of England. Then, the velocity of money associated with a particular monetary aggregate must be stable. The report focused on the difficulty in defining money because money is only one of many indirect securities of financial institutions, implying that the velocity of money is unstable and that the quantity theory of money would not work. The report had a substantial impact on the government policy toward the financial system in subsequent years. See the Radcliffe Committee (1959: para. 389).

   In addition, there are two other comprehensive reports on the UK financial system which have a similar significance. One is the report of the Macmillan Committee on Finance and Industry (1931), which focused on foreign exchange parity issues. The other is the report of the Wilson Committee to Review the Functioning of Financial Institutions (1980), which was concerned about the efficiency of functioning of financial institutions. Its recommendation led to greater competition in financial markets including the stock market in recent years.

2 There were 590 recognized and licensed deposit-takers as of November 18, 1981, which were reported for the first time by the Bank of England after the passing of the Banking Act 1979 (Bank of England 1981: 533–7).

3 M1 included currency in circulation, sight deposits at banks, and interest-bearing sight deposits at banks; M3 included M1 plus additional components (sterling time deposits at banks and sterling certificates of deposit at banks). M2 includes nib M1 plus interest-bearing retail deposits with banks and building societies. Nib M1 includes currency in circulation and non-interest-bearing sight deposits at banks. Note that, except for currency in circulation, the components of monetary aggregates M1 and M3 consist only of the liability items of banks.

4 M3c includes M3 plus foreign currency deposits at banks.

5 M4 includes nib M1 plus interest-bearing sterling sight deposits (equivalent to checkable savings deposits in the United States), sterling time deposits with banks, and shares and deposits and certificates of deposit with building societies; M5 includes M4 plus money market instruments (bank bills, Treasury bills, local authority deposits), certificates of tax deposits, and national savings instruments.

6 National Westminster Bank (1985: 4).

7 See Rybczynski (1973: 107–22).

8 See Committee of London Clearing Bankers (1977: para. 5.20).

9 See Bank of England (1989: 516–28).

BASIC READING

Bank of England (1981) "Money and Banking Figures: Forthcoming Changes," *Quarterly Bulletin*, December: 531–7.
—— (1983) "Revised Presentation of Banking Statistics," *Quarterly Bulletin*, December: 562–8.
—— (1989) "London as an International Financial Centre," *Quarterly Bulletin*, November: 516–28.
—— (1991) "Notes and Definitions to the Tables," *Quarterly Bulletin*, February.
Channon, D. F. (1977) *British Banking Strategy and the International Challenge*, London: Macmillan.
Gilbody, J. (1988) *The UK Monetary and Financial System: An Introduction*, London: Routledge.
Grady, J. and Weale, M. (1986) *British Banking, 1960–85*, London: Macmillan.
Groome, D. R. and Johnson, H. G. (eds) (1970) *Money in Britain 1959–69*, Oxford: Oxford University Press.
Gurley, J. G. and Shaw, E. S. (1960) *Money in a Theory of Finance*, Washington, D.C.: Brookings Institution.
Kindleberger, C. P. (1974) *The Formation of Financial Centers: A Study in Comparative Economic History*. Princeton Studies in International Finance No. 36, Princeton, N.J.: Princeton University Press.
National Westminster Bank (1985) *National Banking System*, London.
Radcliffe Committee on the Working of the Monetary System (1959) *Report*, London: Her Majesty's Stationery Office.
Reed, H. C. (1981) *The Preeminence of International Financial Centers*, New York: Praeger.
Rybczynski, T. (1973) "The Merchant Banks," *Manchester School*, 41 (1): 107–22.
Wilson Committee to Review the Functioning of Financial Institutions (1980) *Report* and *Appendices*, London: Her Majesty's Stationery Office.

FURTHER READING

Banking Act 1979, London: Her Majesty's Stationery Office, Chapter 37.
Banking Act 1987, London: Her Majesty's Stationery Office, Chapter 22.
Committee of London Clearing Bankers (1977) *The London Clearing Banks: Evidence to the Committee to Review the Functioning of Financial Institutions*, London, November.
The Economist (1991) "Why London?", May 4.
Financial Services Act 1986, London: Her Majesty's Stationery Office, Chapter 60.
Hawawini, G. and Rajendran, E. (1989) *The Transformation of the European Financial Services Industry: From Fragmentation to Integration*, New York: New York University Press.
Kelly, J. (1977) *Bankers and Borders: The Case of American Banks in Britain*, Cambridge, Mass.: Ballinger.
Macmillan Committee on Finance and Industry (1931) *Report*, London: Her Majesty's Stationery Office.
Mayer, C. (1990) "The Regulation of Financial Services: Lessons from the United Kingdom for 1992," in Dermine, J. (ed.) *European Banking in the 1990s*, Oxford: Blackwell.

Mullineux, A. W. (1987) *UK Banking After Deregulation*, London and New York: Croom Helm.
Revell, J. S. (1973) *The British Financial System*, London: Macmillan.
Zawadzki, K. K. (1981) *Competition and Credit Control*, Oxford: Blackwell.

Part III

International bank regulation

Chapter 12

Analytic framework for international bank regulation

THE EFFECT OF INTERNATIONAL BANK REGULATION ON BANK BEHAVIOR

The banking industry in the United States, as in many other countries, is a highly regulated industry. Commonly stated objectives of bank regulation are (1) to maintain a sound and efficient payment system which is necessary for smooth commercial transactions, (2) to control liquidity of the banking system which is a key to price stability, (3) to regulate the allocation of financial resources to achieve certain policy objectives, such as promotion of a specific industry, (4) to control cross-border capital flows to insure national interest, and (5) to promote competition and efficiency so that banking services are provided efficiently at competitive prices.

The first four objectives tend to increase bank regulations, resulting in reduced competition and efficiency, while the last one is to offset the ill effect of the first four. Bank regulation is in essence a balancing tool between a variety of objectives — sometimes conflicting ones. For many countries these objectives are equally important, but for some countries certain objectives are more important than others, depending on their past experience and current needs. Thus industrialized countries which depend more on private initiatives in the marketplace may emphasize both soundness of the banking system and promotion of competition coupled with price stability, while developing countries that are anxious for accelerated economic development may emphasize financial resource allocation and control of capital flows.

Since bank regulation will either restrict the permissible area of bank operations or increase costs of operations, the imposition of regulation will cause corresponding changes in bank operations; some changes are directed to overcoming the boundary constraint, while others are to reduce regulatory costs. In contrast with domestic banks, international banks have a wider range of alternatives: (1) location of banking facilities, (2) type of organizational setups, (3) banking products, and (4) accounting and reporting practices. Let us look at each in turn.

Choice of location

When a bank is deciding where to locate its overseas facility, it is natural for it to consider regulatory environments in which it would be operating, in addition to potential business opportunities. In some instances banks may choose a particular location solely on the basis of regulatory advantage. In order to attract such banks, some banking centers (Bahamas, the Cayman Islands, the Ivory Coast, and Kenya) have emphasized regulatory advantage as the single most important selling point.[1]

Choice of organizational forms

Also in some instances differences in regulation are deciding factors for whether banks set up a branch or a subsidiary or some other form of banking organization. As you recall from the discussion of the causes of growth of the Eurocurrency market, international banks frequently use offshore banking facilities instead of their home offices for foreign-source deposit business in order to avoid regulatory costs. Also it has been a common practice for banks to use several specialized subsidiaries to enter a foreign market where branches are prohibited. Furthermore, in deciding which organizational forms to choose, the potential tax burden or advantage is an important consideration. For US tax laws, a foreign subsidiary of a US firm is a foreign entity not subject to US taxation until earnings are remitted to its parent, while a branch is an integral part of the parent subject to US taxation immediately. Therefore, a branch setup must have substantially more advantages in operations than a tax-advantageous form of subsidiary.[2]

Financial innovations

In addition, when a new regulation is imposed, banks often respond by creating new products or techniques to mitigate the impact of a new regulation. We examined the causes behind the supply of financial innovations in Chapter 9 – for instance, banks moved into new areas of business when a new bank capital adequacy requirement was imposed in the mid-1980s. Securitization of bank loans, the issuance of mandatory convertible notes, and business expansion in standby letters of credit were all designed to mitigate the new bank capital requirement.

Choice of transfer pricing, and accounting and reporting methods

In order to reduce regulatory costs including the tax burden, banks also resort to transfer pricing as well as different accounting and reporting methods. For instance, a bank parent located in a high tax country may transfer funds to its subsidiary in a tax-haven country at a lower interest rate to generate profit at the subsidiary rather than at the parent in order to reduce tax liabilities, although tax laws usually require that transactions between affiliated entities be at arm's length. Similarly, how the accrued gains such as discount gains can be categorized, for instance as ordinary income or capital gains, and how such gains can be amortized may result in the use of different accounting and reporting methods.

In short, banks attempt to take regulatory arbitrage as such opportunities are created from the imposition of new regulations. Regulatory arbitrage in turn may negate the original purpose of the regulation to a certain extent but at the same time reduces market segmentation created by the regulation. What is the effect, then, of regulatory arbitrage at a macroeconomic level?

Where to locate their facilities, what kind of organizational form to choose, what kind of financial instruments to use, how to report their performance, all will have a direct effect on the balance of payments of countries that either export or import banking services. Furthermore, such decisions will have an effect on the level and redistribution of income between home and host countries and between owners of different factors of production (capital and labor) within each country, as we studied in Chapter 2. Also, regulatory arbitrage will have an immediate impact on foreign exchange and financial markets at home and abroad, as it changes the availability of funds and services.

CLASSIFICATION OF BANK REGULATIONS BY IMPACT

It would be useful to classify international bank regulations by their effect rather than by *de jure* or formality, because the impact gives a better measure of competitiveness. International bank regulations can be conveniently classified at two levels: at the entry level and at the operational level. Although regulations are imposed by both host and home countries, we will direct our attention to the regulations imposed by the host countries. According to a report by the US Department of the Treasury (1979) to Congress regarding foreign treatment of US banks, a variety of regulatory tools was used by foreign countries to restrict banking activities. Some countries prefer using laws, whereas others prefer administrative decrees or rely simply on conventional practices. When the conditions for entry and the nature and scope of operations are set forth by law, they tend to be less ambiguous, thereby making it easier for new entrants. The opposite will be the case when effective rules are set by frequent changes in administrative decrees or by unwritten convention. In such a case potential entrants may even need a mentor to guide them in the new market.

Regulation at the entry level

What is the extent of the restrictions at the entry level? It varies: (1) total prohibition of the presence of foreign banks, (2) only representative offices; (3) agencies or minority ownership in local banks; or (4) branches or majority ownership in local banks. Obviously, at one extreme is total prohibition of foreign bank presence. With the collapse of centrally planned economies and the encouragement of free capital flows by capital exporting countries together with the IMF and the World Bank, there are hardly any countries which choose this extreme today. Next to this is allowing only representative offices, which essentially function as contact points without banking powers. In less restrictive cases, foreign banks may be permitted to establish agencies or acquire local banks in minority interest. In countries where financial markets are almost completely liberalized, foreign banks are usually permitted to establish their branches or acquire local banks in majority interest. One cannot say which is less restrictive, however, between permission to establish a bank branch and permission to establish a majority-owned subsidiary bank, as it ultimately depends on the extent to which the bank or branch is allowed to engage in banking business.

Regulation at the operational level

Next, what are the types of restrictions imposed at the operational level? Most operational restrictions increase the cost of operations directly or indirectly. Nonetheless, certain restrictions affect cost of funds more directly, while others limit the boundary of business opportunities, thereby

Table 12.1 Examples of restrictions on foreign banks

"Tax-like" restrictions (on liabilities)
Differential reserve requirements
Differential deposit insurance coverage requirements
Differential deposit taking powers
No access to rediscount facilities of the central bank
No access to subsidized funds for export financing
"Quota-like" restrictions (on assets)
Overall credit/lending ceilings
Ceilings on loans in host-country currency
Ceilings on loans in foreign currencies
Specified investment portfolio
Specified loan portfolio (or loan allocation quota)
Currency swap limits

Source: US Department of the Treasury (1979) *Report to Congress on Foreign Government Treatment of US Commercial Banking Organizations*, 15

affecting revenue more directly. The former type of restrictions may be termed "tax-like" restrictions and the latter "quota-like" restrictions. We also note that tax-like restrictions mainly affect the liability side of the bank balance sheet, while quota-like restrictions, for example restrictions on the size of certain asset items such as local currency loans, by and large affect the asset side. Table 12.1 shows examples of these restrictions.

Yet, the above classification is mainly for convenience. For one thing, asset and liability items are interrelated with one another; second, either type of regulatory restrictions will eventually reduce the profit of banking business in that country. Figure 12.1 shows the equivalence of tax-like and quota-like regulations in terms of restricting banking business. In a two-country model with increasing costs of production of banking services, country A exports banking services while country B imports them or acts as a host country, because the latter has a higher equilibrium price. In Figure 12.1(b), the domestic banking supply in country B (the host) is represented by curve S_2 and the sum of the domestic supply and foreign excess supply by S_2', whereas the domestic demand in country B is represented by D_2. Without regulatory restrictions, the equilibrium point is at E' and the volume of imported foreign banking services can be measured as the distance between B_1 and B_3. Alternatively, we can use the excess supply curve $S_1 - D_1$ and the excess demand curve $D_2 - S_2$ directly to determine the equilibrium point, as shown in Figure 12.1(c). The distance $0Q_2$ represents the same volume as B_1B_3. When a tax-like restriction is imposed, the excess supply curve will shift upward, as shown by ES', reflecting a fixed unit cost increase. The same quantitative restriction can be achieved by setting a quota-like restriction equal to $0Q_1$. However, a quota-like restriction results in a loss of government revenue by country B, equal to P_5JKP_4. Nonetheless, this loss can be recouped by selling bank operating licenses. In effect, if an auctioning method is used, the recovery will be greater than the case of a tax-like restriction. Aside from government revenue, the host country can use either method to restrict foreign banking services to a desired level, say, $0Q_1$.

The corollary to this statement is that it is not always necessary for a host country which does not want the presence of foreign banks to resort to outright prohibition. The same objective can be achieved by increasing a tax-like restriction until foreign banks face an excess supply curve that rises above price level P_2, as shown by curve ES".

Another interesting question is how to provide equal treatment to foreign banks should that be an objective of the host government. The effect-oriented approach discussed above recognizes that a rigid application of identical laws or regulations to both foreign and domestic banks results in a differential treatment between them rather than an equal treatment. This is because the scope and nature of their operations are generally different. For example, an even-handed application of strict foreign exchange

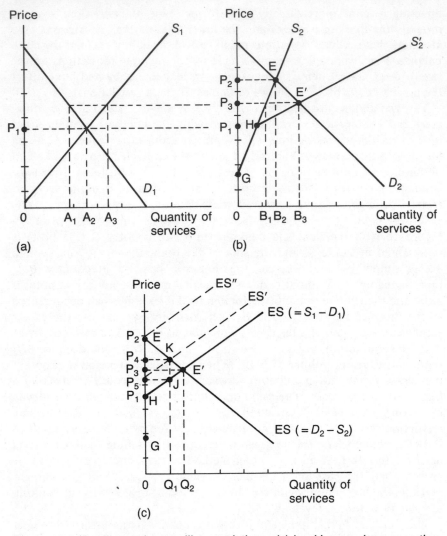

Figure 12.1 Tax-like and quota-like restrictions: (a) banking-services exporting
country; (b) banking-services importing country; (c) excess
demand ($D_2 - S_2$) and supply ($S_1 - D_1$) in the banking-services
importing country

controls may affect foreign banks more because foreign banks are involved
more in foreign exchange dealings. Likewise, an even-handed application of
the interstate branching restriction within the United States would affect
foreign banks more heavily because domestic banks do have a greater
number of alternatives for conducting interstate banking. On the other
hand, a uniformly required ratio of reserves to domestic currency deposits

will act as a regressive tax for domestic banks, particularly for smaller banks, because they depend proportionally more on domestic currency deposits.

Because of inherent differences in the nature and scope of operations of foreign banks compared with domestic banks, the regulatory objective of promoting competition through equal treatment cannot always be achieved by uniform application of laws and regulations to both foreign and domestic banks. Instead, some differential treatment would be needed in some instances to achieve effective equality.

PRINCIPLES OF INTERNATIONAL BANK REGULATORY JURISDICTIONS

When a bank enters a foreign market, it faces the question of regulatory jurisdictions. Which country's rule is dominant? Over the last two decades or so, several principles of regulatory jurisdictions have emerged as a result of major legislative actions in major industrial countries and concerted regulatory harmonization efforts among these countries. Major legislative actions include the US International Banking Act of 1978, the UK Banking Acts of 1979 and 1987, the French Banking Act of 1984, and the First (1977) and Second (1989) Banking Directives of the European Community. At the same time the formation of the Basle Committee in the late 1980s has increased regulatory coordination. [3]

There appear to be five emerging principles of bank regulatory jurisdictions: (1) the host country principle, (2) the home country principle, (3) the reciprocity principle, (4) the principle of regulatory policy harmonization, and (5) the principle of separation of supervisory responsibility for solvency and liquidity. In order to facilitate our discussion, consider the banking facility matrix in Table 12.2, constructed by country of origin and the location of facilities. B_{ij} represents banking facilities (branches) originating from country j and located in country i.

The host country rule

According to the host country principle or rule, all the banks regardless of their country of origin are to be regulated by the government of the host country in which they are located. Thus, this principle is also known as the residence principle. However, it does not necessarily imply that the host country will treat foreign banks in the same manner as domestic banks. An extension of the host country rule is the principle of national treatment, by which foreign banks are treated as if they were host country banks. The regulatory treatment of B_{12} and B_{13} then depends on the treatment of B_{11}, which serve as reference banks. The US International Banking Act of 1978 is guided by this principle of national treatment with large domestic banks as reference banks, as we will examine in more detail in the next chapter.

Table 12.2 Banking facilities matrix

Location	Origin		
	Country 1	Country 2	Country 3
Country 1	B_{11}	B_{12}	B_{13}
Country 2	B_{21}	B_{22}	B_{23}
Country 3	B_{31}	B_{32}	B_{33}

The home country rule

The home country rule permits home country banks to operate in foreign countries, and to establish branches, according to the laws and regulations of the home country as if the foreign country were part of the home country. Thus, this principle is also termed the nationality principle or extraterritorial principle. For example, regardless of their location, banking facilities B_{21} and B_{31} from country 1 are governed by the government of country 1 in the same manner as B_{11}. The EC Second Banking Directive of 1989 which provided the fundamental regulatory framework for credit institutions in the European Community is based on the home country rule. The basic idea behind this rule is so-called "mutual recognition," which means that each host country is expected to honor the judgment of the home country on the soundness of home country banks and their operations.

However, in the past countries were reluctant to accept this principle because it might encroach on the sovereignty of host countries. On the other hand, more recently the principle has been advocated because of its perceived advantage in promoting competition. It is argued that with the home country rule the banks from the least regulated country will have immediate advantage in the host country, competing against banks from more heavily regulated countries. This in turn is expected to cause banks from more restrictive countries to put pressure on their home governments to relax their bank regulations.

On the other hand, the host country rule keeps the host country market segmented from the rest of the world, although such segmentation can be maintained only temporarily. If the residents of each country are permitted to shop around for banking services worldwide, the location of banking facilities becomes less important. Therefore, whether segmented markets created by the host country rule face competitive pressure or not depends on the extent to which residents of such countries are left free to participate in out-of-country banking markets. The wholesale market participants such as large firms face practically no restrictions stemming from the host country rule, while retail market participants such as household units usually do not have the freedom of using banking services worldwide. When the two principles are simultaneously applied, bank regulation becomes more restrictive as the more restrictive rule becomes the effective rule.

Principle of regulatory policy harmonization

The third principle is that of regulatory policy harmonization which is mainly intended to equalize the treatment of B_{11}, B_{22}, and B_{33}. If regulatory policy is completely harmonized among the participating countries, then it does not matter whether the home country rule or the host country rule is applied. A major question here is the level at which rules are harmonized.

Earlier experience based on the EC Banking Directive of 1977 which attempted to harmonize the member country rules as much as possible showed up some difficulties. Because of a high level of regulatory structure in each member country, the host country rule did not produce competitive incentives to integrate the inter-country markets but kept each market segmented. Also, the attempts to centralize the rule-making have proved to be difficult. Subsequent effort has been directed toward harmonization at a minimum level. As noted earlier, the first successful harmonization effort came from the member countries of the Basle Committee on Banking Supervision when they adopted the minimum bank capital requirement based on the weighted risk-assets of banks.

The difficulty in harmonization of regulations partly stems from the fact that the host and home country governments may have different regulatory objectives or may not attach the same degree of importance to each objective. For example, of the several bank regulatory objectives we examined earlier, the US regulatory agencies tend to attach importance more to (1) soundness of the banking system through protection of depositors and (2) stability of liquidity supply, whereas regulatory authorities of developing countries are usually more concerned about (3) financial resource allocation and (4) control of foreign capital flows.

We can show the above situation using the Venn diagram in Figure 12.2. First, the rectangular area is all conceivable banking activities, out of which circles A and B represent the permissible banking activities as defined by the regulatory authorities of country 1 (United States) and country 2 (a developing country) respectively. The distance from the center of the rectangle to each corner measures the relative importance attached by each respective country. The overlapping area formed by the two circles shows the degree of policy harmonization. It is essential to have harmonization of regulatory objectives first in order to achieve overall regulatory harmonization. This overlapping area is also the scope within which a foreign bank must operate when it must comply with both home and host country rules simultaneously.

Soundness of
banking practice
(1)

Control of foreign
capital flows
(4)

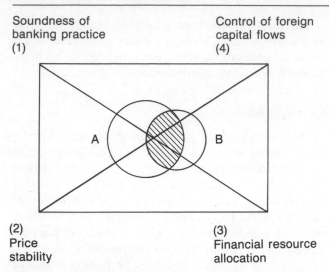

(2)
Price
stability

(3)
Financial resource
allocation

Figure 12.2 Conflicting objectives of bank regulations

The principle of reciprocity

This principle stipulates that in country 1 the treatment of banks from countries 2 and 3, that is, B_{12} and B_{13}, depends on the treatment that B_{21} and B_{31} receive in countries 2 and 3 respectively. Obviously, the net result of application of this principle is to apply different regulatory frameworks for foreign banks coming from different countries, thus creating an administrative nightmare. Without too much administrative burden, the principle may be applied at the entry level, as adopted, for example, in the New York state banking law. The US federal banking law does not require the reciprocity, while the EC Second Banking Directive stipulates the application of this principle to banks of nonmember countries.

The principle of separation of solvency and liquidity responsibility

This principle assigns to the host country the responsibility of providing adequate liquidity and a stable monetary environment in which banks operate, and to the home country the responsibility of supervising the prudential banking practices of their home banks. For prudential supervision, as long as all the countries adopt the same principle, whether home country rule or host country rule, there will be no overlapping or lack of cover in regulatory jurisdictions, thereby avoiding the problems of banks being forced to observe conflicting rules or of being unchecked.

OPTIMAL INTERNATIONAL BANK REGULATION

Using the concept developed for international taxation, we may define neutrality of international bank regulation as a situation in which the imposition of regulation does not interfere with or affect the bank's choice between making direct investment at home and making investment in foreign countries for banking operations.[4] More specifically, bank regulation is neutral if (1) it does not alter the relative rates of return at home and abroad, (2) thereby it does not interfere with the bank's choice between capital investment at home and abroad, and (3) it results in that allocation of resources among sovereign jurisdictions which maximizes worldwide total income. The neutrality which maximizes worldwide total income is said to be worldwide efficiency.

However, worldwide efficiency does not always imply maximization of the income of the banking capital exporting country or that of the capital importing country separately. Then, to what extent should the capital exporting country impose bank regulation, say, in the form of regulatory fees or quantitative restrictions? In order to see the impact of regulation in this context, let us review the basic model of foreign capital flow, which is intended for investment in the banking sector. Worldwide efficiency would be achieved if direct investment for banking operations reached the level where the rates of return at home and aboard became equal.

However, recall equation (2.6) (Chapter 2) which shows the condition needed for maximization of income for the capital exporting country:

$$i_1 = i_2 + I \frac{di_2}{dI} \tag{2.6}$$

which we can rewrite as

$$i_1 = \left(1 + \frac{I}{i_2} \frac{di_2}{dI}\right) i_2. \tag{12.1}$$

We now note that the term $(I/i_2)(di_2/dI)$ represents the elasticity of the rate of return on foreign direct investment and it is a negative value under the condition of a diminishing rate of return. Therefore, in order to maximize income of the banking capital exporting country, the home country should impose a tax-like regulatory fee equivalent to the above elasticity so that

$$i_1 = (1 - c_2)i_2 \tag{12.2}$$

where c_2 is the regulatory fee rate on the rate of return on direct investment in country 2.

If worldwide efficiency is to be achieved, $c_2 = 0$ so that in equilibrium the following holds:

$$i_1 = i_2. \tag{12.3}$$

This condition may be obtained by a hands-off policy or a regulatory harmonization policy applied to both countries.

Figure 12.3 shows the optimal international bank regulation graphically. The basic structure of Figure 12.3 is the same as that of Figure 2.1, the line AA' representing the marginal product of capital of the banking capital exporting country and the line BB' the marginal product of capital of the banking capital importing country. Worldwide efficiency can be achieved by permitting capital to flow from country 1 to 2 by EF.

The optimal capital export for the banking capital exporting country is achieved before the equilibrium point **e** is reached. If the home country imposes a regulatory fee of **mf**, no capital movement will take place, whereas if the regulatory fee is **ac**, the amount of capital movement will be FG. Therefore the total fee collected will be equivalent to the area **cgja**, which consists of two parts, area **cgqb** and area **bqja**. Without regulation, the net gain for the banking capital exporting country is represented by area **efq**. The optimal regulatory fee is the one which maximizes the difference between area **bqja** and area **ecb**.

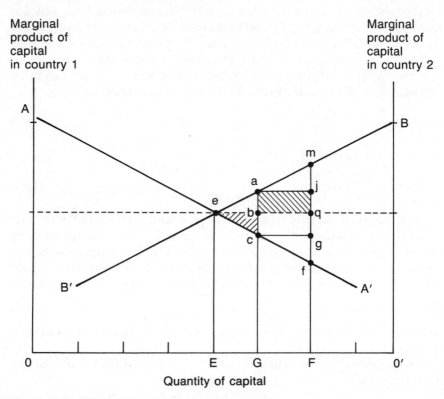

Figure 12.3 Optimal international bank regulation

The same result may be obtained by setting a direct quantitative restriction so that only an amount of capital FG may flow into country 2. In either case, the home country rule would enable the capital exporting country to exercise the needed restrictions.

SUMMARY

This chapter provided a basic framework for analysis of international bank regulation. It is convenient to classify specific bank regulations at the entry level and the operational level according to the impact rather than *de jure*. Certain regulations are "tax-like regulations" mainly raising costs of operations, whereas others are "quota-like regulations" imposing constraints on operations. Nonetheless, it can be shown that both can impart an equivalent impact. There appear five emerging principles of international bank regulatory jurisdiction, namely (1) the home country rule, (2) the host country rule, (3) the principle of minimum regulatory harmonization, (4) the principle of reciprocity, and (5) separation of supervisory responsibility for solvency and liquidity. If a sufficient degree of regulatory harmonization has already been achieved, it may not make any difference which rule, home country or host country, is to be used in promoting competition. Otherwise, the home country rule may be more conducive to promoting competition.

Is there an optimal international bank regulation? If the regulatory cost is set equal to the elasticity of rate of return on foreign banking investment, the banking capital exporting country can maximize its welfare.

REVIEW PROBLEMS AND EXERCISES

1. How does bank regulation affect the behavior of bank decision-making? Explain with examples.

2. What are the advantages and disadvantages for a US bank entering a foreign banking market which is regulated by the following?
   (a) unwritten laws and regulations
   (b) written laws and regulations
   (c) administrative decrees and practices

3. (a) Explain "tax-like" restrictions and "quota-like" restrictions and give some examples of each type.
   (b) Graphically show the equivalence of the impact of a "tax-like" restriction and a "quota-like" restriction.

4. What are the major principles of international bank regulations which have emerged in recent years? Explain them.

5. Which principle of international bank regulation are the following banking acts based on?
   (a) US International Banking Act of 1978
   (b) Council of European Communities, First Banking Directive of 1977
   (c) Council of European Communities, Second Banking Directive of 1989
   (d) 1988 Risk-Based Capital Guideline adopted by the Basle Committee on Banking Supervision

6. Discuss which principle, home country or host country, is more effective in promoting competition.

7. Suppose both home and host country rules are applied simultaneously by the participating countries. Does this create more restrictive regulatory environments than the case of applying only one principle worldwide?

8. What is the condition needed to ensure worldwide efficiency?

9. (a) What is the condition needed to ensure the maximization of welfare of a banking capital exporting country?
   (b) Which principle, home country or host country, is more effective in ensuring the efficiency of a capital exporting country?

10. The supply S_j and demand D_j functions for a tradeable good are given for countries 1 and 2 as below. Find the worldwide equilibrium price after trade takes place.

$$S_1 = -8.333 + 8.333P \qquad S_2 = 11.25 + 3.75P$$
$$D_1 = 100 - 7.143P \qquad D_2 = 140 - 10P$$

NOTES

1 See Effros (1982) for a detailed discussion of the legal and institutional framework for emerging international financial centers.
2 The differences in tax burden are usually reduced by foreign tax credit or deduction.
3 The Basle Committee on Banking Supervision is composed of representatives of the Group of Ten (Belgium, Canada, France, Italy, Japan, the Netherlands, Sweden, the UK, the United States, and Germany), Switzerland and Luxembourg. These representatives are bank regulators and central bankers.
4 A comprehensive theoretical treatment of international taxation can be found in Musgrave (1969).

BASIC READING

Baker, J. (1978) *International Bank Regulation*, New York: Praeger.
Baltensperger, E. and Dermine, J. (1990) "European Banking: Prudential and Regulatory Issues," in Dermine, J. (ed.) *European Banking in the 1990s*, Oxford: Blackwell, 17–40.

Chrystal, K. A. and Coughlin, C. C. (1992) "How the 1992 Legislation Will Affect European Financial Services," *Federal Reserve Bank of St. Louis Review*, March–April: 62–77.

Council of the European Communities (1977) *First Council Directive on the Co-ordination of Laws, Regulations and Administrative Provisions Relating to the Taking up and Pursuit of the Business of Credit Institutions*, 77/789/EEC.

—— (1989) *Second Council Directive on the Co-ordination of Laws, Regulations and Administrative Provisions Relating to the Taking up and Pursuit of the Business of Credit Institutions and Amending Directive*, 77/789/EEC.

Edwards, F. R. (1974) "Relation of Foreign Banking in the United States: International Reciprocity and Federal–State Conflicts," *Columbia Journal of Transnational Law*, 13: 239–68.

Effros, R. C. (ed.) (1982) *Emerging Financial Centers: Legal and Institutional Framework*, Washington, D.C.: IMF.

Hornbostel, P. (1979) *The International Banking Act of 1978*, New York: Practicing Law Institute.

Key, S. J. (1989) "Mutual Recognition: Integration of Financial Sector in the European Community," *Federal Reserve Bulletin*, September: 591–609.

MacDougall, G. D. A. (1960) "Benefits and Costs of Private Investments from Abroad: A Theoretical Approach," *Economic Record*, 36 (March): 13–35.

Pecchioli, R. M. (1983) *The Internationalization of Banking: The Policy Issues*, Paris: OECD, 85–111.

Smaghi, L. B. (1990) "Progressing towards European Monetary Unification: Selected Issues and Proposals," Rome: Banca D'Italia, April.

Spong, K. (1983) *Banking Regulation: Its Purposes, Implementation, and Effects*, Kansas City, Kans.: Federal Reserve Bank of Kansas City.

Ture, N. B. (1975) "Taxing Foreign-Source Income," in *U.S. Taxation of American Business Abroad*, Washington, D.C.: American Enterprise Institute, 47–66.

US Department of the Treasury (1979) *Report to Congress on Foreign Government Treatment of U.S. Commercial Banking Organizations*, Washington, D.C., September.

Whitehead, D. D. (1988) "Moving toward 1992: A Common Financial Market for Europe," *Federal Reserve Bank of Atlanta Economic Review*, November–December: 42–51.

FURTHER READING

Corse, C. T. and Nichols, B. W. (1980) "United States Government Regulation of International Lending by American Banks," in Rendell, R. S. (ed.) *International Financial Law*, London: Euromoney Publications.

Damanpur, F. (1990) *The Evolution of Foreign Banking Institutions in the United States: Developments in International Finance*, New York: Quorum Books.

Dufey, G. and Giddy, I. H. (1978) *The International Money Market*, Englewood Cliffs, N.J.: Prentice Hall, 155–211.

Emerson, M., Aujean, M., Catinat, M., Goybet, P. and Jacquemin, A. J. (1988) *The Economics of 1992: The E.C. Commission's Assessment of the Economic Effects of Completing the Internal Market*, London: Oxford University Press, particularly 1–10, 123–62, 193–265.

Kahkonen, J. (1987) "Liberalization Policies and Welfare in a Financial Repressed Economy," *IMF Staff Papers*, 34 (3): 531–47.

Mayer, C. (1990) "The Regulation of Financial Services: Lessons from the United Kingdom for 1992," in Dermine, J. (ed.) *European Banking in the 1990s*, Oxford: Blackwell, 41–61.

Musgrave, P. R. (1969) *United States Taxation of Foreign Investment Income: Issues and Arguments*, Cambridge, Mass.: Law School of Harvard University.

Pittman, S. L. and Carr, J. L., Jr (1980) "Regulation of Foreign Bank Operations in the United States," in Rendell, R. S. (ed.) *International Financial Law*, London: Euromoney Publications, 115–31.

Santomero, A. M. (1990) "European Banking Post-1992: Lessons from the United States," in Dermine, J. (ed.) *European Banking in the 1990s*, Oxford: Blackwell, 437–57.

Chapter 13

The US regulation on international banking

INTRODUCTION

The international banking business of US banks expanded at a phenomenal rate in the 1960s and 1970s. In 1960, only eight US banks had 131 foreign branches with total branch assets of $3.5 billion. By 1970, seventy-nine banks had 532 branches with $52.6 billion in assets. This rapid expansion continued into the early 1980s. By 1982, a peak year of international banking, 162 banks had 900 branches with assets of $388.5 billion. That year several heavily indebted countries announced their international debt-service problems, causing the overseas banking business to slow down. By 1987, the number of banks which had foreign branches was 153, operating 902 branches with reduced assets of $350 billion.[1] Similarly, the foreign bank presence in the US market rapidly increased. In 1975 there were seventy-nine foreign banks with US branches. By 1985 this number had become 244.[2]

In response to such a rapid increase in international banking, two major legislative acts directly dealing with international bank operations were enacted in recent years, one governing foreign banks and the other US banks. The International Banking Act (IBA) of 1978 deals mainly with foreign bank operations in the United States, whereas the International Lending Supervision Act (ILSA) of 1983 deals with international bank lending in the wake of the third-world country debt crisis.

In this chapter, we will first examine the US regulations on US banks, and we then turn our attention to the US regulations on foreign banks in the United States. In addition to the IBA and the ILSA, there are a number of important laws which jointly form the core of the international banking regulatory framework. These laws have been enacted over the past several decades, providing bits and pieces of regulation. The Federal Reserve Act of 1913 authorized national banks to establish foreign branches. An amendment to the Federal Reserve Act in 1919 empowered the Federal Reserve to grant charters to establish federally chartered international banking corporations. The Bank Holding Company Act of 1956, as amended, largely defined what US banking organizations could do abroad. The Garn–St Germain Act of 1982 set the new per-borrower lending limit for domestic as well as foreign borrowers. The Depository Institutions Deregulation and Monetary Control Act of 1980 specified reserve requirements for all depository institutions including foreign banks in the United States. These regulatory provisions are incorporated and detailed in Federal Reserve Regulation K: International Banking Operations, which essentially serves as a basic reference for our study.

For our analysis, we may group the bank regulation on US banking organizations into two categories, namely organization-oriented regulation and activity-oriented regulation, whereas for the analysis of the regulation on foreign banks in the United States, we focus our attention on the IBA of 1978.

THE ORGANIZATION-ORIENTED REGULATION

Figure 13.1 shows typical organizational setups of US banks engaged in international banking business. As pointed out in Chapter 3, US banks conduct international banking business through (1) the international department of the head office and domestic branches, (2) US subsidiaries (Edge and Agreement corporations), (3) foreign branches, (4) international banking facilities (IBFs), and (5) foreign subsidiaries. Now let us look at more specific aspects of the regulation on these organizations, except for the IBFs which we have examined already in Chapter 8.

Edge Act corporations

Until the turn of the century, US banks played a relatively minor role in international trade finance, although it was the crux of international banking then. The restrictiveness of the existing law spurred US banks to seek new arrangements to compete against foreign banks, particularly British banks which then dominated the international financial markets.

In response to such demand, in 1916 the Federal Reserve Act (Section 25) was amended to permit national banks to acquire stock in corporations which were established to conduct international banking under state or federal laws. However, no federal agency was empowered to issue the necessary permits. In 1919, the Federal Reserve Act was further amended, (it became known as the Edge Act) to empower the Federal Reserve to issue such permits. International banking corporations established under this Edge Act became known as the Edge Act corporations or Edge corporations.[3]

Advantages of having Edge corporations

Why does a bank need an Edge corporation? First, although the international

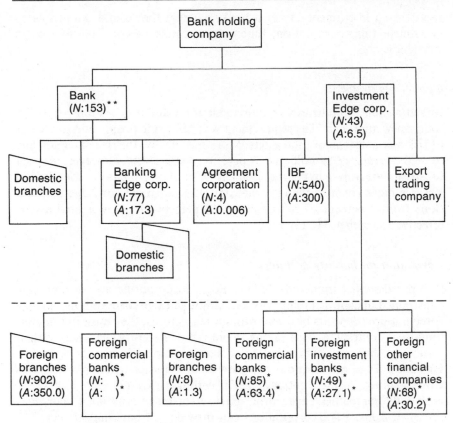

Figure 13.1 Organizational setups for US banks engaged in international
banking: all figures are as of 1987; *N*, number of entities;
A, assets in billions of dollars; *, consolidated, including only
subsidiaries with total assets exceeding $100 million (as of 1986
there were 860 subsidiaries, regardless of size, with total assets
of $132.2 billion); **, banks with foreign branches
Source: Houpt, J. V. (1988) *International Trends for U.S. Banks and
Banking Markets*, Staff Studies No. 156, Washington, DC: Federal
Reserve Board

department of a bank can conduct the bulk of international banking business, the use of an Edge corporation is convenient to separate domestic
banking risks from international risks because it is a separate legal entity
insulating outside risks legally from the bank. Also, it has been used as a
tool to overcome interstate banking restrictions. In addition, an Edge
corporation can serve as a holding company of foreign subsidiaries. Two
Edge corporations are shown in Figure 13.1, one directly under the control
of a bank and the other under the control of a bank holding company. The
first type, known as a banking Edge corporation which receives deposits,

serves as an instrumentality of a bank, whereas the second, known as an investment Edge corporation, functions as a holding company of foreign subsidiaries.

Capital requirements

In setting the capitalization requirement for Edge corporations, the IBA took a new approach. The requirement was defined in proportion to the size of risk assets instead of total assets. More specifically, the size of capital had to be the greater of $2 million or 7 percent of risk assets. However, in order to streamline this capital requirement with that of banks, the Federal Reserve more recently changed the capital requirement for Edge corporations from 7 percent of risk assets to 10 percent of risk-weighted assets, effective December 31, 1992.

Regulation on liability accounts

Compared with commercial banks, Edge corporations are substantially constrained in deposit-taking powers. Although Edge corporations can take foreign source deposits basically without restrictions, they must in principle limit their domestic deposit taking to only those deposits incidental to their business, such as compensating balances and advance repayments. However, Edge corporations can now take deposits without restrictions from qualified business entities (QBEs) within the United States; these are essentially companies engaged in activities of an international character. For such firms, Edge corporations can provide full banking services.

In addition to restrictive deposit taking powers, Edge corporations are subject to reserve requirements and interest rate ceilings in the same manner as member banks. They are not subject to the FDIC deposit insurance, however.

Regulation on asset accounts

The asset-based activities of Edge corporations are rather restrictive. Basically, they are expected to provide credit for business operations carried out outside the United States or for international trade. As part of US export promotion policy, they are permitted to finance even domestic production costs if the production is earmarked for export.

In addition, as international banking institutions, they can engage in international payments and collections, foreign exchange dealings and brokerage, international fiduciary activities (such as acting as payment agents for foreign governments), and international financial advising.

Agreement corporations

As noted earlier, when a state-chartered international banking corporation is to be acquired by a Federal Reserve member bank, this corporation must enter an agreement with the Federal Reserve. The agreement in essence stipulates that the acquired corporation will not exercise any power which is not granted to Edge corporations. Therefore, it practically equalizes the scope and nature of operations of Agreement corporations with those of Edge corporations.[4]

All Agreement corporations are currently state-chartered international banking corporations. However, not all state-chartered corporations are Agreement corporations. As noted in Figure 13.1, there were only four such corporations in 1987 and their role in international banking is rather insignificant today.

Export trading companies

The Bank Export Services Act of 1982 permits certain banking organizations (bank holding companies, Edge corporations, and Agreement corporations) to invest in export trading companies. An export trading company is a firm which derives more than one-third of its revenue from a variety of services provided for exporting goods and services which are produced by parties other than itself in the United States.

One banking organization as a whole may invest in such a company up to 5 percent of the consolidated capital and surplus. In addition, affiliated banks may provide credit to such a company up to a total of 10 percent of the consolidated capital and surplus. All the transactions should be conducted at arms' length. This means that these transactions should be dealt with as if participating parties were unaffiliated with each other.

The main aim of the Act was to create a type of firm backed by banking organizations similar to the general trading companies found in Japan. Unfortunately, the initial enthusiasm and expectations have dwindled greatly because these companies have been unable to amass the necessary resources and to exercise the necessary free hand to challenge general trading companies in Japan or elsewhere.

Foreign branches of US banks

Unlike the case of domestic branch licensing, the Federal Reserve has regulatory power over the establishment of foreign branches of member banks whether they are national or state banks. Foreign branches may be established by member banks (having capital of $1 million or more), Edge corporations, Agreement corporations, or their foreign subsidiary banks. Nonmember insured banks are subject to FDIC regulation.

Branch approval procedures

The Federal Reserve has simplified the approval procedure by taking into account the applicant's international branching experience. Depending on the applicant's global branching experience, the approval procedure is classified into three categories: (1) a specific prior approval, (2) a forty-five-day advance notice, and (3) free to go ahead (no approval or notice required).

When a bank goes into a foreign country for the first time to establish its first foreign branch, it is required to obtain a specific prior approval from the Federal Reserve. The bank is also required to obtain a prior approval when it goes into the second country for the first time. By the time it goes into the third country, the regulatory presumption is that the bank has acquired enough experience in foreign branch operations regardless of the peculiarities of each country, thereby requiring only a forty-five-day advance notice. During this forty-five-day period the Federal Reserve may disapprove the proposed establishment of a branch, or suspend the period for further review, or take no further action. No action by the Federal Reserve implies approval. Once a bank is in a particular foreign country, the establishment of a second branch or any subsequent branch is viewed as routine, not requiring any approval or notice.

Regulatory conflicts between home and host countries

When a branch of a US bank operates in a foreign country, it faces the regulation of the host country as well as that of the home country. Thus, as a general principle it must comply with the regulations of both countries.[5] It must operate within the boundary of the overlapping area of permissible activities, however small the area may be. The difficulty arises when one country imposes mandatory activities which are not permissible from the US regulatory point of view. To some extent this type of conflict is mitigated by permitting additional activities, known as accommodating activities, in order to enable US banks to establish and operate foreign branches. Such expanded activities include (a) investment in certain securities not permitted at home, (b) direct guarantee facilities in addition to standby letters of credit, and (c) underwriting foreign government obligations. Furthermore, some expanded activities are designed simply to enhance the competitive powers of US branches. For example, banks may act as insurance agents or brokers, or engage in repurchase agreements using commodities instead of securities. In addition, these US branches may directly own local banks.

Investment in foreign subsidiaries

US banking organizations such as bank holding companies, member banks, and Edge and Agreement corporations may directly invest in foreign financial institutions. The main consideration of regulation here is to ensure sound banking practices, while promoting competition. To do this, the Federal Reserve in principle permits foreign investment only in those activities closely related to banking, and requires that investments are made with due consideration regarding diversification of risks, provision of suitable liquidity, and maintenance of adequate capital. The "activities closely related to banking" include (1) banking activities proper, (2) other financial intermediation activities which are either substitutes or complements of banking activities, and (3) activities which provide intermediate inputs for the production of final banking products.

Investment in permissible activities

Table 13.1 provides a list of permissible activities according to the nature of the activities, as classified above. As you may note, those permissible activities listed under "other intermediation activities" represent a significant expansion of the banking powers of US banking organizations. Under the newly revised Federal Reserve Regulation K (effective May 24, 1991), they can underwrite the equity securities of any company abroad up to $60

Table 13.1 Major listed activities outside the United States

Banking activities
    Commercial and other banking activities
    Commercial financing, consumer financing, and mortgage banking
    Financial leasing and factoring
    Fiduciary functions
    Underwriting credit-related insurance
    Acting as principal or agent in swap transactions
    Investment through debt–equity swaps arising from loan defaults
Other intermediation activities
    Underwriting, distributing, and dealing in debt and equity securities
    Underwriting life, annuity, and pension-fund-related insurance
    General insurance agency and brokerage
    Overseas mutual funds management
    Acting as a futures commission merchant for futures contracts, etc.
    Travel agency operations
Activities producing intermediate inputs
    Safekeeping of assets on behalf of US customers
    Foreign premise management
    Investment, economic, financial advisory services
    Management consulting services
    Data processing

Source: Federal Reserve Board of Governors (5/24/1991) *Regulation K: International Banking Operations*

million of the investor's Tier 1 capital; they can manage mutual funds; and they can even underwrite life insurance.

Recognizing the fact that activities of a potential target firm in a foreign country may not be confined purely to those listed activities, the Federal Reserve permits certain exceptions. They depend on the degree of a US investor's stake in the invested firm, that is, whether the investment is (1) a subsidiary investment, (2) a joint venture investment, or (3) a portfolio investment. The greater the stake that the US investor holds, the less the invested firm can engage in otherwise not permissible activities.

A subsidiary investment means an investment in more than 50 percent of the voting shares of a firm, while a joint venture investment here means an acquisition of 20 percent or more but not exceeding 50 percent of the voting shares of a firm. A permissible portfolio investment is an investment which does not exceed 20 percent of voting shares of a firm, nor 40 percent of total equity ownership of the invested firm. The rightmost column in Table 13.2 summarizes the extent to which foreign firms invested by US banking organizations can engage in activities other than those listed.

Investment approval procedures

In order to simplify the investment approval procedure, the Federal Reserve

Table 13.2 Permissible activities of foreign subsidiaries

Type of investment	Percentages of voting shares (s)	With US bank as investor	With other US banking organizations as investor	Extent of exemption from otherwise not permissible activities
Subsidiary	50% < s or general partner	Banking	Listed activities	Up to 5% of assets or revenues may come from impermissible activities
Joint venture	20% ⩽ s ⩽ 50%	Banking	Listed activities	Up to 10% of assets or revenues may come from impermissible activities
Portfolio investment	0% < s < 20% and up to 40% of total equity ownership[a]	Any	Any	The amount of assets up to 100% of US bank investor's interest (see Figure 13.3)

Source: Federal Reserve (5/24/1991) *Regulation K: International Banking Operations*
Note: [a] Total equity ownership includes both voting and nonvoting shares.

has established three different categories: (1) a general consent, (2) a forty-five-day prior notice, and (3) a specific consent. This is similar to the foreign branch approval mechanism. However, unlike the foreign branch establishment, the choice of a specific procedure depends on the size of the investment, rather than experience, relative to the investor's capital. If a proposed investment does not exceed the lesser of $25 million or 5 percent of the investor's "Tier 1 capital," it can be made under the general consent procedure, that is, it does not require any prior consent or advance notice, as long as it also satisfies all other established guidelines. On the other hand, a forty-five-day prior notice is required if a proposed investment exceeds the dollar limit set for a general consent but otherwise meets all other requirements. During this forty-five-day period the Federal Reserve may disapprove the proposed investment, suspend the period, or require that the application be filed for a specific consent. Third, a specific consent is the case where the proposed investment requires a specific prior approval by the

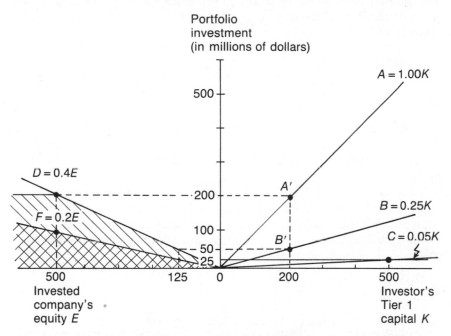

Figure 13.2 Portfolio investment dollar limit: *A*, investment limit for banks; *B*, investment limit for bank holding companies; *C* or $25 million (the lesser of the two), general consent limit; *D*, investment limit in shares (voting plus nonvoting) of the invested company; *F*, investment limit in voting shares of the invested company
Source: Based on the provision of Federal Reserve (5/24/1991)
Regulation K: International Banking Operations

Federal Reserve, as it does not qualify under the general consent or forty-five-day prior notice procedure.

Figure 13.2 shows how the portfolio investment dollar limit is determined by the investor's own capital constraint and by its equity ownership constraint in the invested firm. On the right side of the diagram, line A represents the maximum total portfolio investment which banks can make depending on their own capital, whereas line B applies to bank holding companies. Line C represents the general consent limit. As long as the investment amount is the lesser of $25 million or below this line, it qualifies for a general consent. On the left side, line D represents the total equity investment limit which depends on the invested firm's equity, while line E shows the voting share investment limit. Therefore, for example, a bank having Tier 1 capital of $200 million may invest up to $200 million in any one firm or combination of firms as portfolio investment. However, because of the equity ownership constraint, the bank may invest in the amount which falls within the range represented by the two shaded areas. The amount must satisfy both the lower shaded area (20 percent voting share requirement) and the total shaded area (40 percent total share requirement).

THE ACTIVITY-ORIENTED REGULATION

Regulation on deposit taking

US banks are permitted to take deposits from foreign sources such as individuals, financial institutions, corporations, and government agencies of foreign countries. Such deposits are taken either by banks themselves or by IBFs.

As far as the type of deposits is concerned, there is no distinction between domestic and foreign source deposits. Typically, foreigners place demand deposits with US banks for settlement of individual or correspondent banking transactions, and they place time deposits or certificates of deposit for investment purposes.

Lending limits

For international lending, the applicable per-borrower lending limit today is 25 percent of lender's capital and surplus, which includes Tier 1 and Tier 2 capital.

In determining the per-borrower lending limit, a single borrower is defined as an entity to include the parent corporation and its majority-owned subsidiaries. However, in the case of lending to foreign government entities the definition becomes more complicated. In order to determine whether or not a foreign-government-owned entity is a separate entity for the purpose of the per-borrower lending limit, two tests may be applied, namely the means test and the purpose test. The means test is to determine first whether the borrower will have revenue or resources of its own sufficient to service the debt and second whether its own revenue is greater than the government-supported sources of revenue or subsidies. The purpose test is to see whether the loan is applied for a purpose consistent with the general stated mission of the entity. The borrower must satisfy both tests in order to be considered as a separate entity.

Allocated transfer risk reserves

The 1982 debt crisis raised a fundamental question about the adequacy of regulatory supervision on foreign lending by banks. As a result, the ILSA was enacted in 1983 as part of congressional authorization for an increase in the US contribution to the IMF quota, which was aimed at increasing resources for assistance to debt crisis countries. A key component of the Act stipulated a new set of loan loss reserves, known as "allocated transfer risk reserves" (ATRRs).

According to this provision, the three federal regulatory agencies (Office of the Comptroller of the Currency, the Federal Reserve Board of Governors, and the FDIC) will determine which country's loans are to be classified as problem loans. Then any bank holding such loans must provide an ATRR.

The existence of problem loans is determined by the fact that the named country is unable (a) to make debt service, as evidenced by its failure to pay interest, (b) to comply with restructured terms and conditions, and (c) to make adjustments in accordance with IMF conditionality. Furthermore, it is evidenced by no definite prospects for the orderly restoration of debt service.

The reserve provision for the ATRR is 10 percent of the said loans in the initial year and 15 percent for each subsequent year. Accordingly, the entire amount of the loans will be written off in seven years. These reserves are then to be charged to current income. Now, we turn our attention to the US regulation on foreign banks in the United States.

THE LEGISLATIVE HISTORY OF THE INTERNATIONAL BANKING ACT OF 1978

Prior to the enactment of the IBA in 1978, foreign banks in the United States were regulated mainly by state laws and marginally by federal laws. In the wake of growing activities of foreign banks in the United States, the Joint Economic Committee of Congress undertook a comprehensive study in 1966 on the activities of foreign banks.[6] The study indicated that by and large foreign banks had competitive advantage over US banks in the United

States, because the former were able to take advantage of the differentiated regulations at the state level and the lack of comprehensive regulations at the federal level.

To regulate foreign banks, each state adopted its own regulatory framework, although many state laws were patterned after the New York state banking law. The federal regulation was applied when a foreign bank entered the US market by acquiring a US bank. Only then, as a bank holding company, did the foreign bank become subject to the Bank Holding Company Act administered by the Federal Reserve. The study resulted in various bills that had the intention of restricting foreign bank operations in the United States. However, none of them became law.

At that time, the competitive advantage enjoyed by foreign banks over US domestic banks was mainly in the area of (1) interstate branching, (2) investment banking, and (3) reserve requirements. First, foreign banks were able to establish branches in multiple states, whereas US banks were prohibited by either state laws or the McFadden Act of 1927. Since foreign banks were not chartered by the state in which they established their branches, the state could not stop such banks from establishing branches in other states.

Second, in addition to having US branches, foreign banks were able to acquire investment companies as well as other nonbanking companies in the United States, whereas US commercial banking organizations were prohibited from acquiring such companies because of the separation of commercial and investment banking mandated by either the Banking Act of 1933 or the Bank Holding Company Act of 1956. Here again foreign banks could avoid such mandatory separation because a foreign bank, having banking branches alone without at least one subsidiary bank, was not defined as a bank holding company.

Third, since foreign banks were not member banks of the Federal Reserve System, they were not subject to the reserve requirements imposed by the Federal Reserve. This enabled them to obtain funds at lower effective cost.

Besides the question of fairness, the need to regulate foreign banks at the federal level was prompted by the rapid growth of foreign bank operations in the United States. The number of banking institutions with US operations increased from 111 to 186 and their US assets increased from $30.5 billion to $60.5 billion within the three years from 1973 to 1976.

Meanwhile, the Federal Reserve also created a Steering Committee on International Banking in 1972 to initiate its own study, which resulted in recommendation of a bill, the Foreign Bank Act of 1975. According to this bill, the Federal Reserve Board would become the central regulatory agency and competitive powers would be equalized by stripping the advantages that foreign banks were enjoying. However, during the three-year legislative process, the original proposal was substantially modified. The final version, the IBA of 1978, divided the regulatory powers among the three federal regulatory agencies according to the traditional line and equalized competitive advantage by expanding the banking powers of US banks to the level enjoyed by foreign banks.

PRINCIPLES OF THE INTERNATIONAL BANKING ACT

It is interesting to examine the principles embodied in any act in order to understand the basic tenet and orientation of that law. The IBA of 1978 embodies three basic principles, namely (1) the principle of national treatment, (2) the principle of the dual banking system, and (3) the principle of minimum interference.

The principle of national treatment

From the outset in the legislative debate, two principles were competing with each other for adoption into international banking law, namely the principle of national treatment and the principle of reciprocity.

When the principle of national treatment was considered for adoption, several practical issues had to be resolved. First, what kind of US banks should we use as reference banks to measure whether foreign banks were treated equally or not? There were over 14,000 banks in the United States in the late 1970s. Some were very small ones, each with only one banking facility serving its local community, whereas others were very large, having many banking facilities of one type or another throughout the country. On the other hand, foreign banks already operating or those expected to operate in the United States were relatively large, mostly having assets of $1 billion or more then, and they were likely to be competing mainly against large US banks. Thus, one legislative task of the IBA was to examine the overall banking powers of the large US banks and to accord approximately the same banking powers to these foreign banks.

The next question was how to equalize the treatment between domestic banks and foreign banks when they had different levels of regulations. One method was to expand the banking powers of the banks which were constrained more. The other was to reduce the banking powers of those banks which had more freedom. The IBA chose the first approach. The banking powers of US reference banks were expanded by permitting nationwide branching for Edge corporations. Most large US banks already had several Edge corporations in key cities throughout the United States, which served as a nationwide network for international banking business. At the same time, foreign banks were permitted to establish branches on a nationwide basis as well, although with limited deposit-taking powers.

As can be seen from the above, the equal treatment involves another question, namely formality (*de jure*) versus substance (*de facto*). The 1978 Act recognized differences in the nature of operations and the organizational structures between US and foreign banks. Therefore, instead of treating foreign banks in exactly the same manner as US banks, the Act treated foreign banks in a slightly different way in order to achieve roughly equal competitive advantages. A case in point is limited interstate banking. The banking powers of US banks with Edge corporations would be roughly equal to those of foreign banks with out-of-state branches with limited deposit-taking powers. The limited interstate branch banking also provided a partial restoration of equity between those grandfathered foreign banks and the newcomers.

Another question was how the principle of national treatment would benefit US banks. One underlying reason for the adoption of national treatment was to provide a basis for the US government to negotiate with foreign governments to replicate. We may call such an approach an implicit reciprocity approach.

Now let us examine the problem associated with the principle of reciprocity. According to this principle, banks from countries 2 and 3 may have to be treated differently if countries 2 and 3 treat US banks differently; this creates an administrative nightmare, as pointed out in Chapter 12. Thus, it would be more practical to apply this principle at the entry level rather than the operational level.

The principle of the dual banking system

As noted earlier, the original plan in the Foreign Bank Act of 1975 envisioned the Federal Reserve Board as regulating all the foreign banks in the United States. However, this single regulatory agency concept was replaced by the traditional dual banking system in which regulatory responsibility was shared between the state and federal governments. Therefore, foreign banks were in essence given an option to choose their regulatory master. Consequently, they could apply to either the federal regulatory agency or the state regulatory agency for a license to establish a branch or agency.

Also, at the federal level, the regulatory powers were further divided between the Office of the Comptroller of the Currency, the Federal Reserve Board, and the FDIC according to the traditional line of responsibilities. Nevertheless, the regulatory powers of the Federal Reserve Board were strengthened because, in addition to the traditional powers, the Board was charged with the residual regulatory powers not within the purview of the other two agencies.

The principle of minimum interference

The principle of minimum interference means that the regulatory agencies may impose additional regulatory requirements on foreign banks, if necessary, and that in such instances the additional requirements must be kept to a minimum level. This principle would be unnecessary if the principle of national treatment could be strictly enforced. The incorporation of the principle in the 1978 Act was an admission of the fact that differences exist between domestic banks and foreign banks from a regulatory point of view.

One question related to this principle of minimum interference is how US regulatory agencies should deal with business activities carried out outside the United States by foreign banks which are also operating in the United States. The operations of foreign banks outside the United States will be unregulated in principle as long as they meet the following two criteria. First, their global nonbanking activity is relatively small compared with the size of their banking activity outside the United States. Second, the proportion of banking activity within the United States is also smaller than that conducted outside the United States. A foreign bank satisfying these two requirements is termed a qualifying foreign banking organization (QFBO). Once designated as a QFBO, its activities outside the United States are not under the supervision of the Federal Reserve. In addition, it has reduced reporting and disclosure requirements on its worldwide operations, consistent with the principle of minimum interference.

THE ROLE OF THE "HOME STATE" AND INTERSTATE BANKING

The concept of the "home state" adopted in the IBA of 1978 serves as a cornerstone for the implementation of the principle of national treatment. The foreign bank must choose its home state if it is to establish a branch or to own a US bank. If the foreign bank fails to choose a state, the Federal Reserve may designate one for the foreign bank, which will usually be the state in which the foreign bank first entered by a branch or subsidiary bank.

Once the home state is chosen, the foreign bank will then be treated as if it were a national bank as well as a bank holding company of that state. As a bank, a foreign bank can exercise its banking powers to the fullest extent permitted to the national banks in that state. It can establish multiple branches in the home state, if the state law permits this for its state banks. Furthermore, as a bank holding company, the foreign bank may also own other nonbank subsidiaries, in addition to branches and subsidiary banks. On the other hand, banking activities out of the home state are restricted in substance in a similar manner as to the way that national banks are restricted.

BANKING REGULATION BY TYPE OF BANKING FACILITIES

As shown in Figure 13.3, foreign banks conduct their business in the United

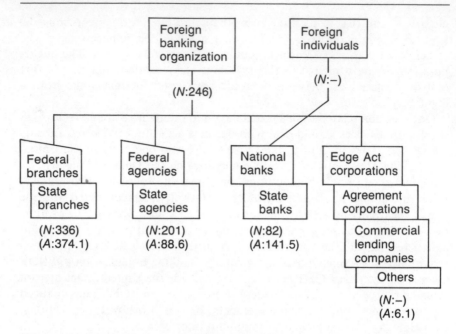

Figure 13.3 Type of banking facilities held by foreign banks in the United
States: all figures are as of the end of 1987; *N*, number of
entities; *A*, assets in billions of dollars
Source: Houpt, J. V. (1988) *International Trends for U.S. Banks and
Banking Markets*, Staff Studies No. 156, Washington, D.C.: Federal
Reserve Board

States primarily through their branches and agencies. As of the end of 1987,
there were 246 foreign banks which had presence in the United States. These
banks had 334 branches with assets of $374 billion and 201 agencies with
assets of $88.6 billion. In addition, they had eighty-two US domestic banks
with assets of $141.5 billion.

As pointed out earlier, foreign banks may apply to either the Office of
the Comptroller of the Currency or the state regulatory agency for a license
to establish a branch or agency. If a branch or agency is established with
a federal license, it is termed a "federal" branch or agency. On the other
hand, if it is established with a state license, it is called a "state" branch or
agency.

Therefore, a foreign bank has four alternatives for establishing a banking
facility as an integral part of the parent bank in the United States: (1) a
federal branch, (2) a state branch, (3) a federal agency, and (4) a state
agency. However, the foreign bank must choose one of these four forms in
any given state. It cannot have a combination of two or more of the above,
because otherwise foreign banks may take undue advantage. Whether

multiple branches can be established in any given state or not depends on that particular state law. The Office of the Comptroller of the Currency can issue licenses only within the purview of the state laws. But it can also do so as long as the state law does not expressly prohibit it.

Now let us examine specific regulations on federal branches, federal agencies, and representative offices. Since many state banking laws follow the New York state law which is in turn similar to the federal law, we will examine only "federal" banking facilities of foreign banks.

Federal branches in home states

The key factors considered for issuing a license for a federal branch are essentially the same as those considered for branching of a domestic bank except that the explicit emphasis is on the effect on international commerce of the United States. No other considerations such as reciprocity or minimum size of the parent bank are expressly required.

A branch is an integral part of the parent organization. However, from the regulatory point of view it is desirable to treat a branch as a separate entity. For this purpose, a US branch of a foreign bank is treated as an accounting unit which must have its own capitalization, the amount of which is the same as for US bank branches in that particular locality, satisfying the principle of national treatment. In place of a capital account, the concept of a capital equivalency account was devised, which serves as (a) a permanent source of funds out of advances made from the parent office and (b) a basis for reserve requirement exemptions, but (c) not a basis of the per-borrower lending limit, which is determined by the size of globally consolidated capital of the parent organization.

A federal branch in the home state may receive deposits from both domestic and foreign sources without restriction. These deposits are subject to reserve requirements. Today, only transactions accounts actually require reserves. The interest rate ceiling applies to their demand deposits. Deposit insurance is not required if the branch is taking only wholesale deposits which are $100,000 or more in size.

Unlike domestic banks, foreign banks must maintain the capital equivalency deposit with a Federal Reserve member bank in order to protect depositors and creditors of the branch. This capital equivalency deposit is an example of the application of the principle of minimum interference.

In addition to the capital equivalency deposit, a foreign branch is required to pledge additional assets to protect the insurance fund of the FDIC, provided that the branch deposits are insured. However, in order to reduce the burden on foreign branches, as manifested by the principle of national treatment, up to one half of the pledge amount may be satisfied by the capital equivalency deposit.

Federal branches in out-of-home states

Now let us look at federal branches in out-of-home states. First, such branches face more restrictive domestic deposit-taking powers. They can take only those deposits incidental to their business. Literally, this restriction is identical to the one applied to Edge corporations, although the effective deposit-taking powers may be somewhat different, depending on their scope of operations. Because of the restricted wholesale nature of deposits, these deposits are not insured. Thus these branches are not required to make an asset pledge to the FDIC. Nonetheless, they must arrange the capital equivalency deposits.

Federal Agencies

There is no regulatory difference between agencies in home states and those in out-of-home states. These agencies are similar to commercial finance companies in terms of their major activities. They are regulated almost as identically as to federal branches in out-of-home states except that the former lack fiduciary functions. A federal agency is permitted to take deposits from foreign sources without restriction but it may take only those deposits incidental to its business from domestic sources. The primary source of domestic funds comes from commercial paper issued in the name of the parent banks. Again, because of the wholesale nature of deposits originating from foreign sources, these deposits are not insured by the FDIC. However, the deposits are subject to reserve requirements and interest rate ceilings as if they were member banks' deposits. On the assets side, federal agencies are subject to the capital equivalency deposit requirement, but not to the asset pledge to the FDIC.

Representative Offices

The IBA requires that any foreign bank that maintains an office other than a branch or agency in the United States must register with the Secretary of the Treasury within 180 days of establishment. A representative office does not have authority to make any business transaction decisions for the account of its head office. It can engage mainly in representing its organization, establishing liaison with customers, soliciting new business, and gathering and disseminating information.

Investment in US banking and other financial institutions

As noted earlier, prior to the enactment of the IBA, one way for foreign banks to enter the US banking market was through acquisition of state-chartered banks. The federal law did not permit a majority ownership of a national bank by a foreign banking organization. As the ban was lifted by the IBA in 1978, foreign banks began acquiring relatively large US banks.

This raised public concern. The Depository Institutions Deregulation and Monetary Control Act, enacted in March 1980, placed a moratorium for three months to investigate the probable adverse impact of such acquisitions. Some major concerns were the potential conflict in national interest and the difficulty in controlling foreign banks. It was argued that the interest pursued by foreign banks would not be consistent with US interests. Foreign banks might favor their home-based multinational corporations, placing American corporations in a disadvantageous position. Besides, they might not allocate overall financial resources according to US priorities. The study gave neither conclusive evidence nor a strong theoretical rationale to prohibit acquisitions of domestic banks by foreign banks. The moratorium was not renewed.

Another major issue was the extent of acquisition of nonbanking subsidiaries by foreign banks. They already held interests in commercial lending companies as well as in investment companies, while US banking organizations were not permitted to acquire investment companies in particular. Such holdings by foreign banking organizations would otherwise become subject to the Bank Holding Company Act. However, the IBA grandfathered them in the light of practices outside the United States. As US banks have increasingly been permitted to move into the investment banking area, the question of disadvantage for US banks not having investment banking affiliates has become moot.

SUMMARY

This chapter outlined the US bank regulation on US banks operating internationally and foreign banks operating within the United States. For the US banks, a number of legislative actions including the Federal Reserve Act of 1913, the Bank Holding Company Act of 1956, the International Banking Act of 1978, and the International Lending Supervision Act of 1983 primarily constitute the main body of governing legislation, which is prescribed more in detail in Federal Reserve Regulation K. Some of these regulatory provisions are organization-oriented ones governing specific forms of banking organizations such as Edge Act corporations, Agreement corporations, IBFs, export trading companies, bank branches abroad, and foreign investment. Meanwhile, other provisions are more specifically aimed at particular activities (e.g. per-borrower lending limit) or balance sheet items (e.g. allocated transfer risk reserves for nonperforming third-world country loans).

On the other hand, the International Banking Act of 1978 was the most comprehensive piece of legislation governing foreign banks. The act is guided by the principle of national treatment, the dual banking system, and minimum interference. Therefore, foreign banks in the United States are treated as if they were US national banks without requiring reciprocity. They may obtain licenses to establish branches or agencies either from the Office of Comptroller of the Currency or state regulatory agencies.

REVIEW PROBLEMS AND EXERCISES

1. Which aspect of international banking business does each of the following acts regulate?
   (a) Federal Reserve Act of 1913
   (b) Amendments to Federal Reserve Act (Section 25) in 1916 and 1919
   (c) Bank Holding Company Act of 1956
   (d) International Banking Act of 1978
   (e) Garn–St Germain Act of 1982
   (f) International Lending Supervision Act of 1983

2. What are the major regulatory differences between an Edge corporation and an Agreement corporation?

3. How different are the domestic deposit-taking powers between Edge corporations and domestic commercial banks?

4. What are the major restrictions on asset items of Edge corporations?

5. For what purposes are Edge corporations used in conducting international banking business?

6. Explain the three different approval procedures for the establishment of a branch in a foreign country.

8. To what extent can a foreign firm in which a US banking organization has invested engage in non-listed activities?

9. Explain the three different approval procedures for foreign investment by US banking organizations.

10. Under what kind of conditions is a US bank required to put aside the allocated transfer risk reserves?

11. What sort of competitive advantage did foreign banks in the United States have over US domestic banks prior to the enactment of the International Banking Act of 1978?

12. What are the basic regulatory principles adopted in the International Banking Act of 1978? Explain them and pinpoint the practical issues involved in applying each principle.

13. What is the role of the "home state" within the context of interstate banking?

14. How is each of the following balance sheet items of a federal branch of a foreign bank in the home state regulated?
    (a) capital equivalency account
    (b) deposit accounts
    (c) capital equivalency deposits

15. What are major regulatory differences between federal branches in home states and those in out-of-home states?

16. Differentiate a federal agency from a federal branch in terms of regulatory constraints.

NOTES

1 For year-to-year data, see various issues of Federal Reserve Board of Governors *Annual Report*.
2 See Houpt (1988: 26).
3 The Edge Act was named after Senator Walter Edge of New Jersey who proposed the amendment bill.
4 However, note that this agreement is effective only when the banking powers authorized by the state laws exceed those of the Edge corporation. It can reduce but cannot increase the banking powers authorized by the states.
5 Note that this principle is different from the Second Banking Directive of the Council of the European Communities of 1989. See Chapter 14.
6 See US Senate Committee on Banking, Housing, and Urban Affairs (1978) for a more specific account of the legislative history.

BASIC READING

Baker, J. C. (1978) *International Bank Regulation*, New York: Praeger.
Billingsley, R. and Lamy, R. (1988) "The Regulation of International Lending, IMF Support, the Debt Crisis, and Bank Shareholder Wealth," *Journal of Banking and Finance*, 12: 255–74.
Corse, C. T. and Nichols, B. W. (1980) "United States Government Regulation of International Lending by American Banks," in Rendell, R. S. (ed.) *International Financial Law*, London: Euromoney Publications.
Edwards, F. R. (1974) "Relation of Foreign Banking in the United States: International Reciprocity and Federal–State Conflicts," *Columbia Journal of Transnational Law*, 13: 239–68.
Federal Reserve Board of Governors (1991) *Regulation K: International Banking Operations*, Press Release, Docket No. R-0703, April 19.
—— (1989) *Risk-Based Capital Guidelines*, Press Release, Docket No. R-0628, January 19.
Hornbostel, P. (1979) *The International Banking Act of 1978*, New York: Practicing Law Institute.
Houpt, J. V. (1988) *International Trends for U.S. Banks and Banking Markets*, Federal Reserve Board of Governors Staff Study No. 156, Washington, D.C.
Key, S. J. and Brundy, J. M. (1979) "Implementation of International Banking Act," *Federal Reserve Bulletin*, October: 785–96.

Martinson, M. G. and Houpt, J. V. (1989) "Transfer Risk in U.S. Banks," *Federal Reserve Bulletin*, April: 255–8.

US Department of the Treasury (1979) *Report to Congress on Foreign Government Treatment of U.S. Commercial Banking Organizations*, Washington, D.C.

US Senate Committee on Banking, Housing and Urban Affairs (1978) *Report Submitted to the Senate, 95th Congress 2nd Session on International Banking Act of 1978*, Report No. 95–1073, August.

FURTHER READING

Aharony, J., Saunders, A. and Swary, I. (1985) "The Effect of the International Banking Act on Domestic Banking Profitability and Risk," *Journal of Money, Credit, and Banking*, November: 493–506.

Baker, J. and Bradford, M. G. (1974) *American Banks Abroad: Edge Act Companies and Multinational Banking*, New York: Praeger.

Hultman, C. W. (1990) *The Environment of International Banking*, Englewood Cliffs, N.J.: Prentice Hall.

Keeton, W. R. (1989) "The New Risk-Based Capital Plan For Commercial Banks," *Federal Reserve Bank of Kansas City Economic Review*, December: 40–60.

OECD (1978) *Regulations Affecting International Banking Operations of Banks and Nonbanks*, Paris: OECD.

Chapter 14

The EC regulatory framework for banking services

INTRODUCTION

Since the creation of the European Economic Community (EEC) in 1957, there have been unmistakable movements, despite occasional slowdowns and stoppages, toward the integration of the fragmented financial markets into one single Communitywide market.[1] The movements can be identified at two levels. At one level the effort has been directed toward the creation of a monetary union, which would be similar to the US Federal Reserve System, providing a single currency and a uniform monetary policy area. At another level, successive efforts have been mounted toward devising a common regulatory framework necessary and sufficient to facilitate and ensure the integration of segmented banking markets which have been laden by twelve different philosophies toward bank regulations and twelve different historical developments.

We first briefly examine historical developments in monetary union movements and the liberalization of capital flows. Then we analyze the structure of the EC regulation on credit institutions, as predicated by the Second Banking Directive.

THE EC MACROECONOMIC INTEGRATION PROCESS

Movements toward creation of a monetary union

Over three decades since the creation of the EEC in 1957, there have been at least three attempts to create a monetary union. These attempts were in large measure reactions to greater changes in exchange rates at times and the Community's desire to maintain a stable exchange rate system.

The first attempt to create a monetary union came in October 1962, in response to the 5 percent revaluation of the deutsche mark and the Dutch guilder in March 1961. This revaluation was the first currency realignment after the signing of the Treaty of Rome (1957). Thus, the question of stable exchange rates was brought to the forefront, leading to the EEC

Commission's proposal to create a monetary union in stages by 1971. However, concerned with the monetary union's potential power to create excessive liquidity, West Germany objected to the proposal.

The second attempt was initiated in December 1969. By then, it became clearer that an alternative exchange rate regime to the existing dollar–gold system was needed, as the credibility of the US dollar value became doubtful because of the continuing deficits in the US balance of payments. In addition, in order to provide the price support program for EC farmers which was regarded as a key purpose of the EC then, a stable exchange rate system was needed just as in the case of creating a customs union. Without stable exchange rates uniform external tariffs could not be maintained because devaluation of a currency would amount to a reduction in tariffs on agricultural goods entering that country.

Following the Barre Report (a Commission memorandum of February 1969) which advocated the creation of a monetary union, a more comprehensive Werner Report (October 1970) proposed the creation of a monetary union in stages by 1980. The monetary union would have the following characteristics: (1) complete liberalization of capital movements within the Community, (2) a single community currency, (3) a common central bank system, (4) a centralized economic policy-making body responsible to the European Parliament, and (5) fiscal policy coordination. In March 1971 the Council adopted a resolution on the gradual implementation of the Werner plan. The first stage of the plan was intended to narrow the fluctuation margins between the EC currencies and to establish the European Monetary Cooperation Fund (EMCF) to administer short-term credit facilities provided by member central banks in support of foreign exchange open market operations. However, the actual implementation was temporarily interrupted by the international monetary crisis of 1971. Nonetheless, the EMCF was established in 1973.

The third attempt was initiated in June 1988 when the European Council established a committee which was chaired by European Commission President Jacques Delors to study and propose concrete stages toward economic and monetary union (European Monetary Union (EMU)), as a logical extension of the Single European Act of 1986. The Delors Committee's "Report on Economic and Monetary Union in the European Community" spelled out specific measures to be taken in three stages with a timetable.

In June 1989 the European Council adopted the first stage program of the Delors Report, which required complete liberalization of capital movements within the Community by July 1990. For the second stage measures which would start at the beginning of 1994, the European Council, except for the UK, agreed in October 1990 to make final preparations which emphasized macroeconomic policy convergence as a necessary condition to create a monetary union. The third and final stage measures would involve the creation of a single currency and a single central bank. These measures were agreed upon in the Maastricht Summit Accord in December 1991 subject to unanimous ratification by the member states. As you recall, we examined the content of the Accord in the light of the optimum currency area in Chapter 4.

What are the bank regulatory implications arising from the EMU? First, with only one currency within the Community, foreign exchange regulation on intra-EC transactions will no longer have a rationale. The regulation on monetary controls such as interest rate ceilings, reserve requirements, credit allocations and rules for the use of central bank liquidity will eventually be centralized in the hands of the central bank of the Community from the host country central banks.

Complete liberalization of capital movements

An essential prerequisite for the integration of fragmented banking markets into a Communitywide single market is free movement of capital. This prerequisite was finally satisfied by July 1990 when most of the member states complied with the Delors first stage plan, as noted earlier. Portugal, Spain, Greece and Ireland were granted an extension for compliance.

Their major concern has been on adverse effects of destabilizing capital movements and capital flight. To cope with such possibilities, member states would be provided with necessary credit facilities, not only a very short-term-financing facility (VSTF), but also short-term monetary support (STMS) and medium-term financial assistance (MTFA). The VSTF is an unlimited credit facility provided among the participating members of the exchange rate mechanism primarily to stabilize exchange rates. The STMS is also a short-term credit facility but is provided to meet the short-term balance of payments deficit. On the other hand, the MTFA is a credit facility administered by the Council to meet the needs of longer-term structural changes. In addition, a uniform withholding tax rate would be applied to capital earnings to prevent capital flight seeking tax arbitrage. Finally, the member states retain the right to reimpose controls on capital movements when such movements are deemed disruptive.

The extent to which a country has removed its capital controls can be measured by the interest rates on comparable financial instruments denominated in the same currency and issued in different countries, such as the Euro-sterling rate and the domestic sterling interbank rate. Evidence presented by Chrystal and Coughlin (1992) and Blundell-Wignall and Browne (1991), for instance, exhibits a close convergence of these rates.

From the bank regulatory point of view, this reinforces our earlier contention in Chapter 8 that the rationale for the Eurocurrency market will probably diminish and there will be less and less distinction between the Eurocurrency market and the domestic market.

THE EC REGULATORY FRAMEWORK FOR CREDIT INSTITUTIONS

Laws governing credit institutions

Within the general framework provided by the Treaty of Rome (1957) and the Single European Act (1986), there are a number of major legislative measures which form the EC banking laws, laws governing credit institutions. They include (1) the First Banking Directive (12/12/1977), (2) the Second Banking Directive (12/15/1989), (3) the Council Directive on the supervision of credit institutions on a consolidated basis (6/13/1983), (4) the Council Directive on the own funds of credit institutions (4/17/1989), (5) the Council Directive on the solvency ratio (12/18/1989), (6) the Commission Recommendation on monitoring and controlling large exposures of credit institutions (4/2/1987), (7) the Commission Recommendation concerning the introduction of deposit guarantee schemes in the Community (4/2/1987), (8) the Council Directive on the complete liberalization of capital movements within the Community (6/13/1988), and (9) the Basle Accord on risk-based capital guidelines (7/11/1988).

The first two banking directives constitute the core of EC credit institution regulations, the first being guided by the host state rule and the second by the home state rule. Credit institutions are defined as those that take deposits or repayable money from the public and grant credits on their own account. These are equivalent to depository institutions in the United States. Note, however, that no attempt is made in the EC regulatory definition to differentiate between different types of depository institutions. The third directive on supervision on a consolidated basis is in line with an earlier Basle agreement (1980) reached by industrial countries requiring commercial banks headquartered within their territories to consolidate their worldwide accounts. This would enable bank examiners to regulate domestic and foreign operations on a consistent basis. The fourth directive defines "own funds," and stipulates the minimum capitalization requirement, while the fifth directive provides guidelines for determining the risk-based capital requirement or solvency ratio. The two Commission Recommendations on deposit guarantee schemes and large market risk exposures were partly incorporated in the Second Banking Directive. The complete liberalization of capital movements by July 1990 was the prerequisite for free financial services, particularly securities investment and cross-border financial services.

Although the Basle Accord (1988) is not a direct legislation of the European Community, major EC member states are parties to the Accord. It involved a package of four measures providing a minimum level of capital (own funds), a harmonized solvency ratio based on risk-weighted assets, rules for large risks undertaken by credit institutions, and deposit guarantee schemes.[2]

The EC legislative bodies and regulatory instruments

The European Commission as the regulatory agency

The Commission is the executive branch of the European Community and is responsible for proposing new laws and policies and for implementing decisions made by the Council. In fact, it is more than an executive branch. All legislative initiatives start with the Commission. It makes supplementary laws necessary to carry out previous Council decisions. As the "Guardian of the Treaties," it oversees proper implementation of Treaties provisions and Community measures and takes action against those member states which do not comply with EC rules. Given a specific mandate from the Council, the Commission represents the Community and negotiates external matters, such as reciprocity issues in banking, with non-EC parties. In the Second Banking Directive the Commission is designated to act as a "Regulatory Committee."

The Council of European Communities

The Council is the ultimate decision-making institution within the European Community. The term "Council" usually refers to the "Council of Ministers," consisting of ministerial-level officials representing their own governments. Depending on the nature of the agenda, participants at the Council meeting vary. For example, a Council meeting on banking issues would be attended by ministers of finance, whereas a meeting on the mutual recognition of professional certification would be attended by ministers of labor or education. Also depending on the significance and technicality, the Council can include working groups of officials representing the individual countries. The highest level of the Council is the "European Council," also known as the "Summit," which consists of heads of states or governments of the member countries. When the Council of Ministers is unable to reach an agreement on a proposed measure, it may pass it up to the European Council which is often in a better position to produce compromised solutions. In order to facilitate implementation of internal market integration, for most single market issues the "qualified majority rule" is used, as predicated by the Single European Act.[3] A practical problem then is how to differentiate 1992-related problems from non-related ones which in most instances require a unanimous ruling.

The European Parliament

The European Parliament, although directly elected, does not have the final authority in legislation except in EC budget and EC membership matters. It has an advisory role on the first reading of a proposed measure submitted by the Commission. Upon its second reading, this time on a revised version approved by the Council known as a "common position," the Parliament may accept it, take no action, propose amendment, or reject it. Even in the case of Parliament's rejection the Council may still adopt its original measure. However, it becomes more difficult to do so, because the passage of legislation in the presence of a Parliament's rejection requires unanimity instead of a qualified majority.

Legislative instruments

There are three main types of legislative instruments used for the EC, namely regulations, directives, and decisions. Regulations are legally binding on all member countries and their citizens and directly applicable without further national legislation. For example, a measure on "changing the value of the unit of account used by the European Monetary Coopera- tion Fund" is a Council Regulation (1984) applicable to all member states in its entirety. In the case of conflict with national law, the Community regulations take precedence.

By contrast, directives are addressed to all the member states giving the stipulated objectives, framework, and timetable for implementation. The member states are then obligated to achieve the results set forth in them, but the means by which the results are achieved are left with the individual member states. For example, the Second Banking Co-ordination Directive (1989) leaves with each member state how to handle business rules of banking, given the minimum harmonization of conditions for authorization and supervision and the home country rule.

The third instrument is decisions; these are legally binding but are directed only to particular governments, organizations, or individuals. For example, Council legislation (1971) "on the strengthening of cooperation between the central banks of the member states of the EEC" is a Council decision specifically addressed to the central banks of the member states.

There are also other types of legislation, such as Council resolutions, Commission recommendations, and Commission statements (opinions), which are not legally binding but have moral suasion or serve as precursors for future legally binding legislation.

The Second Banking Directive

The most relevant EC banking law today is the Second Banking Directive. Its formal title is "Second Council Directive of 15 December 1989 on the Co-ordination of Laws, Regulations and Administrative Provisions Relating to the Taking Up and Pursuit of the Business of Credit Institutions and Amending Directive 77/780/EEC." Let us examine the Directive's major characteristics and its implications on market integration and the treatment of non-EC banks.

The Second Banking Directive is structured on the basis of three inter-related principles: (1) the principle of minimum regulatory harmonization, (2) the principle of mutual recognition, and (3) the principle of home country rule.

Principle of minimum regulatory harmonization

As we studied in earlier chapters, common objectives of bank regulation are to promote competition on one hand and to ensure the safety and soundness of banks (credit institutions) in order to protect depositors and other customers on the other. To promote competition, regulation should be kept as little as possible, whereas to protect credit institutions and their customers regulation should be maintained at a necessary and sufficient level. National differences in bank regulation stem mostly from differences in judgment regarding the "necessary and sufficient" level.

The Second Banking Directive sets the extent of harmonization of conditions needed to establish and operate a credit institution at the level necessary and sufficient to make a single license acceptable throughout the Community. Areas of essential harmonization include initial capital requirements, disclosure of a credit institution's major shareholders, limitations on the size of participation in nonfinancial undertakings, standard solvency ratios, and permissible activities.

The minimum initial capitalization (own funds) requirement for the establishment of a credit institution is set at ECU 5 million. The identity of shareholders having "qualifying holdings" must be disclosed in the license application to establish a credit institution. "Qualifying holdings" means holdings of 10 percent or more of capital or voting rights or holdings which make it possible to exercise significant influence over management. Investment in any one nonfinancial firm may not exceed 15 percent of a credit institution's own funds and the aggregate amount of such investment may not in turn exceed 60 percent of an investor's own funds. The permissible banking activities are provided by member state laws and regulations which can be more restrictive than the EC rule.

Principle of mutual recognition

This requires that each member state recognize that the authority and judgment exercised by other states to grant licenses and to supervise prudential operations of credit institutions are equivalent to its own. Therefore, differences in national rules must not be used as a ground to restrict access. However, in order to accept such a position, there must be a common understanding about the minimum criteria on which regulatory judgment is exercised by other member states. This is the reason for trying to harmonize essential conditions subject to mutual recognition.

Thus, once a credit institution is authorized to operate in a member state, that authorization must be applicable to any member state within the Community. Table 14.1 gives the list of the core business activities of credit institutions subject to mutual recognition. Any listed activity is considered a standard one and therefore it should be permitted throughout the Community, as long as the home state permits it in the first place within its territory. Note that the list includes full investment banking business. It is based on a German-type universal banking model.

Principle of home country rule

This rule states that the home state which gave authorization to establish a credit institution retains the responsibility of prudential supervision over the institution wherever it goes. Therefore when a home state credit institution expands its operations in other member states, this prudential supervision with an open-end license goes with it.

Under the home country rule, also known as the single license or common passport rule, any credit institution that is duly chartered and authorized in one member state may establish branches or Article 18 (2) subsidiaries

Table 14.1 List of activities subject to mutual recognition

1   Acceptance of deposits and other repayable funds from the public
2   Lending
3   Financial leasing
4   Money transmission service
5   Issuing and administering means of payments (e.g., credit cards, travelers' cheques, and bankers' drafts)
6   Guarantees and commitments
7   Trading for its own account or for customers' accounts in (a) money market instruments, (b) foreign exchange, (c) financial futures and options, (d) exchange and interest rate instruments, and (e) transferable securities
8   Participation in share issues and provisions of services related to such issues
9   Advice to undertakings on capital structure, industrial strategy and related questions, and advice and services relating to mergers and the purchase of undertakings
10 Money brokering
11 Portfolio management and advice
12 Safekeeping and administration of securities
13 Credit reference services
14 Safe custody services

Source: *Second Council Directive of 12|15|1989*

without host country authorization. An Article 18 (2) financial institution is a special subsidiary of a credit institution, functioning just like a branch but legally as a separate entity.[4] Regardless of host country law, these branches and special subsidiaries can conduct any or all of the listed banking activities to the same extent as is permitted at home. Also, credit institutions can conduct banking business directly from their home bases and cater for customers in other member states, known as cross-border transactions.

On the other hand, if an ordinary subsidiary is to be established, it is subject to host country authorization.

The role of the host member state

Even under the principle of home country rule, the role of the host member state is not totally passive. In fact, the host member state retains an exclusive responsibility for liquidity and matters arising from the European Monetary System. In addition, the host state has primary responsibility over large market risk exposures of credit institutions operating in its territory. It enforces its own law enacted pursuant to the Second Banking Directive, including on-the-spot verifications of matters under its purview. Therefore, the host country may still dictate how to conduct business within its territory.

Authorization procedures

A credit institution planning to establish a branch, for example, notifies its home regulatory authorities with necessary information, such as the location of the establishment, managers, mailing address, intended activities, and deposit guarantee schemes. Within three months of receipt of the information, the home state authorities communicate that information to the host state authorities. If the home authorities fail or refuse to communicate with the host state authorities, this has the *de facto* consequence of disapproval, which may be appealed against in the home state court. When the host country authorities receive the information from the home country authorities, the former have two months in which to act. If necessary, the host country authorities may indicate the conditions under which the proposed activities must be carried on.

A comparison with the First Banking Directive

According to the First Banking Directive, a prospective credit institution must first satisfy minimum legal requirements for a charter such as adequate capital and management staffing requirements, which are similar to those of the Second Banking Directive. Once chartered by the home state, a credit institution gains a basic right to establish a branch in any member state. However, a credit institution must still obtain a license to establish a branch from the host state, and its branch activities are under the supervision of the licensing state. Furthermore, all activities carried out by the out-of-state branch must conform with those of domestic credit institutions of the host state. In addition, branches must have their own capitalization (endowment funds), separate from their parents. As such, this Directive is distinctively governed by the host country rule.

Treatment of non-EC banks

Non-EC banks may enter EC markets either through branches or through subsidiaries. The treatments of these two approaches are different.

Branch establishment

For third-country banks, branch establishment is not covered by the Second Banking Directive. Therefore they cannot benefit from the single license rule. They must get authorization from each host country in which they plan to establish branches.

Subsidiary establishment

By contrast, subsidiaries of third-country banks, once established in the Community, can benefit from the single license rule. However, in order for a third-country bank to establish or acquire a subsidiary credit institution in the Community, the third country must provide both (1) national treatment and (2) reciprocal treatment for EC country banks.

By national treatment, EC banks once in a third country must be given an effective access to the market and the same competitive opportunities as those given to the domestic banks in that country. It requires *de facto* as well as *de jure* national treatment, so-called "genuine national treatment." Otherwise, the member states receiving applications from banks of that particular country must limit or suspend authorization for a period of three months. Meanwhile, the Commission may initiate negotiation with the country in question. After the three months, whether to continue suspension or not must be decided by the Council.

Similarly, by reciprocal treatment the third country must offer to EC banks an effective market access comparable with that granted by the Community. Otherwise, the Commission may submit proposals to the Council for the appropriate mandate for negotiation. Note that the reciprocal requirement does not require an automatic initiation of negotiation or suspension.

Finally, note that existing subsidiaries of non-EC credit institutions would, in general, be grandfathered and would be treated like any other financial institutions in the member state in which they were chartered. Without a grandfathered clause many non-EC banks located in less restrictive places such as London might have to be suspended.

Effects of the reciprocity requirement

What do these national and reciprocal requirements mean to US banks, for instance? It is rather easy for the US regulatory agency to provide national treatment to EC banks entering the US market. As you recall, the International Banking Act of 1978 is in fact predicated on this principle of national treatment. However, it would be more difficult to meet the requirement of reciprocity, because in order for US banks to receive the benefit of the single license rule, the United States must provide free interstate branching to EC banks. This means that EC banks must be given competitive powers greater than those granted to US banks at this time.

In general, the reciprocity requirement may potentially affect the US banking regulatory system, particularly in the areas of restricted investment banking and differentiated demand deposits taking power among depository institutions, in addition to restrictive interstate branching. The US International Banking Act does not require reciprocal treatment. A strict adherence to reciprocal treatment may result in differentiated treatments of banks from different EC member states.

SUMMARY

Since the creation of the EEC in 1957, there have been unmistakable movements toward the creation of a monetary union at one level and toward designing a common regulatory framework for integration of segmented banking markets at the other. Motivated to stabilize exchange rates among the member country currencies, the first attempt to create a monetary union came in 1962, the second in 1969, and the third in 1988 which eventually led to the Maastricht Treaty in 1991; this mandates creation of the European Monetary Union by 1999. Meanwhile, the liberalization of capital flows was completed by the majority of the member countries by 1990. Such coordinated efforts serve as prerequisites for the liberalization of financial services. Based on the Single European Act of 1986, the Second Banking Directive was issued in 1989. The Directive is guided by the home country rule, coupled with minimum regulatory harmonization plus mutual recognition. The regulatory system is expected to enhance competition within the EC banking industry. For non-EC banks the principle of reciprocity applies.

REVIEW PROBLEMS AND EXERCISES

1. There have been at least three attempts to create a monetary union since the creation of the EEC. What was the major motive behind each attempt?

2. Explain the following regulatory principles in reference to the Second Banking Directive:
   (a) harmonization of conditions for authorization
   (b) harmonization of conditions for prudential supervision
   (c) mutual recognition
   (d) home country rule

3. What are the major differences between the First Banking Directive and the Second Banking Directive?

4. Under the given regulatory structure can the US regulatory authorities meet the national treatment requirement, if it is demanded by the European Commission for EC banks entering the US market? What about the reciprocal treatment requirement?

NOTES

1 The European Economic Community (EEC), the European Atomic Energy Community (Euroatom), and the European Steel and Coal Community (ESCC) formed the European Communities (EC), each having its respective Council and Commission. Later, in 1967, the institutions of the three Communities were merged into a single Council of Ministers and a single Commission. Thus, the terms European Communities and European Community became interchangeable. Also the EEC is simply termed the European Community.

2 The rule on the risk-asset based capital requirements was formally adopted in the Council Directive (12/18/1989).

3 Under the qualified majority voting system, as stipulated by the Single European Act of 1986, a number of votes are assigned to each member state roughly in accordance with its population size and importance in the EC. Britain, France, Germany, and Italy each have ten votes; Spain has eight; Belgium, Greece, the Netherlands, and Portugal have five votes each; and Denmark and Ireland three votes each; and Luxembourg two. A qualified majority means fifty-four votes out of seventy-six from at least eight member states.

4 An Article 18 (2) financial institution must satisfy the following conditions: (i) its voting shares are 90 percent or more owned by the parent credit institution; (ii) its prudent management is pledged by the parent; (iii) its activities must be the same kind of activities as those actually carried out in the parent member state; (iv) the subsidiary must be included in the consolidated supervision of the parent undertakings.

BASIC READING

Baltensperger, E. and Dermine, J. (1990) "European Banking: Prudential and Regulatory Issues," in Dermine, J. (ed.) *European Banking in 1990s*, Oxford: 17–36.

Blundell-Wignall, A. and Browne, F. (1991) "Increasing Financial Market Integration, Real Exchange Rate and Macroeconomic Adjustment," OECD Department of Economics and Statistics Working Paper No. 96.

Chrystal, K. A. and Coughlin, C. C. (1992) "How the 1992 Legislation Will Affect European Financial Services," *Federal Reserve Bank of St Louis Review*, March: 62–77.

De Cecco, M. and Giovannini, A. (eds) (1989) *A European Central Bank? Perspectives on Monetary Unification after Ten Years of the EMS*, Cambridge: Cambridge University Press.

Dixon, R. (1991) *Banking in Europe: The Single Market*, London: Routledge.

EC Council (1989) *Second Council Directive of 15 December 1989*, Brussels.

Giavazzi, F. and Giovannini, A. (1990) *Limiting Exchange Rate Flexibility: The European Monetary System*, Cambridge, Mass.: MIT Press.

Ingram, J. C. (1973) *The Case for European Monetary Integration*, Essays in International Finance No. 98, Princeton, N.J.: Princeton University Press.

Key, S. J. (1989) "Mutual Recognition: Integration of the Financial Sector in the European Community," *Federal Reserve Bulletin*, September: 591–609.

Ungerer, H., Hauvonen, J. J., Lopez-Claros, A. and Mayer, T. (1990) *The European Monetary System: Developments and Perspectives*, Washington, D.C.: IMF.

FURTHER READING

Cordero, R. (1990) *The Creation of a European Banking System: A Study of Its Legal and Technical Aspects*, New York: Peter Lang.

De Grauwe, P. and Papademos, L. (1990) *The European Monetary System in the 1990s*, London: Longman.

Emerson, M., Aujean, M., Catinat, M., Goybet, P. and Jacquernin, A. J. (1988) *The Economics of 1992: The E.C. Commission's Assessment of the Economic Effects of Completing the Internal Market*, Oxford: Oxford University Press.

Hawawini, G. and Rajendra, E. (1990) *The Transformation of the European Financial Services Industry: From Fragmentation to Integration*, New York: New York University Press.

Owen, R. and Dynes, M. (1989) *The Times Guide to 1992: Britain in Europe without Frontier*, London: Times Books.

Part IV

International banking activities

Chapter 15

International portfolio investment

INTRODUCTION

As we studied in Chapter 2, international capital movement takes place as investors seek higher return across national boundaries, for a given risk. For short-term investment, it is usually easier to identify, measure, and hedge risk related to investment. Thus, investors may focus more on the rate of return. For direct foreign investment, investors are more interested in management control, in addition to the rate of return. Nonetheless, in both cases the consideration of risk is an integral part of investment decision-making. For portfolio investment, an explicit consideration of both return and risk comes into play with an equal importance. A consideration of both risk and return enables us to explain the cases in which capital may flow into a country where the rate of return is lower. A simple theory of return maximization would find it difficult to explain such capital movement.

In this chapter, we first examine several basic models of portfolio investment. We then examine the effect of including foreign financial assets in a portfolio. Finally, we examine the role of banks in international portfolio management.

BASIC MODELS OF PORTFOLIO INVESTMENT

In 1952, Markowitz published a path-breaking article entitled "Portfolio Selection," which was based on a mean—variance analysis showing the relationship between the mean and variance of the rate of return on investment. His work became a foundation of modern portfolio theory. Tobin (1958) extended the Markowitz model to a case where all investors can borrow and lend at the riskless rate, arriving at the conclusion that all investors, regardless of their attitude toward risk, should choose the same portfolio of investment assets. Combining with regression techniques, Sharpe (1964) and Lintner (1965) independently developed the capital asset pricing model (CAPM), separating systematic risk and unsystematic risk. Systematic risk of a portfolio is the risk related to changes in the return on the market portfolio. Since the market portfolio is a portfolio which includes all securities, its performance is determined by the entire market conditions in the economy. On the other hand, unsystematic risk is that which arises from variations in individual asset returns unrelated to the market. Such a separation provides a convenient approach for examining the effect of international diversification of investment assets, as we shall see later.

Since the conceptual formulation and testability of the CAPM depends on the market portfolio, the outcome will be different depending on how the market portfolio is defined. Ross (1976) developed an alternative model, known as the arbitrage pricing theory. This theory does not require specification of the market portfolio but divides the systematic risk into smaller component risks stemming from some unspecified fundamental factors. Let us examine these models more specifically so that we can see how they can be modified to account for the effect of international diversification in investment.

The Markowitz model

The Markowitz model, also known as mean–variance analysis, in essence explains the relationship between the expected rate of return on portfolio investment and its variance. Portfolio investment means investing wealth in more than one asset at a given time. Let us first see how the expected rate of return on a portfolio is determined by individual component asset returns and then see how to measure the variance of portfolio returns.

The expected rate of return on a portfolio

We begin with a two-asset model with asset j and asset k (say, asset 1 and asset 2) in which the investor allocates her financial resources in the proportion w_1 and w_2. The one-period return on investment in asset 1, for instance, is

$$R_{1t} = \frac{V_{1t} - V_{1t-1} + D_{1t}}{V_{1t-1}} \tag{15.1}$$

where V_{1t-1} is the market value at the beginning of period t, V_{1t} is the market value at the end of period t, and D_{1t} is the dividend during period t. The rate of return R_{1t} is uncertain because its components V_{1t} and D_{1t} cannot be determined at the beginning of investment. But that is the time when the investment decision must be made. A useful way to deal with this problem is to assign a subjective or empirical probability to each possible outcome. An empirical probability is the frequency distribution of outcomes derived from past data.

Table 15.1 Examples of covariance computations

(a) Return on assets

State	Asset 1	Asset 2	Asset 3	Asset 4	P1 $(w_j = 1/4)$	P2 $(w_j = 1)$
1	1.20	7.40	1.60	7.20	4.35	17.40
2	1.60	1.40	5.80	12.10	5.23	20.90
3	− 1.00	3.20	9.00	8.60	4.95	19.80
4	17.80	7.20	14.20	6.30	11.38	45.50
5	5.30	5.40	15.40	2.90	7.25	29.00
$E(R_j)$	4.98	4.92	9.20	7.42	6.63	26.52

(b) Deviation from mean

State	Asset 1 (d_{i1})	Asset 2 (d_{i2})	Asset 3 (d_{i3})	Asset 4 (d_{i4})	P1 (d_{ip1})	P2 (d_{ip2})
1	− 3.78	2.48	− 7.60	− 0.22	− 6.62	− 9.12
2	− 3.38	− 3.52	− 3.40	4.68	− 1.41	− 5.62
3	− 5.98	− 1.72	− 0.20	1.18	− 1.68	− 6.72
4	12.82	2.28	5.00	− 1.12	4.75	18.98
5	0.32	0.48	6.20	− 4.52	0.62	2.48

(c) Variance–covariance matrix

	Asset 1	Asset 2	Asset 3	Asset 4	P1	P2
Asset 1	56.48	10.55	26.88	− 9.46	21.11	84.44
Asset 2		6.73	1.96	− 5.94	3.32	13.30
Asset 3			33.20	− 12.03	12.50	50.01
Asset 4				11.26	− 4.04	− 16.17
P1					8.22	
P2						131.58

(d) Correlation coefficient matrix

	Asset 1	Asset 2	Asset 3	Asset 4	Portfolio
Asset 1	1.00	0.54	0.62	− 0.38	0.98
Asset 2		1.00	0.13	− 0.68	0.45
Asset 3			1.00	− 0.62	0.76
Asset 4				1.00	− 0.42
Portfolio					1.00

Source: The data used here are those selected randomly from the rates of return on stocks of twenty-eight countries reported in Levy, H. and Sarnat, M. (1970) "International Diversification of Investment Assets," *American Economic Review*, 60 (4): 669, except asset 3 whose returns are hypothetical values

Notes: (a) P1, return on portfolio with averaging equal to $\Sigma_j\, w_j R_{ij}$ where each weight is assumed to be the same so that $w_j = 1/4$; P2, return on portfolio without averaging equal to $\Sigma_j\, w_j R_{ij}$ where $w_j = 1$.

(c) P1, $\Sigma_k (1/4)\text{cov}(R_{ij}, R_{ik}) = \text{cov}(R_j, R_m)$; P2, $\Sigma_k \text{cov}(R_{ij}, R_{ik}) = 4\,\text{cov}(R_j, R_m)$.

The expected rate of return R_1 on asset 1 is the weighted average of all such possible outcomes in period t where each weight is equal to the probability P_{i1} of each possible outcome R_{i1}:

$$E(R_1) = (P_{11})(R_{11}) + (P_{21})(R_{21}) + \cdots + (P_{m1})(R_{m1}). \tag{15.2a}$$

The notation E represents the expected value. For our purpose, we assume that there are m possible outcomes, each having an equal chance of occurrence. Then, equation (15.2a) becomes

$$E(R_1) = \frac{1}{m}(R_{11} + R_{21} + \cdots + R_{m1}), \tag{15.2b}$$

which is a simple arithmetic average. In order to gain a more concrete understanding of each new concept, Table 15.1 is constructed to provide numerical examples. There are four assets in the example; each asset has five possible outcomes on return; each outcome has an equal chance of occurrence. Table 15.1(a) lists the rate of return on each asset and on the portfolio; part (b) shows the deviation of each possible return from its respective mean, from which the variance–covariance matrix is constructed in part (c); and part (d) is the corresponding correlation matrix.

Let us return to the two-asset case. Out of the four assets shown in Table 15.1, let us assume that a portfolio now consists of asset 2 and asset 4. The expected rate of return on asset 2 is:

$$E(R_2) = \tfrac{1}{5}(7.40 + 1.40 + 3.20 + 7.20 + 5.4) = 4.92. \tag{15.3a}$$

Likewise, the expected rate of return on asset 4 is then:

$$E(R_4) = \tfrac{1}{5}(7.20 + 12.10 + 8.60 + 6.30 + 2.90) = 7.42. \tag{15.3b}$$

Therefore the expected rate of return on the portfolio is

$$E(R_p) = w_2 E(R_2) + w_4 E(R_4)$$
$$= w_2(4.92) + w_4(7.42) \tag{15.4}$$

which varies as the mix of investment between asset 2 and asset 4 changes. An example is given in Table 15.2. With $w_2 = 1$ and $w_4 = 0$ the portfolio simply consists of asset 2 alone, while with $w_2 = 0$ and $w_4 = 1$ the portfolio contains only asset 4.

Measurement of portfolio risk

Before measuring the portfolio risk, let us first look at the risk on individual asset returns. We may measure such risk in terms of variance (or standard

Table 15.2 Two-asset portfolios

(a)	Characteristics of assets			
	Asset 2	$E(R_2) = 4.92$	$\mathrm{var}(R_2) = 6.73$	
	Asset 4	$E(R_4) = 7.42$	$\mathrm{var}(R_4) = 11.26$	
	$r_{24} = -0.68$			

(b) Portfolios having various proportions of assets 2 and 4

w_2	1.00	0.80	0.60	0.40	0.20	0
w_4	0	0.20	0.40	0.60	0.80	1.00
$E(R_p)$	4.92	5.42	5.92	6.42	6.92	7.42
$\mathrm{var}(R_p)$	6.73	2.86	1.38	2.29	5.58	11.26
$s(R_p)$	2.59	1.69	1.18	1.51	2.36	3.36

deviation). Formally, we can express the variance, $\mathrm{var}(R_j)$ and standard deviation $s(R_j)$ of the return on asset j as follows:

$$\mathrm{var}(R_j) = \frac{1}{m-1} \sum_{i=1}^{m} d_{ij}\, d_{ij} \tag{15.5}$$

where

$$d_{ij} = R_{ij} - E(R_j).$$

Therefore, the variance of R_2 is

$$\mathrm{var}(R_2) = \tfrac{1}{4}[2.48 \times 2.48 + (-3.52) \times (-3.52) + (-1.72)$$

$$\times (-1.72) + 2.28 \times 2.28 + 0.48 \times 0.48]$$

$$= 6.73 \tag{15.6a}$$

and the standard deviation of R_2 is:

$$s(R_2) = [\mathrm{var}(R_2)]^{1/2} = (6.73)^{1/2} = 2.59. \tag{15.6b}$$

Similarly, we have the variance of R_4 as

$$\mathrm{var}(R_4) = 11.26 \tag{15.6c}$$

and the standard deviation of R_4 as

$$s(R_4) = [\mathrm{Var}(R_4)]^{1/2} = (11.26)^{1/2} = 3.36. \tag{15.6d}$$

Obviously, asset 4, having a higher variance, is riskier than asset 2.

In order to determine portfolio risk, we need to introduce an additional measure of risk, covariance, which measures the risk related to returns on different assets. Now, we can calculate the covariance of R_2 and R_4 as

$$\text{cov}(R_2, R_4) = \frac{1}{m-1} \sum_i d_{i2}\, d_{i4}$$

$$= \tfrac{1}{4}\,[2.48 \times (-0.22) + (-3.52) \times 4.68 + (-1.72)$$

$$\times 1.18 + 2.28 \times (-1.12) + 0.48 \times (-4.52)]$$

$$= -5.94 \tag{15.7}$$

and the correlation coefficient r_{24}, of R_2 and R_4 can be found as

$$r_{24} = \frac{\text{cov}(R_2, R_4)}{[\text{var}(R_2)]^{1/2}[\text{var}(R_4)]^{1/2}}$$

$$= \frac{-5.94}{(6.73)^{1/2}(11.26)^{1/2}} = -0.68. \tag{15.8}$$

With this much preparation, we can now turn to the variance of the portfolio returns as a measure of portfolio risk:

$$\text{var}(R_p) = w_2{}^2\,\text{var}(R_2) + w_2 w_4\,\text{cov}(R_2, R_4)$$
$$+ w_4{}^2\,\text{var}(R_4) + w_4 w_2\,\text{cov}(R_4, R_2) \tag{15.9a}$$

$$= w_2{}^2\,\text{var}(R_2) + w_2 w_4 r_{24} s(R_2)s(R_4)$$
$$+ w_4{}^2\,\text{var}(R_4) + w_4 w_2 r_{42} s(R_4)s(R_2) \tag{15.9b}$$

or, in terms of the standard deviation,

$$s(R_p) = [\text{var}(R_p)]^{1/2} \tag{15.10}$$

As can be seen from equation (15.9a) or (15.9b), the risk of a portfolio is the weighted sum of two variances and two (the same) covariances. If the weighted sum of two covariances is less than the weighted sum of two variances, the overall portfolio risk (measured in standard deviations) is reduced. A negative correlation between R_2 and R_4 will obviously reduce the portfolio risk, but a negative correlation is not a necessary condition. However, the correlation must be less than unity in order to have the portfolio risk less than the sum of the individual asset risks.

Selection of an optimal portfolio

Now, we can construct the relationship between the expected rate of return on the portfolio and its risk (measured in standard deviations) for varying proportions of investment between assets 2 and 4; this is presented in Table 15.2. Although asset 4 yields a higher expected rate of return, it also carries a higher risk in comparison with asset 2.

On the basis of the numerical figures in Table 15.2, the mean–standard deviation relationship is depicted in Figure 15.1 by curve **abcdef**, which we

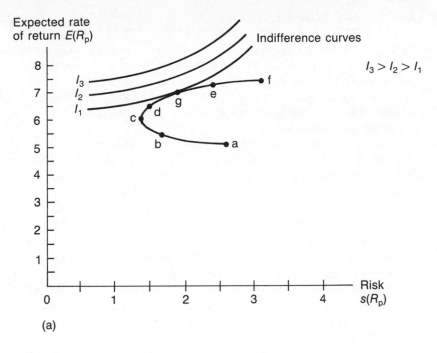

(a)

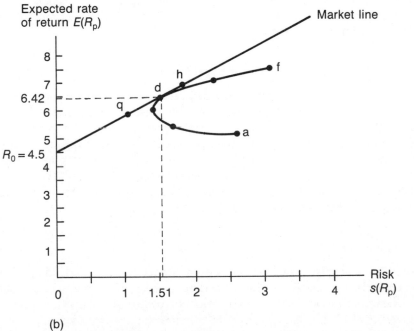

(b)

Figure 15.1 Relationship between the expected rate of return on a portfolio and portfolio risk: (a) selection of the optimal portfolio with indifference curves; (b) selection of the optimal portfolio with the market line

term an investment opportunity curve. If there are more than two assets, the investment opportunity curve becomes the investment opportunity area. In Figure 15.1(a), the segment from point **a** to point **c** represents a set of portfolios from which the portfolio mix can be changed to achieve a higher return without simultaneously increasing risk. We call such a set an inefficient set of portfolios.

On the other hand, the segment from point **c** to point **f** represents a set of portfolios each point of which represents the maximum return for a given risk (or the minimum risk for a given return). In other words, from any point in this set, one cannot move to a point of higher return without also increasing risk. We term such a set an efficient set of portfolios.

Therefore, an optimal portfolio can be found within the efficient set. Then, which combination is an optimal one? To find such a combination we may need to introduce investor's indifference curves. An indifference curve is a utility curve which represents the same level of utility by having various combinations of two goods, in this case, return and risk. An optimal mix of investment is the point where the highest attainable level of the indifference curve is tangent at a point on the efficient set of portfolios. This optimal portfolio is represented by point **g** in Figure 15.1(a). From a practical point of view, identifying such a point **g** is a difficult task because of the subjectivity of the indifference curves. The Tobin model provides a partial solution to this problem.

Modification of the model with foreign assets

Now, assume that domestic investors can invest in foreign financial assets. They may face two possible cases. One is the case in which domestic and foreign markets are still separated. Therefore, initially there are two investment opportunity curves, which over a period of time would merge into one. The other is the case in which the existing investment opportunity curves merge instantaneously through workings of efficient markets. The former is the case of less efficient markets, where perhaps investors can also reap greater return initially.

The Tobin model

From the Markowitz model, the Tobin model introduces lending and borrowing at a given riskless rate. Lending at the riskless rate is equivalent to investment in the riskless asset; and borrowing at the riskless rate is equivalent to issuing the riskless debt instrument.

Suppose that the market condition is such that the rate of return on the riskless investment is 4.5 percent, and that at this rate investors can also borrow to finance their portfolio investment. Drawing a straight line originating from the riskless rate R_0, we may drop this line toward the efficient portfolio investment opportunity curve. The tangent point **d**, as shown in Figure 15.1(b), is then the optimal portfolio. In effect, this new straight line is a new efficient investment opportunity curve. Only one point from the original efficient portfolio set is represented on this new curve, and all others are now inefficient. That is, for each point on the original efficient curve, there is a corresponding point of higher return on the new curve. Only point **d** is efficient with or without the riskless asset. Therefore, regardless of investors' attitude toward risk, investors should choose point **d** as an optimal mix of risk assets. This is known as the portfolio separation theorem. That is, instead of choosing risky assets on the basis of the investor's attitude toward risk, the investor should choose the portfolio that creates the Tobin market line, a line that runs from the point of the riskless rate and is tangent to the efficient portfolio.

Let us now examine the meaning of the distance on the straight line from point R_0. At point R_0, the investor makes all of her investment in the riskless asset; thus, the rate of return is 4.5 percent and risk is zero. At point **d**, the investor is making all the investment in the risk assets whose mix is represented by combination **d** (40 percent in asset 2 and 60 percent in asset 4).

As we move toward point **d** from point R_0, proportionally more assets are placed in the risk asset portfolio. For example, point **q** represents 70 percent of the distance from R_0 to **d**. Then the mix of assets will be (a) 30 percent in the riskless asset and (b) 70 percent in the risk asset portfolio, of which asset 2 is 28 percent ($0.7 \times 40\%$) and asset 4 is 42 percent ($0.7 \times 60\%$) respectively of the total investment.

Thus

$$E(R_p) = 0.7 \times 6.42 + 0.3 \times 4.5 = 5.84 \ (\%) \tag{15.11}$$

$$s(R_p) = 0.7 \times 1.51 = 1.06 \ (\%). \tag{15.12}$$

On the other hand, a point beyond point **d**, say point **h**, which is 1.2 times the line segment $R_0 d$, represents 120 percent of the original investment in portfolio **d** with 20 percent of funds borrowed at the riskless rate. Then,

$$E(R_p) = 1.2 \times 6.42 - 0.2 \times 4.5 = 6.804 \tag{15.13a}$$

which can be rewritten, in order to show the direct impact of borrowing at the riskless rate and reinvesting the borrowed funds in the risk-asset portfolio, as

$$E(R_p) = 6.42 + 0.2 \ (6.42 - 4.5) = 6.804. \tag{15.13b}$$

The portfolio risk is

$$s(R_p) = 1.2 \times 1.51 = 1.81. \tag{15.14}$$

Thus, this new straight line is a new investment opportunity curve touching on point **d** and extending upward without limit. The practical limit comes from the investor's borrowing ability. As pointed out earlier, this line is the set of efficient portfolios and is known as the market line. Although we were able to pinpoint an optimal risk asset portfolio regardless of investors' attitude toward risk, this Tobin model still requires the indifference curves to show the optimal choice on the straight line. Nonetheless, this market line served as a precursor of the CAPM.

The case with foreign assets

Now, assume that domestic investors can invest in foreign riskless assets at the rate R_0^*, which is higher than the domestic riskless rate R_0; at the same time, they can still borrow at home at R_0; when they invest in a risk-asset portfolio, they should now choose a new portfolio d^* which is tangent to the new straight line originating from R_0^*. Under such conditions, the new efficient set with foreign investment opportunities will be a kinked curve consisting of two segments: (1) the portion R_0^*k of line segment between R_0^* and d^* and (2) the portion kk' of line segment between R_0 and k'. In all cases, by definition, each point on the new kinked curve must represent the maximum return for a given risk. Although it is possible that investors may borrow at home at R_0 and invest in the portfolio d^*, it is not an efficient strategy, as is shown by the broken line R_0z in Figure 15.2.

The Sharpe–Lintner model

Separation of systematic risk and unsystematic risk

Suppose now that the market portfolio consists of our four assets, as shown in Table 15.1. Conceptually, the market portfolio is the portfolio which includes every financial asset in the market. At the expense of repetition, we spell out the formula for the variance of the market portfolio to separate systematic and unsystematic risk. The core of the Sharpe–Lintner model which was developed independently by Sharpe (1964) and Lintner (1965) argues that the required rate of return on a security or a portfolio is determined by systematic risk, which can be represented by a function of beta. Furthermore, if the actual rate of return is higher or lower than the required level of return, the market arbitrage will force the former back to the required level, provided that the market is efficient, efficient in the sense that every participant in the market has equal information and he or she will adjust investment position instantaneously as new information becomes available.[1]

Now let us decompose the variance $var(R_m)$ of the market portfolio with four assets to see how systematic risk and unsystematic risk behave as the

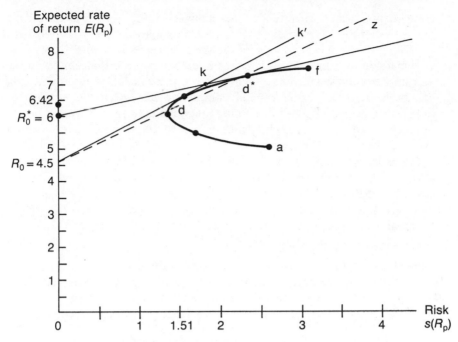

Figure 15.2 An efficient set of portfolios (the kinked curve $R_0 * kk'$) with foreign lending and domestic borrowing: $R_0 * k$, investment in a combination of a foreign riskless asset and risk asset portfolio $d*$ without borrowing; kk', investment in risk asset portfolio d with borrowing at R_0

number of investment assets increases. The variance of the four-asset portfolio is in essence the expansion of the following formula:

$$\text{var}(R_m) = E(w_1 d_1 + w_2 d_2 + w_3 d_3 + w_4 d_4)^2 \tag{15.15}$$

where R_m is the return on the market portfolio and

$$d_j = R_j - E(R_j).$$

In the expanded form, we have the variance of the market portfolio as

$$
\begin{aligned}
\text{var}(R_m) = w_1 &[w_1 \text{ var}(R_1) + w_2 \text{ cov}(R_1, R_2) \\
&+ w_3 \text{ cov}(R_1, R_3) + w_4 \text{ cov}(R_1, R_4)] + w_2 [w_2 \text{ var}(R_2) \\
&+ w_1 \text{ cov}(R_2, R_1) + w_3 \text{ cov}(R_2, R_3) + w_4 \text{ cov}(R_2, R_4)] \\
&+ w_3 [w_3 \text{ var}(R_3) + w_1 \text{ cov}(R_3, R_1) + w_2 \text{ cov}(R_3, R_2) \\
&+ w_4 \text{ cov}(R_3, R_4)] + w_4 [w_4 \text{ var}(R_4) + w_1 \text{ cov}(R_4, R_1) \\
&+ w_2 \text{ cov}(R_4, R_2) + w_3 \text{ cov}(R_4, R_3)]. \tag{15.16}
\end{aligned}
$$

Now, the portfolio risk can conveniently be divided into systematic and unsystematic risk. Unsystematic risk is the weighted sum of the variance components, which is unrelated to changes in the performance of the market portfolio. Systematic risk is the other part of the portfolio risk, consisting of the weighted sum of the covariance components. The risk is systematic in the sense that it is systematically related to the changes in the market portfolio performance. This also implies that this systematic risk cannot be reduced (or diversified) simply by increasing the number of investment assets. On the other hand, unsystematic risk decreases as the number of investment assets increases, provided that the individual variance does not become too large.

Let us look at some numerical examples. Suppose that the total asset is allocated in equal proportions so that $w_1 = w_2 = w_3 = w_4 = 1/n = 1/4$. From equation (15.16) it is clear that the weight of each variance is now $(1/n)^2$ and there are n such variances. Each covariance of R_j and R_k now has weight $(1/n)^2$ and there are $n(n-1)$ such covariances. The variance of the market portfolio can then be expressed as

$$\begin{aligned} \text{var}(R_m) &= (1/n)^2 (n) \text{ (average variance of individual asset return)} \\ &\quad + (1/n)^2 n(n-1) \text{ (average covariance of two asset returns)} \\ &= (1/n) \text{ (average variance of individual asset return)} \\ &\quad + [1 - (1/n)] \text{ (average covariance of two asset returns).} \end{aligned}$$

(15.17)

Therefore, as n increases, $\text{var}(R_m)$ approaches the average covariance of all the assets. This effect is shown in Figure 15.3. Using the numerical figures in Table 15.1(c), we find the average variance and covariance as

$$\text{average return variance} = \tfrac{1}{4}(56.48 + 6.73 + 33.20 + 11.26)$$

$$= 26.92 \tag{15.18}$$

and

$$\text{average return covariance} = \tfrac{1}{12}[2(10.55) + 2(26.88) + 2(-9.46)$$

$$+ 2(1.96) + 2(-5.94) + 2(-12.03)]$$

$$= 1.99. \tag{15.19}$$

Figure 15.3a shows the effect of the number of assets on unsystematic risk, while 15.3(b) shows the effect on systematic risk. Unsystematic risk decreases drastically as n increases; it becomes 1.35 ($= 26.92/20$) or 5.01 percent ($= 1.35/26.92$) of the original risk when n reaches 20. On the other hand, systematic risk starts at zero when there is only one asset and it approaches the average covariance level asymptotically; in our example, it reaches 1.89, which is 95 percent of the asymptotic value of 1.99, when n becomes 20.

What happens to systematic risk and to unsystematic risk when foreign assets are added to the investment portfolio? Foreign asset investment is

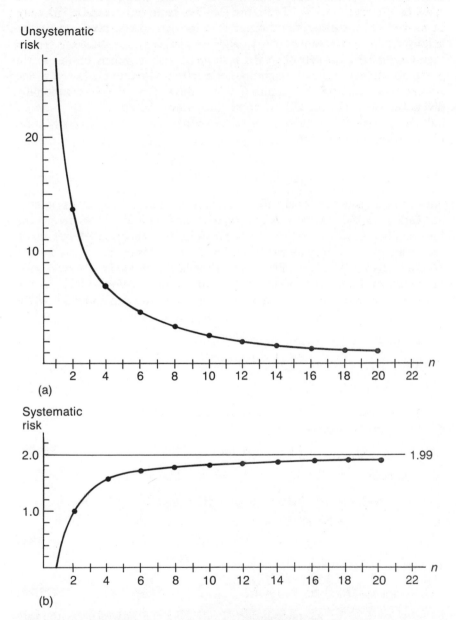

Figure 15.3 The effect of number of assets in the portfolio on
(a) unsystematic risk and (b) systematic risk

accompanied by additional risks such as foreign exchange rate risk and cross-border transfer risk. Therefore the decline in unsystematic risk may be slower. On the other hand, differences in regulations, taxes, and other arrangements cause the domestic and foreign securities markets to be segmented. This is likely to make systematic risk in terms of the world portfolio (domestic plus foreign market portfolios) relatively lower. Some studies, for example by Solnik (1974), show that the internationally diversified portfolio for US investors can reduce the overall risk to about half the US risk.[2] We will examine the effect of international diversification in more detail on pp. 346–51.

Capital asset pricing model

Now let us consider how risk affects the required rate of return. As pointed out earlier, in the CAPM it is argued that the required rate of return (or the equilibrium rate of return) on a portfolio is a function of systematic risk, which is measured by the beta. To see why this is the case, consider Figure 15.1(b), which is modified so that the horizontal axis now represents the return on the market portfolio. Out of the total investment, a certain portion w_m is invested in the market portfolio and the remainder $1 - w_m$ in the riskless asset. Then, the return on this portfolio is

$$R_p = w_m R_m + (1 - w_m) R_0 \tag{15.20}$$

and the expected return on the portfolio is

$$E(R_p) = w_m E(R_m) + (1 - w_m) R_0. \tag{15.21}$$

Being equivalent in the formula to a regression coefficient, the beta for the portfolio can be expressed as

$$\beta_{pm} = \operatorname{cov}(R_p, R_m)/\operatorname{var}(R_m) \tag{15.22}$$

where the covariance of R_p and R_m can be obtained as

$$\operatorname{cov}(R_p, R_m) = E w_m \{ [R_m - E(R_m)] + [(1 - w_m) R_0 - E(1 - w_m) R_0] \}$$
$$\times [R_m - E(R_m)]$$
$$= w_m \operatorname{var}(R_m). \tag{15.23}$$

Therefore,

$$\beta_{pm} = w_m \operatorname{var}(R_m)/\operatorname{var}(R_m) = w_m. \tag{15.24}$$

Substituting β_{pm} for w_m in equation (15.21), we can now express the rate of return on the portfolio as:

$$E(R_p) = \beta_{pm} E(R_m) + (1 - \beta_{pm}) R_0$$
$$= R_0 + [E(R_m) - R_0] \beta_{pm}. \tag{15.25a}$$

This is the CAPM, which shows that the expected return on the portfolio is a function of the beta.

Security market line versus capital market line

Since the portfolio can be any combination of capital assets, the above model has a general applicability in the pricing of capital assets. Furthermore, in one extreme case there may be only one asset in the portfolio, while in the other the portfolio may consist of the entire market assets. In either case we can use the above model. The line which runs from the rate of a riskless asset (or a hypothetical riskless asset) and has a slope of $[E(R_m) - R_0]/\beta_{mm}$ (Figure 15.4) is called the capital market line (CML). The notation β_{mm} which is numerically unity represents the beta of the market portfolio and the numerator term $E(R_m) - R_0$ represents the risk premium for the market portfolio.

On the other hand, if there is only one asset, say asset j, in the portfolio, equation (15.25a) can be rewritten as

$$E(R_j) = R_0 + [E(R_m) - R_0]\beta_{jm}. \tag{15.25b}$$

The curve representing equation (15.25b) is known as the security market line (SML). The expected rate of return on asset j, $E(R_j)$, is also the

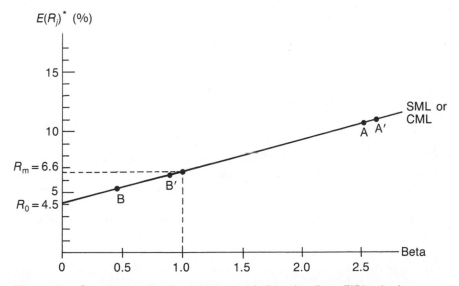

Figure 15.4 Security market line versus capital market line. $E(R_j)*$ is the expected (or required) rate of return on security j. For asset 1: A, held in portfolio, $E(R_1)* = 9.97$, $\beta_{1m} = 2.57$; A', held alone, $E(R_1)* = 10.08$, $\beta_1 = 2.62$. For asset 2: B, held in portfolio, $E(R_2)* = 5.35$, $\beta_{2m} = 0.40$; B', held alone, $E(R_2)* = 6.42$, $\beta_2 = 0.90$

required rate of return for the given level of risk β_{jm}. Note that if (a) the capital market is perfectly competitive and efficient and (b) arbitrage is permitted, the risk–return combination of each security will be on the CML. Therefore, both CML and SML will be on the same line.

For illustrative purposes, let us use the numerical values given in Table 15.1 and find the expected rate of return for asset 1, which has covariance with the market portfolio of 21.11. Then, the beta for asset 1 is

$$\beta_{1m} = \frac{\text{cov}(R_1, R_m)}{\text{var}(R_m)} = \frac{21.11}{8.22} = 2.57. \tag{15.26}$$

Therefore, for the given beta of 2.57, the required rate of return $E(R_1)^*$ on asset 1 is

$$E(R_1)^* = 4.50 + (6.63 - 4.50) \times 2.57 = 9.97 \ (\%). \tag{15.27}$$

It is also possible to measure the risk of a particular security in terms of the ratio of the standard deviation of the security to that of the market portfolio. Again, in the case of asset 1 we have the following:

$$\beta_1 = \frac{s(R_1)}{s(R_m)} = \frac{(56.48)^{1/2}}{(8.22)^{1/2}} = 2.62 \tag{15.28}$$

Thus,

$$\begin{aligned} E(R_1)^* &= 4.50 + (6.63 - 4.50) \times 2.62 \\ &= 10.08 \ (\%). \end{aligned} \tag{15.29}$$

In this case the assumption is that the asset is held alone, not as part of the portfolio.

The case with foreign assets

When foreign assets are introduced, the market portfolio should be replaced by the world portfolio, which in turn changes the position of the rate of return on the portfolio. Also the riskless rate may change. Then, the required rate of return on each individual asset also changes. This implies that the required rate of return on any asset is a relative concept. Furthermore, when major sources of risk associated with foreign investment are more than one, it would be more fruitful to use the arbitrage pricing model, as we shall see below.

The arbitrage pricing theory

In order to see the difference between the traditional CAPM and an alternative model developed by Ross (1976), let us reproduce equation (15.24a) below:

$$E(R_j) = R_0 + [E(R_m) - R_0]\beta_{jm}.$$

Given the variance var(R_j) of asset j and the riskless rate R_0, the required rate of return on asset j depends on the expected rate of return $E(R_m)$ on the market portfolio and its variance var(R_m). Thus, depending on the choice of different proxies for the market portfolio, the expected (or required) rate of return on a given asset will be different. Therefore, whether the model works or not cannot be tested unambiguously, because such a test must include all individual assets. Furthermore, investment assets with a beta of zero tended to have a higher return than Treasury bills, suggesting that the market rewards not only holding systematic risk but also holding unsystematic risk.

Noting these shortcomings in the traditional CAPM, Ross developed an alternative model, known as the arbitrage pricing theory (APT). This theory first decomposes the beta into a number of components, implying that the variability of the market portfolio performance stems from a number of underlying factors:

$$E(R_j) = R_0 + [E(R_m) - R_0] (T_1\beta_{1j} + T_2\beta_{2j} + \cdots + T_k\beta_{kj}) \tag{15.30}$$

where the T_i are non-negative constants normalized so that

$$\Sigma \ T_i = 1. \tag{15.31}$$

For example, if all the β_{ij} are the same, equation (15.30) is then reduced back to equation (15.25a). Equation (15.30) simply tells us that the risk premium on asset j, $E(R_j) - R_0$, is a linear combination of its beta weights multiplied by the risk premium on the market portfolio.

Next, the theory tries to reduce the role of the market portfolio. Let us define

$$\delta_i = [E(R_m) - R_0] T_i. \tag{15.32}$$

Then we can rewrite equation (15.30) as

$$E(R_j) - R_0 = \delta_1\beta_{1j} + \delta_2\beta_{2j} + \cdots + \delta_k\beta_{kj}. \tag{15.33}$$

Then, with a suitable transformation, we can interpret δ_i as the market risk premium on the ith market factor, that is,

$$\delta_i = E(R^i) - R_0 \tag{15.34}$$

where $E(R^i)$ is the expected rate of return on the ith market factor. Then,

$$E(R_j) - R_0 = [E(R^1) - R_0]\beta_{1j} + [E(R^2) - R_0]\beta_{2j} + \cdots$$
$$+ [E(R^k) - R_0]\beta_{kj}. \tag{15.35}$$

This tells us that the risk premium on any given asset is determined by the weighted sum of the factor risk premiums with weights being equal to the corresponding beta coefficients of the asset. The equality of both sides of equation (15.35) is the arbitrage result; hence, it is termed the arbitrage pricing theory.

The explicit role of the market portfolio is thus removed. Instead, the focus is shifted to the underlying factors which might influence the market portfolio performance. These factors are not specified in advance. In principle, any underlying factor which might influence the return on a group of assets – if not the market portfolio – would qualify.

The empirical studies, however, show that by and large asset returns depend on (1) inflation rate, (2) interest rates, (3) industrial production, and (4) investors' changing attitude toward risk.

With international investment opportunities, additional factors which would be important sources of risk may include foreign exchange rate risk and cross-border transfer risk, which we will explore in the next section.

INTERNATIONAL DIVERSIFICATION

Why should anyone diversify one's investment internationally? Up to this point we have briefly touched on how several key models for portfolio analysis might be modified with international investment. In this section we will examine the effect of international investment in a more comprehensive way. As in domestic investment diversification, there are basically two main reasons to diversify internationally, one to reduce risk and the other to increase return.

International diversification to reduce risk

Let us look at what it takes to reduce risk internationally. Suppose that an investor is to invest half of her financial resources in domestic assets and half in foreign assets. The returns on both investments have the same standard deviation of, say, 3 percent. Then, using formula (15.9b), we can find the variance of this internationally diversified portfolio as

$$\text{var}(R_p) = (\tfrac{1}{2})^2(3)^2 + (\tfrac{1}{2})^2(3)^2 + 2(\tfrac{1}{2})(\tfrac{1}{2})(r_{12})(3)(3)$$

$$= 9 \tag{15.36}$$

if the correlation coefficient $r_{12} = 1$. That is, if the variances are approximately the same in both domestic and foreign countries, the internationally diversified portfolio risk can be reduced only when the correlation coefficient is less than unity.

Then, what are the underlying factors which cause the correlation to be relatively small? Basically, it depends on the extent of integration of the domestic and foreign economies. The less the integration is, the lower is the correlation of economic performances of different countries likely to be, contributing to a lower worldwide market covariance. Worldwide economic integration is facilitated by increased international trade, capital flows, human resource movements, and policy harmonization. In particular, policy harmonization is becoming an increasingly important factor for integration, as is manifested in the European Community single-market movement. Different countries pursuing different policy objectives tend to create segmented markets.

Table 15.3 shows the correlation coefficients of GDP (or GNP) growth rates for the Group of Seven countries (Canada, France, Germany, Italy, Japan, the UK and the United States). For example, the French economy which can be presumed to have a greater integration with the founding EC member countries indeed has high correlations with such countries as Germany and Italy. On the other hand, the US economic growth rate has shown relatively low correlations with other economies, suggesting that the correlation of the world portfolio for US investors might be low.

Related to the economic integration, the speed of international transmission of shocks from one country to another also contributes to the determination of the covariance of asset returns. The faster the transmission, the higher the correlation is likely to be. Similarly, the degree of synchronization of the business cycles also affects the correlation. The more synchronized the phases of the business cycles, the higher is the correlation.

At this point we should note that, even if the correlation is low, this would still not guarantee a low portfolio risk. What if variances of foreign investment are substantially higher? For US investors, this is more likely to be the case in many instances. Then the portfolio risk may not decrease readily even when additional foreign assets are included in the portfolio.

Table 15.3 Correlation of the gross domestic products of the Group of Seven countries (1985.IV–1989.II)

	Canada	France	Germany	Italy	Japan	UK	USA
Canada	1	0.18	0.04	−0.31	0.18	−0.47	0.38
France		1	0.77	0.76	0.53	−0.08	−0.02
Germany			1	0.46	0.48	−0.15	−0.48
Italy				1	0.55	0.38	0.07
Japan					1	0.18	−0.11
UK						1	0.10
USA							1

Source: Based on the quarterly growth rates (annualized) data in Federal Reserve Bank of St. Louis (1990) *International Economic Conditions*, October
Note: For Canada, France, Italy, and the UK, figures are those of GDP, whereas for Germany, Japan, and the United States, they are GNP figures.

Additional risks in international investment

Then, what are additional sources of volatility of the return on foreign investment? One important source is the foreign exchange rate volatility. In effect, the variance of the return on foreign investment may be decomposed into two components: (1) the market risk in the local currency, $\text{var}(R_c)$, and (2) the exchange rate risk, $\text{var}(R_f)$:

$$\text{var}(R_2) = \text{var}(R_c) + \text{var}(R_f) + 2r_{cf}s(R_c)s(R_f) \qquad (15.37)$$

where R_2 is the return on the second investment asset which represents the foreign asset in our example here. As we studied in Chapter 7, the interest rate parity condition, for example, suggests that the higher return in local currency R_c will be offset by the depreciation of the local currency R_f, implying that the values of R_c and R_f usually have a negative correlation. Therefore, the foreign investment risk is usually less than the additive sum of the market risk in the local currency and the exchange rate risk. That is,

$$s(R_2) < s(R_c) + s(R_f). \qquad (15.38)$$

Another major source of foreign investment risk is abrupt changes in host government policies which restrict remittance of the return, which we term cross-border transfer risk. Such governmental actions may in turn be caused largely by the unfavorable balance of payments position. Thus, we may hypothesize within the framework of the APT that the additional factor components of the risk premium for an internationally diversified portfolio include foreign exchange volatility and cross-border transfer risk.

International diversification to increase return

Now let us turn to the return side of foreign investment. For domestic investment, total return consists of capital gain (or loss) and dividend (or interest), as shown in equation (15.1). However, for international investment, the total return on a particular asset is the sum of capital gain (or loss) and dividend (or interest) in local currency and foreign exchange gain (or loss):

$$R_{jt} = \frac{V_{jt} - V_{jt-1} + D_{jt}}{V_{jt-1}} + \frac{r_t - r_{t-1}}{r_{t-1}} \qquad (15.39)$$

where r_t and r_{t-1} are exchange rates (expressed in the price quotation method) at the end of the period and at the beginning of the period respectively. The foreign exchange gain (or loss) creates new opportunities as well as new risk.

For example, as shown in Table 15.4, out of the total return on foreign government bond investment, a substantial portion comes from unusual

Table 15.4 Risk and return on foreign government bond investment for US dollar investment and UK pound investment

	Return in local currency (%) (1)	Foreign exchange gain (%) (2)	Total return (%) (3)	Risk in local currency (%) (4)	Implied exchange rate risk (%) (5)	Total risk (%) (6)
$ bonds	6.07	0.00 (−19.95)	6.07 (−13.88)	1.46	0.00 (2.37)	1.46 (3.83)
C$ bonds	3.25	0.60 (−18.93)	3.85 (−15.68)	2.03	0.58 (2.09)	2.61 (4.12)
¥ bonds	−3.79	9.57 (−10.33)	5.78 (−14.12)	1.48	3.39 (1.85)	4.87 (3.33)
DM bonds	−0.12	21.19 (−17.58)	21.19 (−17.70)	1.26	3.10 (1.80)	4.36 (3.06)
FFr bonds	4.46	23.84 (−0.29)	28.30 (4.17)	1.69	2.16 (1.32)	3.85 (3.01)
£ bonds	7.39	24.87 (0.00)	32.26 (7.39)	2.43	2.59 (0.00)	5.02 (2.43)
Lit bonds	15.34	21.68 (−4.09)	37.02 (11.25)	0.50	2.77 (1.67)	3.27 (2.17)

Source: J. P. Morgan (1990) Global Markets, November: 21
Notes: Figures in parentheses are for pound investment. Total return covers the twelve-month period from November 1, 1989, to October 31, 1990. Return in local currency includes interest plus capital gains. Risk is measured in standard deviation of monthly total returns from December 31, 1985, to October 31, 1990. Foreign exchange gain or loss is the difference between the US dollar return and the local currency return. Implied foreign exchange risk is the difference between total risk and market risk in local currency.

foreign exchange gains. More specifically, during a one-year period ending October 31, 1990, US investors who invested in pound-denominated British government bonds could have realized a 32.26 percent return, which is 5.3 times higher than for the domestic investment, while facing a risk about 3.4 times higher. This exceptionally high return was mainly caused by appreciation of the pound.

On the other hand, a higher local currency return may be realized in a country where economic growth is rapid. As Table 15.5 shows, developed countries like the Group of Seven experienced relatively slow economic growth, whereas some Asian countries had substantially higher rates of growth. For instance, during the twenty-three-year period from 1965 to 1988, the annual per capita GNP growth rate in Korea was 6.8 percent; at this rate of growth, the economy expanded 4.54 times in twenty-three years. Under such favorable circumstances, the Korea Composite Stock Price Index went up from 100 in 1980 to over 900 in 1988.[3] The rapid rise was partly caused by inefficient market conditions coupled with a restricted supply of securities. There appears to be an emerging pattern for newly established securities markets. When a market is newly established or revitalized in a developing country, securities tend to be underpriced initially because of weak demand and inefficient market operations; this is followed by a rapid succession of price rises due to expanded demand from home and abroad, and then by slower price rises as the market becomes mature.

Table 15.5 Per capita gross national product growth rates (1965–88)

	Average annual growth rate (%)	Cumulative increase from 1965 (1965 = 1)
Group of Seven countries		
Canada	2.7	1.85
France	2.5	1.76
Germany	2.5	1.75
Italy	3.0	1.97
Japan	4.2	2.63
UK	1.8	1.51
USA	1.6	1.44
Asian countries		
Hong Kong	6.3	4.08
Korea	6.8	4.54
Singapore	7.2	4.95

Source: World Bank (1990) *World Development Report 1990*, New York: Oxford University Press, 178–9

A number of Third World country stocks funds have been established, first starting with newly industrializing countries (NICs) (such as Korea, Hong Kong, Singapore, Taiwan, and Turkey) and followed by new NICs (such as Thailand and Indonesia) and some Latin American countries (such as Chile and Argentina). However, investment in these funds is accompanied by high risk in local currency earnings as well as foreign exchange rate risk, of which the magnitude is not well understood because of insufficient experience.

THE ROLE OF COMMERCIAL BANKS IN INTERNATIONAL PORTFOLIO MANAGEMENT

International commercial banks perform several functions directly related to international portfolio management. Unlike the case of restrictive investment banking operations at home, US banking organizations can engage in investment banking business including mutual funds management abroad. They can however manage such funds at home only as trust activities. UK banks do manage investor portfolios at home or abroad directly by themselves or indirectly using subsidiaries. Being universal banks engaged in both commercial and investment banking, German banks have found no problems in managing investor funds. Japanese banks are sanctioned in ways similar to US banking organizations by the so-called "Article 65" of the Securities Exchange Law, the Japanese equivalent of the Glass–Steagall Act. However, Japanese banks have the added advantage that they are able to control a number of securities companies even with five percent ownership.

Their portfolio management activities include (1) global custodianship services, (2) international investment research, (3) foreign assets management for domestic pension funds, (4) other investor funds management, and (5) banks' own assets management.

Global custodianship services

Large commercial banks having an extensive global banking network have competitive advantage in the business of custodianship services (known as backroom services) which include (a) safekeeping of the indicia (evidence of ownership), (b) settlement of transactions, (c) collection of dividends and interest, (d) currency translation and conversion, and (e) centralized reporting.

The sources of banks' strength come from their extensive branch network supplemented by a correspondent banking network. Also their efficient telecommunications system gives them a competitive edge in this business. Armed with such arrangements, large international banks have accumulated detailed and comprehensive information relating to investments, varying standards applied to settlement procedures, and legislative developments and requirements in each market, all of which are useful for providing supporting services to portfolio managers. Thus, they are capable of executing timely and accurate settlement, dividend collection, and currency conversion and remittance to investors.

A number of US banks provide the so-called global master custodianship services which are standardized services provided for portfolio managers whether they are bank-affiliated portfolio managers or not. Chase Manhattan Bank, Citibank, and Mitsubishi Bank of California became active in this area by the early 1980s. [4]

International investment research

Spurred by the pension funds management business since the mid-1970s, large US banks, for example, have become active in acquiring expertise more directly related to securities transactions. Through international lending, they already had substantial expertise on foreign economies, industrial sectors, specific companies, and currency markets. What they needed was expertise on securities analysis, transactions and regulatory requirements, as well as local procedures. They also needed to cover uncovered territories. For the former need, a few banks put securities analysts in existing foreign branches, while others gathered information through extensive visits abroad. Over time some banks established new merchant banks abroad, partly for investment research purposes. For the latter, banks established further correspondent banking relationships with foreign banks in the countries where they did not have branch presence. In fact, larger banks already had some readily usable infrastructure for investment research through the established foreign credit analysis system, which conducted country risk analysis, currency risk analysis, as well as individual company credit analysis.

Foreign asset management for domestic pension funds

In recent years, the portfolio investment of pension funds has been the single largest source of funds for the US capital markets, reaching over $1 trillion by the mid-1980s. In a large measure this was spurred by the passage of the Employee Retirement Income Security Act (ERISA) in 1974, which provided that underfunded corporate pension funds be fully funded. In addition, the law stipulated that funds fiduciaries must diversify the investments within portfolios so as to minimize the risk of large losses, instead of just "investing as a prudent man would do." This resulted in the encouragement of the use of modern professional portfolio management practices. Note the influence of portfolio theory in action.

There were then three main categories of portfolio managers of pension funds, namely bank trust departments, insurance companies, and traditional funds managers (such as lawyers and corporate treasurers). Banks as a whole were managing about one-third of total funds by 1984. Many of these managers were replaced by professional funds managers equipped with techniques suggested by modern portfolio theories. Nonetheless, a number of large banks were able to win back their business through internal reorganization and their strength in familiarity of foreign markets.

A rapid growth of pension funds was also witnessed in the UK and other European countries, as well as in Japan in the past decade or so due to the increasing recognition of societal obligations for past services of retirees. A typical UK pension fund has 20–30 percent of its investments in non-UK assets, whereas US and Japanese funds typically have foreign assets somewhat below the 10 percent level.[5]

They all became interested in cross-border investments, particularly in the mid-1980s. As the international portfolio theory which we examined in the previous section would suggest, they became interested in investing in foreign assets for three major reasons. First, greater foreign exchange rate fluctuations created greater exchange rate risk but also provided opportunities for exchange gains, as we saw in Table 15.4. Second, certain countries exhibited an unusually high economic growth which would more probably provide a higher return on investment. Third, they were also interested in the diversification effect. Foreign assets provided an alternative opportunity to take advantage of the portfolio effect. Fund managers invested not only, for example, in domestic automobile companies, but also in foreign competitor companies. They also diversified between industrial countries in Europe and Japan, as well as between newly emerging industrializing countries and untapped countries.

Other investor funds management

In addition to pension funds, there are other institutional investors around the world which retain banks as their funds managers. They include foundations and other nonprofit organizations, central banks of foreign countries, and international organizations. In addition, there are a variety of specialized investment funds to meet the taste of individual investors. Bank trust departments manage the whole or part (particularly the foreign asset portion) of such funds. Finally, as a private bank, banks manage the private accounts of high net worth individuals, providing a complete set of investment services.

Banks' own assets management

To a greater extent, the whole asset-based banking operations are guided by the concept of portfolio management. The bank assets can be broadly classified into three categories: reserve assets, securities investment assets, and loan portfolios. The need for reserve assets is basically determined by regulatory requirements and the stochastic pattern of deposit additions and withdrawals.[6]

Securities investment assets are mainly short-term money market instruments. In the case of investment in domestic money market instruments, the major source of risk for banks is the interest rate risk. Thus, the minimization of interest rate risk is an important objective for bank asset management. When a bank has a foreign branch, it acquires foreign money market instruments in the course of business. Therefore, banks must consider additional risks, particularly the exchange rate risk. In order to hedge such risk, banks use versatile tools such as currency and interest rate swaps in addition to traditional forward, futures, and options contracts.

For the management of international loan portfolios, banks face quite a different set of risks in terms of composition and importance. Now they directly face cross-border risk in addition to credit risk and possibly also exchange rate risk. To mitigate the risk arising from changes in valuation of the loan portfolio including default risk, the lending bank may function more as an originator of loans than a holder of loans. Thus, as soon as the bank acquires loans, it may package them and sell them to other investors in the secondary market. This process is termed securitization of loans. We shall see more of cross-border risk in Chapter 17.

SUMMARY

This chapter outlined the characteristics of several major theories of portfolio investment and how inclusion of foreign assets can be accommodated in them. Adding foreign assets in the Markowitz theory of mean-variance trade-off means a shift in the investment opportunity curve. Similarly, foreign asset investment would shift the Tobin market line. Due to the effect of national boundaries segmenting one national market from others, foreign asset investment would reduce the systematic risk faster in the Sharpe–Lintner model of capital asset pricing.

However, the Ross arbitrage pricing theory is most versatile to account for risks arising from foreign investment, since it permits decomposition of the systematic risk into a number of underlying fundamental factors including foreign exchange rate risk and cross-border transfer risk, in addition to interest rate risk, inflation risk, and fluctuations in industrial production. It can also be shown that the international portfolio risk is less than the sum of the local currency investment risk and foreign exchange rate risk.

In relation to international portfolio management, commercial banks provide global custodianship, settlement of transactions, collection of dividends and interest, third-party (such as pension) funds management, and banks' own funds management.

REVIEW PROBLEMS AND EXERCISES

1. Explain the characteristics of the following models of portfolio analysis:
   (a) Markowitz model; (b) Tobin model; (c) Sharpe–Lintner model; (d) arbitrage pricing theory.

2. Explain how each of the above models may be modified when foreign investment assets are included in the portfolio.

3. Explain the difference between systematic risk and unsystematic risk.

4. Explain the differences between the capital market line and the security market line.

5. How does the foreign exchange rate risk affect the portfolio risk?

6. What would be a necessary condition to reduce the portfolio risk through international diversification?

7. What is the major risk faced by banks in managing their asset portfolio? What kind of tools can banks use to hedge the interest rate risk?

8. Suppose that three assets are available for investment. Each asset has the possible rates of return given in the table below depending on the state of market conditions. Each state has the same chance of occurrence.

State	Asset 1	Asset 2	Asset 3
1	5.4	14.1	5.2
2	4.2	10.6	6.6
3	7.9	9.2	7.4
4	8.2	-1.0	6.5
5	10.5	8.0	8.0

Calculate the following:
(a) the expected rate of return on each asset
(b) the variance of the rate of return on each asset.

9. Using the same information as given in Problem 8,
   (a) construct the variance–covariance matrix of the three assets;
   (b) construct the correlation matrix of the three assets.

10. Now assume that investment is made in an equal proportion in the three assets. Find
    (a) the expected rate of return on the portfolio
    (b) the variance of the rate of return on the portfolio
    (c) the covariance of each asset return and the portfolio return
    (d) the beta coefficient of each asset.

11. Using the results in Problem 10 above, find the following:
    (a) the required rate of return for each investment asset as an independent investment
    (b) the required rate of return for each investment asset as part of the portfolio.
    Assume the riskless rate is 4 percent.

12. Suppose that the investor has the following options:
    (a) investing in a portfolio consisting of assets 1 and 2 as characterized by the above data
    (b) investing in a foreign riskless asset at 6%
    (c) borrowing at a domestic riskless rate of 4%.
    Draw the efficient set of the portfolios.

NOTES

1 Although the efficient markets theory assumes that there is no investor who possesses information better than the market's information, Fama (1970: 383–417) classified three possible cases of market efficiency depending on the extent of available information: (a) "weak-form efficient," (b) "semi-strong efficient," and (c) "strong-form efficient."
2 In addition to Solnik (1974), see Lessard (1975) and Levy and Sarnat (1970) in particular.
3 See Korea Stock Exchange (1989: iii) for a phenomenal growth of the market.
4 See Ehrlich (1986: 31) for other banks which were also involved.
5 See Smith and Walter (1990): 521–2.
6 For a full discussion of stochastic deposit additions and withdrawals, see Kim (1979: 569–84).

BASIC READING

Ehrlich, E. E. (1986) "International Diversification of US Pension Fund Portfolio," in Tapley, M. (ed.) *International Portfolio Management*, London: Euromoney Publications, 25–40.
Emery, D. R. and Finnerty, J. D. (1991) *Principles of Finance: With Corporate Applications*, St Paul, Minn.: West Publishing.
Grimsey, C. G. (1986) "Global Custody," in Tapley, M. (ed.) *International Portfolio Management*, London: Euromoney Publications, 139–46.
Hayes, S. L., III and Hubbard, P. M. (1990) *Investment Banking: A Tale of Three Cities*, Boston, Mass.: Harvard Business School Press.
Korea Stock Exchange (1989) *Fact Book*, Seoul: Korea Stock Exchange.
Lessard, D. (1975) "The Structure of Returns and Gains from International Diversification: A Multivariate Analysis," in Elton, E. J. and Gruber, M. J. (eds) *International Capital Markets*, Amsterdam: North-Holland, 207–20.
Levy, H. and Sarnat, M. (1970) "International Diversification of Investment Portfolios," *American Economic Review*, 60 (4): 668–75.
Lindsay, J. (1986) "International Investment Research," in Tapley, M. (ed.) *International Portfolio Management*, London: Euromoney Publications, 109–18.

Lintner, J. (1965) "The Valuation of Risk Assets and the Selection of Risky Investments in Stock Portfolios and Capital Budgets," *Review of Economics and Statistics*, 47 (February): 13–37.

Markowitz, H. (1952) "Portfolio Selection," *Journal of Finance*, 7 (1): 77–91.

Roll, R. (1977) "A Critiques of the Asset Pricing Theory's Tests," *Journal of Financial Economics*, 4 (March): 129–76.

Ross, S. A. (1976) "The Arbitrage Theory of Capital Asset Pricing," *Journal of Economic Theory*, 13 (May): 341–360.

Sharpe, W. F. (1964) "Capital Asset Prices: A Theory of Market Equilibrium under Conditions of Risk," *Journal of Finance*, 19 (4): 425–42.

Simonds, R. R. (1978) "Modern Financial Theory," *MSU Business Topics*, Winter: 54–63.

Smith, R. C. and Walter, I. (1990) *Global Financial Services: Strategies for Building Competitive Strengths in International Commercial and Investment Banking*, New York: Harper & Row.

Solnik, B. H. (1974) "Why Not Diversify Internationally Rather Than Domestically?" *Financial Analysts Journal*, July–August: 48–54.

—— (1991) *International Investment*, 2nd edn, Reading, Mass.: Addison-Wesley.

Tobin, J. (1958) "Liquidity Preference as Behavior Toward Risk," *Review of Economic Studies*, 25 (February): 65–85.

FURTHER READING

The Economist (1991) "Schools Brief: Risk and Return," February 2: 72–3.

Fama, E. F. (1970) "Efficient Capital Markets: A Review of Theory and Empirical Work," *Journal of Finance*, 25 (2): 383–417.

Frankel, J. A. (1979) "The Diversifiability of Exchange Risk," *Journal of International Economics*, August: 379–93.

Grinblatt, M. and Titman, S. (1987) "The Relation between Mean–Variance Efficiency and Arbitrage Pricing," *Journal of Business*, 60 (1): 97–112.

Grubel, H. G. and Fadner, K. (1971) "The Interdependence of International Equity Markets," *Journal of Finance*, 25 (1): 89–94.

Kim, T. (1979) "Stochastic Reserve Changes and Expansion of Bank Credit," *Journal of Monetary Economics*, 5(4): 569–84.

Litan, R. E. (1987) *What Should Banks Do?*, Washington, D.C.: Brookings Institution.

Martin, J. D., Cox, S. H. and MacMinn, R. D. (1988) *The Theory of Finance: Evidence and Applications*, Chicago, Ill.: Dryden Press.

Ross, S. A. (1977) "Return, Risk, and Arbitrage," in Friend, I. and Bicksler, J. L. (eds) *Risk and Return in Finance*, Cambridge, Mass.: Ballinger, 189–218.

Solnik, B. (May 1983) "International Arbitrage Pricing Theory," *Journal of Finance*, 38 (2): 449–57.

Chapter 16

International trade finance

INTRODUCTION

Traditionally, international trade financing has been one of the most important functions of international banking. Retreating from sovereign lending as a result of the recent world debt crisis, many banks have returned to trade financing as the core of their business.

As we studied in Chapter 5, international trade involves two-way transactions. One is the delivery of goods or services and the other is making payment. Banks provide services to facilitate both delivery of goods and making payment. Since a seller and a buyer in international transactions are separated by distance as well as by national boundaries, each party faces greater potential risks. The exporter is particularly concerned about the buyer's potential payment default, while the importer is concerned about the seller's potential delivery default, as shown in Figure 16.1.

In addition, when there is a time gap between the shipment of goods (or delivery of services) and the payment, either the seller or the buyer must bear trade financing cost. If the payment is made after the shipment of goods, the exporter bears that cost. Conversely, if the payment is made before receiving goods, the importer bears the burden.

In this chapter, we first study how different methods of payment shift risks and trade financing cost between the seller and the buyer. We then examine the required documentation for international trade transactions. A precise documentation is essential to discern clear responsibility of each party involved so that disputes arising from ambiguity can be minimized. We then take a look at how various methods of payment result in alternative methods of trade financing. Finally, we discuss nonconventional methods of trade financing.

METHODS OF PAYMENT IN INTERNATIONAL TRADE

For exporters and importers, the method of payment is important because it determines who is going to bear greater risk and who is going to pay trade

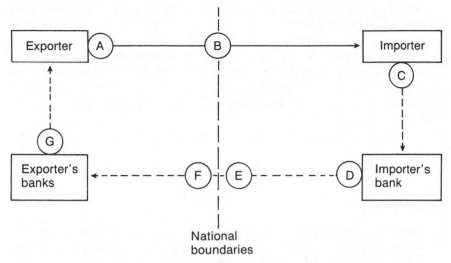

Figure 16.1 International trade transactions and sources of risk: A, delivery
default risk originating from the exporter; B, transit risk
originating from third parties or nature; C, credit risk originating
from the importer; D, credit risk originating from the letter of
credit bank; E, currency risk originating from the markets;
F, cross-border transfer risk; G, credit risk originating from the
home country bank; ⟶, flow of goods; – – ➙, flow of payment

financing cost. The incidence of trade financing cost depends on the selling
price, which is in turn determined by the supply and demand for the goods.
For example, even if the exporter assumes trade financing cost, he may be
able to shift such cost to the buyer through a higher price. The extent to
which the seller can transfer depends on the price elasticity of demand and
supply curves. The more elastic the demand, the less likely it is that the seller
can transfer the cost. An elastic supply curve shifts the burden to buyers.

Here, we will examine four basic methods of payment and their relative
advantages and disadvantages for exporters and importers. They are (1)
cash deposit in advance, (2) open account, (3) documentary draft for
collection, and (4) documentary letters of credit.

Cash deposit in advance

Under cash deposit in advance terms, the seller requests payment in cash in
whole or in part before shipping the merchandise. Obviously, this method
is most advantageous for the seller because it provides the greatest protection for him and the burden of trade financing cost is borne by the buyer.
Conversely, this method puts the foreign buyer in an unprotected position
against the seller's potential delivery default.[1]

Although this kind of arrangement is infrequent, it is more often observed in the seller's market. Even in the buyer's market, the seller may still insist on advance payment when the probability of default is unusually high, so that the expected loss cannot reasonably be covered without advance payment. Such instances may arise when the foreign buyer's credit is very questionable, or when political conditions in the country of destination are very unstable, or when the government policy on foreign exchange allocation is very uncertain.

In addition, advance payment is customarily requested when a buyer places a special order to the seller to produce tailor-made products for which the seller may not be able to find ready buyers other than this one.

Open account

In the United States, it is common to sell goods or services on an open account basis to domestic buyers. According to this method, goods are sold on credit terms, as agreed between the seller and the buyer, and payment is due in a specified number of days after the invoice date. An open account sale does not accompany any negotiable instrument such as a bill of exchange or a promissory note evidencing the buyer's payment obligation. It simply results in an accumulation of accounts receivable on the seller's balance sheet.

Under this payment method, the importer has the major advantage, since she receives the merchandise before making payment. On the other hand, the seller may have to rely solely on the buyer's ability and willingness to pay. As a consequence, the seller faces payment default risk and bears trade financing cost.

The advantages of selling on open account are its simplicity and the avoidance of additional charges related to other payment arrangements. It is simple because no third party is involved. No bank services such as collection or guarantee are involved so that fees related to such services can be avoided. However, in the event of default, it is more difficult to enforce collection than with other methods, because in this case the seller must first demonstrate that the buyer has a payment obligation.

As a result, this method is used primarily for transactions between affiliate firms in different countries or between parties having a long-standing relationship or between parties relatively well known to each other because of the proximity of their locations. In certain countries, this method of payment is not permitted because it is more difficult for the import country governments to monitor foreign exchange flows.

Documentary drafts for collection

After shipment of goods, the exporter forwards shipping and other documents plus a payment order (a draft drawn on the importer) through his bank to the importer's bank for collection. The draft orders the importer to pay now or to pay later, as stipulated in the sales contract. The draft accepted by the buyer for a later payment is termed a trade acceptance.

In forwarding a set of documents, the exporter instructs the collection bank not to release the documents to the importer unless the latter makes sight payment or accepts the draft for time payment. In this way, the exporter is reasonably assured of payment. That is, in the case of sight payment, the forwarded documents will be released to the importer only in exchange for payment. However, in the case of time payment, the exporter is not totally protected because, by the time the payment is due, the importer's financial conditions may have changed so that the importer might not be able to fulfill her payment obligation. In order to reduce such risk, the exporter may request an endorsement of a third party on the accepted draft. Frequently, the third party is the parent organization of the importer. Also, the importer's bank may provide a standby letter of credit for payment guarantee.

Unlike the case of an open account, the seller now has a negotiable draft evidencing the buyer's payment obligation, which makes it easier to enforce collection in the event of default. We also note that a time payment under the documentary collection method results in transfer of the trade financing burden to the exporter. However, if it is a sight payment, the importer must assume delivery default risk as well as trade financing cost, as shown in Table 16.1.

The documentary collection method is one of the most widely used methods of payment for exports of goods and services to foreign buyers.

Table 16.1 Relative advantages of alternative methods of payment

	Exporter		Importer	
	Financing cost	Default risk	Financing cost	Default risk
Cash in advance	No	1	Yes	6
Open account	Yes	6	No	1
Draft collection				
Sight	No	4	Yes	5
Time	Yes	5	No	4
Letter of credit				
Sight	No	2	Yes	3
Time	Yes	3	No	2

Note: Numbers indicate the approximate degree of risk; 1 represents the least risk and 6 the highest risk.

It is particularly suitable when the protections provided by a letter of credit for commercial risk are deemed unnecessary. For issuing letters of credit, banks charge letter of credit opening fees as well as acceptance fees. Therefore the cost saving brought about by not using letters of credit may be shared by both parties. Note that under this payment method the importer's bank is merely acting as a transmittal agent of the exporter, not as a guarantor of payment.

Documentary letters of credit

A letter of credit is one of the most common instruments used to facilitate international trade and its financing. By definition, a letter of credit is a notification letter issued by a bank to the seller stating that it will make payments on behalf of the buyer under specified conditions. Instead of the buyer, the letter of credit bank is now the first obligor, whose credit standing is purportedly higher than that of the buyer.

Not only is the seller protected but the buyer is also protected by a letter of credit in a manner similar to documentary collection, because the letter of credit sets forth specific pre-conditions for payment, which are in essence to require presentation of stated documents.[2] Without fulfilling his delivery obligations, the exporter would not be able to assemble such a set of required documents.

Once the shipment of goods is made, the exporter forwards the shipping and other documents including a payment order (draft drawn this time on the letter of credit bank) to the letter of credit bank through his house bank. Upon receiving and reviewing the documents to check the conformity with the letter of credit conditions, the bank makes a sight payment or accepts the order of the draft for a time payment, as required. A draft accepted by a bank for future payment is known as a bankers' acceptance.

Letters of credit may be issued in revocable or irrevocable form. A revocable letter of credit, which is not commonly used in international trade, can be modified or canceled by the letter of credit bank without prior consent of the seller. It therefore merely serves as a letter of intent without firm commitment, creating greater uncertainty for the seller. An irrevocable letter of credit cannot be altered or canceled without mutual consent of all parties.

With a letter of credit, the source of credit risk shifts from the buyer to the letter of credit bank. Nonetheless, the exporter still faces two types of risks: (1) credit risk originating from the letter of credit bank which may be unknown to him and (2) cross-border transfer risk. To remove these risks, the exporter may request that a bank in his country assume payment obligations on behalf of the letter of credit bank. The bank assuming this function is termed a "confirming" bank. This confirming bank collects fees of about 1/8 percent of the invoice value from the beneficiary for the confirming service. If there is substantial cross-border transfer risk, this confirming bank may purchase political risk insurance from the Eximbank, for instance, and may charge the premium to the exporter. If the function of the bank in the exporter's country is merely to notify the exporter when a letter of credit arrives, such a bank is termed an advising bank. Table 16.1 summarizes the relative advantages of alternative methods of payment for exporters and importers.

EXPORT/IMPORT DOCUMENTATION AND TERMS AND CONDITIONS OF SALES

Documentation

For international trade transactions, we have already noted the importance of documents, which are commonly used for several purposes. First, they are used to give a general indication that the exporter has fulfilled his obligations. Documents issued by third parties such as bills of lading, warehouse receipts, forwarders' receipts, and air waybills cannot be obtained without physical delivery of the merchandise by the exporter to the above document-issuing parties. Therefore, presentation of such documents by the exporter implies that the exporter has performed his contractual obligations. In addition, these documents establish the right to claim control of the merchandise.

Second, a certain document is specifically prepared to claim payment. A draft (also termed bill of exchange) is such a document. A commercial invoice which provides a list of what the buyer is to receive and what the buyer has to pay serves as a direct supporting document for the payment claim.

Third, some documents are used to give further indications that the merchandise to be shipped by the exporter purportedly meets the specifications of the contract. Documents certified by independent parties such as certificates of analysis, inspection certificates, and certificates of weight and measurement may serve such purposes. Obviously, in order to reduce delivery default risk, the importer may request additional documents. Then, where to stop? Preparation of each additional document incurs additional cost which must be borne by either the exporter or the importer. There is therefore a trade-off between additional assurance with more cost and less assurance but with less cost.

Fourth, in addition to other documents, certain documents are specifically required to clear the merchandise through ports of entry or exit. Such documents include consular invoices, customs invoices, and certificates of origin. Fifth, documents are also prepared for the buyer's convenience in handling and warehousing merchandise. They include packing lists. Finally, because of high (often catastrophic) transit risks in transporting goods between countries, documents are needed to give evidence of reasonable coverage of such risks to comfort and to protect parties involved. Insurance policies or certificates of insurance are needed for this purpose. Now let us take a look at individual documents.

Bill of lading

Among the various documents cited above, the bill of lading is one of the most important. A bill of lading is a receipt issued by a carrier for merchandise to be delivered to a designated destination. It has three main functions: (a) it is a contract obligating the carrier to carry goods from the port of shipment to the port of destination; (b) it is a warehouse receipt issued by the carrier, evidencing that goods are under the carrier's custody; and (c) it is the document establishing the right to control or to claim the goods. When goods are sent by air, the document equivalent to a bill of lading is called an air waybill (or airway bill).

Export drafts

An export draft is an unconditional order drawn by the exporter (drawer) on the importer or the letter of credit bank (drawee) giving an order to pay the amount of the draft upon presentation of the draft (a sight draft) or at an agreed future date. Time drafts usually specify 30 days, 90 days, 180 days, etc. after sight (after presentation) or after date (after the date of the draft). The basis of authority to give such an order to pay is given by the importer in the sales contract or in the letter of credit by the letter of credit bank.

Commercial invoice

This is a document prepared by the exporter, which shows individual goods shipped, the amount to be paid by the importer including any charges connected with the shipment, terms of sale, and terms of shipment such as free on board (FOB) or cost, insurance, and freight (CIF). In short, the commercial invoice tells the importer what she gets and what she pays.

There are some documents which are marginally different in form from a commercial invoice but serve quite a different purpose. A consular invoice which is prepared by the exporter generally contains the same information as the commercial invoice but is officially signed or stamped by the consulate of the importing country. It is used as a means of monitoring movements of goods and money into and from the importing country. Similarly, a customs invoice, as required for importation to the United States, is an invoice prepared by the exporter on a special form supplied by the Department of the Treasury. It is used to clear goods through US customs houses.

Insurance policy or certificate

An insurance policy is a document issued by an insurance company promising to indemnify a party against loss due to certain perils which are covered by the premium charged. An insurance certificate is an individual insurance policy issued under a master insurance policy.

Other certificates

A certificate of weight and measurement is prepared by the exporter or by an independent entity indicating the weight or dimension of goods. A certificate of analysis is a report of an analysis, prepared by experts, of the substance or compounds shipped. Similarly, an inspection certificate is a document prepared by an independent entity to certify the condition, quality or quantity of goods shipped. These certificates individually as well as jointly constitute a body of evidence that the goods shipped by the exporter meet the specification of the sales contract.

Terms and conditions of sales

In order to minimize potential disputes, the international sales contract should be drawn to stipulate the exact obligations of each party. It should include a description of the merchandise sold, price, method of payment, shipping arrangements, and designation of the payers of various charges such as shipping charges, insurance, taxes, analysis fees, and weighing fees.

The merchandise price is affected by whether or not some of the fees and charges are included in the price. It is also affected by shipping arrangements, which specify the transportation point where the title passes from the exporter to the importer. Let us take a look at specific shipping arrangements.[3]

Ex factory (or ex mill, or ex warehouse, etc.)

The merchandise is transferred to the buyer at the point of origin (point A in Figure 16.2), usually at the factory site. Under this term, the seller is responsible for making the merchandise available for the buyer, usually at the factory site.

Free on board

The title to the merchandise passes to the buyer when the merchandise is loaded on the carrier's means of transportation (railroad cars, trucks, aircraft, vessels, etc.). There are several variations. FOB may be at the named loaded inland point of departure (point B in Figure 16.2), at

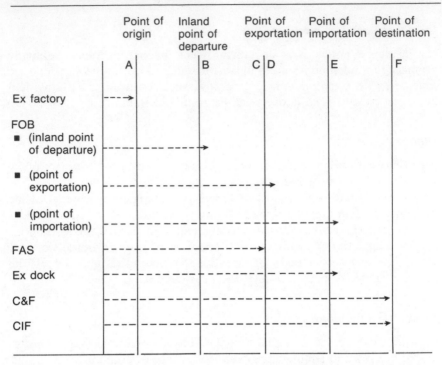

Figure 16.2 Different price quotations and title transfer points: A, before loading on inland carrier; B, on board (inland carrier); C, delivery to dock; D, on board (ocean vessel); E, delivery to dock; F, delivery to destination; – – →, coverage of the seller's responsibility

the loaded point of exportation (point D), or at the unloaded point of importation (point E).

Free alongside

Under the term free alongside (FAS) the seller quotes a price including delivery of the merchandise alongside an overseas vessel within reach of its loading tackle. The title passes at that point (point C) of loading.

Ex dock

Under this term, the title passes when the goods are placed on the dock at the named port of importation (point E). Accordingly, the seller quotes a price including the costs of the goods and all additional costs to deliver the goods there. This term is used primarily in the US import trade.

Cost and freight

The seller delivers the goods to the named point of destination (point F), where the title passes. The price quoted by the seller includes the cost of goods and all the transportation costs except expenses incurred for the convenience of the buyer, such as obtaining the certificate of origin and the consular invoice. Fees for these services are charged separately.

Cost, insurance, and freight

Under this term, the seller quotes a price which includes the cost of the goods, marine insurance, and all transportation charges to the named point of destination. This is similar to cost and freight (C&F) except that the seller additionally is responsible for marine insurance. However, usually war-risk insurance is not included.

INTERNATIONAL TRADE FINANCING

Now let us look at financing methods in international trade. A variety of financing arrangements are available: short term, medium term, export oriented, import oriented, domestic source, foreign source, etc. However, the basic guiding principle of financing is to choose the method which will minimize the cost of funds, given risk and other considerations. As we note below, the choice of payment methods by and large predetermines trade financing methods, and vice versa.

Financing through buyer credits

Recall the case of cash deposits in advance, or that of sight payments in documentary collections and letters of credit. There, cash payment is due in advance or due as documents are presented. To meet such an immediate payment obligation, a financing arrangement may be necessary for the buyer. If the amount of the payment is relatively large, say over $1 million, a buyer credit is a suitable method.

A buyer credit is a loan provided usually by international banks to an importer of goods or services. The credit can be used to cover down payment for the imported goods as well as the remainder of the payment. Since the credit is specifically earmarked for the import of goods or services, it cannot be used for other purposes.

Major providers of this type of credit include Eurocredit banks as well as trade finance specialty banks such as accepting houses in London. The terms and conditions of credit are similar to those of other Eurocurrency credit with a medium-term maturity. A major advantage of a buyer credit is the flexibility it offers. It can be arranged rather quickly even for a large amount; it can be provided in any number of currencies; and the maturity can be adjusted to meet the need of the importer.

Financing through accounts receivable

When the exporter sells goods and services on an open account basis, the net result is an accumulation of accounts receivable on the exporter's balance sheet. To support such credit sales, the exporter may need financing. Here, however, the exporter may utilize accounts receivable in two alternative ways: he may assign accounts receivable to lenders as collateral for borrowing (accounts receivable financing) or he may sell accounts receivable at a discount (factoring).

Accounts receivable financing

Many banks and their affiliate finance companies are active in this field of financing. In accounts receivable financing, credit is provided to the exporter, not to the importer. Therefore, the main credit risk for the lender is the creditworthiness of the exporter backed by the value of the assigned accounts receivable, which in turn depends on the buyer's creditworthiness.

Since accounts receivable arising from international sales involve additional risks because of unfamiliar buyer credit standing, uncertain exchange control policy, and exchange rate fluctuations, the lender usually will not provide credit up to the full value of the assigned claims. It is customary to provide only up to about 70 percent of the assigned value. In accounts receivable financing, the buyers are usually not informed of the debt assignment. The repayment schedule is tailored to the accounts receivable maturity schedule.

Since it is pure financing to the exporter with accounts receivable as collateral, the lender does not assume international transaction risks (international commercial risk, cross-border transfer risk, and currency risk). These risks remain with the exporter.

International factoring

Factoring is financing through sales of accounts receivable. A buyer of accounts receivable is termed a factor. The factoring involves several functions: (1) credit checking, (2) financing, (3) risk bearing, and (4) collection. Factoring companies, which in many instances are banks and other subsidiaries of bank holding companies, provide all or some of the above functions. Accounts receivable are sold at a discount. The exact discount price is the risk-adjusted present value of the accounts receivable. Typically, the factor pays about 80 percent or more of the invoice value at the time of purchase of the accounts receivable and the balance later after reduction of discounts or returns. Fees for other services may be charged separately or figured in the discount price.

As pointed out earlier, accounts receivable financing is pure financing, that is, to provide funds for use of a borrower for a certain duration. On the other hand, factoring may be pure financing or something more than that. If the main purpose of factoring is pure financing as in accounts receivable financing, the accounts receivable may be sold to the factor with recourse. However, if it is desirable for the exporter to transfer credit risk to the factor, they may be sold without recourse.

The factor in the exporter's country, known as an export factor, then passes credit risk on to a factoring partner in the importer's country, known as an import factor. This is accomplished when the import factor provides guarantees for importers' payment obligations.

Generally, the export factor, before purchasing accounts, conducts a credit evaluation of importers in different countries through a network of factoring partner companies. The factors in the importers' countries are better informed about local situations and better equipped to assess the economic risks of the accounts receivable from the local importers. They then usually take over the commercial risk from the export factor for fees, and carry out local collection again for fees, if necessary. These services (credit checking, risk bearing, and collection) are known as import factoring. Note that the essence of the export factor's function is pure financing, while other accompanying services are carried out by import factors.

Currency risk and cross-border transfer risk are not usually assumed by the export factor. Currency risk could be removed from the beginning if the exporter could invoice in his home currency units. Cross-border risk can be transferred, if desired, by purchasing a political risk insurance from the Eximbank, for instance.

Financing through letters of credit

Timing of payment

Whether financing is through a documentary collection or a documentary letter of credit, the importer must negotiate whether to pay now or later. Let us consider the case of a US importer buying goods from a UK exporter at the pound price of $P_£$. Then, using the same notation as in Chapters 6 and 7, we can express the dollar amount for immediate payment as

$$P_£ r_{00}. \qquad (16.1)$$

On the other hand, credit payment (say, to be paid a year from now) requires the dollar amount of

$$P_£(1 + i_f)r_{01} \tag{16.2}$$

the present value of which is then

$$\frac{P_£(1 + i_f)r_{01}}{1 + i_d}. \tag{16.3}$$

Since the US importer will choose the least costly method of financing, she will make an immediate payment if the following condition holds:

$$\frac{P_£(1 + i_f)r_{01}}{1 + i_d} > P_£r_{00}. \tag{16.4}$$

Alternatively, the above condition may be rewritten as

$$(1 + i_f)\,\frac{r_{01}}{r_{00}} > 1 + i_d \tag{16.5}$$

which means that the US importer will make an immediate payment to the UK exporter by borrowing in the US money market.

Similarly, a UK importer importing goods from the United States must pay the pound amount of $P_\$(1/r_{00})$ per unit of import if he chooses to pay now. On the other hand, if he chooses to pay later, say one year later, the pound amount needed will be $P_\$(1 + i_d)(1/r_{01})$. Therefore, this importer should make an immediate payment under the condition

$$\frac{P_\$(1 + i_d)(1/r_{01})}{1 + i_f} > P_\$\,\frac{1}{r_{00}} \tag{16.6}$$

or if the following condition holds:

$$1 + i_d > \frac{r_{01}}{r_{00}}\,(1 + i_f). \tag{16.7}$$

This also means that under the condition of equation (16.7) the UK importer should be borrowing at home to make a sight payment. However, if the market conditions are such that equation (16.5) holds, then the UK importer should choose a time payment method.

In sum, to choose a sight payment is equivalent to financing from the domestic money market. If the money and exchange market conditions are such that US importers should be making sight payments, then UK importers should be making time payments. To take advantage of the interest rate differentials between exporting and importing countries and the exchange rate differentials between spot and forward rates so that trade is financed in the least costly market is termed trade finance arbitrage or simply trade arbitrage.

Bankers' acceptances

Under the arrangement of a letter of credit, the exporter draws either sight draft or time draft on the letter of credit bank. A sight draft involves trade financing by the importer, whereas a time draft involves financing by the exporter. Instead of keeping the accepted time draft until maturity, the exporter may sell it at a discount to a buyer, who can be the confirming bank, or the letter of credit bank, or an acceptance investor.

The recent statistics shows that a bulk of bankers' acceptances are held by investors other than accepting banks. For example, only $7.9 billion out of $54.8 billion of total bankers' acceptances in the United States as of the end of 1990 were held by accepting banks.

What, then is the discount price at which the exporter can sell his accepted draft? Since it is sold at a discount, the proceeds P are the difference between the principal amount A and the discount charge D:

$$D = A \times i \times (N/360) \tag{16.8}$$

and

$$P = A - D \tag{16.9}$$

where N is the number of days to run and i is the discount interest rate. For example, a draft with an invoice value of $1,000,000 and 182-day tenor is discounted at the rate of 8.20 percent. The discount charge is then

$$D = \$1,000,000 \times 0.082 \times (182/360) = \$41,456 \tag{16.10}$$

and the proceeds are

$$P - \$1,000,000 - \$41,456 = \$958,544. \tag{16.11}$$

One important question is whose interest rate this discount rate represents, the exporter's or accepting bank's. Once a draft is accepted by a bank, it is equivalent to the bank's own debt instruments. Therefore the market would discount accepted papers accordingly. How much is the value of acceptance by a bank? As Figure 16.3 shows, it depends on the relative creditworthiness of the borrower and the bank. Suppose that the exporter is an A-rated customer and he can borrow at 9.0 percent without bank guarantee, while his accepting bank is a prime-name bank (class A bank) and its borrowing rate is 8.0 percent. Then, once the exporter's instrument is accepted by this bank, the interest rate will drop from 9.0 percent to 8.0 percent.[4] This difference of 1 percent is due to the bank guarantee. Thus, the maximum fee that this particular customer is willing to pay for the guarantee facility will be 1 percent. Note that, for another exporter with BBB-rating, the value of class A bank acceptance is 1.5 percent. Also note that the prime-name banks tend to attract better rated customers. For an

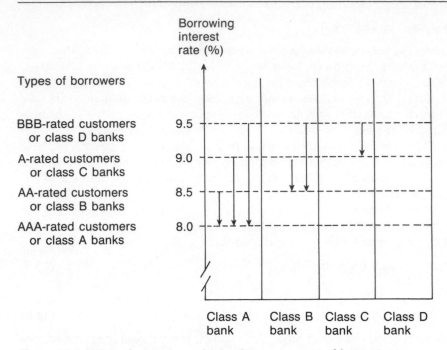

Figure 16.3 Value of acceptance by banks: →, amount of interest rate
reduction due to acceptance by a bank

AA-rated exporter, class B or lower rated banks have no value in reducing
the borrowing interest rate.

In practice, acceptance fees are charged to the importer when a letter of
credit is open. Acceptance fees vary depending on the credit standing of the
applicant, the tenor of the credit, the amount of the credit, and the
prevailing credit market conditions. Typically, the fees may range between
1/16 to 1/8 percent per month. In addition, a letter of credit opening fee
of about 1/4 percent of the invoice amount is charged.

Banks are originators, investors, and dealers of bankers' acceptances. As
originators, they receive acceptance fees; as investors, they receive interest
income; and as dealers, they make profit by buying acceptances at lower
prices and selling them at higher prices. A bank may enhance the quality
of acceptances which it is holding by exchanging with similar quality acceptances held by another bank. A swapped bankers' acceptance has three
names, namely the current owner bank, the previous owner bank, and the
exporter. The quality of this so-called three-name paper approaches that of
US Treasury bills because the probability of two banks in a row going into
bankruptcy in the United States is still very slim.[5] Thus these two banks

would be able to sell swapped acceptances at higher prices. Their rates are only a few basis points above Treasury bill rates.

Today, bankers' acceptances are used as a tool not only for international trade financing but also for any short-term working capital financing purposes. Finance bills are created when borrowers draw drafts on their banks under a prearrangement in which the banks commit to accept the drafts when presented. The accepted drafts are then sold in the bankers' acceptances market. There are no underlying transactions in this instance; accepted drafts are used simply as alternative means of financing. By financing in this way, the maturities of the asset item (loan to the borrower) and the liability item (payable to the investor) on the bank's balance sheet are automatically matched.

When the amount of trade financing need is large, no one bank may be willing or able to undertake a full commitment to finance the entire amount. Then a lead bank may arrange a bankers' acceptances syndication in which each participating bank commits to accept a certain amount of financing need with the same terms and conditions. Note that the discount applicable to each participating bank may be different.

Trade financing through trade acceptances and forfaiting

Now consider the case of documentary drafts for collection, where no letters of credit are involved. However, documentary collections result in either sight payment or trade acceptances or the creation of promissory notes. For short-term financing, trade acceptances with or without endorsement are usually used, while for medium-term financing, forfaitings are increasingly used.

Trade acceptances

In documentary collection, the exporter presents a draft with other documents to the importer through a collection bank. As we mentioned earlier, when the draft is accepted by the importer, the accepted draft is termed a trade acceptance. The trade acceptance may be sold in the market at a discount to an investor. In order to enhance the quality of the instrument, a third party endorsement or banker's guarantee may be used.

Forfaiting

Forfaiting means the purchase of debt instruments (promissory notes or trade acceptances) arising from the import of goods and services without recourse to the previous holder (exporter) of the instruments. The word forfaiting originates from the French *à forfait*, which implies forgoing of the right of claims.

This method of financing is often used in a case where import of capital goods is involved and the importer makes a series of installment payments which are determined by the invoice price divided by a number of payments. In making payment, the importer makes promissory notes or the exporter draws bills of exchange usually at six-month intervals for three to five years. Each promissory note or trade acceptance is *avalled* or guaranteed by a guarantee bank, which is usually the importer's house bank. Acting as an agent of the importer, this guaranteeing bank forwards the debt instrument with bank guarantee to the exporter, who in turn sells these documents to a forfaitor without recourse.

For the exporter, forfaiting is similar to factoring, as claims against the importer are sold at a discount. However, in forfaiting, practically all commercial, currency, and cross-border risks are transferred to the forfaitor, whereas in factoring only commercial risk is transferred to the factor. For the importer, installment payments are similar to the loan repayment schedule of a medium-term Eurocurrency credit. If the exporter's bank is the forfaitor, its function is similar to a confirming bank purchasing the exporter's draft (which is guaranteed by the letter of credit bank under a set of stipulated conditions). For the importer's bank, its function in forfaiting is to issue a standby letter of credit instead of a letter of credit.

ALTERNATIVE APPROACHES TO INTERNATIONAL TRADE FINANCING

New financing techniques are constantly being developed to meet new needs of international trade transactions, and at the same time old techniques which have successfully been applied to domestic trade financing are extended to international trade financing.

Leasing

In a leasing arrangement, the lessee (user) does not buy an equipment but rather buys services of the equipment for a given period of time and pays service fees (leasing rental) to the lessor who owns the equipment.

There are two types of leasing. In an operating leasing, it is the producer of capital goods who provides a leasing arrangement for the user (lessee) of capital equipment. Such a producer as the lessor usually provides technical services and replacement with updated products, as in the computer industry, for example. Banks are typically involved in the second type of leasing, known as capital leasing or financial leasing. It is a pure financing arrangement. No technical services are provided.

There are two types of leasing involving two countries. One is cross-border leasing. This is the case in which a lessor in one country leases his equipment directly to a lessor in another country who in turn leases to the end-user. There are a number of questions in this type of arrangement, such as whether import duty should be applied in this case and whether the lessor has the priority claim on the leased equipment in the event of lessee bankruptcy.

Another type is international leasing. This is the case of selling an equipment by the exporter to his country's leasing company which in turn sells to a foreign leasing company in the country where the lessee resides. Then the foreign leasing company leases to the lessee instead of the lessee importing the equipment. Usually such a arrangement is facilitated through the international network of leasing companies in different countries.

What makes this type of financing arrangement more attractive than conventional financing? One potential benefit stems from favorable tax treatment on depreciation which the lessor (bank) can reap. Such benefit can be shared with the lessee in the form of more favorable terms and conditions than is the case with conventional credit. Since the lease payment is in substance an installment payment, it will impact less on the balance sheet of the lessee than the case of borrowing. This is also true for the capital importing country as a whole. As leasing will impact the balance of payments less adversely than the case of outright borrowing and purchase of the equipment, some governments concerned with their balance of payments deficit encourage this kind of financing approach.

Government-subsidized financing and guarantee facilities

Since the export sector of the economy creates jobs and income, it has become standard for a designated government agency, for instance the Eximbank in the United States, to provide export credit subsidies and to absorb excessive export credit risks which cannot reasonably be covered in the private insurance market. The rationale for providing such subsidies is twofold: first to neutralize the effect of subsidies provided by other governments so that their country companies can effectively compete in winning sales contracts, and second to facilitate flows of external finance to developing countries.

Export credit subsidies and insurance coverage vary. For instance, the Eximbank provides (1) guarantees to commercial lenders who provide loans to foreign buyers of US exports, (2) export credit insurance to protect US exporters, (3) working capital guarantees to commercial lenders who provide loans to small US companies which have export commitments, and (4) direct loans to foreign buyers of US exports at subsidized terms and conditions.

The export credit insurance program is provided by the Eximbank in cooperation with the Foreign Credit Insurance Association (FCIA) which is a joint enterprise of some sixty insurance companies in the fields of marine, casualty, and fire insurance. Basically political risk is covered by the Eximbank, whereas commercial risk is covered by the FCIA. Guarantee fees (exposure fees) charged to commercial lenders are determined by the actual amount of exports financed, the terms of credit, the classification of the borrower or guarantor, and the country category of the borrower. Current exposure fees (as of June 1991) range from $0.50 to more than $8.00 per $100. Export credit insurance premiums charged to exporters are determined by the credit terms, the exporter experience, the quality and number of buyers insured, and the category of the importing countries.

In addition to insurance/guarantee programs, the Eximbank provides direct loan programs for foreign buyers. Furthermore, direct loans are also provided to foreign buyers by the Private Export Funding Corporation (PEFC), usually in the form of co-financing with commercial banks and the Eximbank. The PEFC is owned by some fifty commercial banks plus a number of corporations specializing in medium-term loans for sales of large ticket items.

In the UK, the Export Credits Guarantee Department (ECGD) which was established as early as 1919 started out to provide insurance cover against the risks of buyer default and now provides a variety of services including medium-term credit facilities. La Compagnie Française d'Assurance pour le Commerce Extérieur (COFACE) in France performs functions similar to the ECGD. In Germany, Hermes Kreditversicherungs-AG (Hermes), which is a private company with a federal government mandate, provides export insurance and Kreditanstalt für Wiederaufbau (KfW), which is a state-owned development bank, provides medium-term credit. In Japan, the Export–Import Bank of Japan provides medium-term loans to support exports and to some extent imports and foreign direct investment. The Export Insurance Scheme (Scheme) provides export insurance programs.

In order to mitigate undue competition, the twenty-two-member Organization for Economic Cooperation and Development (OECD) has established guidelines for export credit arrangements including the interest rates to be charged. According to the guidelines, there are three categories of importing countries, namely, relatively rich, intermediate, and relatively poor. Differentiated rates are charged depending on the category of the importer's country, with more favorable rates for relatively poor countries.

Countertrade

Countertrade is trade involving payment in kind or payment in a mix of goods and hard currency. For this type of transaction, the shipment of goods and its payment are usually not made simultaneously, thereby requiring trade financing. Thus, we may consider countertrade not only as alternative methods of payment but also as alternative methods of trade financing. For countries facing an acute shortage of hard currencies, such as most Eastern European and debt-stricken developing countries, this is considered a viable alternative financing method in spite of the known inefficiency inherent in it.

Several different arrangements are practiced in countertrade today, including (1) barter, (2) buyback agreements, (3) compensation agreements, and (4) counterpurchase agreements.[6]

Barter is the oldest form of exchange transactions and involves direct, simultaneous exchange of merchandise of equivalent value without using means of payment. The major disadvantage of this method is the difficulty in matching a double coincidence of wants. That is, wants of the two parties in the transaction must be matched simultaneously and the two parties must be able to agree on the exchange ratio to be applied to the barter transactions. Once suitable counterparties are matched, usually letters of credit are used to guarantee the performance of both parties. The seller's bank guarantees the delivery of goods by the seller to the counterparty, while the counterpart's bank guarantees the delivery of compensation products by its client. Compensation products are those used in lieu of means of payment.

A buyback agreement is more commonly used to finance export of capital equipment. In this arrangement, the exporter of the equipment agrees to buy the products produced with the equipment that the exporter supplied. This is similar to a medium-term loan with repayment in kind. A compensation deal involves an agreement similar to a buyback but partial payment is made "in kind" and partial payment in cash. This provides some flexibility for the exporter.

Counterpurchase is designed to provide further flexibility to overcome the difficulty inherent in a double coincidence of wants. With this arrangement, the exporter agrees to purchase goods produced by a company nominated by the importer. Then, the importer settles the purchase payment with the nominated company in local currency. Also, a variation of this arrangement is that the exporter takes products from the importer within the specified future period. Again, the exporter is selling products on a credit basis and receiving payment in kind later.

Since it is more difficult to find counterparties interested in countertrade, the market search cost is substantial. Such market search may be unnecessary if foreign exchange is used as the means of payment. Therefore, countertrade has high transactions costs and its transactions costs are largely hidden. Thus the cost of financing is now implicit rather than explicit. The very fact that certain compensation products can be exported only through countertrade implies that such products are marginally in demand. Therefore continuous support of the export of such products through countertrade would distort global resource allocations.

Then, why countertrade? For Eastern European and developing countries, countertrade is a means to utilize the national resources which were not tapped by major international trading companies. At the company level, countertrade is equivalent to gaining a priority in foreign exchange allocation in the country where importation of such equipment may not necessarily receive a high priority. By directly linking the export of compensation products, the importing company is in effect receiving the first priority in foreign exchange allocation to purchase the capital goods in question.

SUMMARY

International trade financing has been one of the core international banking businesses. Varying payment methods not only shift the incidence of payment and performance default risks, but result in different types of financing. A cash deposit in advance may require buyer credit; an open account may result in accounts receivable financing or factoring; documentary collection may lead to forfaiting; and documentary letter of credit leads to bankers' acceptance financing.

For international trade transactions, documents serve a number of purposes; some, such as bills of lading, commercial invoices, and consular and customs invoices, are used either as evidence of claims or facilitation of claims on merchandise, while others such as export drafts and insurance certificates are prepared for the purpose of payment claims. In deciding whether to make sight payment or time payment, the importer should be guided by trade arbitrage opportunities. In international trade financing, leasing, government-sponsored financing, and countertrade can be considered as alternatives.

REVIEW PROBLEMS AND EXERCISES

1. Identify the major sources of risks in international trade and payment transactions.

2. Compare the advantages and disadvantages of using the following payment methods for exporters in terms of (i) risk transfer, (ii) incidence of trade financing cost, (iii) fees and charges related to each method, and (iv) other considerations.
   (a) Cash in advance
   (b) Open account
   (c) Documentary draft for collection
   (d) Letter of credit

3. A number of documents are used in international trade transactions. What purposes are they used for?

4. What are the functions of bills of lading?

5. Explain the point of transfer of the title of goods from the seller to the buyer in each of the following cases: (a) CIF; (b) ex factory; (c) FAS; (d) FOB; (e) C&F.

6. Rank the above shipping arrangements according to the costs to the seller.

7. The choice of certain payment methods results in certain trade financing methods. Explain the probable financing methods resulting from the payment methods cited in Problem 2 above.

8. How can the accounts receivable from export sales be used for trade financing?

9. How different is international forfaiting compared with the following financing methods?
   (a) Trade acceptance
   (b) Bankers' acceptance
   (c) Factoring

10. Banks are originators, investors, dealers, and users of bankers' acceptances. Explain.

11. Rank the following countertrade methods according to the flexibility of compensation product payments and explain why.
    (a) Barter
    (b) Buyback agreement
    (c) Counterpurchase
    (d) Compensation deal

12. Explain how the value of acceptance by a bank is determined.

13. What is the rationale used for providing export credit subsidies by the Eximbank? Does it make sense to subsidize foreign buyers? What about domestic buyers?

14. A US importer is trying to choose either sight payment or six-month time payment for his import of goods from Japan under the following market conditions:

    spot rate ¥200/$1   six-month forward rate ¥196/$1
    US interest rate 8.00%   Japan interest rate: 5.00%

    (a) Which method should the US importer choose?
    (b) What if this is a Japanese importer facing exactly the same market conditions?

15. Given the following market conditions, determine the proceeds of a discounted bankers' acceptance.

    Principal, $500,000   Tenor, 91 days
    Interest rate, 8.25%

NOTES

1 However, the buyer may reduce or remove the seller's performance default risk using a surety bond or a bank's guarantee. See, for example, Beckers (1981: 149–71).
2 Under clean collection, a draft may be sent without requiring commercial documents.
3 For more precise definitions, see Chase World Information Corporation (1979: 74–86) in which US Chamber of Commerce (1941) *Revised American Foreign Trade Definitions – 1941* is reprinted.
4 This assumes that the exporter's endorsement is without recourse.
5 The probability of two banks going into bankruptcy in a row in the United States in 1990 was on the order of 0.016 percent.
6 Other types of arrangements include switch deals, offsets, linkages, and industrial cooperations. See, for instance, Korth (1985) for the detailed mechanics of their arrangements.

BASIC READING

Beckers, L. (1981) "Contract Guarantees and International Bonding Practices", in Gmür, C. J. (ed.) *Trade Financing*, London: Euromoney Publications, 149–71.
Chase World Information Corporation (1979) *Methods of Export Financing*, 3rd edn, New York.
Continental Bank (undated) *Guide to Export/Import Documentation*, Chicago, Ill.
Eximbank (1991) *An Introduction to Eximbank*, Washington, D.C., July.
Gmür, C. J. (ed.) (1981) *Trade Financing*, London: Euromoney Publications.
Hervey, J. L. (1989) "Countertrade – Counterproductive?" *Federal Reserve Bank of Chicago Economic Perspectives*, January–February: 17–24.
Johnson, G. G., Fisher, M. and Harris, E. (1990) *Officially Supported Export Credits: Developments and Prospects*, Washington, D.C.: IMF.
Korth, C. (1985) *International Countertrade*, New York: Quorum.
Melton, W. C. and Mahr, J. M. (1981) "Bankers' Acceptances," *Federal Reserve Bank of New York, Quarterly Review*, Summer: 39–55.
OECD (1990) *The Export Credit Financing Systems in OECD Member Countries*, 4th edn., Paris: Organization for Economic Co-operation and Development.
Stern, R. M. (1973) *The Balance of Payments: Theory and Economic Policy*, Chicago, Ill.: Aldine, 45–7.
Venedikian, H. M. and Warfield, G. A. (1986) *Export–Import Financing*, 2nd edn, New York: Wiley.

FURTHER READING

Ball, J. and Knight, M. (eds) (1989) *The Guide to Export Finance 1989*, London: Euromoney Publications.
Demarines, R. J. (1982) *Analysis of Recent Trends in U.S. Countertrade*, USITC Publication No. 1237, Washington, D.C.: US International Trade Commission.
Kingman-Brundage, J. and Schulz, S. (1986) *The Fundamentals of Trade Finance*, New York: Wiley.
de Miramon, J. (1982) "Countertrade: A Modernized Barter System," *OECD Observer*, 114 (January): 12–15.
—— (1985) "Countertrade: An Illusory Solution," *OECD Observer*, 134 (May): 24–29.

Chapter 17

Country risk analysis, international lending, and debt rescheduling issues

INTRODUCTION

In this chapter, we will examine three sequentially related topics: country risk analysis, international bank lending, and debt restructuring issues. We start with an examination of the methodology of country risk analysis, which is preparatory work needed for international bank lending. The result of the analysis serves as a basis for prior- and post-lending decision-making.

International bank loans are provided for a variety of purposes including development financing, project financing, leveraged buyout financing, and even refinancing. The magnitude of financing for such purposes often exceeds $100 million and in some instances is even billions of dollars. For instance, in 1989 one major leveraged buyout of a US-based multinational corporation involved a net cost of $25.96 billion of which 49 percent or $12.63 billion was senior debt financing. Mobilizing large-sized credits in a swift, competitive manner can conveniently be accomplished by loan syndications or note issuance facilities (NIFs).

Once credits are provided, lenders' concerns naturally turn to the debt servicing performance of debtors. Since the announcement of payment difficulties by Mexico in August 1982, and by several other Latin American countries later, two major approaches to resolutions of the debt crisis have emerged, namely the concerted renegotiation approach and the market-oriented approach. We will examine each of these topics in this chapter.

COUNTRY RISK ANALYSIS

Purposes of country risk analysis

For international banks, country risk analysis is to assess the political and economic factors of a borrowing country which can interrupt the sustainable inflows of foreign credits to the country and the timely repayment of principal and interest from the debtor country. Why do we need to consider country risk as a separate risk instead of part of credit risk of individual borrowers? It is because an individual borrower's ability to meet external debt-service obligations is influenced not only by its own ability but also by the ability of the country as a whole. The latter depends on other borrowers' ability, the availability of foreign exchange relative to total external payment obligations, and the extent of government interventions.

Often, country risk is equated with sovereign risk, although they are not the same in a strict sense. As noted above, country risk is the credit risk of borrowers in a country as a whole viewed from a specific country perspective, whereas sovereign risk is the credit risk of a sovereign government as a borrower. However, if the government is the only external borrower within the country, or the government takes over all external debt obligations, then country risk and sovereign risk become indistinguishable. Nonetheless, there are some noteworthy subtle differences. A sovereign government, as a direct debtor or guarantor, may exercise sovereign immunity to commercial lawsuits, thereby making it difficult for creditors to attach debtor government properties in the event of default or even to bring the debtor to court. In addition, a debtor government may exercise its authority to change laws and regulations which in turn materially alter the contractual terms and conditions of its debt obligations, whereas private debtors do not have such powers.[1] When a sovereign government exercises its power to force a reduction or a delay or default on foreign credit, there will be possible losses for creditors, which we call cross-border transfer risk.

Figure 17.1 shows the major determinants at each step for loan repayment. The first step determinants are the debtor country's willingness to repay and its ability to repay. The willingness to repay in turn depends on relative costs and benefits of default. The main cost of default is loss of a country's access to financial and export markets, resulting in reduced income and less ability for the country to make multi-period adjustment in consumption. The benefit is the increased resources available for domestic use, which otherwise would have been transferred out to meet debt service.

The extent of willingness in turn determines a priority list in allocating available foreign exchange for debt service, and it also determines the extent to which an economic adjustment program is to be carried out. On the other hand, the ability to repay is determined by the existing economic structure and economic adjustment programs. It also depends on the external market conditions and the country's ability to borrow new funds.

How then do banks use the results of country risk analysis? The results are used as pre-lending as well as post-lending decision tools. Prior to lending, the measured risk will serve as a basis for the lender to decide whether or not to lend, how much to lend, and how much risk premium it should charge. After lending, periodic country risk analysis serves as a monitoring device, providing a pre-warning system. The result of the analysis is also used to determine the need for bank loan portfolio adjustment and the discount prices of loans when they are sold in the secondary market.

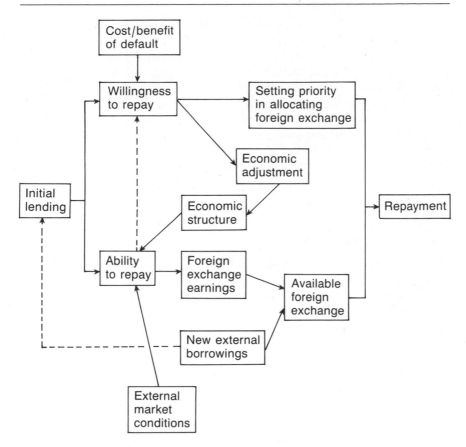

Figure 17.1 Determinants of external debt repayment

Approaches to country risk analysis

In 1977, the Eximbank conducted a survey of thirty-seven US banks with regard to their approaches to country risk analysis. Although the total number of banks surveyed was small, the sample included the twelve largest US banks and accounted for almost 30 percent of the total US banking industry assets and over 50 percent of the total US bank international assets. The survey revealed that banks were using a variety of methods, which the survey report classified broadly into four categories: (1) a fully qualitative method, (2) a structured qualitative method, (3) a checklist method, and (4) some other quantitative method.

The fully qualitative method usually involved an in-depth analysis of a country without a fixed format. It was more of an *ad hoc* approach which made it difficult for users to compare country with country. On the other hand, the structured method used some standardized format with specifically stipulated scope and focus of analysis. It was easier to make comparisons. Still, considerable subjective judgment had to be exercised by analysts. The checklist method involved checking a list of specific variables, such as inflation rate, government deficit, etc. Each item was scaled from the lowest to the highest score. The sum of scores was then used as a measure of country risk. The fourth procedure was to use econometric methods or some other statistical method to explain and predict potential default risk. Explanatory variables were chosen on theoretical and statistical bases and also by an intuitive approach. Although this last procedure was methodologically the most sound, only 2 percent of the sampled banks used it.

Statistical discriminant analysis

If the objective of country risk analysis is correctly to classify countries into debt rescheduling and nonrescheduling countries in advance, our task is to choose appropriate variables which would separate these two groups of countries. As noted earlier, the ability to repay depends on the country's economic conditions on one hand and a favorable external market structure on the other. To relate the debt-service capacity of a country to its macro-policy measures, particularly monetary policy measures, is known as a monetary approach, whereas to look at the market structures as determinants of debt-service capacity is known as a structural approach.[2]

First, consider the monetary approach. This approach is concerned with the overall determination of the balance of payments by monetary and fiscal policy. For example, a fiscal deficit may cause an increase in money supply, which in turn causes higher inflation. Under less than a flexible exchange rate system, the foreign exchange rate will be slower in reflecting the deterioration in the value of domestic currency. This in turn results in a balance of payments deficit, causing debt-servicing problems.

On the other hand, the structural approach emphasizes the specific component structure of the balance of payments, usually expressed in terms of ratios, such as the debt-service ratio and the import cover. Here, for example, the deterioration of the debt-service ratio, the ratio of debt service (DS) to export earnings (EX), gives a signal of the likelihood for debt rescheduling. Since the debt-service amount (sum of interest payments and repayments of principal) is rather contractually fixed, fluctuations in export earnings cause problems. However, if the export earnings are fluctuating because of price fluctuations in both directions, the problem is short term in nature and regarded as a liquidity problem. Some primary commodities exporting countries often face this kind of problem. On the other hand, if the price is permanently depressed or the market has disappeared, the problem is of a long-term nature, resulting in an insolvency problem. This requires structural changes. However, the pressure on export earnings can be relieved if imports can be reduced. The extent to which the imports should be reduced becomes the core of an austerity program.

Another frequently used ratio is the import cover, which is the ratio of official reserves (RE) to imports (IM) and measures the reserve adequacy.

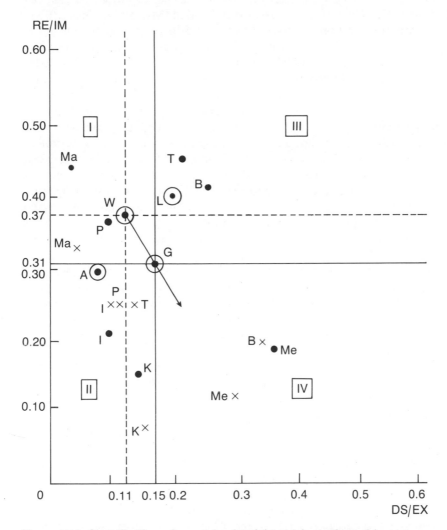

Figure 17.2 Classification of countries by debt service ratio and import cover: for individual countries, ● average (1971–81), x yearly data (1981); G, seven country average; A, Asian countries average; W, worldwide average; L, Latin American average

Source: Kim, T. (1985) "Assessment of External Debt Servicing Capacity: an Alternative Methodology," *Journal of Economic Development*, 10 (2): 48

That is, it measures the percentage of annual imports which can be met by using up reserve holdings. Under a perfectly flexible exchange rate system there is no need for reserve holdings, because any excess demand for foreign exchange will automatically be removed through the adjustment in the exchange rate.

Figure 17.2 shows the classification of seven countries (Brazil (B), Indonesia (I), Korea (K), Malaysia (Ma), Mexico (Me), Philippines (P), and Turkey (T)) using both debt-service ratio and import cover for the eleven year period (1971–81) ending just prior to the Latin American debt crisis. By then, Brazil and Mexico surfaced as potential problem countries, exhibiting high debt-service ratios and low import coverage ratios.

Now let us return to the discussion of the classification of countries by statistical discriminant methods. As mentioned earlier, our first task is to find a variable which would ideally separate rescheduling countries from nonrescheduling countries, as shown in Figure 17.3(a). In most instances, however, we may have two groups overlapping each other so that statistical type I and type II errors both occur. Type I error occurs when debt rescheduling countries are incorrectly classified as nonrescheduling countries, whereas type II error occurs when nonrescheduling countries are incorrectly classified as rescheduling countries.

Our second task is to determine the optimal cutoff value for the chosen variable so that type I error or a combination of two errors can be minimized. For example, a study by Sargen (1977) which covered forty-four countries during the period 1960–76 found the inflation rate to be a statistically significant variable; and a 10 percent inflation rate as the cutoff rate yielded four of fourteen countries which rescheduled their debt incorrectly classified as nonrescheduling countries (type I error), while four of the thirty countries which did not reschedule were classified incorrectly as rescheduling countries (type II error). Which error is of greater concern for banks? Obviously, it is costlier for banks to classify rescheduling countries as nonrescheduling ones. In such instances, different weights may be assigned with a heavier weight to type I error.

In their discriminant analysis, Frank and Cline (1971) found the debt-service ratio, the debt amortization ratio, and the import cover as statistically significant. Similarly, in their logit analysis, Feder and Just (1976) found three additional variables, the export growth rate, per capita income, and the ratio of capital inflows to debt-service payment as significant. On the other hand, using a variety of statistical techniques, Solberg (1988) reconfirmed that the monetary variable (slower foreign exchange rate adjustment to price changes) is the most significant variable. In a more recent study Di Mauro and Mazzola (1989) found drastic movements of the LIBOR a significant variable.

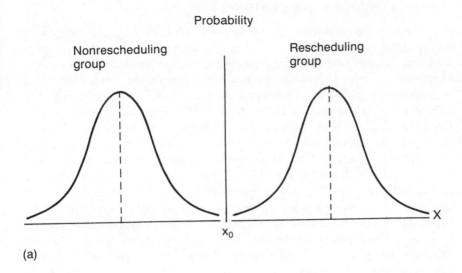

(a)

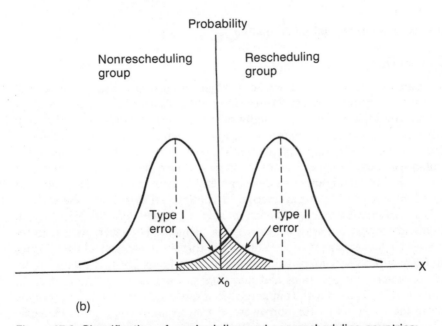

(b)

Figure 17.3 Classification of rescheduling and nonrescheduling countries: (a) case without type I and type II errors; (b) case with type I and type II errors; x_0, cutoff value

INTERNATIONAL BANK LENDING

Now we turn our attention to international bank lending. As their name would imply, commercial banks have traditionally provided short-term commercial loans as their main stable. However, by the time US banks were establishing banking facilities in London, term loans were their main competitive tools. When oil prices quadrupled in 1973 and again tripled in 1979–80, a worldwide balance-of-payments imbalance was created requiring the transfer of funds from oil exporting countries to oil importing countries. By default, commercial banks assumed the role of recycling so-called petro-dollars. This led commercial banks to engage in balance of payments deficit financing and development project financing. With the heightened debt crisis beginning with Mexico in 1982, commercial banks retreated from less developed country lending to merger-and-acquisition financing. Meanwhile, banks have long been involved in individual project financing, which can be traced back to bank financing of independent oil company projects in the 1930s in the southern states of the United States. Let us examine bank lending more in detail.

Types of international bank lending

Development loans

Developing countries borrow from abroad for current consumption as well as for investment purposes. Depending on the stages of economic development, developing countries usually receive external funds from different sources with different degrees of grant element. Figure 17.4 shows the Rostow-type (1971) stages of economic development and the corresponding balance of payments position of a country. It also shows typical sources of funding at different stages of development. A country in an early stage of development would not have access to commercial credit markets because of its poor credit standing. Therefore, such a country depends primarily on bilateral foreign aid with a heavy grant element. However, as a country moves to higher stages of development, the grant element changes from outright gift to soft loans to hard loans. Soft loans are those with highly concessionary interest rates and maturity and are even repayable in local currency. Compared with commercial loans, official hard loans still provide more favorable terms for borrowers as they contain some grant element. They are provided by the World Bank, regional development banks, and official export credit agencies of exporting countries. When they reach this stage, developing countries begin to enter international commercial credit markets where commercial banks play a major role.

Development loans are provided to finance infrastructure construction, such as highways, telecommunications facilities, utility facilities, water and

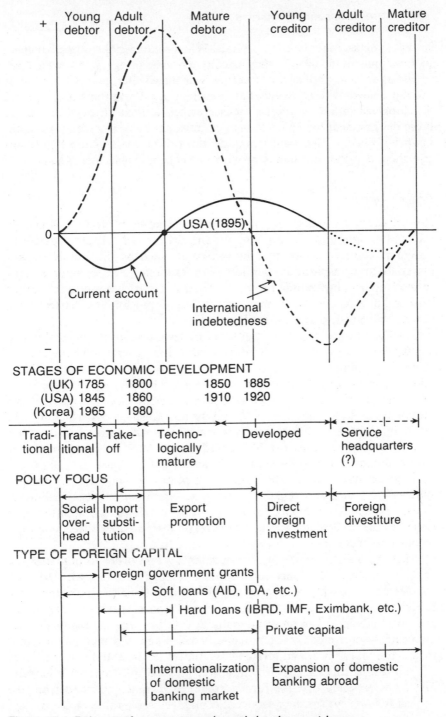

Figure 17.4 Balance of payments cycle and development loans
Source: Kim, T. (1990) "Internationalization of Banking: With Special Reference
to the Case of Korea," Journal of Economic Development, 15 (1): 71

sewage systems, schools, and hospitals. When commercial banks participate in development financing, they usually provide bridge loans which are repaid as soon as permanent financing is arranged. Permanent financing is often provided by development banks such as the World Bank and regional development banks. In order to preserve their limited financial resources, these development banks encourage commercial bank participation in co-financing under which banks provide short-term construction-type loans and these development banks provide permanent replacement loans.

Project financing

Project financing is financing provided to a specific project. It is usually initiated by sponsors who are interested in the project because it performs functions complementary to their activities, such as the supply of raw materials or transportation services. For example, steel companies may sponsor an iron ore mining project in order to secure long-term sources of iron ore, and oil companies may sponsor an oil pipeline project to have a cost-effective transportation facility.

Usually, a project is jointly sponsored by several sponsors each taking up a minority interest. Such a joint-ownership has several advantages. For example, pooling their resources together, sponsors may be able to undertake a needed project otherwise not possible because of its sheer size. Also, they may be able to undertake a significantly larger project to reap economies of scale. Likewise, they may be able to share risk which may be more than one company alone can assume. Minority interest in the form of a partnership or trust can also avoid double taxation which otherwise may be imposed at two levels, project and sponsor levels.

A typical approach to the structuring of project financing is for the sponsors to establish a vehicle company and let it assume legal liabilities. Thus, financing is provided to the project. By doing so, sponsors can minimize the adverse impacts of financing on their balance sheets and limit recourse to them.

What are major sources of project financing? In order to minimize the costs of financing, all conceivable sources of funds are tapped. Although sources of funds vary according to the nature of the projects, there are fairly standard sources of funding, namely sponsor equity contributions and loan advances, commercial bank loans, supplier credits and lease financing, export credit agency loans, World Bank and regional development bank loans, local and foreign government loans, and investor credits.

Project financing usually provides three layers of protection for lenders. First, it is expected that the future stream of income generated from the project is sufficient for debt service. Second, the asset value of the project is sufficient to cover the loan value in the event of liquidation. Third, further assurance is provided to lenders by third parties. These third parties are in many instances sponsors of the project. How to arrange a suitable repayment guarantee to satisfy lenders and at the same time not to impact the balance sheets of sponsors adversely is indeed a matter of so-called financial engineering.

Typically, sponsors provide a repayment guarantee in the form of a long-term purchase commitment of services or products produced by the sponsored project, such as (1) through-put agreements, (2) take-or-pay contracts, and (3) hell-or-high-water leasing. A through-put contract is an agreement entered by sponsors to ship certain minimum amounts of crude oil or refined products through a pipeline constructed and operated by the project vehicle company. In exchange, each sponsor is unconditionally bound to make periodic minimum payments, in total sufficient to cover operating expenses and debt service. All the sponsors are obligated to make minimum payments whether they use the pipeline service or not during the given time period. Both take-or-pay contracts and hell-or-high-water leasing contracts are similar to through-put contracts in the sense that sponsors enter a long-term contract to purchase products or to lease a ship at predetermined prices sufficient to cover debt service.

In recent years, there has been a decline in project financing in the private sector after it reached a peak in the late 1970s when energy prices were high. However, public-sector project financing has gained in popularity. Mainly it takes the form of "build, operate, and transfer" (BOT). Under a BOT agreement, sponsors of the project receive a concession from the government to build an infrastructure (a toll highway or Eurotunnel, for instance) and operate (or lease) it for a period of time at a profit. After acceptable recovery of investment, sponsors transfer the project to the government.

In project financing, international banks perform the financial advisers' role as well as lenders' role. As financial advisers, they put all the puzzles together to complete the necessary financing. As lenders, they provide short- and medium-term loans to fill the residual gap in financing.

Leveraged buyout loans

After the collapse of international lending to developing countries in the early 1980s, many banks turned their lending to customers in industrial countries. This was when leveraged buyout activities took off. A leveraged buyout is an acquisition of a firm that is financed principally, sometimes more than 90 percent, by borrowing on the basis of the assets of the firm to be acquired. The financing approach is similar to project financing. Lenders look to the assets of the acquired firm as collateral and the net cash flows as sources of debt service. In general, there are four components of financing for a leveraged buyout, namely senior debt, subordinated debt, preferred equity, and common equity. Commercial banks are major providers of senior debt financing which is often used as an asset sale bridge facility with medium-term maturity. Senior debt constitutes about 50 percent or more of total financing. Subordinated debt instruments, often rated as junk bonds, are sold to institutional investors. Also preferred shares are sold to institutional investors, whereas a bulk of common shares are kept by the sponsors of the leveraged buyout.

Usually, common target companies are extensively diversified in terms of their products and geographical markets. However, highly leveraged buyouts proved to be very risky, as the worldwide recession in the early 1990s amplified the systematic risk of shares of such companies.

International loan syndications and note issuance facilities

Syndication mechanism

For international bank lending one of the most efficient methods of providing large-sized credits, regardless of the purposes of the funds, is loan syndication. With syndicated loan a group of financial institutions (usually banks) make funds available on common terms and conditions to one borrower. The amount of funds committed by each lender may be different. In order to facilitate the formation of such a loan, the borrower designates a lead bank which then manages the syndication process.

Syndicated loans are attractive for both lenders and borrowers. For lenders, a syndicated loan is a convenient tool to spread credit risk among many lenders. For borrowers, it provides the means to raise a large amount of funds on competitive terms within a short period of time. The accepting houses in London have generally been credited for initiating Eurocurrency loan syndications since the early 1960s. However, more recently, large commercial banks from industrial countries, notably the United States, the UK, Canada, Germany, and Japan, have become the dominant force acting as lead banks facilitating Eurocurrency loan syndications. This shift in dominance from accepting houses to commercial banks is largely due to the fact that accepting houses with their limited financial resources primarily relied on the best effort basis, whereas commercial banks with larger asset resources were able to make firm commitments.

The loan syndication process begins with a mandate, an instruction given by the borrower to the lead bank to form a loan syndication, as shown in Figure 17.5. A study by Wellons (1977) shows that, in choosing a lead bank, the borrower employs several criteria including (a) experience of the lead bank in syndication, (b) prior ties with the borrower, (c) geographic proximity of the bank to the borrower, (d) the size of the bank, (e) the country of the currency in demand, and (f) willingness to bid even under some difficult or sometimes questionable situations.[3] These factors in a broader sense are the elements needed to ensure a successful syndication.

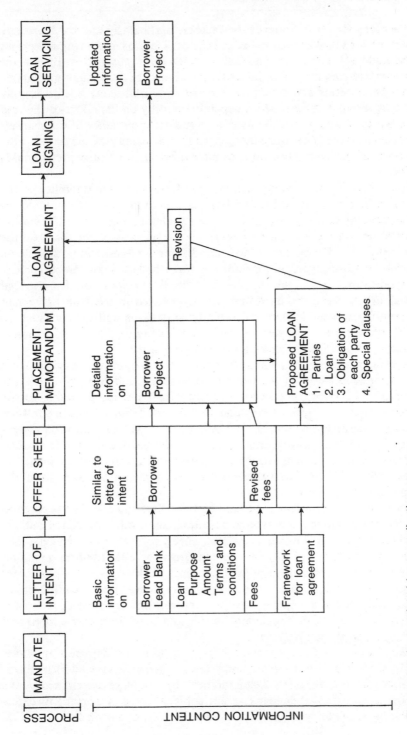

Figure 17.5 International loan syndication process

In a narrower sense, some of the factors, particularly the first three, are important for the borrower to reduce the problem of measuring the extent of the lead bank's effort in syndication which is not observable. Even if the borrower can acquire some information about the lead bank's effort to obtain better terms and conditions for the proposed loan, it is given only by the observed outcome, which depends not only on the effort of the lead bank but also the state of the market. Repeated experience in the market, prior ties with the borrower, and geographic proximity of the bank to the borrower all enable the borrower to have a better sense of the lead bank's performance.

Upon receiving a mandate, the lead bank tests the marketability of the proposed loan and then submits a letter of intent in which the basic terms and conditions of the proposed loan are stipulated. The basic information in the letter includes (a) the borrower, (b) the purpose of the loan, (c) the loan amount, (d) the terms and conditions (interest rate, drawdown schedule, maturity, special provisions in the proposed loan contract, etc.), (e) syndication fees, and (f) the lead bank's responsibilities. Special provisions are those special clauses to be included in the loan agreement primarily to protect lenders individually as well as collectively, such as "yield protection," "waiver of sovereign immunity," "cross-default," "negative pledge," and "sharing clause" among others.

In giving a mandate to a bank the borrower is assigning an underwriter's role to the lead bank. In the letter of intent, the lead bank proposes the extent of its commitment about the funds to be made available to the borrower under the given terms and conditions. It may be either full (or partial) commitment or best effort basis. Eager to get a syndication assignment, the lead bank may offer terms and conditions that are too favorable, only later finding it difficult to sell purchased instruments without incurring losses. This is known as underwriting risk, which originates from the unknown demand curve.

Once the letter of intent is accepted by the borrower, it then becomes a firm mandate. Based on this firm mandate, the lead bank sends out the offering telex or fax, known as an offer sheet, to prospective lenders. The offer sheet contains basically the same information as in the firm mandate. Upon receiving favorable responses, the lead bank sends out a placement memorandum, which is a printed brochure giving more detailed information usually on three parts: (a) the borrower and the project for which the loan is intended, (b) the detailed terms and conditions of the loan, and (c) the proposed loan agreement.

Like the case of domestic underwriting of securities depicted by Hayes (1971), there is a distinctive hierarchy among prospective lenders in Euro-currency markets, although the hierarchy is by and large determined by the size of each participating bank. Such a hierarchy is important in determining the share of syndication management fees, as shown in Table 17.1.

Table 17.1 Syndication fee structure

Category	Recipients of fees		Nature of fees		
	Characteristics of banks	Functions in syndication	Advance interest payment[a]	Underwriting fees	Administrative fees
Whole participants			Management fee (syndication fee)		
Lead bank	Over $100 billion assets	Mandate Underwriting Lending Administrative work	Manager's fee	Share of pool	Praecipuum Agent fee
Management group banks	Over $100 billion assets	Underwriting Lending Administrative work	Manager's fee	Share of pool	Agent fee
Co-manager banks	$50–100 billion assets	Large sum participation	Co-manager's fee		
Participant banks	$10–50 billion asset	Small sum participation	Participation fee		
Special bracket banks	Special relationship with the lead bank or the borrower	Support of syndication			Special bracket bank fee

Note: [a] Facility fees and utilization fees may be added.

For instance, the lead bank and management group banks receive proportionally higher points (advance interest payment) in the name of the manager's fee and they share residual underwriting profit (share of the pool). The lead bank is also rewarded for obtaining the mandate (praecipuum).

There is usually asymmetric information between the borrower and the lenders possibly leading to market failure unless an incentive system is provided to encourage the borrower to furnish full information. One such incentive system is the repeated access to the Eurocredit market permitted to the borrower. Another point related to information asymmetry is the relationship between the lead bank and other lenders leading to a possible conflict of interest. Since the lead bank would be interested in successful syndication of the loan, there is an incentive for the lead bank to depict the borrower's condition more favorably. This may mislead other lenders, causing a potential lawsuit.[4]

Whether or not banks participate in this particular loan syndication depends on a number of factors such as (a) prior knowledge of the lead bank and the borrower, (b) the portfolio and country limit of the lender, (c) the desire to do business with this borrower, and (d) the liquidity in the Eurocurrency market.[5]

When accepted, the proposed loan agreement which was part of the placement memorandum will become a formal loan contract between the borrower and the lending group (lead bank, other lenders, and guarantors). The loan signing represents the culmination of the syndication process and marks the end of the lead bank as the agent of the borrower. After signing of the loan, the lead bank usually becomes the administrator of loan servicing. Limiting the "sell down" by the lead bank may ensure that the interest of the lead bank coincides with that of other lenders.

Variations in terms and conditions

The loan is usually priced as follows:

$$\text{lending rate} = \text{LIBOR} + \text{spread}. \tag{17.1}$$

Given the reference rate LIBOR, lenders still have a number of options to adjust terms and conditions to reflect credit risk properly, as shown in Table 17.2. Thus, the spread alone does not represent an accurate risk premium.

Note issuance facilities

As noted in Chapter 9, a note issuance facility is a credit facility provided by a group of banks under which a borrower can issue short-term Euronotes in its own name over a given medium term but underwriting banks are committed either to purchase unsold notes or to provide guarantees for

Table 17.2 Variations in terms and conditions in loan pricing

		Low-risk borrower	High-risk borrower
Amount			
	Drawdown	Faster	Slower
	Commitment fee	Lower	Higher
Maturity			
	Grace period	Longer	Shorter
	Repayment schedule	Longer	Shorter
	Option of early repayment	Yes	No
Interest rate			
	Basic reference rate (LIBOR) reference banks	Prime-name banks	Lesser-name banks
	Spread	Fixed	Adjustable
	Interest payment interval		
	When the rate is expected to rise	Longer	Shorter
	When the rate is expected to fall	Shorter	Longer[a]
	Management fees	Smaller	Larger

Note: [a] This is equivalent to a prepayment penalty.

repayments of notes. Increasingly, these facilities are used as alternatives to syndicated loans. Note that syndicated loans are asset-based activities for banks, whereas note issuance facilities are basically fee-based activities. Nevertheless, both facilities accomplish the same purpose, making large funding available to borrowers in a swift, competitive, and flexible way.

DEBT RESCHEDULING ISSUES

With Mexico's announcement of its payment difficulties in August 1982, widespread debt crises erupted almost simultaneously in most Latin American countries. Debt crises spread further in other regions as well. As a consequence, the so-called Baker 17 countries alone (mostly Latin American severely indebted countries) had $9.6 billion interest arrears for their long-term credits by the end of 1985.

What were the major causes for these simultaneous debt service crises? Causes were manifold: (a) there was a severe recession in the industrial countries, particularly in the United States between 1980 and 1982, which were their main export markets; (b) the value of commodity exports fell sharply, reducing the debt-service capacity of primary commodity exporting countries; (c) there was a sharp escalation in interest rates in the world credit market due to the contractual monetary policies pursued by industrial countries, raising debt-service costs for the debtor countries; (d) there was a large decline in bank lending after the Mexican announcement of the debt-service problem, precisely when more was needed; (e) there was massive capital flight from severely indebted countries, depleting sources of funds further; and (f) there was a rise in the dollar exchange rate, increasing the burden of debt service.[6]

By the end of 1989, the total amount of external debt of all developing countries reached $1,290 billion from $839 billion in 1982. The major increase came from government sources. With this magnitude of external debt, it is unlikely that debt issues can be resolved in a short period of time.

Debt restructuring

Before examining debt-service issues, let us define a few related terms. Debt restructuring or debt reorganization is any change in terms and conditions associated with an existing debt mutually agreed upon by the borrower and the lender. Debt refinancing is new credit provided to meet debt-service obligations on the existing problem debt. Debt rescheduling is a new arrangement for postponing payments of principal or interest or otherwise changing the terms of repayment or of interest charges. Debt relief is similar to debt restructuring but changes are made in favor of the borrower, for example, lower interest rates, reduced principal repayment, or full or partial forgiveness of any payment.

A country with debt-servicing difficulties has four choices. If the country has no intention of repayment, it may repudiate the loan repayment outright. Obviously, there are costs associated with this option. The repudiating country may be denied future access to the financial markets. The second option is to cease repayments on its debt, resulting in service arrears. This is simply putting the problem aside and not solving it. The third alternative is to service debt at any cost. This may require both present and future sacrifice, which may not be bearable. The fourth approach is to rearrange the debt service. In most instances, this fourth method is used. If it takes too long for renegotiation, this has the same effect as the second approach.

As noted earlier, rearranging debt service may include (a) principal rescheduling which usually involves stretching the grace period and maturity, (b) interest rescheduling which may include one or more of interest rate reduction, amortization of interest in arrears, and lengthening of the grace period and maturity, and (c) debt stock reduction.

Two major approaches have emerged, for the solution of debt restructuring issues. One is a concerted approach by which the creditor governments, commercial banks, and debtor government direct their concerted effort to resolution of the debt problem. The second is the market-oriented approach by which loan repayment problems are resolved through the market mechanism. Let us look at each approach in more detail.

Concerted approach to debt restructuring

There are two main *ad hoc* institutional arrangements for debt restructuring: the Paris Club for governmental debts or guarantees, and the London Club for private debts.

The Paris Club

In 1956 a group of creditor country government representatives met in Paris to renegotiate Argentine debt which was owed to export credit agencies of these countries. This *ad hoc* governmental organization became known as the Paris Club. The Club only deals with restructuring of official bilateral loans and officially guaranteed export credits. It has become a major forum for renegotiation of official debts. It had dealt with at least fifty-four renegotiations by the end of 1984.

The meeting is held at the request of the debtor country. Although there are no written rules for the format of renegotiations, a certain pattern has emerged: (a) out of eligible debt, 85–90 percent of the amount is rescheduled with maturity stretched to eight to ten years and with a grace period of four to five years; (b) the debtor should not accord better treatment to debt renegotiated outside the Paris Club and seek to renegotiate other debts on comparable terms; (c) the debtor country should have placed a stabilization program with the IMF before rescheduling provisions become effective.[7]

The London Club

By contrast, the London Club which began in the 1970s consists of *ad hoc* consortia of commercial banks aiming to renegotiate problem debt owed to commercial banks. Since much of this debt consists of syndicated loans, uninsured trade finance, or project finance, the number of participant banks in each case tends to be well over a hundred. In order to facilitate renegotiation, banks form an "advisory" committee whose membership usually comes from the banks that have the greatest stake. Their renegotiation pattern is becoming similar to that of the Paris Club, as the Baker and Brady plans called for a comprehensive approach to both official and private debts.

The Baker initiative

The first three-year period of the debt crisis was the period of rescheduling debts, monitoring the progress, and avoiding further crisis. The international financial system withstood enormous stress and severely indebted countries began showing signs of improvement. However, renewed momentum was needed to spur a more positive approach to the solution of debt problems rather than a defensive approach. In 1985, the then US Secretary of the Treasury James Baker proposed a plan, known as the Baker initiative, the essence of which consists of

1 an increase in lending of $20 billion by the international lending community over a three-year period;
2 a $9 billion increase in lending by the World Bank and Inter-American Development Bank to fifteen severely indebted countries over the three years, which later became known as the Baker 15 countries;[8]
3 major adjustment policies on the part of debtor countries that would promote growth within a market-oriented framework.

The Baker initiative was based on the premise that the solution of the debt problems would require a combination of three ingredients: economic growth, structural reform, and new lending. That is, new lending combined with structural changes would lead to economic growth of the debtor countries, which in turn would safeguard the world financial system and restore the creditworthiness of debtor countries.

However, commercial banks were reluctant to provide additional credits. From 1985 to 1988, long-term private source funds increased by only about 10 percent from $486 billion to $537 billion and short-term funds remained virtually unchanged, increasing from $132 billion to $141 billion. At the same time, for debtor countries investment at the expense of current consumption appeared less attractive, because the anticipated drainage of future output to debt service was so great as to make sacrifice of current consumption in order to increase investment unattractive. This disincentive effect of existing debt is termed the debt overhang.

The Brady plan

Recognizing such problems, in 1989 US Secretary of the Treasury Nicholas F. Brady proposed a new approach, known as the Brady plan. The new approach[9]

1 builds on the fundamental principles of the Baker plan;
2 focuses on more broadly based, voluntary debt reductions;
3 recognizes the continuing needs of commercial bank participation in lending for investment funds and repatriation of flight capital;
4 emphasizes the central role for the IMF and the World Bank in assistance for economic adjustments of debtor countries;
5 redirects and increases available IMF and World Bank resources to support debt and debt-service reduction transactions agreed upon by the commercial banks and debtor countries.

There are two major differences from the Baker initiative. First, debt forgiveness is now officially recognized as a needed element of debt restructuring. This will reduce the debt overhang and encourage investment in debtor countries. In order to enable each lender to negotiate on an individual basis, the plan urges waiver of sharing and negative pledge clauses in loan syndication contracts. Second, the IMF and the World Bank are now asked to redirect some portion of their resources specifically for debt and debt-service reductions for the countries having a high debt burden and strong adjustment programs. Both institutions are committed to set aside an amount of funds up to 25 percent of adjustment lending program funds to support debt reduction.

How to handle a debt crisis?: the case of Mexico

How private lenders, creditor governments, and Mexico responded to Mexico's debt crisis is a useful lesson on how to handle future debt crises.[10] Soon after Mexico announced its payment difficulties on August 12, 1982, two distinct problems were identified: a liquidity problem and an insolvency problem. The immediate need of Mexico for the summer of 1982 was for liquidity. The week following Mexico's shock announcement a special meeting of the central banks of the Group of Ten (G-10) was held, resulting later in the month in a financial package of $1.85 billion. In addition, through a bilateral arrangement, the United States immediately provided an additional $1 billion. This prompt arrangement of liquidity enabled the international financial system to override the crisis situation and to function well without major interruptions.

Dealing with the insolvency problem was much more complicated and took longer. Nonetheless, some key patterns of renegotiation emerged: (1) use of the advisory committee format for renegotiation, (2) additional concerted lending, (3) the imposition of mutual conditionality between new bank lending and placement of IMF programs, and (4) the scope of the debts to be renegotiated.

An advisory committee was set up to contact the hundreds of banks worldwide which had Mexican debt and to draw as many of them as possible into agreement on restructuring. In general, banks having the largest stakes stayed in, while banks having marginal stakes left.

Unlike the previous practices, the IMF this time insisted that banks commit new loans associated with the IMF adjustment programs before the adjustment plan was fully negotiated. An IMF program presumes a certain amount of private capital inflows to determine official funding needs. Without definitive commitment from private creditors, the program would be left with uncertainty. In the past, banks usually would not commit any new loans until an IMF adjustment plan was agreed to.

Obviously, debt owed to banks by the government and its agencies was included for renegotiation. But government bonds which happened to be relatively small were excluded because it would have been more difficult to renegotiate with a relatively large number of widely dispersed shareholders. Also excluded were interbank placements and private loans. Interbank placements in London and New York which amounted to some $6.5 billion were then rolled over, while private sector debts were to be negotiated on an individual basis. However, the central bank of Mexico agreed to provide foreign exchange to service rescheduled debt when private borrowers present peso payments in line with an agreed maturity schedule.

Thus, official reschedulings, bank financial packages, and IMF agreements were linked with each other, providing carrots and sticks for both banks and the Mexican government. But that was not enough. Only after substantial debt relief was made, as urged by the Brady plan, has significant economic progress been witnessed. The Mexican case nonetheless laid down a basic pattern for handling bank loans to developing countries in case of debt crisis.

Market-oriented approach to debt restructuring

The use of a market-oriented approach to debt restructuring has been advocated, because it would minimize the cost for creditor governments and it is voluntary in nature. Most transactions of debt instruments in the secondary market may eventually result in a reduction in indebtedness of debtor nations, but some of them may not have a direct bearing on the reduction of debts immediately as in the case of debt-for-debt swaps. We examine several commonly used techniques here.

Debt-for-debt swaps

These swaps, estimated to be about 75 percent of secondary market transactions, involve banks exchanging claims on one country for claims on another, or exchanging claims on different parties within the same country. Swapping of their debt holdings for those held by other banks is an effort to optimize the bank's portfolio within its constraints. A bank may desire diversifying its portfolio to reduce risk, or to increase concentration of its holdings of a certain country to meet its strategic business interests. Also it may want to partition its holdings to minimize the accounting impact of discount sales on the overall value of its assets when the bank sells some of its holdings.

Discount sales of debt instruments

Some banks, particularly US regional banks, sell their holdings to reduce their debt exposure or simply to exit from international lending business. Some feel compelled to do so if they are to increase their ability to raise capital which is needed for their survival. Such sales are made largely to corporations for direct investment abroad through debt–equity swaps, and marginally to nonprofit organizations for environment, education, or charity swaps. In turn, those who bought such debt instruments sell them to debtor governments at a discount in debtor country currency. Thus, the benefit to debtor nations is that they can retire their hard-currency debts for their own currency at a discount. However, the disadvantages are that such transactions may be inflationary and may impede inflows of new foreign capital which might be substituted by these swaps.

Direct cash buyback

Since banks sell their debt holdings to third parties, then why not sell directly to debtor nations? However, most bank loan agreements have a sharing clause which prohibits individual lenders from renegotiating individually with the debtor unless waivers are given by other participating banks. This clause hampers the use of this direct cash buyback method despite its directness and convenience. As noted earlier, the Brady plan urges waiver of this kind of contractual provision in the loan agreements.

Debt conversion

This is the case of directly converting existing debt instruments into alternative instruments, namely debt for equity swaps, or old debt for new debt swaps. Usually banks sell their debt holdings to their affiliates which in turn swap debts for equity holdings of the debtor, such as government-owned corporation shares. Federal Reserve Regulation K permits a US banking organization to acquire up to 100 percent of shares of a government-owned corporation and up to 40 percent of shares of a private corporation. Also banks may exchange their debt holdings for new debt instruments, which may pay less principal and interest but with better assurance of repayment, as in the case of the 1988 Mexican debt–bond exchange. Another type of conversion is hard-currency debts for local currency debts.

Which debt reduction technique to use?

A recent IMF study conducted by Dooley and others (1990) shows that the amount of debt reduction it is possible to carry out with given resources is the same regardless of the technique employed. In order to illustrate the case in point, let us assume that the debtor faces the following market conditions: (a) the contractual amount of the outstanding debt is $100 million; (b) its market price is $0.40 per face value; (c) this market price fully reflects all the effects of the announcement of the debt reduction plan;

and (d) the country newly borrows $10 million from a third party in the London interbank market.

If the country chooses to use a cash buyback technique, it is able to retire $25 million of existing debt in exchange for the newly borrowed money. Since this country incurred $10 million of new debt, the net reduction is $15 million. By contrast, suppose now that the country chooses to use a debt–debt swap, that is, swapping old debt for new enhanced debt. For the enhancement of new debt, the country is going to use new money to purchase zero coupon, riskless US Treasury bonds having the same maturity as the outstanding debt (say twenty years). The going interest rate on bonds is 8 percent. Then, the $10 million will be sufficient to buy zero coupon bonds with a face value of $46.610 million, which is to be used as collateral for new debt to be issued by the borrower in order to retire old debt:

$$\$10 \text{ million}(1 + 0.08)^{20} = \$46.610 \text{ million}. \tag{17.2}$$

The market value of the new debt will be the sum of the 40 percent discount value plus the enhancement (collateral) value of $10 million, which is $28.644 million:

$$\$46.610 \text{ million} \times 0.4 + \$10 \text{ million} = \$28.644 \text{ million}. \tag{17.3}$$

The market price in fractions is thus

$$\frac{\$28.644 \text{ million}}{\$46.610 \text{ million}} = 0.6145. \tag{17.4}$$

Compared with the market price of the old debt ($0.40 per face value), the value of the new debt is 1.536 25 times higher. Therefore a new debt of $46.610 million should be sufficient to retire $71.10 million of old debt. Since total new debt (including a loan from London) is $56.610 million, the net reduction is $15 million as in the case of cash buyback. This is true regardless of bond interest rates and maturity. In fact, the net reduction (NR) can be expressed as

$$NR = (1/D - 1)L \tag{17.5}$$

where D is the initial ratio of market price to face value and L is new money. Furthermore, it does not matter which technique is used in an efficient secondary market where problem debt instruments are traded.

Economic adjustments

In parallel with massive debt restructuring, debtor countries were in turn asked to make economic adjustments. Countries with debt restructuring would in most instances be borrowing also from the IMF and would be required to follow the IMF-prescribed stabilization programs aimed at reducing the current account deficit. Such requirement is known as IMF conditionality. Even though the amount loaned by the IMF is relatively small compared with the total new credit amount, the IMF involvement is important. When the debtor agrees to IMF conditionality, it is more likely that new capital flows into the borrower country, as commercial lenders may presume that the economic conditions will improve and that the debtor country will be able to resume normal debt servicing in the near future.

SUMMARY

This chapter presented sequentially related topics, namely country risk analysis, international bank lending, and debt rescheduling issues. Country risk is credit risk of borrowers in the country as a whole. Sovereign risk may converge to country risk when the government is only the borrower or the government takes over all external debt obligations. Broadly, country risk analysis may be approached either as a structural problem or as a monetary problem. From the lenders' perspective, the use of statistical technique in classifying rescheduling and nonrescheduling countries would require consideration of how to minimize Type I error.

International bank lending has changed its character since the worldwide oil crisis erupted in the early 1970s, placing banks by default in nontraditional financing businesses such as balance of payments and economic development financing. Likewise, as a typical size of such financing tends to be large in the Eurocurrency credit market, syndicated loans or note issuance facilities are often used.

Since the announcement of debt-service problems in Mexico in 1982, debt rescheduling issues have been one of the most pressing issues in the banking industry. In addition to the concerted renegotiations, both lenders and borrowers having problem loans are increasingly resorting to the market-oriented approach, which employs new instruments such as debt-equity swaps, debt-debt swaps, and buybacks in the secondary market. Under reasonable assumptions, we can show that regardless of methods (e.g. debt-debt swaps or buybacks), the amount of debt stock reduction would be the same, given the amount of new money.

REVIEW PROBLEMS AND EXERCISES

1. Explain the differences between the monetary approach and the structural approach to the assessment of debt rescheduling possibilities.

2. What does a seemingly simple ratio, the debt-service ratio, tell us about the debt-servicing capacity of a county? Elaborate.

3. Which statistical error, type I or type II, should a country risk analyst weigh more heavily? Why?

4. According to the Frank–Cline and Feder–Just studies, several variables turned out be statistically significant. Are they monetary variables or structural variables? Why?

5. Depending on the stages of economic development, external capital provided to less developed countries may have different degrees of grant elements. Compare the differences at each stage of economic development.

6. In project financing, how can lenders be protected from repayment default in such a way that the impact on sponsors' balance sheets is not too great?

7. Explain the advantages of syndicated loans, compared with straight loans, for borrowers and for lenders.

8. Explain the role of the lead bank in a syndication process.

9. What are the factors considered by the borrower of a syndicated loan in giving a mandate to a bank?

10. What were the major causes of the widespread debt-service crises that erupted in many Latin American countries in the early 1980s?

11. What are the major differences between the Baker and Brady plans?

12. Explain how the Paris Club and the London Club work in debt renegotiations.

13. The following market approaches are used to resolve debt rescheduling problems. Explain the characteristics of each approach.
    (a) Debt-for-debt swaps
    (b) Cash buyback
    (c) Debt conversions (old debt for new debt, debt for equity, etc.)

14. Why do banks engage in debt-for-debt swaps?

15. What is meant by debt overhang? What should creditors and debtors do to resolve this problem?

16. Suppose that new debt is collateralized with zero coupon US government bonds. The new debt is going to be used to retire old debt. Does the US government bond interest rate affect the amount of net debt reduction? Using the same assumptions except for the interest rate on bonds (say now 6 percent), show your conclusion.

NOTES

1 In order to protect the original return on a loan, a "yield protection" clause is usually included in a loan agreement.
2 See Sargen (1977: 19–35).
3 See Wellons (1977: 60–5).
4 For a real case issue, see Donaldson (1979: 78–90).
5 Wellons (1977: 70–1).
6 For specific discussions, see Griffith-Jones and Sunkel (1986: 96–119).
7 See IMF (1983: 28).
8 These fifteen countries were Argentina, Bolivia, Brazil, Chile, Columbia, the Ivory Coast, Ecuador, Mexico, Morocco, Nigeria, Peru, Philippines, Uruguay, Venezuela, and Yugoslavia. Later, Jamaica and Panama were added to make the Baker 17 countries.
9 See US Department of the Treasury (1989: 7). Also see Brady (1989: 69–76).
10 This part is a condensed version of Frydl and Sobol (1988: 5–29).

BASIC READING

Avramovic, D. *et al.* (1964) *Economic Growth and External Debt*, Baltimore, Md: Johns Hopkins University Press.

Brady, N. F. (1989) "A Reexamination of the Debt Strategy," in Fried, E. R. and Trezise, P. H. (eds) (1989) *Third World Debt: The Next Phase*, Washington, D.C.: Brookings Institution, 69–76.

Cline, W. R. (1987) *Mobilizing Bank Lending to Debtor Countries*, Washington, D.C.: Institute for International Economics.

Donaldson, T. H. (1979) *Lending in International Commercial Banking*, New York: Wiley.

Dooley, M. P., Folkerts-Lonau, D., Haas, R. D., Symansky, S. A. and Tyron, R. W. (1990) *Debt Reduction and Economic Activity*, Washington, D.C.: IMF.

Eichengreen, B. and Lindert, P. H. (eds) (1989) *The International Debt Crisis in Historical Perspective*, Cambridge, Mass.: MIT Press.

Export and Import Bank of the USA (1976) *A Survey of Country Evaluation Systems in Use*, Washington, D.C.

Feder, G. and Just, R. (1976) "A Study of Debt Service Capacity Applying Logit Analysis," *Journal of Development Economics*, 4: 25–39.

Frank, C. R. and Cline, W. R. (1971) "Measurement of Debt Servicing Capacity: An Application of Discriminant Analysis," *Journal of International Economics*, 1: 327–44.

Frydl, E. J. and Sobol, D. M. (1988) "A Perspective on the Debt Crisis, 1982–87," in Federal Reserve Bank of New York, *Annual Report 1987*, 5–29.

Griffith-Jones, S. and Sunkel, O. (1986) *Debt and Development Crises in Latin America: The End of an Illusion*, Oxford: Oxford University Press.

Hayes, S. L., III (1971) "Investment Banking: Power Structure in Flux," *Harvard Business Review*, March–April: 136–52.

IMF (1983) *External Debt in Perspective*, Washington, D.C.

—— (1989) *World Economic Outlook*, Washington, D.C.

Kim, T. (1985) "Assessment of External Debt Servicing Capacity: An Alternative Methodology," *Journal of Economic Development*, 10 (2): 35–52.

—— (1990) "Internationalization of Banking: With Special Reference to the Case of Korea," *Journal of Economic Development*, 15 (1): 63–82.

Khoury, S. J. (1985) *Sovereign Debt: A Critical Look at the Causes and the Nature of the Problem*, Columbia, S.C.: University of South Carolina.

Nevitt, P. K. (1979) *Project Financing*, London: Euromoney Publications.

Rostow, W. W. (1971) *The Stages of Economic Growth: A Non-Communist Manifesto*, 2nd edn., New York: Cambridge University Press.

Sargen, N. (1977) "Economic Indicators and Country Risk Appraisal," *Federal Reserve Bank of San Francisco Economic Review*, Fall: 19–35.

Solberg, R. L. (1988) *Sovereign Rescheduling: Risk and Portfolio Management*, London: Unwin Hyman.

US Department of the Treasury (1989) *Interim Report to the Congress Concerning International Discussions on an International Debt Management Authority*, Washington, D.C., March.

Wellons, P. A. (1977) *Borrowing by Developing Countries on the Euro-currency Market*, Paris: OECD.

World Bank (1985) *World Development Report 1985*, Washington, D.C.

—— (1989) *World Debt Tables 1989–1990, vol. 1, Analysis and Summary Tables*, Washington, DC.

FURTHER READING

Di Mauro, F. and Mazzola, F. (1989) *LDCs' Repayment Problems: a Profit Analysis*, Banca D'Italia Termi di Discussione No. 116, Rome.

Eaton, J. and Gersovitz (1981) "Debt with Potential Repudiation: Theoretical and Empirical Analysis," *Review of Economic Studies*, 48: 289–308.

Fischer, S. and Husain, I. (1990) "Managing the Debt Crisis in the 1990s," *Finance & Development*, June: 24–7.

Lessard, D. R. and Williamson, J. (1987) *Capital Flight and Third World Debt*, Washington, D.C.: Institute for International Economics.

Lieftinck, P. (1966) *External Debt and Debt-Bearing Capacity of Developing Countries*, Essays in International Finance, Princeton, N.J.: Princeton University Press.

Smith, R. C. and Walter, I. (1990) *Global Financial Services: Strategies for Building Competitive Strengths in International Commercial and Investment Banking*, New York: Harper Business.

Solomon, R. (1977) "Perspective on the Debt of Developing Countries," *Brookings Papers on Economic Activity*, 2: 479–510.

Index